D1154936

A Dictionary of
Education

SEE WEB LINKS

Many entries in this dictionary have recommended web links. When you see the above symbol at the end of an entry, go to the dictionary's web page at http://www.oup.com/uk/reference/resources/education, click on **Web links** in the Resources section, and locate the entry in the alphabetical list, then click straight through to the relevant web sites. Sites that are not free to access include '(subscription)' in their description.

A Dictionary of
Education

Edited by

SUSAN WALLACE

OXFORD
UNIVERSITY PRESS

OXFORD
UNIVERSITY PRESS

Great Clarendon Street, Oxford OX2 6DP

Oxford University Press is a department of the University of Oxford.
It furthers the University's objective of excellence in research, scholarship,
and education by publishing worldwide in

Oxford New York
Auckland Cape Town Dar es Salaam Hong Kong Karachi
Kuala Lumpur Madrid Melbourne Mexico City Nairobi
New Delhi Shanghai Taipei Toronto

With offices in
Argentina Austria Brazil Chile Czech Republic France Greece
Guatemala Hungary Italy Japan Poland Portugal Singapore
South Korea Switzerland Thailand Turkey Ukraine Vietnam

Oxford is a registered trade mark of Oxford University Press
in the UK and certain other countries

Published in the United States
by Oxford University Press Inc., New York

First published 2008

British Library Cataloguing in Publication Data
Data available

Library of Congress Cataloging in Publication Data
Data available

Typeset by SPI Publisher Services, Pondicherry, India
Printed in Great Britain on acid-free paper by
CPI Antony Rowe, Chippenham, Wiltshire

ISBN 978–0–19–921206–4

1 3 5 7 9 10 8 6 4 2

Contents

Preface

One of the pleasures of writing a Dictionary of Education has been the knowledge that it focuses on a topic which is of relevance to everyone at some stage in their life, and of enduring interest to many in their personal or professional capacity. Moreover, such a dictionary is an additionally valuable and necessary resource today, when education policy in Great Britain remains in a state of development and change, and where new terminology is generated with a rapidity which can prove bewildering, even to those within the educational professions themselves.

However, that very factor of constant change creates enormous difficulties for anyone attempting to compile a dictionary in this field. There will always be the temptation to take the easiest approach, which would be a historical one, with an emphasis on educational legislation over the past two centuries, and on organizations and qualifications which have had their day and passed into recent history. These are 'safe' entries which can be described definitively, and are therefore a great comfort to a compiler of dictionaries. Unfortunately, however, it is unlikely that this sort of information is what users of the dictionary will be most frequently looking for. Indeed, it has been my assumption that parents, pupils, students, teachers, governors, social workers, and others for whom this Dictionary is intended will be most concerned with current terminology, qualifications, and legislation. So, although the reader who wishes it will find a historical perspective here, it will be in the form of entries on recognized landmark legislation, publications, and provision; and, in addition, a Time Line in Appendix 1, which sets out in sequence the major developments of the past century.

The approach taken, therefore, has been wherever possible to identify trends in educational policy and philosophy and, through the use of extensive cross-referencing, to allow the reader to explore key topics such as assessment, research, and the national curriculum, in all their complexity and across a range of contexts. Links to relevant and reliable Internet sources are provided wherever appropriate in order to ensure, as far as it is possible to do so, that readers are guided towards additional information which is both current and accurate. In terms of trends, some clear themes are emerging in the development of educational policy and provision in the early years of the 21st century. These include a growing emphasis on children's and young people's welfare and safety as central to ensuring their access to educational opportunity; and a trend in 14–19 policy towards the creation of closer links and equivalencies between academic or general qualifications and the acquisition of work-related skills. Both of these developments are reflected in the expansion of Ofsted's role and title from 'Office for Standards in Education' to 'Office for Standards in Education, Children's Services, and Skills'. Another theme to emerge is the increasing focus on personalized learning, and the ideal of a curriculum tailored to meet the needs of the individual learner. This has gone hand in hand with a gradual increase in the flexibility with which the national curriculum is applied, allowing for developments such as the 14–19 Diploma.

Also emerging is a growing recognition that policies affecting schools' recruitment and admission of pupils, such as the emphasis on parental choice and on competition between schools, may have an impact on wider issues of concern, such as social cohesion. These themes—the welfare and safety of young learners, the tension between a national curriculum and personalized learning, and the contradictions between market forces and inclusion—emerge as common factors in many otherwise disparate entries.

In an era when 'lifelong learning' has become a buzzword in education, particularly at a policy level, it is important that the Dictionary reflects this concept by not restricting entries to matters relating only or mainly to schools, but giving due coverage also to vocational education and training, to adult education, and to the further and higher education sectors, and exploring the relationships and distinctions between these. Special education at all levels has not been treated as a separate or discrete topic, but has been addressed extensively through a comprehensive range of entries integrated into the order of the Dictionary as a whole.

The Dictionary also sets out to identify the points of comparison and contrast in education and training provision across England, Northern Ireland, Scotland, and Wales, in terms of structures, organizations, qualifications, and legislation. Each of these has a lengthy entry which provides an overview of educational policy, provision, and trends. Additional entries relating to each, and providing detailed and specific definitions, are cross-referenced, where appropriate, to the relevant main entry. For readers of the Dictionary who wish to refer to British education in the wider context of English-speaking countries worldwide, a comparative table is set out in Appendix 2.

In the current process of rapid development and change, education is notorious for its steady proliferation of acronyms and other forms of abbreviation which prove a bane to students, teachers, and parents alike. For convenience, a comprehensive list of these is provided below. Within the text of the Dictionary itself, definitions are listed in almost all cases according to the full-length form of words, which is followed by the abbreviation in parentheses, thus: *National Vocational Qualification (NVQ)*.

Finally, and appropriately for a dictionary, a word about language. Many of the entries relate to subjects which are not sector-specific but which may be applied to all phases of education from primary to higher. In such cases the word 'learner' has been used as a generic term for pupil, student, and trainee. The term 'trainee' itself is in some senses problematic, referring as it usually does to learners engaged in further education on programmes of vocational training, but also used in government discourse to describe student teachers. I have used both terms here, according to the context, in describing those undertaking a teaching qualification. Then again, some of the vocabulary we readily employ in relation to education repays closer critical consideration, too: words such as 'deliver' and 'choice' and 'standards'. These terms are subjected here to a certain amount of critical scrutiny as part of the process of exploring their meaning. Lastly, faced with a choice between the two synonymous terms 'educationalist' and 'educationist' I have chosen to use the former throughout.

The writing of this Dictionary has been a team effort, and my thanks go to the contributors, who include specialists from all sectors of education and from a range of professional backgrounds: academics, advisers, classroom practitioners, and educational managers. Their specialist entries are followed by their initials, and a brief biographical note on each of them can be found in the Notes on the Contributors. All other entries are written by me; but I would also like to acknowledge here the very helpful suggestions and advice I have received from a number of colleagues whose professional practice gives them a national or regional perspective on developments in the field; these include Pat Hollingworth and Dr Alan Morris. To all those others who gave generous advice on the compiling and writing of this Dictionary, very many thanks.

S.W.

Notes on the Contributors

Robert Bowen is Advisory Editor on this Dictionary. He is Associate Dean in the School of Education at Nottingham Trent University. He has responsibility for leading the School's Initial Teacher Education provision for all sectors and has carried out an extensive range of consultancy work for the Training and Development Agency for Schools. He has published widely in the field of primary design and technology. His most recent research work explores junior age children's use of handheld computers when designing.

Liz Atkins (L.A.) is a principal lecturer and researcher in higher education and has a key role in the provision of professional development for teachers in the lifelong learning sector. Her published work focuses on issues of class and identity in tertiary education.

Karl Aubrey (K.A.) is a senior lecturer at Bishop Grosseteste University College, Lincoln, where he is the Academic Coordinator for the Foundation Degree in Educational Studies for teaching assistants as well as the BA (Hons) Professional Studies in Education. His research interests include inclusive practice and access routes into the teaching profession.

Trisha Bowen (T.B.) is Head of a Special Needs Support Service in the East Midlands. She has been involved in the field of special educational needs, and in particular physical disability, for over 20 years. She is an active SEN school governor; a steering group member of the National Network for Advisory Teachers of Physically Impaired Pupils; and also an MA Education tutor at Northampton University.

Viv Channing (V.C.) is a teacher educator at Lincoln College, where she coordinates initial teacher training and is involved in the provision of continuing professional development for experienced teachers.

Liz Ellis (L.E.) is a Learning Director and local authority special educational needs coordinator, leading enhanced resource facilities for students on the autistic spectrum. She has worked as an advisory teacher for SEN, writes and delivers training programmes for educational professionals on SEN and inclusion, and is co-author of the guidance for teachers on differentiation in literacy, *See the Light* (2007).

Heather Graham (H.G.) is the Associate Director (Wales) of the Leadership Foundation for Higher Education. From 2003 to 2007 she was the Director of the Open University in Wales, and in that role she served as Chair of the Welsh Assembly's review into funding and support for part-time students at Welsh universities.

Morwenna Griffiths (M.G.) is Professor of Classroom Learning in the Moray House School of Education at Edinburgh University. She has taught in primary schools in Bristol, and at the University of Isfahan, Iran, at Christ Church College of Higher Education in Canterbury, and at Oxford Brookes, Nottingham, and Nottingham Trent universities. Her recent research has included philosophical theorizing and empirical investigation related to epistemology of (auto)biography, social justice, public spaces, the nature of practice, feminization, and creativity. Her books include *Action for Social Justice in Education: Fairly Different* (2003), *Educational Research for Social Justice* (1998), and *Feminisms and the Self: The Web of Identity* (1995).

Julia Hardwick (J.H.) is an Advanced Practitioner for Creative Studies at Burton College. She has many years of teaching experience, both in the UK and overseas, and has a particular interest in lexicography.

Chris Hudson (C.H.) is a lecturer and researcher working in higher education.

Susan Meggett (S.M.) teaches in the secondary sector. She has worked on local authority initiatives for gifted and talented pupils and as a General Certificate of Secondary Education examiner. Her previous experience includes teaching and researching in higher education.

Lindsay Paterson (L.P.) is Professor of Educational Policy at Edinburgh University. His current research interests are in the 20th-century history of Scottish education, social mobility, and the relationship between education and civic values. His books include *Crisis in the Classroom: The Exam Debacle and the Way Ahead for Scottish Education* (2000), *Education and a Scottish Parliament* (1996), *A Diverse Assembly: The Debate on a Scottish Parliament* (1998), and *The Autonomy of Modern Scotland* (1994).

Isabella Wallace (I.F.W.) is an author and Advanced Skills Teacher working in the secondary sector. As well as research on innovative teaching and learning, her publications include the guide for teachers *Pimp Your Lesson* (2007).

Susan Wallace is Reader in Post-Compulsory Education at Nottingham Trent University. She previously taught for ten years outside the higher education sector, and has worked in a local authority advisory role for 14–19 education. Her research interests and publications focus on the motivation and behaviour of learners, and she has written widely on the professional development of teachers.

Annie Woods (A.W.) is an academic team leader in higher education for continuing professional development, and has also had many years' experience as a lecturer in initial teacher training for the primary sector. She has recently taken a year's secondment to act as assistant head teacher in an inner-city primary school which takes an innovative approach to early years education.

Abbreviations

AAC augmentative and alternative communication
ABE adult basic education
ACCAC Qualifications, Curriculum, and Assessment Authority for Wales
ACE Advisory Centre for Education
ACEG Association for Careers Education and Guidance
ADHD attention deficit hyperactivity disorder
AEA Advanced Extension Award
AfL Assessment for Learning
A4e Action for Employment
AiFL Assessment is for Learning
AIUTA International Association of Universities of the Third Age
A level Advanced Level
ALI Adult Learning Inspectorate
Alp Accelerated Learning Programme; Association of Learning Providers
AMMA Assistant Masters and Mistresses Association
AoC Association of Colleges
AP advanced practitioner
APEL accreditation of prior experience and learning
APL Accreditation of Prior Learning
APR age participation rate
APVIC Association of Principals in Sixth Form Colleges
AQA Assessment and Qualifications Alliance
ASD Asperger's Syndrome
ASE Association for Science Education
AS level Advanced Subsidiary Level; Advanced Supplementary Level
AST advanced skills teacher
ATL Association of Teachers and Lecturers
AUT Association of University Teachers
AV audio-visual
AVA audio-visual aid
BA Bachelor of Arts
BA British Association for the Advancement of Science; Bachelor of Arts
BAC British Accreditation Council for Independent Further and Higher Education Colleges
Becta British Educational Communications and Technology Agency
B.Ed. Bachelor of Education
BEI British Education Index
BELB Belfast Education and Library Board
BERA British Educational Research Association
BESd behavioural, emotional, and social difficulties
BSA Boarding Schools Association
B.Sc. Bachelor of Science
BTEC Business and Technology Education Council
CACHE Council for Awards in Children's Care and Education
CAF Common Assessment Framework
CAL computer-assisted learning
CAMHS Child and Adolescent Mental Health Services
CASE Cognitive Acceleration through Science Education
CAT credit accumulation and transfer; cognitive abilities test
CCEA (Northern Ireland) Council for the Curriculum, Examinations, and Assessment
CCMS Council for Catholic Maintained Schools
CCW Curriculum Council for Wales
CDT craft, design, and technology
CEDP Career Entry and Development Profile
CEFRL Common European Framework of Reference for Languages
CEL Centre for Excellence in Leadership
CERI Centre for Educational Research and Innovation
Cert. Ed. Certificate of Education
CETT Centre for Excellence in Teacher Training
CfE Curriculum for Excellence
CIF Common Inspection Framework
CNAA Council for National Academic Awards

CoP Code of Practice
COVE Centre of Vocational Excellence
CPD continuing professional development
CPS Centre for Policy Studies
CPVE Certificate of Pre-Vocational Education
CQFW Credit and Qualifications Framework for Wales
CSE Certificate of Secondary Education
CSIE Centre for Studies in Inclusive Education
CSYS Certificate of Sixth Year Studies
C2K Curriculum 2000
DCSF Department for Children, Schools, and Families
DEETI Department of Education's Education and Training Inspectorate
DELNI Department for Employment and Learning, Northern Ireland
DENI Department of Education, Northern Ireland
DES Department of Education and Science
DfE Department for Education
DfEE Department for Education and Employment
DfES Department for Education and Skills
DIUS Department for Innovation, Universities, and Skills
D. Phil. Doctor of Philosophy
DtS Determined to Succeed
EAL English as an Additional Language
EAZ Education Action Zone
EFL English as a Foreign Language
EiC Excellence in Cities
EIS Educational Institute of Scotland
ELWa Further Education Funding Council for Wales
EMA Education Maintenance Allowance
EOTAS education otherwise than at school
ERA Education Reform Act 1988
ESF European Social Fund
ESOL English for Speakers of Other Languages
ESRC Economic and Social Research Council
e2e entry to employment
ETP employer training pilot
ETS Excellent Teacher Scheme
EV external verifier
EWS Education Welfare Service
EWO education welfare officer
EYFS Early Years Foundation Stage
FE further education
FEDA Further Education Development Agency
FEFC Further Education Funding Council
FENTO Further Education National Training Organization
FEU Further Education Unit
FTE full-time equivalent
GCE General Certificate of Education
GCSE General Certificate of Secondary Education
GMS grant maintained school
GNVQ General National Vocational Qualification
GTC General Teaching Council
GTCE General Teaching Council (England)
GTCNI General Teaching Council (Northern Ireland)
GTCS General Teaching Council (Scotland)
GTCW General Teaching Council (Wales)
GTP Graduate Teacher Programme
GTTR Graduate Teacher Training Registry
HE higher education
HEFCE Higher Education Funding Council for England
HEFCNI Higher Education Funding Council for Northern Ireland
HEFCW Higher Education Funding Council for Wales
HEI higher education institution
HEW Higher Education Wales
HLTA higher-level teaching assistant
HMI Her Majesty's Inspectorate
HMIE Her Majesty's Inspectorate of Education (Scotland)
HNC Higher National Certificate
HND Higher National Diploma
IAPC Institute for the Advancement of Philosophy for Children, New Jersey
IB International Baccalaureate
ICR income-contingent repayment
ICS integrated community school
ICT information communication technology
IE instrumental enrichment
IfL Institute for Learning
ILA Individual Learning Account

ILP individual learning plan
ILT Institute for Learning and Teaching; information learning technology
INSET in-service education of teachers
IQ intelligence quotient
ISP Intensifying Support Programme
IT information technology
ITA initial teaching alphabet
ITT initial teacher training
IV internal verifier
JCGQ Joint Council for General Qualifications
JCNVQ Joint Council for National Vocational Qualifications
JCQ Joint Council for Qualifications
JISC Joint Information Systems Committee
JNCHES Joint National Committee for Higher Education Staff
KAL knowledge about language
KS key stage
LA local authority
LAC looked-after children
LDSS Learning Development and Support Services
LEA local education authority
LEC Local Enterprise Company
LGA Local Government Association
LLM Master of Laws
LLS language-learning strategies
LLUK Lifelong Learning UK
LMS Local Management of Schools
LSC Learning and Skills Council
LSDA Learning and Skills Development Agency
LSN Learning and Skills Network
LSU Learning Support Unit
LTS Learning and Teaching Scotland
MA Master of Arts
M.Ed. Master of Education
mfl modern foreign language
MLE managed learning environment
M. Phil. Master of Philosophy
M.Sc. Master of Science
MSC Manpower Services Commission
NAB National Assessment Bank
NACETT National Advisory Council for Education and Training Targets
NACGT National Association of Careers Guidance Teachers
NAEIAC National Association of Educational Inspectors, Advisers, and Consultants
NAgC National Association for Gifted Children
NAHT National Association of Head Teachers
NARE National Association for Remedial Education
Nasen National Association for Special Educational Needs
NASUWT National Association of Schoolmasters Union of Women Teachers
NATFHE National Association of Teachers in Further and Higher Education
NC national curriculum
NCB National Children's Bureau
NCC National Consortium of Colleges; National Curriculum Council
NCE National Commission on Education
NCSE National Council for Special Education
NCSL National College for School Leadership
NCVQ National Council for Vocational Qualifications
NEC National Extension College
NEET not in employment, education, or training
NEELB North Eastern Education and Library Board
NET National Education Trust
NFER National Foundation for Educational Research
NGfL National Grid for Learning
NIACE National Institute of Adult Continuing Education
NICIE Northern Ireland Council for Integrated Education
NJF National Joint Forum
NLS National Literacy Strategy
NLSC National Learning and Skills Council
NLT National Literacy Trust
NNATPIP National Network for Advisory Teachers of Physically Impaired Pupils
NNEB National Nursery Examination Board
NNS National Numeracy Strategy
NOCN National Open College Network
NOF New Opportunities Fund
NPA National Progression Award
NPQH National Professional Qualification for Headship
NQs National Qualifications

NQF National Qualifications Framework
NQGA National Qualification Group Award
NQT newly qualified teacher
NRA National Record of Achievement
NTET National Targets for Education and Training
NTO national training organization
NUS National Union of Students
NUT National Union of Teachers
NVQ National Vocational Qualification
NYA National Youth Agency
OCN Open College Network
Ofqual Office of the Qualifications and Examinations Regulator
Ofsted Office for Standards in Education; from 2007 the Office for Standards in Education, Children's Services, and Skills
O Grade Ordinary Grade
OLASS Offender Learning and Skills Service
O level Ordinary Level
OU Open University
PANDA Performance Assessment National Data
PAT Professional Association of Teachers
PAYP Positive Activities for Young People
PCAS Polytechnics Central Admissions Systems
PCET post-compulsory education and training
PCFC Polytechnics and Colleges Funding Council
PE physical education
PECS picture exchange communication system
PEP personal education plan
PGCE Postgraduate Certificate of Education; Professional Graduate Certificate of Education
PGDE Professional Graduate Diploma in Education
Ph.D. Doctor of Philosophy
PHE Postgraduate Certificate in Higher Education
PI performance indicator
PLP Primary Leadership Programme
PNS Primary National Strategy
PoS programme of study
PRU pupil referral unit
PSCL primary strategy consultant leader
PSE personal and social education
PSHE personal, social, and health education
PTA Parent–Teacher Association
QAA Quality Assurance Agency for Higher Education
QCA Qualifications and Curriculum Authority
QCF Qualifications and Credit Framework
QIA Quality Improvement Agency
QTLS qualified teacher learning and skills
QTS qualified teacher status
RAE Research Assessment Exercise
RE religious education
RLD reference-level descriptor
Rosla raising of the school leaving age
RP received pronunciation
RSA Royal Society of Arts
RSG revenue support grant
RTP Registered Teacher Programme
SAAS Student Awards Agency for Scotland
SAR self-assessment report
SATs Standard (Assessment) Tasks
SCAA School Curriculum and Assessment Authority
SCE Service Children's Education
SCOTCAT Scottish Credit Accumulation and Transfer
Scotvec Scottish Vocational Education Council
SCQF Scottish Credit and Qualifications Framework
SCRE Scottish Council for Research in Education
SCT senior curriculum team
SDP school development plan
SEAC Schools Examinations and Assessment Council
SEAL social and emotional aspects of learning
SEB Scottish Examinations Board
SEED Scottish Executive Education Department
SEELB South Eastern Education and Library Board
SEF self-evaluation form
SELB Southern Education and Library Board
SEN special educational needs
SENCO special educational needs coordinator
SENDA Special Educational Needs and Disability Act 2001
SENDIST Special Educational Needs and Disability Tribunal

SEU	Standards and Effectiveness Unit
SFC	Scottish Funding Council
SFCC	school facing 'challenging circumstances'
SFEU	Scottish Further Education Unit
SGA	Scottish Group Award
SHA	Secondary Heads Association
SIP	school improvement partner
SLC	Student Loans Company
SLSU	Skills for Life Strategy Unit
SLT	senior leadership team
SMT	senior management team
SNCT	Scottish Negotiating Committee for Teachers
SPA	Scottish Progression Award
SQA	Scottish Qualifications Authority
SQC	Scottish Qualifications Certificate
SQH	Scottish Qualification for Headship
SRE	sex and relationship education
SSA	standard spending assessment
SSC	sector skills councils
SSDA	Sector Skills Development Agency
SSR	staff–student ratio
StAR	Strategic Area Review
STRB	School Teachers' Review Body
SVQ	Scottish Vocational Qualification
SVUK	Standards and Verification UK
TA	teaching assistant
TAT	Third Age Trust
TDA	Training and Development Agency for Schools
TEC	Training and Enterprise Council
TESOL	Teachers of English to Speakers of Other Languages
TfW	Training for Work
TLR	teaching and learning responsibility
TMA	tutor-marked assignment
TOPS	Training Opportunity Scheme
TP	teaching practice
TTA	Teacher Training Agency
TVEI	Technical and Vocational Education Initiative
UCAS	Universities and Colleges Admissions Service
UCCA	Universities Central Council on Admissions
UCEA	Universities and Colleges Employers' Association
UCU	University and College Union
UFC	University Funding Council
UfI	University for Industry
UHI	UHI Millennium Institute
U3A	University of the Third Age
VET	vocational education and training
VLE	virtual learning environment
VOCA	voice output communication aid
VSO	Voluntary Service Overseas
WBL	work-based learning
WEA	Workers' Educational Association
WELB	Western Education and Library Board
YOP	Youth Opportunities Programme
YOT	youth offending team
YT	Youth Training
YTS	Youth Training Scheme
ZPD	zone of proximal development

A* A *grade awarded for exceptionally good performance in any subject at *General Certificate of Secondary Education. Previously, the highest grade awarded was an A grade. When the introduction of an A* grade also for *General Certificate of Education *Advanced Levels was proposed in 2002, it became part of the debate about *standards. Those who supported the introduction argued that the additional grade was necessary to reward and acknowledge the achievement of outstanding candidates, while opponents suggested that it represented an inflation of the grading system and was indicative of a general lowering of standards.

A Basis for Choice (ABC) *See* KEY SKILLS.

ability Used in education in the sense of 'potential for performance'. It is unclear, however, how ability might be accurately measured, if not in terms of performance. Nevertheless, it is synonymous neither with 'achievement' nor with 'attainment', and refers rather to what a student is capable of, than to what they have proved themselves able to do. This is best illustrated by the fact that a student may be described as having high ability but performing poorly; or as having low ability but performing well. The idea of ability as a potential is evident in such phrases as 'late developer', commonly used to describe someone whose innate ability does not become evident until late in their school career, or even after they have left formal education.

ability grouping Grouping pupils together in classes to be taught according to their *ability. In the United Kingdom this is not usually the case, as pupils are normally grouped according to age, and within a national framework of *key stages of development. However, *primary schools often use **target grouping** for *literacy and/or *numeracy, which is, in effect, grouping by ability for the purpose of teaching in these *curriculum areas. Similarly, in secondary schooling, pupils may be grouped according to ability within their age group cohort for specific subjects, so that there might be, for example, three Year 9 classes for English: one for high achievers, one for those pupils of average achievement, and one for those expected to do less well.
See also SETS.

Abitur The German *examination equivalent to the *General Certificate of Education *Advanced Level. It is often held up by educators in the United Kingdom as a model to be emulated as it offers the *academic rigour necessary for a *university entrance qualification as well as the breadth required to prepare school-leavers for employment. In this sense it can be cited as an example of how the academic–*vocational divide may be successfully bridged.
See also BACCALAURÉAT.

academic 1. An adjective used to describe learning and related activities which are largely of a *cognitive nature and involve the acquisition, exploration, or application of knowledge, often of an abstract kind or for its own sake. It is often applied to point up the distinction between this type of activity and the more practical or instrumental types of learning which fall into the category of *vocational. In this context it can be used in a derogatory sense, as in the phrase, 'too academic', meaning that the learning in question is too far removed from the practicalities of life. This understanding of the term emerges also in the phrase 'That's academic', applied to a question raised about a merely hypothetical or fictional issue, about which further discussion would be fruitless.

2. A *teacher or researcher, usually in *higher education. This sector itself is sometimes referred to as Academe.

academic board A committee of staff and managers in a *university or *college which meets regularly for the purpose of regulating and monitoring the academic affairs of the institution. Staff members are usually nominated and elected by their peers, although such a board will normally include some co-opted members.

academic monitoring The process of observing students' academic progress in one or more subject over a period of time. It is used by teachers to compare the performance of a particular student to that of his/her classmates and to identify students who are struggling, excelling, or underachieving. Information for examining students' progress is usually collected in the form of *test marks and *teacher assessment levels or grades. These are often recorded on **tracking sheets**, or **progress reports**, which can then be issued to parents at intervals during the academic year. Usual practice is for these documents to be completed three times annually in order to illustrate a student's level of achievement at the beginning, middle, and end of the school year. The same documentation can also be used on a whole-school level by the *senior leadership team, in order to assess the success of intervention strategies, and also to monitor the effectiveness of teaching across all subjects. Academic monitoring is useful to pupils because it allows them to become aware of their *examination prospects and any disparity between their current and predicted performance. I.F.W.

academy 1. A *specialist school or *college, usually providing training in the arts or in a specific profession; for example, a music academy or a military academy. It may also be applied to a secondary school, although usually a private one. The term was used in the naming of the *city academies, secondary schools set up as a trust with private sponsorship and government funding, as part of a 2002 government initiative aimed at improving the standards of performance in English inner-city schools in areas of social deprivation. The word 'academy' itself derives from the garden near Athens where Plato taught his students and from which his school of philosophy took its name. In this sense the term carries connotations of serious scholarship and learning suggestive of high status and academic respectability.

2. A generic term used to describe comprehensive schools in Scotland.

accelerated learning A range of techniques which are claimed to increase the learner's capacity to absorb and retain information by focusing on learning how to learn. Proponents suggest that we use only a small percentage of our potential mental capacity, and that we could increase this by, for example, identifying our preferred learning style and adopting strategies such as the use of memory maps. Training in accelerated learning often draws on the theory of *multiple intelligences.

SEE WEB LINKS

- Summarizes the claims made for accelerated learning and how it can be applied in various sectors of education and training. **I.F.W.**

access arrangements Adjustments which are made which enable students with particular needs to access *tests and *exams. Such arrangements must not give students an unfair advantage. Students entitled to access arrangements are those who have a *statement of *special educational needs (SEN), who are at school action or school action plus of the SEN Code of Practice, and who receive special educational provision. Students whose access to the tests is significantly impaired by a *learning difficulty or a disability may also qualify. Students who have difficulty concentrating may also be entitled, as are those whose first language is not English or who lack fluency in English. Typical access arrangements include the use of readers, *amanuenses, scribes, and transcripts. Rest breaks can be given. Schools and colleges are required to give evidence of a history of special provision in support of a request for special access arrangements. Guidance for the correct use of access arrangements can be found in the *Qualifications and Curriculum Authority's guidance on access arrangements for pupils with particular needs.

Further Reading: Department for Education and Skills *Code of Practice for Special Educational Needs (Revised)* DfES/581/2001 (DfES, 2001). **T.B., L.E.**

Access course Known in full as an 'Access to Higher Education course', this is a programme of study specifically designed for adults without formal entry qualifications such as *Advanced Levels (A levels) seeking to gain access to *higher education. Since their inception into education provision in the late 1970s, Access courses have been regarded as the 'third route' into higher education, differentiating them from A levels and diplomas. It is, though, worth noting the difference between 'access' and 'Access'. The former refers to any educational courses which provide entry into education, while the latter is specifically designed as a pathway for adults into higher education. Although the development of access courses can be seen to be part of a long history of *adult educational programmes in tertiary education, dating back as far as the original *mechanics institutes of the mid-19th century, more recently they have been shaped by specific governmental education policies which emphasize the role played by education and a highly trained workforce in creating economic health and stability. To this end, *widening participation in higher education has been the focus of policy reports and research, such as the *Dearing Report, the *Kennedy Report, and of the subsequent *Green Paper *The Learning Age* (DfEE, 1998). In this context, Access courses represent one major route towards widening participation in higher education. They are subject-based and are taught mainly in *colleges of further education, offering subjects such as sociology, psychology, English, and philosophy. They are internally assessed by *continuous assessment; and academic references from tutors play a key role in securing students' progression to undergraduate study. C.H.

Access Fund A source of financial support for students aged 16 or over in full-time education whose studies involve costs (for example, for specialist equipment) which they are not able to meet; or who face leaving their studies for reasons of financial hardship; or who have additional costs incurred by a disability or childcare responsibilities. The Access Fund is intended to facilitate wider access to further education and higher education. It is financed by central government and is administered through *local authorities for claimants in *schools, and through *universities and *colleges for disbursement to their own eligible students. The Access Fund cannot normally be used simply for the purpose of paying tuition fees.

accessibility plans Since 2003 it has been a requirement that all schools possess an accessibility plan. These must describe how the school intends to improve access for pupils with disabilities to the curriculum, environment, and information (which includes all written information including signage, handouts, and textbooks). Plans must be in writing and adequately resourced. They must be implemented, reviewed, and revised as necessary. Before drafting their plan, schools are required to consult widely. Plans are renewable every three years and must be published annually. T.B., L.E.

Access to Employment (A2e) A pathfinder project which aimed to enable adults, including people with disabilities or learning difficulties, to gain the skills needed to enter employment. The project concentrated on *literacy, language, and *numeracy, as well as the generic skills needed for employment. Managed by the *National Institute of Adult Continuing Education, in 2006 the project produced the *Skills for Working* document that was mainly based on the experiences of the learners involved at the various A2e pathfinder sites. *Skills for Working* is a set of guidelines which offers advice in meeting the needs of individuals in such matters as work experience, various courses and training opportunities, *mentoring, and travel. V.C., K.A.

accountability Educational institutions, in the persons of their managers and governing bodies, are required to account publicly and, in the case of schools, particularly to parents for their performance through such means as *performance indicators and *league tables. This is termed 'accountability'. It is an example of the trend for a vocabulary more usually associated with business and commerce being applied in the context of schools and other educational institutions following measures to create a *market in education since the 1980s.

accreditation 1. The awarding of credit to an individual student for achievement of, or towards, a qualification. *See also* ACCREDITATION OF PRIOR LEARNING.

2. A process by which an organization or institution, such as a college or university, wins approval for one or more of its awards, involving confirmation from a panel including representatives of peer institutions that the award or awards in question meet nationally accepted standards. *See also* VALIDATION.

accreditation of prior learning The process or practice of awarding *credits which can be counted towards a qualification, based on the candidate's previous experience, learning, or achievements. This practice has become widely used in the *learning and skills sector since the introduction of *National Vocational Qualifications (NVQs), as the nature of these qualifications allows a candidate to be assessed on their current *competence, rather than requiring attendance on a *course or the successful completion of *examinations. Candidates for *accreditation are usually required to present a portfolio of evidence which may include observer or assessor reports, witness statements, previously gained certification, evidence of competence in the workplace, photographs, or recordings. The process of compilation is usually supported by a qualified adviser and the portfolio is assessed by a qualified assessor, both of whom are required to hold the NVQ units appropriate to their role. The process of compiling a portfolio can be time-consuming and, in terms of support and assessment, can prove as costly as the enrolment fee for a course of study. Accreditation of prior learning is also used outside the system of NVQ qualifications; for example, for some candidates applying for a university course in teacher training for further education. In such a case, the assessment of portfolios does not require an NVQ-qualified assessor but is instead subject to the quality assurance system operating within that institution.

achievement The performance or *attainment of a *student or *pupil. It may be measured in a number of ways, such as the successful demonstration of a pre-specified *competence, the award of a pass mark, or the gaining of a satisfactory *grade for work accomplished. A learner's achievement is based on their performance, rather than on their potential or their *ability. A learner with high ability might, under some circumstances, perform less well than a learner with lower ability.

Action for Employment (A4e) Originally formed in 1986, A4e is now an international organization which helps people to return to work as well as providing a *training and recruitment support service for businesses. The organization works closely with other agencies such as **Jobcentre Plus** in supporting and preparing people who wish to re-enter work. Those whom A4e assists include black and non-white British groups, the disabled, and people from disadvantaged areas. The organization also operates *learndirect centres and delivers a variety of *basic skills and *vocational programmes.

SEE WEB LINKS

- Provides the historical rationale for the foundation of the organization.
- Provides details and statistics of the groups and businesses supported, as well as links to specific aspects such as welfare to work, financial inclusion and education, and business support.

V.C., K.A.

a

action research A *research methodology in which the researcher investigates practice through cycles of reflection, identification of issues, action, data collection, analysis, and more reflection in order to identify further areas for investigation. The emphasis is on improving practice. Researchers usually investigate their own practice, and may be working alone or collaboratively with one or more co-researchers. Most models of action research encourage collaboration as being optimal at every stage of the cycle. Action research may be narrowly instrumental: simply a method of problem-solving. However, most models emphasize reflection focused on the self of the researcher, the wider context of the research issue, the theoretical background, and the social and political assumptions governing the articulation of the research issue.

There are various kinds of research, all closely related to action research, which use cycles of action, collection of evidence, and reflection on the researcher's own practice. They include reflective practice, action inquiry, action learning, double loop learning, critical action research, and self-study. They differ in the emphasis placed on, for instance, collaboration, the focus on self, or social and political change. These differences in emphasis distinguish different models. All of them unite in having an *epistemological perspective which prioritizes improved practice. Evidence only has to be strong enough to warrant changes in practice in the specific context of the research. Research methods are likely to be qualitative, and are also often creative. 'Small-scale classroom research' and 'practitioner research' are allied to action research but they are not cyclical. Rather, they follow the pattern of identifying a research question, gathering evidence, and using the analysis of the data to formulate conclusions for dissemination.

Further Reading: B. Somekh and S. Noffke *Handbook of Educational Action Research* (Sage, 2008).

SEE WEB LINKS

- Details of the Collaborative Action Research Network.

M.G.

active learning Learning which encourages the pupil or student to engage actively with what is being learned through activities such as *group discussion, role play, or experimentation, rather than passively receiving and memorizing knowledge or instruction from the teacher in order to be able to repeat it accurately, as was the practice in many 19th- and early 20th-century schools. Active learning became the norm in most schools, as the value of being able to reproduce information uncritically and 'parrot fashion' came increasingly under question in the 20th century. However, the facilitation of active learning becomes more difficult the larger the *class size. The implementation of an active approach to learning, therefore, can depend as much on *pupil–teacher ratio as on beliefs about effective approaches to learning.

active vocabulary The range of words which an individual is able to use accurately in their speech (active spoken vocabulary), or their writing (active written vocabulary), or both of these. The active vocabulary does not include words which are only recognized and understood, either by reading or hearing, but not actually used. At most stages of learning of a language, the learner's active vocabulary will be more limited than their comprehension. In other words, their understanding will outstrip their ability to express themselves. *See also* AGE, READING; PASSIVE VOCABULARY.

activity A task or exercise undertaken by the learner, and usually set by the teacher, which has an intended learning outcome. Such activities range from the fairly passive—for example, listening attentively to the teacher—to the dynamic and active—for example, carrying out an experiment, conducting a survey, or painting a picture. The types of activity the learner is required to undertake will be determined by a number of factors, which include the learner's age, the subject matter being learned, and the level of study. *See also* ACTIVE LEARNING; LESSON.

admissions The process of gaining a place at—being admitted to—a school, college, or university. Schools have been required since 2007 to ensure that their **admissions code** promotes social cohesion. This requirement was introduced as a result of evidence that pupils from less advantaged homes were more likely to fail to gain admission to the most popular schools, since these tend to be located in areas of social advantage. Some local authorities, in an effort to address this issue, have introduced the use of an admission **lottery**, where pupils are allocated places by chance rather than by parental *choice. In larger institutions, such as universities and colleges, it is often the title of the department or section which deals with the administration relating to applications, offers, and admissions. *See also* ADMISSIONS APPEAL; SOCIAL CLASS; UNIVERSITIES AND COLLEGES ADMISSIONS SERVICE.

admissions appeal If a child does not gain admission to their first *choice of school, their parents are entitled to lodge an appeal against this decision. Such appeals are heard by independent appeal panels whose membership must exclude all members of the *local authority and the *governing bodies of the schools in question. A decision made by the appeals panel is deemed to be final. The number of admissions appeals made in England annually continues to rise.

adult basic skills *See* BASIC SKILLS; BASIC SKILLS AGENCY; MOSER REPORT.

adult education Courses of study offered for learners over the age of compulsory schooling. Sometimes used synonymously with *evening classes, adult education encompasses a very wide range of provision, including prison education, education in the armed forces, *adult literacy classes, and church-based learning groups, as well as *local authority and *Workers' Educational Association provision. It has a long history closely associated with ideals of social reform, self-help, and self-improvement, particularly among *social classes who could not access adequate schooling or higher education. Direct forerunners of adult education were the 'adult and benevolent evening schools', the 'young men's reformation and mental improvement societies', and the *mechanics' institutes of the 19th century. By the 21st century, however, adult education has lost much of its earlier, radical image. Theory related to the education of adults constitutes in itself a field of academic study, sometimes referred to as **androgogy**, to distinguish it from *pedagogy, the theory related to the teaching of children. It is argued, for example, that some key characteristics can be associated with adult learners, which must be taken into account if they are to be helped to learn effectively. These include:

- their adult responsibilities and commitments, which will inevitably compete for time with their studies;
- their motivation, which has brought them back to education;
- their need to feel they are getting good value, in terms of learning, from the time and money they have invested;
- their level of anxiety at returning to education, which may be much higher than they are willing to disclose.

The education of adults can also necessitate a reconfiguration of the teacher–pupil paradigm into a more egalitarian, negotiated relationship in which it will usually not be appropriate for the teacher to use the same forms of encouragement and sanctions which they might employ with younger learners. *See also* NATIONAL INSTITUTE OF ADULT CONTINUING EDUCATION; RADICAL EDUCATORS.

Further Reading: Roger Fieldhouse and Associates *A History of Modern British Adult Education* (NIACE, 1996).

Adult Learning Inspectorate (ALI) A specialist inspectorate whose function was the inspection of *adult education provision and *work-based learning for 16–19-year-olds. Created in 2000 and operational from 2001, it had its own chief inspector. In *colleges of further education its specialist remit meant that it shared responsibility for inspections with *Ofsted (then the Office for Standards in Education). On 1 April 2007, following the reorganization of inspectorates embodied in the Education and Inspections Act 2006, ALI was incorporated into the Office for Standards in Education, Children's Services, and Skills.

adult literacy It is estimated that 7 million adults in England possess *literacy skills which are below the level of that expected of 11-year-old pupils. The figures for the UK as a whole are unavailable, but are likely to reflect similar levels. To address this problem the *Skills for Life Strategy Unit was set up in 2000, operating at first within the *Department for Education and Skills and later, following departmental reorganization, within the *Department for Innovation, Universities, and Skills. Since the level of adult literacy is particularly low among the prison population, the Unit works closely with the Prison Service, as well as with the Qualifications and Curriculum Authority, to implement the Skills for Life strategy. This has involved the development of National Standards for Adult Literacy (NSAL), which are set at *entry level and levels 1 and 2 of the *National Qualifications Framework. These standards act as a benchmark against which an adult's level of literacy skills can be assessed. They cover a range of literacy skills, encompassing not only *reading and writing, but also speaking and listening. In order to ascertain whether an adult is in need of literacy support, the individual is first screened, and may then go on to an initial assessment, which is designed to identify their level of *functional literacy as measured against the NSAL. This process is also used to ascertain the learning needs of adults for whom English is not their first language and who are seeking literacy support for their speaking, listening, reading, or writing skills. The assessment materials used also function to identify underlying problems such as *dyslexia.

Part of the strategy has included the development, begun in 2006, of a series of books, known as **Quick Reads**, designed to engage the interest of adult emergent readers and to encourage them in reading as an enjoyable leisure pursuit. Although simplified, edited versions of popular novels have been in existence for several decades, often aimed specifically at the prison population, the Quick Reads series takes a rather different approach, commissioning well-known celebrities to write original work which aims to build the confidence of adults who are in the process of developing their literacy skills. *See also* BASIC SKILLS; MOSER REPORT.

Advanced Extension Award (AEA) Aimed at the most able 10 per cent of *Advanced Level (A level) students, these awards are designed to encourage a critical and analytical approach to the study of a subject. They require the student to study in depth, and are available in a more restricted range of subjects than the standard A level. By making it possible to identify outstanding students, the AEA was intended to make it unnecessary for *universities to develop their own entrance examinations as a response to the increasing number of applicants with good A level results.

SEE WEB LINKS

- Lists the subjects available for the AEA.

Advanced Higher An advanced qualification made up of internally and externally assessed *units, which was introduced in Scotland in 2000/01 to replace the *Certificate of Sixth Year Studies. This is equivalent to level 7 of the *Scottish Credit and Qualifications Framework. S.M.

Advanced Level (A level) The generic term applied to the *General Certificate of Education advanced level *examinations taken by some students in Years 12 and 13 of their schooling, and by others, including adult learners, through other educational institutions, such as *colleges of further education. It is the most usual entrance requirement for *higher education, each A level *grade achieved carrying a number of 'points', which, added, must achieve the total specified for entry. Until 2000 the candidate would normally choose two or three subjects to study from a wide range of options. Following the reforms of *Curriculum 2000, the A level curriculum is now divided into two stages. During the first year, candidates are encouraged to choose four or five subjects to study at *Advanced Subsidiary Level (AS level), and to narrow their choice down to two or three in their second year, following the *assessment of their achievement at AS level. The final assessment is now known as **A2**, to distinguish it from the AS stage of the *curriculum. The intention of this structural reform was to broaden the post-16 curriculum. Both students and teachers have reported that the increased number of assessments and examinations, as well as the additional subjects for study, are proving onerous.

Schools and students receive the results of the A level examinations in August, an annual event widely covered by the national press. For 21 consecutive years the results have shown an improvement in performance overall, with more students achieving top grades each year. Perhaps inevitably, this has led to accusations by some of falling standards, and the suggestion that perhaps the

A level examinations themselves are becoming easier, rather than students' performance improving year by year. Others argue, however, that such accusations at that juncture each year are ill-judged and do not give sufficient credit to successful students for their hard work and achievement. The debate over this issue of performance and standards remains unresolved. *See also* UNIVERSITIES AND COLLEGES ADMISSIONS SERVICE.

SEE WEB LINKS

- Current information about A level choices.

advanced practitioner (AP) A title awarded to outstanding teachers in *colleges of further education in acknowledgement of their skills at teaching and supporting learning. APs are usually expected to take on the role of *mentor to newly appointed teachers or those with professional development needs, and to contribute generally to the professional development of colleagues within their institution. In this sense, the role may be seen as roughly equivalent to that of *excellent teacher in the schools sector. Unlike teachers with an *advanced skills teacher role in schools, the AP is not required to contribute to *local authority led professional development, since colleges of education fall outside local authority remit.

advanced skills teacher (AST) A teacher who has been recognized through external *assessment as having excellent classroom practice. The teacher must pass a national assessment and subsequently be appointed to an AST role. This scheme was introduced to reward the very best teachers who wish to remain in the classroom rather than being promoted up the management scale or taking on extra responsibilities for additional payment. ASTs should have 80 per cent of their timetable given over to supporting other teachers within their own or other schools; to helping colleagues to develop their skills; and to sharing excellent practice, approaches, and ideas.

They receive additional payment on a separate pay scale, and increased non-contact time in order to carry out their AST duties. These duties often involve supporting staff in other local schools, but can also include activities such as:

- producing high-quality teaching materials for use in their own and other schools;
- teaching 'model' lessons with staff observing;
- observing lessons and advising other teachers on good classroom practice and *lesson planning;
- supporting and *mentoring teachers who are experiencing difficulties;
- participating in the induction and mentoring of *newly qualified teachers;
- leading professional research groups or working parties;
- supporting professional development through performance management and quality assurance systems.

I.F.W.

Advanced Subsidiary Level The first stage of the *Advanced Level (A level) curriculum, introduced in 2000, following a recommendation in the *Dearing Review (1996) that the existing *Advanced Supplementary Level (AS level), which covered about half a full A level syllabus and was assessed against the same criteria, should be retitled Advanced Subsidiary Level, and should be assessed at a lower level which reflected the shorter length of study. Candidates are expected to select four or five subjects, which are assessed after a year. From these they will choose the subjects (usually two or three) with which they will continue to A2 level. *See also* CURRICULUM 2000.

Advanced Supplementary Level (AS level) A *General Certificate of Education (GCE) qualification whose syllabus covered about half that of a full GCE *Advanced Level (A level) syllabus and which was assessed against the same criteria, at the same level as a full A level. These AS levels were normally studied over two years, were often taken alongside one or more full A levels, and were designed to allow sixth form pupils access to a broader curriculum. In 2000, following a recommendation in the *Dearing Review (1996), the Advanced Supplementary was replaced by the *Advanced Subsidiary, which constitutes the first half of the two-year A level programme, and is accordingly assessed against a less demanding set of criteria than the original AS level. *See also* CURRICULUM 2000.

adviser *See* ADVISORY SERVICE.

Advisory Centre for Education (ACE) An independent registered charity offering advice to parents and carers on issues related to state-funded compulsory schooling in England and Wales. Founded in 1960, it provides telephone advice lines as well as printed guidance on a range of topics, including *bullying and *special educational needs. It is particularly active in providing advice on *admission appeals and *exclusions.

advisory service The education departments of *local authorities usually offer an advisory service to schools in order to support them in meeting national standards in teaching and learning and in school management. Those carrying out this work may be full-time **advisers** or, in some cases, *advisory teachers. The advisory service is normally responsible for providing *continuing professional development, such as updating on national initiatives, for teachers within the authority; and will also carry out trial-run 'inspections' to aid schools preparing for imminent *Ofsted inspections. One of its additional functions may be to place advisers in schools temporarily to carry out essential roles, such as *head teacher or subject leader, where this is deemed necessary.

advisory teacher A teacher, normally seconded from a teaching post in order to join their *local authority *advisory service and take up an advisory role for local schools in a specific *curriculum area, *key stage, or specific issue, such as *assessment or *inclusion, of which they have expert knowledge and experience. As well as visiting schools and supporting teachers, their remit includes organizing and delivering *continuing professional development for teachers in their area of expertise. The role of advisory teacher has now been largely superseded by the introduction of *advanced skills teachers, who carry out a similar role while remaining based in their own school.

affective One of the three **domains** of *knowledge, the others being the *cognitive and the *psychomotor domains. It is used to describe *learning which involves a development or change in attitudes or feelings, and is applied in contexts where such development is an implicit goal, such as spiritual and moral education, or the development of an aesthetic appreciation of art, poetry, or music. Learning in the affective domain is difficult to express in terms of observable outcomes, and difficult to assess, since a change in feelings or attitudes usually cannot be reliably or accurately measured. The term derives from **affect**, in its sense of 'emotion' or 'feeling'.

after-school activity *See* OUT-OF-HOURS ACTIVITY.

age participation rate (APR) The number of a specific age group participating in *further or *higher education as a proportion of the total. A major use of the APR by providers of *post-compulsory education is to calculate trends in the demand for places, both to the institution as a whole and in specific subject areas.

age, reading The measurement of a child's *reading ability in terms of the average ability expected at a particular age. Thus, a very competent reader at the age of 6 might be deemed to have a reading age of 9. The idea of a reading age in years, however, can be misleading, particularly when related to *adult literacy levels, and does not necessarily correspond to thinking and comprehension age, especially for children with *dyslexia. The very concept of 'reading age' was challenged in the **Bullock Report** as early as 1975, and continues to be questioned by educationalists such as Stierer and Maybin (1994). It is more usual now to express competence in reading in terms of **readability levels** rather than reading age. The *National Literacy Trust defines readability levels by sentence length and complexity of vocabulary, where levels can be calculated for any piece of prose using a simple formula. In schools, *National Foundation for Educational Research tests are now widely used to provide a 'reading quotient', or standardized score.

A child's reading age was commonly appended to a child's school *report prior to the onset of the *National Literacy Strategy (1997). Children are now expected to reach national levels for reading and writing; level 3 at 7 years of age, level 4 at age 11, and level 6 at age 14. Government research suggests that reading skills have improved in the UK since 1997. The *Department for Education and Skills has produced lists of words that children should be able to read, depending on what school year they are in. These are known as high-frequency words. These are part of the framework for literacy teaching.

Further Reading: Barry Stierer and Janet Maybin (eds) *Language, Literacy and Learning in Educational Practice* (Multilingual Matters in association with the Open University, 1994).

SEE WEB LINKS

- Data on reading skills assessment.
- Guidance on national standards.

aggregation The adding together of marks awarded for separate pieces of a student's assessed work within an *assessment scheme. In *national curriculum testing or on a programme of study made up of a number of individually assessed *modules or *units, for example, an aggregate summative assessment for the student will be arrived at by a calculation based on all the marks they have been awarded.

Aimhigher A programme which aims to *widen participation in *higher education, it was developed from the **Excellence Challenge** and **Partnerships**

for Progression initiatives, and is managed by the *Higher Education Funding Council for England and supported by the *Department for Education and Skills. Aimhigher encourages young people from diverse, non-traditional backgrounds to enter higher education; the government's target in 2007 was that, by the year 2010, 50 per cent of 18–20-year-olds should be engaged in study at higher education level. It particularly focuses on raising aspirations among those with disadvantaged socio-economic backgrounds, minority groups, and those with physical and learning disabilities.

SEE WEB LINKS

- Gives details about the programme and its target group.

V.C., K.A.

aims A statement of intent by a teacher or *curriculum designer, encapsulating what they are setting out to achieve in a lesson, a series of lessons, a *programme of study, or a *syllabus. Aims are phrased in such a way as to make it clear that they refer to the purpose of the lesson. For example, 'to provide the pupils with a clear understanding of the difference between primary and secondary sources of evidence'. They should not be confused with *objectives, which are a statement of what the learner will achieve, and are constructed with the learner as subject. (For example, 'The learner will demonstrate an understanding of ...'.)

alternative schooling Education which does not conform to that provided in state schools, in terms of either the *curriculum or the approaches to teaching and learning, or both of these. Widely recognized examples of such schooling include provision based on the educational theories of *Steiner, *Montessori, *Malaguzzi, and A.S. *Neill. These approaches to schooling are firmly *learner-centred and place an emphasis on *discovery learning and the learner's right to self-determination. Rather than following solely an externally imposed and standardized curriculum, the *lesson planning and teaching in these forms of alternative schooling take into account primarily the learners' needs in relation to their social, emotional, and personal development; take as their starting point those topics which are of direct interest and relevance to the learners; and encourage learner control over the methods and activities employed. This emphasis on individual development rather than upon national standards means that examples of alternative provision such as these may be difficult to reconcile with the requirements of externally imposed targets and testing and standardized curriculum levels. In its most radical form, alternative schooling, such as that provided at *Summerhill School, may take the form of a democratic community of learning where learners and teachers are considered to have equal status.

However, although often associated with radical philosophies of education, alternative schooling can also include private tuition in the pupil's own home, or schooling in a curriculum shaped by ideological or religious beliefs. *See also* EDUCATION OTHERWISE THAN AT SCHOOL; ILLICH, IVAN; REGGIO EMILIA.

amanuensis A person who scribes the dictated answers to questions from pupils or students whose independent writing skills are extremely limited through a learning difficulty, injury, or sensory or physical impairment. If a learner has a temporary or permanent disability, such as a broken wrist or *dyslexia for example, an amanuensis may be provided who will accompany the learner to classes and take notes which the learner is unable to do themselves; or will write an examination or a piece of coursework at the learner's dictation. Permission to use an amanuensis during examinations can be requested from the examining bodies for students who regularly access this type of support as part of their normal provision. Specific guidance for amanuenses is clearly defined in the *Qualifications and Curriculum Authority's guidance on *access arrangements for pupils with particular needs. Also sometimes called 'scribing', the use of an amanuensis in formal assessments raises a number of questions about validity, arising from the possibility that the candidate's actual ability might be misrepresented.

SEE WEB LINKS

- Debates the issues arising from the use of an amanuensis in GCSE examinations. T.B., L.E.

ancillary staff The staff employed by an educational institution whose responsibilities do not include teaching. Also referred to as non-teaching staff, they include those in technician and administrative roles.

APEL (accreditation of prior experience and learning) *See* ACCREDITATION OF PRIOR LEARNING.

appeals *See* ADMISSIONS APPEAL; CHOICE.

application of number One of the original six *key skills which *General National Vocational Qualification students were required to demonstrate, and one of the three which were formally assessed, the other two being communication and *information technology. It is concerned with skills of *numeracy, and, more specifically, how numeracy is applied in practical situations, both in the workplace and in day-to-day problem-solving and transactions.

appraisal A system for assessing the performance and *continuing professional development needs of teachers and managers in *schools, *colleges, and *universities. It normally involves an interview during which the individual's performance is reviewed and their development needs and career trajectory discussed. It may also involve an observation of the teacher's classroom practice. The appraisal of teachers and lecturers are carried out internally by designated staff, usually senior to the appraisee, although some institutions operate a system of peer appraisal. In schools, the appraisal of *head teachers is carried out by *school improvement partners, who make a report to the governing body on the head teacher's performance.

apprenticeship The traditional method of learning the specialist skills and knowledge of a trade or a craft. Apprentices were indentured to a master—someone who had mastery of the trade or craft they required to learn—for a period of seven years. This element of 'time-serving' was criticized in the 1981 *White Paper *A New Training Initiative*, which abolished traditional apprenticeships in favour of *competence-based training where the qualification was based upon the achievement of competence regardless of time served. When the term was reintroduced in 1995 as *Modern Apprenticeship, it was as a competence-based qualification.

In 2004 participation in apprenticeships was widened by the introduction of *Young Apprenticeships for 14–16-year-olds, which enabled pupils in compulsory education to spend up to two days a week in a workplace to learn on-the-job skills, and by removal of the upper age limit of 25 for those wishing to enter an apprenticeship scheme.

aptitude The potential of a learner to assimilate knowledge, skill, or understanding successfully. This is not quite synonymous with *ability, denoting rather a potential to learn effectively. It is often used in relation to specific areas of knowledge or skill, so that one might speak of an individual having 'an aptitude for scientific enquiry', or 'an aptitude for spot welding', for example. Tests designed to measure such aptitudes are referred to as **aptitude tests**. Although the purpose of these is to assess candidates' potential, they are necessarily based on those candidates' current performance, and therefore the extent to which they are predictive rather than a measure of ability is open to some debate. These tests, however, are more widely used in selection procedures for employment than in assessment for educational purposes.

articulated progression A clearly defined progression route through the qualification system, which enables the learner to choose the appropriate next step in education or training towards their goal, whether it be university entrance or access to a trade or profession. The concept of articulated progression also involves establishing a clear statement of value or equivalence for each qualification. For example, following the introduction of *foundation degrees, it was necessary to establish a clear articulation and progression route from the foundation degree to the *bachelor's degree, which, depending upon the *higher education institution concerned, is now established as involving either a bridging course or direct entry to the final year of the bachelor's degree.

Asperger's syndrome (ASD) A syndrome on the continuum of autistic spectrum disorders. Asperger's is often referred to as 'high-functioning *autism'. Those affected by Asperger's syndrome often have normal language development, which autistic individuals generally do not. T.B., L.E.

ASSESSMENT

The measurement of a learner's potential for *attainment, or of their actual attainment. The assessment of potential can be carried out through **aptitude tests** or tests of intelligence or verbal acuity. In a general educational context, however, most assessment focuses on the measurement of attainment. This may be *diagnostic, *formative, *ipsative, or *summative. Diagnostic assessment measures the learner's achievement on entry to their course of study in order to identify their individual learning needs and their strengths. Formative assessment is the ongoing process of assessment which takes place throughout the learner's course of study and provides them with the feedback and guidance necessary to enable them to improve their performance. Ipsative assessment is where learners are assessed against their own previous level of attainment. Summative assessment takes place at the end of their course of study, and measures the learner's attainment against the specified learning *objectives of the syllabus or programme. Thus, coursework, *assignments, and other methods of *continuous assessment offer opportunities for formative assessment and a consequent learning from performance which the more traditional style of assessment, involving only summative assessment through an end-of-course *examination, does not allow. A debate continues over the relative merits of end examinations and coursework as methods of assessment, the examination lobby arguing that summative assessment under examination conditions provides a more accurate, rigorous, and reliable measurement of the candidate's ability; while proponents of continuous assessment maintain that the skills necessary to perform well in end examinations may be gender-specific, and that continuous assessment gives a more accurate measure of whether a candidate can attain the required standard consistently over time. Linked to this debate has been the argument about the relative merits of internal and external assessment. Some contend that teachers themselves are best placed to assess their pupils' work, while others, notably the examinations lobby, maintain that assessment by external examiners and assessors is more likely to be both rigorous and reliable. The direction, over the past half-century, has, on the whole, been towards continuous and partly internal assessment, although there have been a number of minor reversals to this trend, for example the introduction of additional external assessment on the *General National Vocational Qualification (now the *Vocational A Level). On the other hand, the introduction of a system of continuous, *modular assessment for Advanced Levels, which had previously been assessed solely through an end examination after two years of study, is more clearly illustrative of the overall trend.

Three key concepts which apply to assessment are *sufficiency, **validity**, and **reliability**. Sufficiency refers to the requirement that there be sufficient evidence on which to base an assessment decision. Validity refers to the requirement that assessment measures what it claims to measure. For example, an assessment of a candidate's driving skills based on their ability to write an essay about driving would be invalid, as would an assessment of a candidate's knowledge of art history based on their own skill at painting a picture. To be valid, an assessment must measure what it claims to measure. For an assessment to be reliable, the candidate should be awarded the same result, regardless of which assessor is marking their work. For example, a *multiple choice test has a much higher degree of reliability than an essay because the latter may be open to a subjective response from assessors. The use of *assessment criteria and *marking schemes is designed to increase the reliability of assessment; but, to some extent, the question of reliability of assessment will differ from subject to subject, with a higher level of reliability in the assessment of subjects where facts or quantitative data play an important part, such as mathematics and chemistry, and relatively more problems over reliability in subjects which call for a subjective response, such as English literature. *See also* ASSESSMENT INSTRUMENTS; ASSESSMENT PLAN; EXTERNAL ASSESSMENT.

Assessment and Qualifications Alliance (AQA) The largest of the three major *awarding bodies responsible for *academic and *vocational qualifications for 18–19-year-olds. It was formed in 1997 as the result of an alliance between three awarding bodies: the City and Guilds of London Institute, which had been responsible for the *assessment and award of a range of vocational qualifications, including teacher training qualifications for the *further education sector; and the Northern and the Associated Examining Boards, both awarding bodies for *General Certificate of Secondary Education and *Advanced Level.

SEE WEB LINKS

- Provides a detailed description of the Alliance's role and function.

assessment criteria A list of requirements against which a piece of work or the performance of a task is measured in order to judge whether it has been successfully completed. An *assessor will use *assessment criteria in order to distinguish between work which is a pass and work which is a fail, and in order to determine what percentage or category of mark to award. The purpose of such criteria is to ensure a degree of objectivity in the forming of an assessment decision. They may be devised and employed within one awarding institution, such as a *university; or, in the case of work leading to national awards, they may be devised and imposed externally by a national *awarding body. In all cases their purpose is to support the standardization and reliability of assessment decisions. *See also* GRADING CRITERIA.

Assessment for Learning (AfL) An approach to *assessment which is applicable to all *key stages and is based on ten underlying principles drawn up by the Assessment Reform Group in 2002. It centres on the processes by which learners find and interpret evidence which enables them and their teachers to decide what stage they are at with their learning, and what they need to do to progress to the next level. AfL encourages *self-assessment by pupils, which helps them to decide how they can improve their own learning. This approach allows pupils a measure of control in their own learning, and one of its central tenets is that assessment should focus on the work, not on the individual. It is based on the belief that it is as important to consider 'how' learning takes place as it is to consider 'what' has been learned. AfL fosters a sense that it is all right to make mistakes, and thereby it develops risk-taking, one of the 'soft skills' which the *creativity initiative aims to foster. Weaknesses are therefore handled constructively so that the pupil is helped to identify for themselves how they might improve. At the heart of AfL is the belief that everyone can make progress. Teachers give feedback to, and receive feedback from, pupils; and this feedback should be used to inform future lesson planning in a way that links teaching more effectively to learning. The use of open questioning and listening to pupils' reasoning while they work are among methods used to help teachers assess understanding and knowledge. AfL is most successful when pupils are shown models of what is expected so that they have an understanding of what is required and can use the model to check their own work against these criteria without fear of criticism. It is essential to provide success criteria which learners understand so that they are clear about the learning goals. The intended outcomes of AfL are that self-esteem increases, and pupils learn to identify their own strengths and weaknesses and the best ways in which they learn. It develops *thinking skills and encourages pupils to reflect on their work and how to improve. The emphasis on *formative assessment is shared between pupil and teacher with the aim of increasing pupil motivation and engagement, as well as learning. AfL is based on a *constructivist approach to learning, and its ten underlying principles are, in summary, as follows:

- lesson planning should incorporate opportunities for formative assessment;
- pupils' full range of achievements should be recognized;
- the focus should be on how, as well as what, pupils learn;
- pupils should be encouraged in self-assessment, reflection, and self-management;
- AfL should be central to classroom practice;
- it should also be considered as an essential professional skill for teachers;
- it should encourage a commitment to appropriate goals and involve a clear and shared understanding of the criteria to be met;
- pupils should be given, as part of formative assessment, constructive advice on how to improve their performance;
- assessments and feedback should be conducted sensitively and constructively;
- assessment should always take account of the need to encourage and sustain pupils' motivation to learn. T.B., L.E.

assessment grid *See* ASSESSMENT PLAN.

assessment instruments A means of assessing learners' progress or level of ability. Such instruments may take a variety of forms, including the essay, the short answer test, the *multiple-choice test, observation of practice, and presentations. The choice of instrument will usually be dictated by the purpose of the *assessment, the skill or knowledge being assessed, and the characteristics of the learners. For example, the essay may be considered an appropriate assessment instrument to test the comprehension skills of older, more able pupils; while younger, less literate learners might be more appropriately assessed by means of oral question and answer.

Assessment is for Learning (AifL) A Scottish national initiative with representation from all parts of the Scottish education community, aimed at raising *standards in teaching and learning. It covers three concept areas of assessment: that which supports classroom teaching and learning; that which supports learners' own learning; and the assessment of learning which gathers and interprets evidence.

SEE WEB LINKS

- Learning and Teaching Scotland web site with further explanation of features of AifL. S.M.

assessment outcome The result of an *assessment, whether by *assignment, essay, *test, *examination, or some other means, which is designed to ascertain a learner's current level of knowledge, ability, or achievement. The outcome might be expressed in terms of a simple pass or fail; or it might be graded using categories such as pass, credit, distinction. Alternatively, the outcome might be expressed numerically, in the form of a percentage mark, for example, or in a score out of ten. In the case of assessment for *bachelor's degrees, the outcome is expressed as a class or classification, according to the student's performance, using first, second, and third class, in descending order of merit, to denote the student's achievement. Other ways of presenting assessment outcomes is by using an alphabetical system, as in the case of *Advanced Levels, for example; or by combining alphabetical grading with plus and minus markers, so that, for example, an A– denotes a slightly better level of achievement than a B+.

In whatever form the assessment outcome is presented—numerical, alphabetical, graded, or classified—the outcome as expressed should be securely grounded in an agreed and transparent set of *assessment criteria so that both assessor and student or candidate are clear about what the assessment outcome means in terms of the student's level of achievement. In order for assessment outcomes to have reliability, a grade B awarded by one assessor for a particular assignment must mean the same in terms of student achievement as a B awarded by a different assessor to a different student for the same assignment.

assessment plan A scheme, grid, or other format which sets out clearly how and where each learning objective is covered by the tasks or questions in a *test, *examination, *assignment, or other means of *assessment, and the relative *weighting given to each in the calculation of a final mark, score, or assessment decision. It should demonstrate that specified outcomes are assessed appropriately, validly, and reliably, and in a sequence compatible with the sequence of teaching. Such grids are required as a matter of course for public examinations such as the *General Certificate of Secondary Education; but individual teachers may also draw up assessment grids for their own use when setting *homework or carrying out assessment in the classroom.

assessor One who assesses candidates' work or performance against pre-specified criteria for the purpose of awarding a mark or grade, or ascertaining whether the required criteria have been met. A distinction is made between an **internal assessor**, who belongs to the same institution as the candidate and is normally responsible for first-line assessment, and an **external assessor**, who comes from outside the institution and whose role is usually to ensure *standardization and reliability of assessment, leading to a specific qualification, between institutions, regionally or nationally.

assignment A task, usually written, which can be used for the dual purposes of *learning and *assessment, and is in the first instance internally assessed. Usually involving some degree of research or preparatory reading, and often consisting of more than one task, an assignment may be set for completion by individual learners, or may require the collaboration of a small group. They are often used as a means of *continuous assessment; and the term is sometimes used interchangeably with *coursework. They were widely used in the first phase of *General National Vocational Qualifications (GNVQs) in the 1990s, when they were presented as a helpful alternative to *examinations for those pupils who did not perform well under examination conditions. In this respect they became the subject of some controversy, considered by some to be an unreliable and insufficiently stringent alternative to external testing. This growing concern led to the introduction into GNVQs of externally set and externally assessed assignments. *See also* ASSESSOR.

assistant head A relatively new post in schools, having been formally established in 2000. The assistant head occupies a rank below that of the *deputy head but senior to that of head of department. The post carries no nationally specified role or set of duties. Instead, these are decided by the individual school according to its circumstances and needs.

Association for Careers Education and Guidance (ACEG) Formerly the National Association of Careers and Guidance Teachers, this association began operating under its current name on 1 January 2006, and provides support and information to teachers and others engaged in providing careers education and guidance, as well as acting as a lobbying group through its links with other, related national organizations. Among the services it offers to its members are in-service professional development support for careers and guidance teachers, support for relevant research, and the dissemination of relevant policy initiatives. The Association operates in England and Wales, but not in Scotland or Northern Ireland.

Association for Science Education (ASE) A professional body whose aims are to promote science education and to support the professional development of science teachers. Its membership is open to educational professionals, including technicians, involved in science education at all levels and for all age groups, from *pre-school to *higher education. It holds an annual conference, publishes a specialist journal, and provides professional advice on all matters relating to the teaching of science.

SEE WEB LINKS

- Details of journals for science teachers, and advice for contributors.

Association of Colleges (AoC) An association formed in 1996 to represent and promote the interests of general further education *colleges, *sixth form colleges, specialist colleges, and other *tertiary institutions in England and Wales. Membership is corporate rather than individual. Its board of management consists of 24 chairs and principals of colleges, including one representative of Northern Ireland colleges, and one representative of Scotland's further education institutions. Board members, excluding the chief executive and any co-opted members, are elected to the board by member colleges for a term of four years. The Association holds an annual conference, and its other activities include consultancy and parliamentary lobbying. The **Association of Scotland's Colleges (ASC)** fulfils a similar function for Scotland's 43 further education colleges. Welsh colleges, in addition to their membership of AoC, are supported by **fforwm**, set up as a charity in 1993 and representing college interests within the principality. *See also* ASSOCIATION OF LEARNING PROVIDERS.

SEE WEB LINKS

- A list of the AoC's regional offices.

Association of Learning Providers (Alp) A UK subscription organization that acts as a lobby for independent learning providers. The main aim of Alp is to influence the education and training agenda by working with government departments, the *Learning and Skills Council, **Jobcentre Plus**, the *University for Industry, and **Business Link**. Most Alp members are private, not-for-profit, and voluntary sector training providers involved in *work-based learning. The organization also contributes to the formation of government strategy for the *lifelong learning sector in collaboration with the *Department for Education and Skills and other national agencies and institutions. *See also* ASSOCIATION OF COLLEGES.

SEE WEB LINKS

- Alp web site.

V.C., K.A.

Association of Teachers and Lecturers (ATL) Originally known as the Assistant Masters' and Mistresses' Association (AMMA), this teachers' union changed to its current name in 1993 in acknowledgement of the growing numbers of lecturers from further education *colleges taking up membership. It is affiliated to the Trades Union Congress and has approximately 160 000 members, whose interests it supports through campaigning and negotiation.

SEE WEB LINKS

- Sets out the history of the Association from 1884 to the present day.

Association of University Teachers *See* UNIVERSITY AND COLLEGE UNION.

asynchronous learning Usually applied to *online or other modes of *distance learning, where pupils are undertaking the same course of study but are accessing the learning materials and interacting with their tutors individually and at different times. By contrast, conventional courses of study normally involve **synchronous** learning, which is to say that all learners are participating or receiving input at the same time.

attainment A level of learning or skill arrived at, as measured against specific targets or criteria, and confirmed by evidence such as test or examination results, or assessment by a teacher. It is part of the vocabulary of the *national curriculum, and, as such, is more often encountered in the schools sector than in further education, where *'achievement' is more commonly used to convey the same meaning.

attainment test A test which measures the learner's achievement against a set of specified learning *objectives in order to assess how much they have learned. *See also* ASSESSMENT; ATTAINMENT.

attendance It is mandatory that all children aged between 5 and 16 years should receive a suitable education, and to this end parents and guardians are required to ensure that this is the case for their school age children, usually (but not always) by regular attendance at a school. Two registers are maintained by every school, with the exception of boarding schools. One is the admissions register, usually referred to as the **school roll**, and the other is the **attendance register**. It is a requirement of *head teachers to ensure that the attendance register is taken twice each day, once at the beginning of the school day and again in the afternoon. Pupils are marked as present, or as engaged off-site in an educational activity (for example, a field trip), or as absent. For those pupils who are absent, it must be indicated on the register whether that absence has been authorized by the school (for example, in cases of sickness or where some other satisfactory explanation has been provided). Unauthorized absences, which include unexplained or unjustified absences, are closely monitored, and it is a requirement of head teachers that they inform the *local authority of any pupil whose attendance is irregular or who has had a continuous unauthorized absence of ten days. The enforcement of attendance is usually a role carried out by the local authority Welfare Service, whose personnel work closely with the school and family concerned to improve the pupil's attendance. Since 1 March 2001 parents who fail to ensure their child's attendance have been liable to a penalty of up to £2 500, or up to a three-month prison sentence, or both of these. *See also* EDUCATION OTHERWISE THAN AT SCHOOL; TRUANCY.

Further Reading: Department for Education and Skills *Social Inclusion: Pupil Support* Circular 10/99 (DfES, 1999) sets out the requirements for marking registers and the categories of authorized and unauthorized absence.

Attention Deficit Hyperactivity Disorder (ADHD) A term which describes overactive impulsive behaviour. Typical features of the condition are: having difficulty in completing tasks, failure to listen to instructions, and restlessness which often results in children being out of their classroom seats. Becoming distracted and forgetful are also common features, together with poor socializing skills, finding it hard to turn-take, and blurting out answers before being asked. ADHD has a negative consequence for learning for both sufferers and their peers. It alienates the individual with the condition from others, who find it difficult to tolerate their behaviour. T.B., L.E.

audio-visual aid (AVA) Sounds or pictures used to support or reinforce learning. These include such resources as slide projections, DVDs and videos, overhead projectors, sound recordings, radio, and television. Increasing use of electronic resources has led to this term falling increasingly out of use, to be replaced with information learning technology. Nevertheless, in many educational institutions the department or team responsible for supplying or maintaining teaching resources of this kind will still carry the designation 'AV' in its title.

augmentative and alternative communication (AAC) This term used to describe methods of communication which can add to the more usual methods of speech and writing when these are impaired. AAC includes unaided systems of communication such as signing (for example, *Makaton) and gesture, as well as aided techniques. These aided techniques range from the use of low technology such as picture or symbol charts to the most sophisticated computer technology currently available. A well-known user of a sophisticated high technology device is the scientist Stephen Hawking. AAC can be a way to help someone understand what is being communicated to them, as well as a means of expression. *See also* PICTURE EXCHANGE COMMUNICATION SYSTEM.

SEE WEB LINKS

- Provides a wealth of information about AAC including details of suppliers, publications, assessment centres, and online forums. T.B., L.E.

authenticity In relation to the *assessment of learning, this term has two distinct usages.

1. When arriving at an assessment decision, the *assessor must consider whether the work or performance being assessed is genuinely the learner's own, and therefore represents an accurate picture of that learner's ability and achievement. In the case of a pupil who has received substantial covert help with their coursework, or a pupil who has purchased an essay answer from the Internet, the lack of authenticity in their work offered for assessment would invalidate any mark or grade awarded. *See also* PLAGIARISM.

2. An *assessment instrument may be judged to lack authenticity if it is deemed inadequate to assess the knowledge or skill being assessed; for example, the use of an essay to assess a practical skill. The call for authenticity in this sense was one of the factors which led to the increased use of *continuous assessment and *portfolios of evidence, particularly for the assessment of *General National Vocational Qualifications. Ironically, these means of assessment inevitably raised questions about authenticity in its first sense as set out here.

autism A term deriving from the Greek word *autos*, meaning 'self'. A person who is autistic has significant difficulty relating to others, and the world at large. Autistic spectrum disorder is a continuum of difficulties which impact on three areas of development: social interaction, social communication, and behaviour and imagination. These are commonly referred to as the 'triad of impairments'. At one end of the spectrum are those cases of moderate *Asperger's syndrome, with severe autism at the other. T.B., L.E.

autodidact One who is self-taught, having achieved their knowledge or skills through their own efforts, without having gone through the formal processes of further or higher education.

autonomous learner One who is self-motivated to learn and is able to do so without direct supervision and prompting. Most educators in the United Kingdom would claim that one of the aims of education is to produce such learners. This is sometimes expressed as helping individuals to 'learn how to learn'. For autonomous learning to become a possibility, the learner needs to be equipped with appropriate skills, including those necessary for carrying out research, problem-solving, or analysis. For the autonomous learner, the teacher becomes a **facilitator** of the learning process, rather than a source of information or instruction.

awarding body An organization responsible for the conduct of *assessment leading to recognized awards such as the *General Certificate of Secondary Education (GCSE), *Vocational Advanced Levels, and *key skills certification, and for the issuing of certification. Before 1996 the term applied largely to bodies awarding vocational qualifications, most notably national organizations such as the *Business and Technology Education Council (BTEC) and the Royal Society of Arts, which were responsible for awarding qualifications such as the *General National Vocational Qualification. At this time, bodies responsible for general education awards such as GCSEs were referred to as *examination boards. However, in line with the Department for Education and Employment's policy to close the gap between vocational and general qualifications, manifested in the replacement of the *School Curriculum and Assessment Authority and the *National Council for Vocational Qualifications by the *Qualifications and Curriculum Authority (QCA) in 1997, mergers took place between the major awarding bodies and examination boards. The University of London Examination and Assessment Council and BTEC were the first to form a **unitary awarding body**. The RSA awarding body and the Oxford and Cambridge examination boards formed the Oxford, Cambridge, and Royal Society of Arts (*OCR) examining board; and the City and Guilds merged with the Northern and the Associated Examining Boards to form the *Assessment and Qualifications Alliance. These three awarding bodies are responsible for academic and vocational qualifications for 18–19-year-olds. There remain, however, a large number of smaller awarding bodies, each responsible for qualifications in a specific area, which operate nationally and regionally within the *learning and skills sector.

The specific operating procedures of awarding bodies vary, but their role will usually include advising on, or specifying, *curriculum content; devising, monitoring, and administrating assessments; operating a system of verification to ensure standardization of *continuous assessment; carrying out *summative assessment and moderation; and issuing certification of awards.

All awarding bodies, and the qualifications they award, are regulated by the QCA as part of its responsibility for maintaining the reliability of the *National Qualifications Framework.

SEE WEB LINKS

- Provides information on QCA's requirements of an awarding body.

baccalauréat The national school-leaving qualification in France, which occupies roughly the same status in the French education system as the *General Certificate of Education *Advanced Level occupies in the English system. Often cited, by those who would wish to reform the 16–19 *examination system in Britain, as an example of good practice, *le bac* reflects a broader and less specialized post-16 curriculum, which allows students to combine subjects from the arts, sciences, and humanities. As well as the general, or academic, *baccalauréat*, which prepares students for further academic studies at *university, *lycées* also offer the less prestigious *baccalauréat technologique* and the *baccalauréat professionel*, which focus on vocational skills and knowledge and were designed to prepare the student for direct entry to the workforce. *See also* British Baccalaureate; International Baccalaureate; Welsh Baccalaureate.

bachelor's degree An award conferred for the successful completion of *undergraduate studies. The general field of study is indicated in the title of the degree. Thus, a **Bachelor of Arts (BA)** is awarded for successful undergraduate studies in some branch of the arts or humanities; a **Bachelor of Science (B.Sc.)** is awarded for successful undergraduate studies in a branch of the sciences; and a *Bachelor of Education (B.Ed.) is awarded for successful undergraduate studies in the field of education. The conferring of a bachelor's degree marks the elevation of the student from undergraduate to *graduate status. In the case of an *honours degree there are four classes, which are used as grading indicators of the level achieved. These are known as a **first** class, an **upper second** class (sometimes referred to as a **2.1**), a **lower second** class (sometimes referred to as a **2.2**), and a **third** class, the first class degree being the highest and most coveted award. Most bachelor's degrees awarded fall into the second class category. A current controversy exists over the classification of degrees, with some academics arguing that the classifications are not being applied consistently, making it easier to gain a higher classification in some universities than in others. One specific concern expressed has been that a disproportionate number of the bachelor's degrees awarded by some universities fall into the first and upper second class category, thus risking a devaluation of these higher classes of the award. In order to progress to *master's degree level, a graduate will normally be required to have achieved a first or upper second class in their undergraduate studies. A BA or B.Sc. may be awarded with **honours**. Where this is the case, the title of the award is abbreviated as **BA (Hons)** or **B.Sc. (Hons)**. Where the degree is awarded without honours, it is known as an **ordinary** degree, and is usually considered to indicate a lesser academic achievement.

The bachelor's degree title may also be used to refer to someone who holds that degree. So, for example, a graduate who holds a B.Sc. may be referred to as a Bachelor of Science, regardless of their gender. *See also* GRADUATION.

Bachelor of Arts (BA) *See* BACHELOR'S DEGREE.

Bachelor of Education (B.Ed.) An award conferred for the successful completion of undergraduate level studies in education. Following the recommendation in the *Robbins Report (1963) that all teachers should be *graduates, teacher training courses leading to Certificates in Education were largely phased out and replaced, in *universities and *colleges of higher education, by courses leading to a B.Ed. for teachers in the *primary and secondary sectors. Entry requirements usually include English and mathematics at *General Certificate of Secondary Education grade C or above, and two *General Certificate of Education *Advanced Level passes. As well as covering educational theory, *national curriculum, and specialist subjects, these full-time courses for student teachers also require participants to undertake substantial periods of practical teaching practice within schools, the assessment of which contributes towards their assessment for their final degree.

Some universities and higher education institutions also offer part-time B.Ed. courses for teachers already in employment who hold a *Certificate of Education but wish to upgrade their qualification. To accommodate teachers' working lives, such courses usually involve evening or weekend attendance, and are aimed at professionals engaged in teaching or training in the *tertiary sector, the health service, social services, police, and armed forces, as well as teachers in schools.

Bachelor of Science (B.Sc.) *See* BACHELOR'S DEGREE.

Bain Review (2006) This independent report was commissioned by the government in Northern Ireland to examine the provision of education for 14–19-year-olds. It was published as *Schools for the Future* and recommended an end to academic selection and increased collaboration between schools. New schools are to cater for the needs of a geographical area rather than a particular section of the community. Schools will be expected to share lessons and some will become *specialist schools providing expertise in specific areas of the curriculum. This scheme will replace the former grammar school system. The Education Order (NI) 2006 determines these changes and the *Eleven Plus was scheduled to be phased out in 2008. *See also* NORTHERN IRELAND, EDUCATION IN.

SEE WEB LINKS

- The Office of Public Sector Information web site for more information.

J.H.

banding The practice of dividing year groups of pupils in secondary education into bands or sub-groups, according to their *ability or learning needs. Each band may then be divided into a number of separate classes whose members may be selected according to ability within that band, or according to some other criteria, or simply at random. It was common practice in grammar schools in the mid-20th century for the curriculum subjects provided to differ according to band. For example, pupils in the most able band of a girls' grammar school might study Latin, while the middle band might instead be taught an additional modern language, and the least able band might be offered instruction in a practical skill such as 'domestic science' or sewing. Such differentiated (and gender-specific) provision would not be considered acceptable today, although decisions about the number and type of *General Certificate of Secondary Education subjects for which a pupil is entered might well be based on which band they find themselves in.

barriers to learning Events and conditions in pupils' lives which make it difficult or less likely that they will be able to learn effectively; for example, hunger, emotional upset, illness, family separation, and bereavement. On the other hand, barriers might include less obvious factors such as inflexible school systems or an inappropriate *curriculum. *Bullying, too, has a profound effect on some victims' ability to learn. Existing and potential barriers to learning may go undetected, particularly in those cases where the root cause is linked to aspects of young people's lives outside school. Where good home–school partnerships exist, these barriers can more easily be overcome. Barriers to learning may arise unexpectedly and may be of a permanent or temporary nature. For this reason it is important that schools and other educational institutions remain vigilant in order to spot changes in learning and behaviour patterns. This enables appropriate support and interventions to be implemented promptly, and for planning and *assessment to take into account the type and extent of the learner's difficulties. T.B., L.E.

baseline assessment The instrument for collecting **baseline data** and the method used by teachers to find out a pupil's learning needs, their natural ability, and potential. Tests are given to pupils across an entire year group to establish where each pupil is in relation to a national and institutional norm. The purpose of baseline *assessment is to establish a point from which future measurements and predictions can be calculated. The assessments are not standardized, and different formats may be used in different schools. These tests, such as *Cognitive Abilities Tests, are used to generate a predicted or expected level of achievement for future performance, for example at *General Certificate of Secondary Education (GCSE) level. They can also function to highlight specific issues such as whether a pupil should be placed on the *gifted and talented register, or whether they are underachieving in relation to their potential. Teachers can use baseline data to plan effectively for each pupil's learning needs and, for this reason, baseline assessments are usually carried out throughout a pupil's schooling, often starting within six weeks of their entering full-time education. Baseline assessment can also be used on a whole-school level to measure the quality of education which the school is providing, by comparing a pupil's performance with their baseline assessment. The results of baseline assessments are formally registered. The baseline data that are generated form part of each pupil's school records. Subsequent data are then added to this, such as the results of *Standard Tasks and GCSE results. Baselines should be both reliable and valid to enable statistical validity. I.F.W.

baseline data *See* BASELINE ASSESSMENT.

basic skills The *Basic Skills Agency defines basic skills as 'The ability to read, write and speak in English or Welsh, and to use mathematics at a level necessary to function and progress at work and in society in general'. Although initiatives have covered all age groups since the creation of the Basic Skills Agency in 1995, the term is most commonly used to refer to the skills of adults rather than of those under 19 years old, where *General Certificate of Secondary Education and *key skills qualifications tend to define levels of skill.

Development of basic skills has been a particular focus of UK government policy since 1975, when the **Adult Literacy Resource Agency** was created to support a high-profile *adult literacy campaign. This function was then taken over first by the **Adult Literacy Unit** (1978–80) and then by the **Adult Literacy and Basic Skills Unit** (1980–95). Currently it falls under the remit of the Basic Skills Agency.

The state of adult UK citizens' basic skills has been the subject of several reviews, the most influential of which is probably that of the committee chaired by Sir Claus *Moser, which published its report, *A Fresh Start: Improving Literacy and Numeracy*, in 1999. This stated that up to 7 000 000 adults in England have difficulties with literacy and numeracy inasmuch as that their skills are below level 2 on the *National Qualifications Framework. In 2000 the final report of the International Adult Literacy Survey, *Literacy in the Information Age*, concluded that Great Britain ranked in the lower third of the 20 countries that form the Organization for Economic Cooperation and Development. Both studies relate the findings to personal socio-economic factors, such as employment, income, and mental health; and to the consequences for national economic prosperity.

As a result of the Moser Report, the **Skills for Life Quality Initiative** was established and given the task of improving basic skills, broadened to include *English for Speakers of Other Languages (ESOL) and information technology through *widening participation; this includes workplace and community projects, and work with adults with learning difficulties or disabilities. Key outcomes of the Initiative were the launch of the **Adult Core Curriculums**, developed by the *Qualifications and Curriculum Authority and the Basic Skills Agency and published from 2001; the development of subject-specific qualifications for teachers, first introduced in 2002; and a system for reporting on the quality of provision of adult basic skills training, carried out since 2002 by the *Adult Learning Inspectorate. The Initiative ceased in August 2006, and responsibility for development now lies with the **Skills for Life Improvement Programme**, under the *Quality Improvement Agency umbrella. *See also* FUNCTIONAL SKILLS.

SEE WEB LINKS

- Source of information and advice on implementing Skills for Life provision.
- Gives further information, including a forum for sharing good practice and resources, and availability of professional development opportunities.
- As previous web site.
- Provides an outline of research into adult literacy, numeracy, ESOL, and information communications technology. The site includes research and development projects, reports, and reviews.

V.C., K.A.

Basic Skills Agency Instituted in 1995, the Basic Skills Agency is an independent, not-for-profit organization working in England and Wales. Its aims are to identify, develop, and disseminate innovation and knowledge in *basic skills teaching and learning. Funded by the *Department for Education and Skills, and working with a variety of providers, the Agency's innovation and development activities encompass initiatives from *early years to adult. Since 2006 these have included projects with the Army and financial literacy, the 14–19-year-old phase of learning, families, and schools, who can work towards the Agency's Quality Mark. V.C., K.A.

Beacon Award A scheme overseen by the *Association of Colleges which annually rewards those in the *further education sector who have demonstrated excellence in teaching, learning, and student support. The scheme aims to celebrate and disseminate good practice. There are a variety of categories in which Awards are available, including teaching, leadership, community development, employer engagement, support provision, and equality and diversity.

SEE WEB LINKS

- Details of application procedures and profiles of previous recipients of the Award. V.C., K.A.

beacon schools Schools identified by their *local authority or by central government as national examples of best practice. They may be *nursery, *primary, secondary, or *special schools. In being awarded this status, it is expected that they will act as beacons of achievement to other schools, working in partnership with them, sharing their successful practice, and thereby helping to raise standards nationally. To this end, they are awarded extra funds on an annual basis to finance development activities. The majority of schools chosen as beacon schools are in urban areas, and they are partnered with schools whose performance is deemed to be in need of improvement, often in areas of urban or rural social deprivation. The initiative itself, which was based on an idea originating from the United States of America, was first implemented in England in 1998. The 2001 *Green Paper *Schools: Building on Success* argued for an increase in the number of beacon schools, and suggested a scheme for the creation of advanced beacon schools which would identify those which demonstrated exceptionally high performance.

BEHAVIOUR

For learners to engage effectively with their learning, it is necessary for there to be a level of cooperation and compliance on their part. Pupil or student behaviour which acts as a barrier to their own learning, and often also to that of their classmates, is of crucial concern to teachers since it can prevent them from carrying out their prime responsibility, which is to support effective learning. Such behaviours are referred to as *disruptive, as they disturb or destroy the learning process. Even one disruptive pupil in a class can have a negative impact on the quality of teaching and learning. While responsibility for decisions about what rules are to be applied within the school lie largely with the *head teacher, it is the teacher in the classroom who has first-line responsibility for applying and enforcing them. The ability to do so has traditionally been regarded as a necessary skill for teachers, known by such terms as 'classroom discipline' and 'classroom control'. A more usual term today is 'behaviour management', which has become a popular focus for *continuing professional development programmes and staff development events. Books for teachers on this topic proliferate, reflecting what many commentators, and particularly the tabloid press, consider to be a continuing decline in standards of behaviour in both primary and secondary schools. Disruptive behaviour is also reported as a growing problem in the *post-compulsory sector, particularly in *colleges of further education, where, in theory, students attend through their own *choice.

A difficulty for teachers in general is the assumption that problems of behaviour have their origins in what is happening in the classroom, and that it is therefore within the teacher's power to address this by changes in approach, lesson content, or their own behaviour. This notion is predicated on a deficit model of the teacher—the belief that teachers can address and solve problems of pupil behaviour by making changes to their own practice and approach. An equally popular 'common-sense' understanding of the issue is based on a deficit model of the learners themselves. This assumes that the pupil or student who presents with non-compliant or challenging behaviour is deficient as an individual and that the solution to the problem lies in changing the individual, modifying their behaviour, or even removing them altogether from the learning situation, either through permanent *exclusion or by some temporary measure.

Many educationalists, psychologists, and sociologists, however, would suggest that the causes of disruptive behaviour and disengagement from learning may arise not from a deficit in the individual teacher or learner, but from wider demographic or socio-economic factors which are beyond any individual teacher's capacity or remit to address, and beyond many individual learners' capacity to overcome. Nevertheless, within their own classroom teachers acknowledge that they have a professional responsibility to do what they can to encourage cooperative and appropriate behaviour which is conducive to learning. The issue of behaviour in schools and colleges is now generally recognized as being closely related to questions of *motivation. Among the effective strategies which teachers use to encourage learner motivation are systems of rewards and sanctions, based on *behaviourist psychology, which in practical terms may mean such strategies as the liberal use of praise for acceptable behaviours and the withholding of 'treats' such as free time at break as a response to disruption or aggression. Alternatively, a strategy based on *humanist psychology may employ determined good humour, a recognition that their teaching needs to take the learner's interests and enthusiasms as a starting point, and the demonstration of a positive attitude towards those misbehaving, though not towards their behaviour.

Enthusiastic teachers are also often reported as having fewer problems with disruptive behaviour, perhaps because their enthusiasm engages even the demotivated.

The use of *corporal punishment or beating, once common as a sanction in primary and secondary schools, was made illegal in state schools in 1986, since when teachers have been precluded from using physical force or restraint, except in extreme circumstances such as the prevention of injury. *See also* ATTENTION DEFICIT HYPERACTIVITY DISORDER; ZERO TOLERANCE.

Further Reading: S. Cowley *Getting the Buggers to Behave* (Continuum, 2004) gives practical guidance on behaviour management for teachers in schools.

behavioural, emotional, and social difficulties (BESd) The effective learning of students with BESd is impeded on different levels. At a personal level, BESd can be manifested through the destruction of students' own work, pre-empting of failure, a low tolerance of frustration, attention-seeking behaviours, and having difficulty forming relationships. It is common for students with BESd to develop anxieties about going to school. At a verbal level it takes the form of making frequent interruptions, being argumentative or abusive, or even refusing to speak. Non-verbal indicators could be school phobia, destructive and aggressive behaviour, making inappropriate responses to perceived provocation, and difficulty with following rules. At a work skills level the following are typical signs of BESd: students find it difficult to work with others in a learning setting; they are unable to follow instructions or complete tasks; they might possess a short concentration span and have poor organizational skills. It is not uncommon for students with BESd to interrupt and impede the learning of others.

In addition to the above descriptors there is usually evidence of underachievement which does not reflect general levels of ability. Very often the young person is unable or unwilling to accept responsibility for their own actions. The above indicators are not a finite list.

Where there is an escalation of BESd, students will not make adequate progress despite *special educational needs support intervention, and these difficulties become a significant barrier to learning. This is usually an indicator that support and advice should be sought from the appropriate external agencies, and highly individual and differentiated educational plans need to be implemented. T.B., L.E.

behavioural learning objective A statement of what a learner is expected to have achieved or learned by the end of a *lesson or *programme of study, expressed in terms of observable behaviour. The objective will usually be prefixed, therefore, by a phrase such as 'By the end of the lesson the learner will be able to ...'. There should then follow a description of what is expected, including the standard to which it must be achieved. Thus, the sentence 'By the end of the lesson the learner will be able to use the apostrophe correctly and appropriately indicate (*a*) possession and (*b*) abbreviation, and will be able to explain correctly the rules governing apostrophe use' indicates exactly what is to be learned and what behaviours the learner must be required to demonstrate in order that valid assessment of their learning can take place. Such observable objectives can be helpful to the teacher in structuring the lesson, since they indicate not only what is to be learned, but also what learner activities are essential, and how the learning is to be assessed. For this reason, they are often used as a basis on which to construct a *lesson plan, and appear within the lesson plan itself as pre-specified learning outcomes. With the growth of *competence-based education and training in the last quarter of the 20th century, behavioural objectives flourished in the guise of competences in *National Vocational Qualifications. However, useful as they may be in subjects where learning takes the form of observable behaviours, behavioural objectives may be irrelevant or inappropriate in other subject areas, particularly those involving higher-order *cognitive skills, or where learning takes place in the *affective domain. Expressing an understanding of particle physics or an appreciation of Yeats's poetry, for example, in terms of observable behaviours to be assessed would almost certainly prove extremely difficult to do. Moreover, useful as pre-specified outcomes may be in many learning situations, it can be argued that the setting of very precise behavioural objectives inevitably imposes constraints on the teacher and learner alike, and could act as an obstacle to inspiration on both sides. *See also* BLOOM'S TAXONOMY.

behaviourist A school of learning theory which argues that all behaviour can be predicted, measured and controlled, and that learning is simply a matter of stimulus and response. Of the behaviourists, **Ivan Pavlov's** (1849–1936) is perhaps the most widely recognized name. His experiments with dogs are often cited to illustrate the central behaviourist claim. These experiments involved 'teaching' them to associate a specific sound with their feeding time, so that eventually they began to salivate at the sound alone, having learned to associate this with food. The sound was the stimulus; salivation was their response. The stimulus–response theory was applied not only to animal behaviour; it was also used, for example by John Watson (1878–1958), to explain human behaviour. It is currently viewed by many as a rather reductive and mechanistic view, and one which it would be difficult to apply to the practicalities of teaching and learning in any humane way.

Considered generally to be more relevant to current educational practices is the work of the **neo-behaviourists**, the best known of whom is perhaps **B. F. Skinner** (1904–90). The neo-behaviourists, or new behaviourists, built upon the work of Pavlov and Watson and introduced two additional ideas into behaviourist theory which are of more practical relevance to teachers. One was the suggestion that human behaviour is goal-oriented—that someone learning something may have a sense of purpose in doing so. The other was the importance of **reinforcement** and **behaviour modification**. Reinforcement refers to rewarding a desired behaviour in order to encourage its repetition; and behaviour modification describes the process and result of doing this. Applied to education, it is the idea that a teacher may modify someone's behaviour—that is, teach them something—by rewarding or reinforcing the desired behaviour. Conversely, the teacher might use **negative reinforcement** to discourage undesired behaviour, for example by withholding their attention from a student until they comply with instructions. According to this model, all teaching and learning is a form of behaviour modification.

behaviour management *See* BEHAVIOUR.

benchmark A target level of achievement, usually derived from national data, and applied on an organizational level. It may be used in relation, for example, to numbers of students successfully completing their qualification, or gaining specific grades. Schools, colleges, universities, and other training organizations may use benchmarking to establish in which areas they need to improve in order to match best practice elsewhere. The term derives historically from workforce monitoring practices in industry. It is said that, in the process of measuring productivity, managers would make a chalk mark on the benches of those workers who were successfully meeting productivity targets, so that other workers could look to them and follow their lead.

Further Reading: J. Owen *Benchmarking for the Learning and Skills Sector* (LSDA, 2002).

Big Brother syndrome A growing tendency among younger learners to voice an ambition for celebrity without notable achievement. Derived from a reality television programme of the same name, the term is now in widespread use by teachers and other professionals involved in work with young people. It expresses a concern not only about values, but also about the difficulties of motivating learners towards academic achievement or useful qualifications which learners themselves may dismiss as irrelevant to their goal of being thrust into a celebrity lifestyle, since their Big Brother role models often make a virtue of having achieved fame despite having little or no academic success at school.

bilingual Having the ability to speak two languages equally fluently. This is often applied to pupils where the language spoken in the family home is other than English. It is sometimes also applied, although technically inaccurately, to pupils whose first language is other than English and who need substantial support from their school in developing their skill in spoken English.
See also MULTILINGUAL.

binary system The two-tier system of *higher education which existed between 1966 and 1992 when the *further education sector was expanded to create *polytechnics and other *colleges which delivered higher education separately from, but in parallel with, universities in the higher education sector. The policy for this expansion was set out in the 1966 *White Paper *A Plan for Polytechnics and Other Colleges: Higher Education in the Further Education System*. Because further education was at that time within the strategic control of *local authorities, the creation of polytechnics was heralded by many as representing the final step in the creation of a 'seamless' route of progression from primary school education right through to the awarding of higher degrees, all under the aegis and financial control of the *local education authority. The creation of polytechnics enabled much *wider participation in higher education, although they never achieved equal status with universities in the public perception. The binary system came to end following the *Further and Higher Education Act 1992, which granted the polytechnics university status and removed them from local authority control. *See also* COLLEGE OF EDUCATION.

b

bipartite system A system based on selection, where some schools select their pupils by ability while others do not. In England this was typified by the system of *grammar schools and secondary modern schools, where the former selected pupils by ability and the age of 11, and the latter provided for those not selected. The bipartite system is still operated formally through the *Eleven Plus by some *local authorities in England; and continues to operate in practice, if not in name, in areas where oversubscribed schools are able to carefully select their intake. *See also* BUTLER ACT; TRIPARTITE SYSTEM.

Birth to Three Matters A framework of support and learning for children in their earliest years. It provides carers and childcare professionals with advice on, and observation notes for, approaches in four broad areas of learning opportunities, with the aim of developing a strong child, a skilful communicator, a healthy child, and a competent learner. The framework is the core approach promoted by *Sure Start, and *children's centres. In 2008 it became fully integrated with the *Early Years Foundation Stage.

SEE WEB LINKS

- Details of Birth to Three Matters framework.

A.W.

Black Papers The name commonly used to refer to a series of publications on education which began to appear in 1969 and continued through the early 1970s, whose authors and contributors were politicians, academics, and writers from the political right wing. Their common theme was the claim that educational standards had declined as a result of modern teaching methods, the philosophy of *liberal education, and the introduction of *comprehensive schools. The approach to teaching under criticism in the Black Papers is sometimes referred to as the *Plowden philosophy, against which these Papers levelled three specific accusations. These were that it had led to declining standards of *literacy and *numeracy, declining standards of behaviour, and the danger of pupils being unduly influenced by 'left-wing' teachers. The Papers argued, among other things, for the retention of, or return to, *selection for secondary education.

Further Reading: C. B. Cox and A. E. Dyson (eds) *The Black Papers on Education* (Davis-Poynter, 1971) presents a selection of these papers.

blended learning A combination of modes of learning. It is currently normally used to describe a combination of *e-learning (or some other form of *distance learning) and face-to-face student–teacher contact. Thus, a student undertaking a *programme of study via a blended learning model of delivery will access much of the learning materials and make regular contact with their tutor and other learners online, but will also attend at least one lesson or tutorial—or perhaps a more lengthy weekend or residential course—where tutor and students can all meet in the same place and at the same time. This represents a blend of *asynchronous, *distributed learning with traditional synchronous, non-distributed provision. The inclusion of face-to-face contact is designed largely to overcome one of the problems associated with distributed (online) learning, which is that students can come to feel isolated and demotivated, and may miss the social contact and stimulation which traditional attendance with a group of peers can provide.

block release Used mainly in the *further and *higher education sectors to describe a period of time for which an employer 'releases' an employee from their work duties in order to follow a course of study or skills training. The length of time allowed for this may be anything from a few days to several months. During this time, the employee usually continues to be paid their salary or wages; and, in addition, the employer will often pay the necessary college or university fees. The concept of block release originates, and is still associated, with vocational or skills training. In academic or professional contexts, such a release from duties would normally be referred to as a *'secondment'. *See also* DAY RELEASE.

Bloom's Taxonomy A classification of *behavioural learning objectives into **domains** and levels of learning, first developed in 1956 by a group of educational psychologists headed by Benjamin Bloom (1913–99). Their work led them to the conclusion that over 90 per cent of assessment questions which students were required to answer tested only their ability to recall and reiterate information. Three domains of learning were identified: *cognitive, *affective, and *psychomotor. The recall or recognition of facts was classified as occupying the lowest level of the cognitive domain, followed by, in ascending order of complexity and abstraction, comprehension, application, analysis, synthesis, and, identified as the cognitive skill of the highest order, evaluation. Similarly, in the other two domains, a range of skills was identified and categorized according to its complexity. For each level of each domain, a list of behaviours was identified by which that level of skill could be assessed. So, for example, in the cognitive domain, the lowest-order skills—those involving the recall of facts—can be recognized by such examples of intellectual activity as the following: define, label, list, memorize, name, order, recognize, repeat, state; while the highest-order cognitive skills will require the learner to appraise, assess, defend, evaluate, predict, support.

Bloom's Taxonomy is useful to the teacher in formulating learning *objectives and planning learning activities which challenge the learners at the appropriate level. It is also useful in helping them to articulate clearly what behaviours a learner must demonstrate in order for learning to be deemed successful. It is widely used in the education and training of teachers for the *learning and skills sector. *See also* KNOWLEDGE.

SEE WEB LINKS

- Details of the levels in all three domains, with more examples of level-related key words.

boarding school A school at which some or all pupils are resident during term-time. Most boarding schools belong to the *independent schools sector, although some are to be found under the aegis of *local authorities. In addition, some local authority day schools, not classed as boarding schools, may include a small number of pupils who are **boarders**. The majority of local authority boarding schools are for the education of pupils with a disability or *special educational needs. In most cases, boarding schools in the independent sector follow the *national curriculum and enter pupils for national examinations. The image of the boarding school has recently been popularized among schoolchildren by the cultural phenomenon of Harry Potter and his experiences at Hogwarts School.

Boarding Schools' Association (BSA) A body which represents those boarding schools, about five hundred in number, which have accreditation from the *Independent Schools Council (ISC). It provides professional development for teachers and governors, and supports research into all aspects of residential compulsory education. It also offers a consultancy service to parents who are considering a boarding education for their child.

SEE WEB LINKS

- Details of publications available from the BSA relating to boarding and boarding schools.

board of corporation The governing body of a *further education college, which came into use following incorporation in 1993. The composition of the board was changed by the *Further and Higher Education Act 1992, which removed *local authority representation and increased the proportion of representation by local commercial and industrial interests. Members of the board are not required to have a detailed knowledge of the minutiae of the college's provision, but are expected to monitor and take responsibility for the quality of that provision, its funding and finances, and its responsiveness to local and wider community needs. A board will normally operate a number of specialist subcommittees with responsibility for reporting back to the full committee on matters of finance, equal opportunities, and quality assurance, for example. The minimum number of members for a board is twelve and the maximum is twenty, with specified categories of membership within these figures. *See also* COLLEGE OF FURTHER EDUCATION.

SEE WEB LINKS

- Explains the distinction in roles between college management and college governance.

Bologna Process An initiative launched in 1999 by governments of 29 European Union member countries to create a European Higher Education Area. This involves the development of a common structure of higher education, and agreement on equivalence or credit levels of qualifications in order to enable students to transfer their studies and their qualifications between member countries, and to facilitate the mobility of staff. It also requires the recognition of a common structure of higher education study which involves both undergraduate and postgraduate levels. The development of the credit transfer system necessary to facilitate student mobility and progression between member countries is an integral part of the Bologna Process, and is known as the **European Credit Transfer System (ECTS)**.
The Process, named after the city where the original meeting of government representatives took place to set the initiative in motion, operates outside the decision-making framework of the EU. All decisions taken require the consent of all participating countries, of which there are now over 40. As well as working towards a common higher education framework, the Process also has the declared aims of improving the quality of higher education across Europe in order to enhance the economy by raising the qualification level of the workforce, and of enhancing the reputation of European higher education and qualifications throughout the world. These economic aims make the Bologna Process a significant factor in the EU's *Lisbon Strategy. The Process also places an emphasis on *'lifelong learning' in the sense of developing provision which

will enable the necessary updating of the workforce at every level in order to keep abreast of rapid developments in technology. Since the initial meeting in 1999, ministers representing the member governments have met every two years in a major European city. In 2007 the meeting was hosted by the UK government in London.

The Process is promoted in UK higher education institutions (HEIs) by a national team of fourteen **Bologna Promoters**, funded by the European Commission. The Promoters' role is to advise HEIs on the implementation of the ECTS and on the implementation of student and teacher mobility between member states. They also provide HEIs with current information about the progress of the Bologna Process. Under the terms of the Process, HEIs are encouraged to develop courses whose content reflects a European perspective, and to engage in partnership activities with HEIs from other member states, including, for example, collaboration in creating joint provision of degrees by institutions in two different member states. *See also* BRUGES–COPENHAGEN PROCESS.

borderline Used to describe a *grade or score arrived at in the *assessment of a candidate's work or performance, which falls on the dividing line between two grades or categories. Thus, if the candidate needed to achieve at least a mark of 40 per cent in order to gain a pass grade, and was awarded 39–41 per cent, they may be said to be a borderline case. Similarly, if the candidate needed to gain 70 per cent in two consecutive pieces of work in order to achieve a distinction, but gained 69 per cent in one and 71 per cent in the other, their work may be said to be a borderline distinction. Such borderline work is often double-marked, *moderated, offered for the consideration of an external examiner, or all three of these, in order to ensure the reliability of the final assessment decision.

Bourdieu, Pierre (1930–2002) A prominent French cultural anthropologist and sociologist whose work covered a wide area of research interests ranging from considerations of cultural taste to the function of education. Bourdieu was interested in how cultural and social understanding and values are transmitted in educational contexts from one generation to the next. Much of the groundwork for his ideas and approach was developed during the Algerian War of Independence (1958–62) when, while serving in the French army, he undertook ethnographic research into Algerian peasant communities. This shaped his desire to focus his approach to research on actual lived experience rather than simply on theory.

One of Bourdieu's principal concerns was to examine the experience and processes of learning. He was interested in how we, as individuals, navigate our lives, making choices, encountering forces which might inhibit these choices, and experiencing hierarchical power relationships which imply symbolic values. This involved an exploration of how unequal and competitive power relationships continue from one generation to the next. Bourdieu sought to find a middle ground between the more objectivist conception of *ideology as a purely external force that constrains and determines human subjectivity of **Louis Althusser** (1918–90), and the emphasis of **Jean-Paul Sartre** (1905–80) upon the power of the agent voluntarily to create meaningful social action, ignoring the influence of constraining external forces.

The two main concepts which distinguish Bourdieu's work are **habitus** and field. What is crucial to Bourdieu's theory is that these two concepts work together and, doing so, explain the relationship between the subjective agent and the objectifying external force. 'Habitus' refers to the 'feel for the game' that agents acquire through the lifelong process of learning and socialization: these are the flexible 'cultural competencies' which serve to account for both the stability of the social order and the transformations that initiate cultural change. When a student arrives in a new class at university, she will bring with her a very particular set of cultural competencies learned in various contexts: these might range from her family, to the various cultural texts and genres she has experienced, to perhaps the most immediately relevant, the previous school she attended. If she had been studying English literature, she might perhaps have a feel for how we might study a play or a poem; she might have learned some of the critical terms used. What she will be confronted with on that first day at university is a whole range of cultural competencies yet to be learned.

If 'habitus' accounts for the agent, 'field' accounts for the objectivity of any given situation. According to Bourdieu, society is made up of a structured set of relatively autonomous fields such as politics, economics, and education. Each field is characterized by a set of cultural and political relationships that exist between the positions occupied by the agents within it. For Bourdieu, these fields are not as rigid as a fixed structure but are flexible as they interact with the agents within them. Power relationships are maintained or reproduced, and to an extent transformed, by the agents operating within them. Thus, agents operating in these 'fields' are in competition over the resources available (material and symbolic), and success in competing is dependent on the agent's cultural 'capital' or 'competence'. For instance, in the educational field, there will be other fields within it such as *primary, *secondary, *tertiary, and higher education, and each of these will compete for resources or funding. Even within a particular institution there will be different faculties such as the humanities, the sciences, or business, with academics competing for funding and pre-eminence in their chosen fields.

In *Homo Academicus*, first published in 1984, Bourdieu conducted research into the intellectual landscape of French university teachers, a world in which he, too, worked. He delved into the social background and practical activities of his contemporaries, examining their social origins, how much they published and where, what their connections were within the institution as well as in the media, and what their political involvements were. In doing so, Bourdieu related the issue of reputations within the intellectual map of France to the distribution of power and capital. He was an influential academic in his day, and his methods of research and his ideas about education continue to inform current concerns regarding educational funding and the relationship between education and the needs of the market. He held the post of Director of Studies at the École Pratique des Hautes Études from 1964, and the Chair of Sociology at the Collège de France from 1981. C.H.

Brain Gym An educational programme based on using physical movement to develop an integrated and coordinated approach to learning, using not only cognition, but also physical and sensory skills. Known as Educational

Kinesiology because of its emphasis on movement, this approach was originally developed in the United States to support the learning of children and adults with learning difficulties such *dyslexia or *attention deficit hyperactivity disorder. It is used in some schools to help raise standards of pupil learning, *behaviour, and attention; and is also used outside education by some adults as a means of stress management or memory improvement. The idea that such exercises can effectively improve brain function have, however, come under criticism and have been accused of being based upon 'bad science'. The terms 'Brain Gym' and 'Educational Kinesiology' are both registered trademarks.

brainstorming A means of generating ideas, often by a group of people, whereby immediate responses are written down and collected uncritically and without editing so as not to impede the creative process. These can then be explored and considered at more leisure in order to identify what is useful. It can be used as a *method for teaching and supporting learning, either when learners are working in small groups and recording their own ideas; or when a teacher is working with a larger group, encouraging all to contribute ideas, and writing them on a board or flip chart. There have been objections from some to the use of the term 'brainstorm' on the grounds that it may cause offence to sufferers from epilepsy. Various expressions, including 'thought shower', have been suggested as an alternative. Although 'brainstorm' remains in common usage, teachers may wish to ascertain, before using it, whether such use will cause offence to any of their learners.

British Accreditation Council for Independent Further and Higher Education Colleges (BAC) The function of the Council is to monitor and improve standards in independent institutions of *further and *higher education which offer British-accredited awards, including *General Certificate of Education *Advanced Level, degrees, and postgraduate qualifications. Such institutions include independent universities overseas; independent professional colleges in the United Kingdom which undertake specialist vocational training; and independent colleges—so-called *crammers—which specialize in preparing candidates for public examinations. To maintain their accredited status, colleges undergo an inspection every five years, in addition to a visit by BAC inspectors between formal inspections. The Council currently accredits more than 200 colleges in the UK, and almost 30 overseas in countries such as the United States, Pakistan, and Switzerland. The Council's membership includes nominees from bodies such as the *Association of Colleges and the *British Council.

SEE WEB LINKS

- Further details of the BAC's role and procedures.
- Full list of accredited colleges.

British Association for the Advancement of Science (BA) Established in 1831 and commonly referred to simply as the British Association, this registered charity aims to promote public understanding of science and to ensure that scientific developments have a positive impact upon society. Its board of trustees acts as a governing council. In addition to its central office in London, there are approximately 30 local branches of the British Association throughout the United Kingdom. Early members of the Association were responsible for coining the term 'scientist'. Among other activities, it organizes an annual Festival of Science and a National Science and Engineering Week. *See also* NATIONAL COMMISSION ON EDUCATION.

SEE WEB LINKS

- An account of the history of the BA.

British Baccalaureate Debate about the desirability of a coherent *examination system for post-16 pupils which placed value on vocational or applied skills and knowledge as well as on academic achievement has its origins in a pamphlet published by the Institute of Public Policy Research in 1990 which called for the introduction of a British Baccalaureate. This would provide a broader range of study than the traditional *General Certificate of Education *Advanced Level curriculum which then dominated the post-16 examination system, and would attract a wider range of pupils to stay on in education after the age of 16. One of its co-authors was David Miliband, who later went on to become Schools Minister at the *Department for Education and Skills. Taking as its models the French **baccalauréat* and the *International Baccalaureate, it was proposed that a British 'Bac' would be *modular, with an educational core and subject-based options. All students would take core *modules in three domains: social and human sciences; natural sciences and technology; and arts, languages, and literature. In addition, they would undertake at least one work or community module in which their theoretical studies could be practically applied. The idea behind this model was that a unified examination system of this type would encourage late selection and high participation. The government's disinclination to engage with these proposals in the early 1990s coincided with a shift in policy emphasis to the reform of the vocational route as a means of providing breadth in the post-16 curriculum. It was this line of reform which eventually led to the development of *General National Vocational Qualifications. The argument for a British Baccalaureate reignited as speculation grew over the possible outcomes of the Tomlinson review of 2003 of the post-16 qualifications framework.

Further Reading: D. Finegold et al. *A British 'Baccalauréat': Ending the Divisions between Education and Training* (Institute for Public Policy Research, 1990).

British Council Set up in 1934, and operating under its current name from 1936, the Council's purpose is to promote a wider knowledge of the United Kingdom and of the English language overseas, and to support and develop cultural relations between the UK and other countries. It is funded through the Foreign and Commonwealth Office, and is best known for its work in teaching English as a second language and providing education in developing countries. Its full title is the British Council for Relations with Other Countries.

SEE WEB LINKS

- Details of the Council's history, including archived films and recordings.

British Educational Communications and Technology Agency (Becta) Set up to support the use of *information and communication technology in education, the agency works with the *Department for Children, Schools, and Families to support and develop *e-learning. It works with both industry and education, and acts as a strategic adviser to government and other national organizations, as well as promoting inclusiveness through its *special educational needs (SEN) strategy. *See also* NATIONAL GRID FOR LEARNING.

SEE WEB LINKS

- Details of Becta's role and SEN strategy.

British Educational Research Association (BERA) An association open to all educational professionals and those working in related fields which aims to promote and sustain a professional research culture with the purpose of informing policy and practice. BERA provides a forum for communication, dissemination, and debate, and supports the professional development of educational researchers. It holds events for researchers, including an annual conference, and publishes current research in the *British Educational Research Journal*.

SEE WEB LINKS

- An account of the history and purpose of BERA.

British Education Index (BEI) A database, updated quarterly, which lists all papers on education which have appeared in British academic *journals, web sites, and periodicals. Papers and articles are analysed and listed according to subject matter. The BEI is also available in hard copy as a quarterly journal and as a CD-ROM. Maintained within the library of Leeds University and available by subscription only, it is a key resource in educational *research.

SEE WEB LINKS

- A list of the journals indexed by the BEI.

Bruges–Copenhagen Process An initiative by governments of the European Union member countries to create a policy of Europe-wide cooperation in vocational education and training designed to develop an enhanced knowledge-based economy and to ensure that the European labour market is open to all. The Process has two main thrusts: to establish recognition and transparency in the standards and content of vocational qualifications, and compatibility between the qualification frameworks of member states; and to introduce measures for quality assurance in relation to mutually recognized qualifications. The overall purpose of the Process is to facilitate the mobility of qualified workers between the member states of the EU, and, to this end, the measures taken are aimed at making it possible for employers in any member country to understand clearly the level and scope of the qualifications possessed by a job applicant from any other participating country in the EU. This emphasis on workforce mobility makes the Bruges–Copenhagen Process an important component of the EU's *Lisbon Strategy, which aims to improve the competitiveness and status of the European economy. The Process itself originates with an agreement by representatives of EU member states in Bruges in 2001 to move towards a greater degree of transparency and cooperation over vocational education and training. This was followed by a signed declaration by member states in Copenhagen in 2002. The Bruges–Copenhagen Process followed the example of the initiative established earlier to promote a European framework for higher education, now known as the *Bologna Process.

b

Bruner, Jerome (b. 1915) An American psychologist who continues to exert an influence on education and the development of curriculum theory. In his work on cognitive psychology, Bruner's interest in the cognitive development of children and how they represent ideas has drawn him to consider the cultural, environmental, and experiential factors influencing the process of education, as set out in his work *The Process of Education* (1960). In the early 1970s Bruner continued his research at Oxford University into the question of infant agency and began a series of explorations into children's language, establishing the concept of LADs (language acquisition devices) and LASSes (language acquisition support systems), which help to explain the nature of cultural–linguistic development. The emphasis on talk as a 'scaffold' to successful learning was influenced by *Vygotsky and demonstrates 'how learning shapes the mind ... [providing] us with the toolkit by which we construct not only our worlds but our very conception of ourselves and our powers' (Bruner 1996).

Bruner sees learning as an active process in which learners construct new understanding based on past knowledge. These accommodated *schemas reflect the cognitive theories of *Piaget but are expanded to encompass the social and cultural aspects of learning. Bruner has more recently worked with the *pedagogistas* in *Reggio Emilia, where children are recognized as competent learners who actively contribute to the emerging curriculum through the encouragement of dialogue, narrative, problem-solving, and documentation—all devices to support the development of the ways in which children and adults make internal sense of the world as a shared construction.

In *The Process of Education*, Bruner presents four key themes: the role of structure in learning and how it may be made central in teaching; readiness for learning and the spiral curriculum; intuitive and analytical thinking (through shared and sustained dialogue); and motives for learning. These themes have been explored further by Donald Schön (1930–97) and Howard Gardner (b. 1943), who have looked at ways in which teachers and schools might create ideal conditions for learners to be able to use their individual *learning style and type of *intelligence to create meaning.

Bruner's cognitive approach to his work in the *early years phase of childhood has made him a key figure in educational theory in the United States and United Kingdom. His three modes of instruction—enactive, iconic, and symbolic—have been interpreted and developed most recently into visual, auditory, and kinaesthetic (VAK) teaching methods, and have informed Gardner's theory of *multiple intelligences.

Further Reading: J. Bruner *Towards a Theory of Instruction* (Belknap Press, 1966); *The Relevance of Education* (Norton, 1971); *Child's Talk: Learning to Use Language* (Norton, 1983); *Actual Minds, Possible Worlds* (Harvard University Press, 1986); *Acts of Meaning* (Harvard University Press, 1990); *The Culture of Education* (Harvard University Press, 1996). A.W.

BTEC National *See* BUSINESS AND TECHNOLOGY EDUCATION COUNCIL.

bulge A sharp rise in the number of pupils or students reaching a particular stage in the education system at any one time. It was coined as a term to describe the demographic phenomenon following the end of the Second World War, when birth rates rose sharply, creating a succession of unusually large cohorts of pupils which proceeded through the various stages of schooling and *higher education in the 1950s and 1960s. The existing number of teachers and the available classroom space in state schools was insufficient to meet this demand. However, when the bulge had moved through the system and the number of children entering compulsory education began to fall, schools found themselves with a surplus of teachers, while local authorities were, in some cases, forced to close down schools for lack of pupils. Some educationalists saw this as an opportunity for introducing smaller *pupil–teacher ratios for the benefit of the pupils; but in policy terms the problem was viewed as financial and addressed accordingly with a reduction in teaching posts and classroom space.

bullying The Elton Report on discipline (1989) confirmed that bullying in school was widespread. It recommended greater vigilance on the part of teachers to identify and address such pupil behaviour. Nevertheless, bullying has continued to present a problem in many schools and other educational institutions, although it is difficult to quantify, on the one hand because victims are often reluctant to come forward, and on the other because of a continuing lack of awareness about exactly what behaviours constitute bullying. All schools, colleges, and universities are required to have an anti-bullying policy, which will normally also cover the bullying of teachers by other teachers or managers. The policy must conform to the Equality Act 2006, which makes some forms of bullying—for example, on the grounds of sexual orientation or religious beliefs—liable to prosecution. In extreme cases which have been reported, bullying at school has led to pupils attempting or committing suicide. As a result, a number of organizations, such as ChildLine, offer advice and support for victims of bullying, while web sites such as Bullying UK, Donthideit, and the unfortunately named Bully OnLine have been designed specifically to help victims by offering definitions of bullying behaviour and encouraging them to report incidents. Since the use of mobile phones and home computers has become widespread, various forms of **cyberbullying** have developed, which are more difficult for teachers to see and prevent. These include the sending of malicious texts and the practice known as 'happy slapping', in which perpetrators carry out a physical attack on their victim while making a visual recording of the incident on their mobile phone for sending to others. Growing concerns about all types of bullying are reflected in the fact that in 2007 an anti-bullying week was introduced; and that a web site has been set up by the *Department for Children, Schools, and Families (DfES) called Don't Suffer in Silence, which presents advice to schools in relation to their mandatory duty to address the issue. This includes reminders that all schools should cover cyberbullying in their anti-bullying policy; that the curriculum should cover instruction in the dangers of new technologies; that schools must monitor all on-site electronic communication, and extend this to off-site communication if this involves a school activity; that they must have a clear policy on phone use within school; that they should employ Internet blocking technologies where appropriate; and that security systems such as firewalls should be in place to prevent information about pupils or staff from being accessed from outside the school.

SEE WEB LINKS

- An introduction to the DfES anti-bullying web site, and information on tackling cyberbullying.

bunching Used to describe a situation where marks or grades awarded to assessed work show very little variance from student to student, but are closely bunched within a few marks of one another. This could indicate either that the ability of the students within the group being assessed is fairly uniform, or, more worryingly, that the *assessment may be invalid or unreliable. If there is bunching at the lower end of the marking scale, this may indicate a problem either with the selection and recruitment of students, or with the quality of the teaching, or with the effectiveness of the learning.

Burnham scale A single national pay scale for teachers in primary and secondary schools. It takes its name from Lord Burnham, who, in 1919, chaired the committee which devised a national pay scale for teachers in elementary schools. Subsequently, the Burnham Committee was tasked with drawing up a scale for secondary school teachers and for those in further education. As a consequence, the agreement of the single national scale in 1945 was known as the Burnham Agreement.

bursary A grant or financial award offered by an institution such as a *university or private school to help students pay their tuition fees or other expenses related to their course of study. A limited number of bursaries are available at any one institution in any one year, and students must make an application stating their case if they wish to be considered. University bursaries are usually offered to support studies in specific subject areas, or for specific awards, such as a *master's degree. Trainee teachers on school-focused *Postgraduate Certificate of Education *initial teacher training programmes are entitled to bursaries as a right.

In Scotland eligibility for bursaries may be assessed on individual students' circumstances or may be awarded on successful achievement of an academic standard, and can be available to assist with travel and living expenses, or other costs incurred through study. They are available through individual institutions or through the Student Awards Agency for Scotland (SAAS).

SEE WEB LINKS

- Details of bursaries available through the Student Awards Agency for Scotland.

Business and Technology Education Council (BTEC) An *awarding body for the *further education sector formed in 1974 as a result of a merger between the Business Education Council (BEC) and the Technician Education Council (TEC). It now operates under the name of Edexcel and, having taken over the examination of the *General Certificate of Education (GCE) *Advanced Level (A level) and *General Certificate of Secondary Education (GCSE), formerly carried out by the University of London Schools' Examination Board in 1995, it is now one of the three unitary awarding bodies which offer both *academic and *vocational qualifications in both the schools and the further education sectors. During the 1980s and early 1990s BTEC awards in a range of general vocational areas such as business studies and sports studies formed one of the few alternative progression routes into higher education available to those who did not choose to study for GCE A levels. A BTEC First Diploma claimed equivalence with four or five good GCSE passes, and provided a means of progression to either A levels or a BTEC National Diploma, which some *universities accepted, at distinction level, for the purpose of university entry, as the equivalent of two sound A level passes. On the introduction of the *General National Vocational Qualification (GNVQ) in 1993, BTEC initially resisted allowing their qualifications to be subsumed under the GNVQ umbrella; and it is a measure of its reputation that many providers continued to refer to these BTEC qualifications by their original BTEC titles even after they had been endorsed as GNVQs. In some vocational areas, the qualifications remained as BTEC National awards, while others, such as the BTEC National Health and Social Care, have survived the demise of the GNVQ to re-emerge with the original BTEC title.

business education *See* BUSINESS AND TECHNOLOGY EDUCATION COUNCIL; BUSINESS STUDIES.

business studies A *curriculum subject which focuses on business-related topics such as marketing, organizational structures, business legislation, finance, and human resource management. Courses and awards are available at most levels, including at *General Certificate of Secondary Education (GCSE), *General Certificate of Education (GCE), *Advanced Level, degree, and postgraduate levels. A well-established subject in further education colleges from the 1970s onwards, it has more recently been included in the curriculum of some secondary schools, particularly as an option in Year 12. It is classed as a *vocational subject, and was one of the most popular options for students enrolling on a General Certificate of National Vocational Qualifications in the 1990s. It now forms one of the options on the *14–19 Diploma. *See also* BUSINESS AND TECHNOLOGY EDUCATION COUNCIL.

Butler Act The name by which the *Education Act 1944 is popularly known. The reforms enacted in this legislation were largely attributed to R. A. Butler (1902–82), who was at that time President of the Board of Education, and with whose name the Act was associated. This legislation is an important milestone in education policy and reform. It established the three progressive stages or sectors of education with which we are now familiar: *primary, secondary, and *further education. It was also responsible for the introduction of the *Eleven Plus, and the system of selecting pupils at the end of the primary stage of their schooling in order that they should receive the education or training which was judged best suited to their ability and their aptitude. The three routes of schooling provided—the grammar schools, the (secondary) modern schools, and the technical schools—were described as having *'parity of esteem', an early use of this phrase, which has since become a familiar part of policy rhetoric. The Act also replaced the Board of Education with a more powerful **Ministry of Education**, whose Minister was empowered to enforce the statutory duties of *local education authorities. This Act was not superseded until the passing of the Education Act 1988.

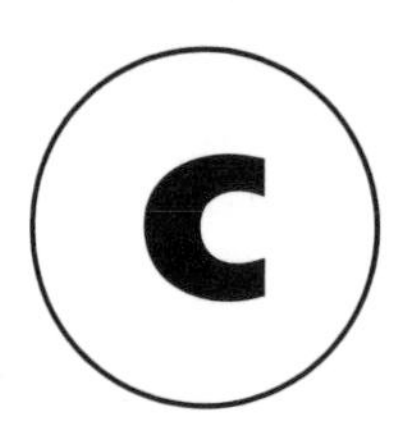

campus The grounds and buildings of a school, university, or college. The expressions 'on-campus' and 'off-campus' are used to indicate whether a location or event is situated on university premises or away from them respectively. Some institutions operate across a number of campuses, with students and teachers travelling between different sites. This is sometimes referred to as **split-site provision**. The word 'campus' is the Latin for 'field', and seems to have been first used in its current sense in the United States.

capitation Funding which is calculated literally 'per head'. Prior to the *Education Act 1988 and the introduction of devolved budgets, *local authorities would provide *maintained schools with a capitation allowance for the purchase of resources, calculated on the number of pupils on roll. Devolved funding to schools is also calculated on the basis of capitation.

Career Entry and Development Profile (CEDP) Trainee and *newly qualified teachers (NQTs) are required to fill in a CEDP, in consultation with their tutor or mentor, at three 'transition points' in their development. The first is towards the end of their *initial teacher training (ITT), the second and third at the beginning and end of the *induction process. The profile sets out their goals, their achievements, and their development needs. The school which employs the NQT can refer to the CDP in order to set objectives for the induction period in order to ensure that the NQT reaches the required induction standards. The statutory requirements for ITT state that all providers of ITT must ensure that trainee teachers have a CEDP and are supported in completing it.

Careers Advisory Service *See* CONNEXIONS.

Careers Wales An all-age careers guidance service for Wales which draws together the skills provided by adult guidance networks, including the national telephone helpline *Learndirect and some elements of the **Youth Gateway**, which provides links between education, business, and specialist assessment and support services for young people. The interactive web site has been live since November 2004.

SEE WEB LINKS

- The web site for Careers Wales.

H.G.

case study Although it has a number of meanings outside an educational context, a case study, in terms of teaching and learning, is a *method of developing learners' understanding by enabling them to engage actively with a problem or issue relevant to their studies. It presents an account or a scenario, either fictional or real, which allows the student to apply what they have learned and make sense of it in a realistic context. It may also encourage the student to draw on their own ideas, experience, and *tacit knowledge. The case study is a method or resource which encourages active, rather than passive, learning.

In the context of education *research, however, a case study has a different meaning and purpose, and is usually understood as a means of conducting a small-scale investigation (literally, a study of a specific case) in order to explore a theory or research question.

catchment The area around the school, college, or university from which it draws its learners. The *Education Act 1980 permitted parents to state a preference for the school which their child would attend. The Education Act 1988 required schools to comply with parental preference as long as they had places to offer. These two Acts changed the pattern of enrolment from one in which secondary schools drew their intake almost entirely from the *primary schools in their catchment area, to one in which they may recruit pupils from other areas and even other *local authorities. Conversely, many universities, which traditionally have enrolled students from all parts of the country, are noting, since the introduction of tuition *fees, a rising trend of applications from students living locally, possibly influenced by the fact that it is less expensive for students to remain living in the parental home.

Catholic maintained schools Schools in Northern Ireland which are owned by the Roman Catholic Church through a system of trustees, and managed by a board of governors. The education and *library boards provide funding and direct the employment of non-teaching staff. Teachers are employed by the Council for Catholic Maintained Schools. *See also* DENOMINATION; FAITH SCHOOLS. J.H.

CAT score *See* BASELINE ASSESSMENT.

Centre for Educational Research and Innovation (CERI) The Centre's purpose is to support the promotion and development of educational *research and the trialling of innovations. Founded in 1968 as part of the Organization for Economic Cooperation and Development, it works to promote cooperation in educational research and development between member countries.

Centre for Excellence in Leadership (CEL) Created in 2003 as part of the *Success for All initiative, CEL's role is to support the development of leadership skills in the *learning and skills sector, particularly in *further education (FE) colleges, but also in work-based learning provision, offender learning, and adult and community provision. The 2006 *White Paper *Further Education: Raising Skills, Improving Life Chances* widened its remit to include the introduction of a mandatory qualification for principals of FE colleges, and a strategy for improving quality of provision in that sector. CEL is a national agency operating through a charitable trust.

SEE WEB LINKS

- Provides a summary of development programmes offered by CEL.

Centre for Excellence in Teacher Training (CETT) Institutions recognized for their good practice in the provision of initial training and *continuing professional development for teachers working for further education colleges or providers of *work-based and adult and community learning in the UK. They are charged with contributing to the further raising of national standards in this field, and are central to the reforms in *initial teacher training for the *learning and skills sector set out in the 2004 policy document *Equipping our Teachers for the Future: Reforming Initial Teacher Training*. Institutions were invited to apply for CETT status through a system referred to as 'bidding'. Those which were successful became operational in September 2007 under the supervision of *Lifelong Learning UK, at the same time as staff undergoing teacher training for that sector began working towards qualifications that would gain them *qualified teacher learning and skills status. Each Centre is required to gather together bodies of best practice, both in materials and in the deployment of human resources, to be disseminated regionally. They are also responsible for directing potential teachers to appropriate institutions, a function which is particularly important in *Skills for Life teacher education, where subject-specific qualifications were unlikely to be available at the majority of colleges at any one time. V.C., K.A.

Centre for Policy Studies (CPS) A right-wing pressure group which is often outspoken in its criticism of the education system.

Centre of Vocational Excellence (COVE) A *further education (FE) *college or other training provider which is judged to provide high-quality specialist *work-based learning in a specific vocational area. Thus, an FE college might become a COVE for Construction and the Built Environment, for example. The programme was launched in 2001 by the *Learning and Skills Council with the aim of improving the further education sector's capacity to provide *vocational training of a high quality in response to employers' needs.

Certificate of Education (Cert. Ed.) A non-graduate teaching qualification, now applicable only to teachers training for *qualified teacher learning and skills status for the *post-compulsory sector. It is normally awarded at *National Qualifications Framework level 5, and is subject to verification and endorsement by *Lifelong Learning UK.

Certificate of Pre-Vocational Education (CPVE) Introduced in 1983, and a short-lived forerunner to the *General National Vocational Qualification, although designed for a slightly different type of student; in this case for 16–18-year-olds who had left the schooling system with few qualifications. It was developed in response to an initiative from the Department of Education and Science, and offered young people an opportunity to experience different types of college-based *vocationally related training as well as providing them with an element of *work experience. Its failure to recruit widely was attributed at the time to the fact that, unlike the *youth training schemes then on offer, it did not carry a financial incentive in the form of weekly payments to the student.

Certificate of Secondary Education (CSE) A school-leaving qualification introduced in 1965 as an alternative to the *General Certificate of Education *Ordinary Level (O level) for those candidates for whom O levels were considered too demanding. At the time, it was claimed that a grade 1 CSE was equivalent to an O level for the purpose of progression to employment or to further study. Thus, school-leavers in possession of grade 1 CSEs in English and mathematics were able to use them as equivalent currency to O levels in these subjects. There was a view among many teachers and pupils at the time, however, that a grade 1 at CSE was more difficult to achieve than a grade C at O level. Like the O level, the CSE was replaced in 1988 by the *General Certificate of Secondary Education.

Certificate of Sixth Year Studies (CSYS) Before 2002 a sixth year study qualification was the highest level of qualification available in a Scottish school. Undertaken in the sixth year of schooling, the qualification was roughly equivalent to an English *General Certificate of Education *Advanced Level, but with elements of *undergraduate level study. It was replaced in 2002 by the *Advanced Higher. S.M.

certification The awarding of a certificate which confirms achievement in an *examination or course of study.

challenging behaviour *See* BEHAVIOUR; DISRUPTIVE.

charitable status Some private schools have claimed charitable status, which has allowed them to benefit from certain taxation exemptions. However, since 2002 schools which claim such status have been permitted to retain it only on the condition that they can demonstrate that the school operates to the benefit of the public.

chartered teacher Traditionally the term for fully *qualified teacher status in Scotland. Completion of teacher training concluded in the award of a 'parchment'; hence the term 'chartered'.

SEE WEB LINKS

- The web site of the General Teaching Council of Scotland, which provides detailed information on achieving qualified teacher status in Scotland. S.M.

Child and Adolescent Mental Health Services (CAMHS) A community-based service for young people who have mental health difficulties. CAMHS often supports young people together with other members of their families. It is a multi-professional service which includes psychiatrists and psychologists, social workers, and nurses. CAMHS work is linked closely with schools, particularly through educational psychologists and educational welfare staff. It offers support and guidance to young people involved in substance misuse including drugs and alcohol as well as mental health problems. Children between the ages of 0 and 14 are supported by child mental health teams. T.B., L.E.

child-centred A conceptual framework for education, popularized in the 1960s as a result of the *Plowden Report (1967), in which children's personal, social, physical, and learning needs were to be at the centre of the education process. This was not a new idea and can be traced back to the educational philosophy of *Rousseau, *Dewey, *Montessori, *Isaacs, *Piaget, and *Erikson. Child-centredness identifies children as unique and special who deserve an education appropriate to their individual needs, rather than a prescribed formal curriculum defined by *behaviourist and narrow models of teaching.

The following notions are central to child-centred education theories:

- education should meet the needs of those being educated;
- these needs are best met if identified with the interests of children;
- the curriculum should be based on experience and discovery;
- rather than being subject- or content-based, educational programmes should focus on activity.

There were, and are, critics of child-centred *ideology who claim that to cater for all individual children's needs might be to embrace learner autonomy to the point of anarchy and an absence of taught and learned curriculum. However, the experiential and active learning *pedagogy of *early years teachers reflects a commitment to encouraging children to be independent, creative, responsible, and autonomous, recognizing their competences and supporting the construction of knowledge through social facilitation rather than didactic teaching. This is reflected in *Reggio Emilia pre-schools and within the *Te Whaariki curriculum. Furthermore, the UK government has embraced child-centred ideology within their *personalized learning agenda and *Assessment for Learning as set out in the Primary National Strategy (Excellence and Enjoyment, 2003), encouraging teachers to plan for the needs of individual children within their classrooms.
See also LEARNER-CENTRED.

SEE WEB LINKS

- Details of the current Primary National Strategy. A.W.

childminder A registered carer providing play and learning opportunities for children within a home setting. Inspected annually by the Early Years Directorate of *Ofsted against national day care standards, a childminder usually looks after children under 5 in their own home, but can also look after older children before or after school and during school holidays. Childminders have a duty to follow the guidelines for the *Early Years Foundation Stage for children aged 0–5, and the statutory ratio for adult:child as specified in national standards. The majority of childminders are self-employed, but they can be employed by *local authorities to look after vulnerable children at risk of neglect or abuse. Qualifications are not necessary, but many childminders belong to a self-support network and work towards a level 3 Certificate in Childminding Practice. A.W.

Children Act 1989 Statutory legislation which defined orders with respect to the welfare of children in the following areas:

- reform of the law relating to children;
- provision for children in need;
- amendments to the law with regards to fostering, children's homes, *childminding, day care, and adoption;
- children in family proceedings;
- *local authority support for children and families, including *looked-after children;
- care and supervision orders and powers of the court;
- protection of children;
- statutory supervisory functions and responsibilities.

This Act brought together, under one framework, a whole raft of legislation with regard to children, young people, and the law over the previous half-century. It was superseded by the *Children Act 2004.

SEE WEB LINKS

- Provides details of legislative framework: Children Act 1989.

A.W.

Children Act 2004 This Act superseded the *Children Act 1989 and sets out a legislative spine for the government's wider strategy in England and Wales, for improving children's lives, covering universal and parental responsibility, the *Every Child Matters agenda, services accessed by children, and the targeted services for those with additional needs. The aim of this Act was to legislate for and encourage multi-disciplinary working and delegate responsibility to local authorities to implement the provisions outlined. Following the *Education Act 2005, schools undergoing inspections by *Ofsted were judged not only against quality of teaching but also against the principles set out in this 2004 Children Act.

SEE WEB LINKS

- Provides details of changes to the series of Children and Child Care Acts.

children's centres The centres are places where children under 5 and their families can receive 'seamless' holistic and integrated services and information, and where they can access help from multi-disciplinary teams of professionals. The core offer includes integrated early learning, care, family support, health services, and outreach support for those not attending the centre. High-quality teacher input is also one of the core components of a children's centre. The *Sure Start children centres are at the heart of a government ten-year strategy (2000–10) to deliver better outcomes for children and families. The centres build on the success of Sure Start local programmes, *early excellence centres, and neighbourhood nurseries developed since 1997. Children's centres are based in the 20 per cent most disadvantaged *local authority wards in England. Since 2005, 188 children's centres have been designated, and it is anticipated that there will be a network of 3 500 centres by 2010.

SEE WEB LINKS

- Information regarding aims and strategy.

A.W.

Children's Plan A government-led initiative to enhance provision of education, play facilities, and care for children up to 19 years of age. Launched in December 2007, the Plan followed a public consultation, initiated by the *Department for Children, Schools, and Families, entitled Time to Talk, carried out during the autumn of 2007. It drew on the reports of three 'Expert Groups', whose brief was to examine the needs of children and young people in a specific age group: birth to 7 years, 8–13 years, and 14–19 years. The Plan sets out a ten-year strategy and is supported by £1 billion of government funding. One of its targets is the replacement of *Standard Tasks testing by *single-level testing for 7–14-year-olds as part of the emphasis on a *personalized curriculum. Other target measures include upgrading 3 500 playgrounds and creating 30 additional supervised adventure play areas; introducing more flexibility into the school start dates for children whose birthdays fall in the summer months; and introducing free childcare for 20 000 2-year-olds from economically disadvantaged families. The Plan also includes reviews of sex education provision in schools, and of child and adolescent mental health services. Other measures include improved communication and contact between schools and parents; the setting up of *parents' councils in every secondary school; and additional support for children with *special educational needs. The initiative also has long-term implications for *higher education and for the professional development of teachers, since one of its ten-year targets is that all new teachers should be able to study for a *master's degree.

choice The issue of parental choice in decisions about their child's schooling has been a key feature of education policy and debate since the 1980s. The *Education Act 1980 permitted parents to state a preference for the school which their child would attend; and the Education Act 1988 took this further by requiring schools to comply with parental preference as long as there were places to offer. These two Acts allow parents to express a choice over their child's schooling, even to the extent that the preferred school might be some distance away and in a different *local authority from that in which the child lives. The principle of choice was an integral part of the introduction of *market competition into the schooling system. By expressing a choice, parents were able to indicate those schools for which there was a market demand, and at the same time provide an incentive to less popular schools to improve their performance in order to be able to compete for pupils. The word 'choice' became prominent in educational policy discourse, appearing, for example, in the title of the 1992 *White Paper *Choice and Diversity*. In September 1995 the *Secretary of State for Education, Gillian Shephard, was quoted as saying, 'We must emphasise the words that people find attractive, such as standards, discipline, and choice' (*The Guardian*, 19 September, 6). The concept of parental choice, however, remains a much-debated one. Those schools which have thrived as a result of market competition, and are fully subscribed or oversubscribed, are now in a position where it is they, rather than parents, who are able to exert an element of choice over which pupils they enter on their rolls. *See also* SCHOOL ADMISSIONS.

CILT, the National Centre for Languages Operates as a centre of expertise whose purpose is to promote and disseminate good practice in the teaching of languages in order to raise levels of capability nationally, across all age groups and sectors. It was established in 2003 as the result of a merger between the Centre for Information on Language Teaching and the Languages National Training Organization as part of the National Languages Strategy. It offers support to businesses and language services, as well as to teachers and learners, and is financed partly by central government grants and public funding for specific projects.

SEE WEB LINKS

- Provides details of CILT's regional language network.

circular The formal means by which the *Department for Children, Schools, and Families communicates its guidance to *local authorities. Circulars are signed by the *Secretary of State or the Permanent Secretary.

citizenship Citizenship education became a compulsory part of the *national curriculum in 2002 at *Key Stages 3 and 4. There are also non-statutory guidelines for citizenship in Key Stages 1 and 2.

SEE WEB LINKS

- Provides details of programmes of study and attainment targets.

city academy A secondary school set up as a trust with private sponsorship and government funding, as part of a government initiative to establish city academies aimed at improving the standards of performance in inner-city schools in England, particularly in areas of social deprivation. Those who support the initiative, which was introduced in 2002, argue that schools which are well resourced with the latest learning technology will be more likely to succeed in motivating disaffected and disengaged learners; and that the example of success provided by the city academy sponsors themselves will encourage and inspire young people to work hard at school and aspire to worthwhile goals in terms of career and qualifications. It is also suggested that the existence of city academies and the example they set of high pupil achievement will encourage other, competing schools to raise their own standards. The government target is to have established 200 city academies by 2010.

To become an academy, a school is required to raise up to £2 million in private sponsorship. The government then contributes a further sum—usually in the region of £25 million—towards the school's start-up costs. The establishment of an academy sometimes involves the demolition and replacement of old school buildings on existing sites; or it may involve the creation of an entirely new school. Sponsors may include private business organizations, private schools, religious organizations, and charities. The influence, expertise, and business acumen of such external sponsors is, it is argued, vital to the regeneration and improvement of inner-city schools. To this end, sponsors occupy the majority of places on the governing body which controls the academy's trust.

Although city academies, like state secondary schools, must follow the *national curriculum, they do not have to employ staff who are registered with the *General Teaching Council. In effect, this means that their teachers are not required to have full *qualified teacher status, and that the academies are not required to adhere to nationally agreed guidelines on teachers' salaries. Teachers' hours and conditions may also vary from those in state schools.

One of the claims made for city academies is that they will create a positive ethos, and that each will have the freedom to establish its own specific ethos, which will be significantly influenced by the values and beliefs of its sponsors. This has led to some criticisms on the grounds that the curriculum could be employed to reflect contentious beliefs, such as that of creationism. The academies have also been criticized on the grounds of their performance, since, in almost half of those established by 2007, pupils' results in the *General Certificate of Secondary Education examinations had not improved under the trust arrangement, and, in some, achievement was actually lower than under the state school system.

Although the government requires academies to take pupils of all abilities, the substantial government funding invested in the academies, and the publicity surrounding the implementation of the initiative, has created significant pressure on them to succeed; and this, according to many education commentators, may be why pupil *exclusion and expulsion figures for some academies have been relatively high, and why there are fears that the pressure to succeed may result in their seeking to recruit mainly pupils with good test results and with no learning difficulties. At this stage, therefore, educational opinion on the role and principle of city academies is divided. *See also* ACADEMY.

City and Guilds *See* AWARDING BODY.

city technology college Introduced as a result of the *Education Act 1988 to provide an alternative to *local authority schools. They were financed by industrial and commercial sponsors, and were non-selective and non-fee-charging. Only fifteen were established, and some have since become *beacon schools, while others have adopted *maintained status.

class 1. A collective noun for learners, used to refer to a group of pupils or students taught together. Used in this sense, we find such expressions as 'top of the class' and *'class size'. In secondary schools, the term may be used synonymously with **form**. In schools, classes usually consist of pupils of the same age, except in those minority of *primary schools where *vertical grouping is applied.

2. May be used synonymously with *lesson, as in 'After break, the pupils have their geography class'.

3. Denotes level of achievement in an *honours degree, which may be awarded at first, upper second, lower second, or third class. *See also* PUPIL–TEACHER RATIO.

class, social *See* SOCIAL CLASS.

classroom assistant *See* TEACHING ASSISTANT.

class size Recent research designed to discover whether there is a correlation between the number of learners in a class and levels of attainment has produced conflicting findings. Common sense suggests that the smaller the class, the more time and attention the teacher will be able to devote to each individual learner, and therefore the more effective the learning. However, recent government-funded research in the UK calls this assumption into question. For example, a study of pupil progress in over 200 primary schools conducted between 2002 and 2003 found that, although pupils aged 8–11 in larger classes receive less individual attention from the teacher, this has no measurable effect on their attainment in any subject, which is more likely to be affected by the economic circumstances of their home background, children from poorer homes making least progress. Similarly, a government-funded review of international research into the effects of class size on pupil achievement concludes that it has less impact on learning than the level of skill and experience possessed by teachers.

Research carried out in America, on the other hand, suggests that small class sizes in the first four years of schooling can lead to higher attainment by the time the pupil reaches secondary education. A report in the *Economic Journal* (January 2001) on research carried out at Princeton University presented findings which showed that pupils taught in smaller classes during the primary phase of their education were more likely to go on eventually to apply for *higher education, and that smaller classes were of particular benefit in raising the attainment of pupils from impoverished backgrounds and from minority groups. The positive impact of reduced class size on the learning of the very youngest pupils, particularly in literacy, is also reflected in a 2000 research report from the London Institute of Education, based on a study of 300 schools.

Class sizes in state schools in the UK, both primary and secondary, tend to be larger than those in other developed countries, and figures suggest no immediate trend towards reduction, having recently remained fairly static. For example, between 1996 and 2000 the average class size across all state schools was around 28 pupils to every teacher. Between 1985 and 2005, however, the average number of pupils in each class in the UK's fee-paying schools fell from almost 14 pupils to 10. There is no statutory maximum class size beyond *Key Stage 1 in the UK, except in Scotland, where there is an upper limit pledge of 18 pupils per class in primary 1 and primary 3. *See also* PUBLIC SCHOOL; PUPIL–TEACHER RATIO.

Further Reading: P. Blatchford *The Class Size Debate: Is Small Better?* (Open University Press, 2003) explores both sides of the debate.

clearing *See* UNIVERSITIES AND COLLEGES ADMISSIONS SERVICE.

coach Someone who provides advice to help a learner improve their performance. For example, a pupil might be provided with coaching to help them improve their examination performance or their game of tennis. The distinction between coaching and *mentoring sometimes appears unclear; and on occasion the two terms are used interchangeably. As a rule, coaching suggests a more restricted role than mentoring, often time-constrained and tightly focused on performance.

Code of Practice (CoP) A framework which provides practical advice to local authorities, maintained schools, early years settings, and others on carrying out their statutory duties to identify, assess, and make provision for children and young people's *special educational need (SEN). The first CoP came into effect in 1994 and has been changed, following consultation, to the new Code, which has been effective since January 2002. It includes new rights and duties introduced by the Special Educational Needs and Disability Act 2001. The CoP document includes guidance under the headings of principles and policies, working in partnership with parents, pupil participation, identification, assessment and provision in all educational settings from early years to the secondary sector, statutory assessment of SEN, statements of SEN, and annual reviews. Working in partnership with other agencies is also addressed. Within the foreword of the document is information regarding the status and implementation of the CoP. It describes the implementation and monitoring guidelines, and information about the process of SEN tribunals which deal with appeals from parents. Relevant regulations and guidance on inclusion are also set out. There is also clear instruction concerning the Disability Rights Code of Practice for Schools.

The advice clearly defines SEN and tracks the development of the CoP through changes in various *Education Acts and *Children Acts. Roles and responsibilities are outlined with regard to principles and policy and working in partnership with parents. The Code also has a comprehensive glossary. All settings which must have regard for the Code of Practice for SEN should demonstrate that they have referred to the framework when developing their own policies and practice for the identification, assessment, and provision for all children and young people who have SEN.

co-education The teaching of girls and boys together in the same school and the same class. Whereas *primary education has generally always been co-educational (although up to the 1950s there were often separate entrance doors for boys and girls), it was often the case in the first two-thirds of the 20th century that boys and girls would attend separate schools for their secondary education. Since the *Education Act 1944 (*Butler Act) the trend has been towards co-educational secondary provision. Some researchers suggest that boys achieve better in mixed (co-educational) classes, while girls may achieve more highly, particularly in science subjects, in single-sex schools. *See also* GENDER.

cognitive 1. One of the three domains of learning (the others being *affective and *psychomotor) and denoting that area of learning which is to do with **thinking** (cognition) and understanding. *See also* KNOWLEDGE.

2. A branch of *learning theory concerned with how and why learning takes place, which argues that thinking is central to the learning process. **Cognitivists** argue that learning is not, as *behaviourists claim, simply a matter of behaviour modification, but involves the student gaining *knowledge not only through the acquisition of new learning, but also through a process of adapting or discarding old constructs or ideas which no longer fit their developing insight into the world. Cognitivist learning theory argues for a *learner-centred approach to teaching and learning, where the structuring and sequencing of learning is of key importance to the success of the learning experience. It suggests that knowledge is not an object to be dispensed or acquired, but a process. In terms of learning theory, two of the most widely recognized names among the cognitivists are *Dewey and *Bruner.

Cognitive Abilities Test (CAT) A *test used by some schools to assess the reasoning skills of *Key Stage 3 pupils. The test consists of three parts: verbal, quantitative, and non-verbal reasoning. The verbal reasoning element assesses reasoning processes using the medium of words, and the quantitative reasoning element assesses reasoning processes using numbers. The non-verbal part of the test uses shapes and figures to assess the pupil's reasoning processes, and can therefore be used as an effective way of assessing the ability of pupils with underdeveloped *numeracy or *literacy skills, or pupils with little knowledge of the English language. The results are referred to as pupils' 'CAT scores'. *See also* BASELINE DATA; MIDDLE YEARS INFORMATION SYSTEM; STANDARD TASKS; VALUE ADDED. I.F.W.

cognitive development *See* BRUNER; PIAGET.

collaborative provision *Programmes of study which are run jointly by more than one institution, as is the case, for example, when two or more schools pool their sixth form teaching in order to offer pupils a wider choice of options; or as might also be the case where one institution teaches and assesses a programme of study validated by another. This latter example might apply where a *college or an overseas institution offers a course which is validated, verified, and partly taught by a *university.

collective worship It is a statutory duty, under the School Standards and Framework Act 1998, for all *maintained schools to provide a daily act of collective worship for all pupils except those who have been withdrawn from this through the wishes of their parent or guardian. This is usually provided through a daily assembly which must be of a broadly Christian character. The exact nature of the provision is agreed between the *head teacher and the governing body and set out in a school policy.

SEE WEB LINKS

- Provides information about the collective worship policy.

college 1. A generic term popularly used to refer to institutions providing *post-compulsory education, including *colleges of education, *colleges of further education, and *sixth form colleges. Following the American usage, the expression 'going to college' may also be employed by some to denote 'going to *university'.

2. An administrative or nominal subdivision of a university, which may have considerable autonomy, in the case of *collegiate universities, or may operate in a similar way to the **house** system in some secondary schools in providing students with a team or sub-group with which to identify.

3. A colloquial term in Scotland for any form of further or higher education.

college of education Teacher training colleges were renamed colleges of education following the recommendation of the *Robbins Report in 1963. Many of these later closed or merged with *polytechnics or *colleges of further education when teacher training places were greatly reduced in the 1970s. Those which remained often did so in partnership with a university which validated their awards, or became autonomous **colleges of higher education.**

college of further education A *tertiary institution offering a wide curriculum which provides *vocational education and training from *entry level up to *foundation degree level across a broad range of areas, and can also include *basic skills programmes, *General Certificate of Education *Advanced Level programmes, teacher training for the sector, and *adult and community education. Many were originally known as **technical colleges.** The *Further and Higher Education Act 1992 removed colleges from local authority control and funding and established them as independent corporate bodies which received funding through the *Further Education Funding Council, a function currently served by the *Learning and Skills Council. The removal of colleges from local authority control and the granting of their right to manage their own budgets became known as incorporation. Colleges' role as centres of skills training was defined in the *Foster Report of 2005. Since 2007 teachers in the sector are required to have *qualified teacher learning and skills status. *See also* COLLEGE SELF-ASSESSMENT; FURTHER EDUCATION; PARITY OF ESTEEM. V.C., K.A.

college of higher education *See* COLLEGE OF EDUCATION.

college self-assessment The process of evaluating the effectiveness of their own provision by all further education *colleges and providers of adult training and education in the UK, in particular to inform the judgements of *Ofsted and the *Adult Learning Inspectorate (ALI). It is based on the principle that providers are accountable for monitoring the standard of what they offer, and for improvements to it, which was set out in the 1999 White Paper *Learning to Succeed*.

Self-assessment began as a preparation for inspection by Ofsted or ALI, though managers reported that they recognized the benefits of the process and its outcomes, both as a means of assessing their progress towards meeting the goals of their *strategic plans, and because the information gathered could be used as evidence for a number of quality assurance purposes. The process is continuous, and results annually in the production of *self-assessment reports.

The self-assessment process is intrinsically linked with the roles of those who plan and fund *post-compulsory education, the Inspectorate, and the *Quality Improvement Agency (QIA). The summary report, together with the quality improvement plan that derives from it, was central to the Annual Planning Review held between a provider and its local *Learning and Skills Council, and to the drawing up of three-year development plans. Since May 2005 representatives of the Inspectorate have undertaken annual assessment visits to providers, during which they measure what is reported against evidence of changes in performance; from this, they draw conclusions about the institution's capacity to offer a high-quality service. One of the key purposes of the QIA is to support providers in responding to students' and industry's needs, including working where provision has been assessed as inadequate by the Inspectorate.

SEE WEB LINKS

- Provides a link to *Quality Improvement and Self-Assessment* (2005), which sets out guidance for learning providers.

V.C., K.A.

collegiate university A *university in which the separate colleges, while subject to university regulations, have a high degree of autonomy in relation to management of their funds and property and their admissions procedures. Oxford, Cambridge, and Durham are collegiate universities.

Common Assessment Framework (CAF) A generic assessment tool available to all practitioners in statutory agencies and voluntary organizations across England working with children and young people. Its use is aimed at children and young people, including unborn babies, who have been identified as having additional needs for which either short- or long-term support is required. The intention is that assessments are carried out early and effectively, with involved professionals fully aware of all issues affecting the child or young person, planning and working together to address these additional needs. When a CAF is in existence, a lead professional will be allocated to coordinate the team around the child or young person, and act as the single point of contact for parents or carers. The CAF has a standard form (although some local areas may have modified this) considering three areas: the development of the child, parents and carers, and family environment. It replaces some existing assessments but sits alongside specialist assessments such as statutory assessment for *special educational needs and universal health checks.

T.B., L.E.

Common Entrance Examination An examination for pupils applying to enter an *independent school between the ages of 11 and 13. Not all independent schools apply this as an entry condition, some preferring to set their own entry *examinations. It is not a public examination, although pupils from state schools can apply to sit it. It is usually conducted in the candidate's own school. *See also* PREPARATORY SCHOOL.

Common European Framework of Reference for Languages (CEFRL) A set of descriptors relating to levels of language ability, which apply to any language and can be used as stage markers in language acquisition and use. Disseminated widely from 2001 and translated into about 30 languages, the CEFRL is an established and worldwide means of providing *benchmarks in language ability, and is used to underpin the teaching and certification of language skills in most countries of the European community. It provides a framework consisting of learning objectives at six progressive levels, A1, A2, B1, B2, C1, and C2, together with associated competence descriptors in speaking, reading, writing, listening, and interacting. The descriptors are generic in that they can be applied to any language. In order to address language-specific learning issues, however, specifications are under development to provide CEFRL frameworks for each European language, both national and regional. These are known as **reference-level descriptors (RLDs)**. The project for the development of RLDs for English language learning is known as English Profile, and is led by bodies including Cambridge University's Research Centre for English and Applied Linguistics, and the *British Council. *See also* ENGLISH FOR SPEAKERS OF OTHER LANGUAGES.

SEE WEB LINKS

- Provides details on the development of RLDs for English.

community college This may take a number of forms, but is often the name taken by a large secondary school which opens up some of its provision and resources to adults in the local community both during the day and in the evening.

community education A concept and practice often linked to *adult education, and involving the provision of courses and educational events outside the *school or *college premises in public or private buildings within the community. This type of provision is also referred to as 'outreach', since it reaches out to the community rather than requiring people to travel to the institution. *See also* WIDENING ACCESS; WIDENING PARTICIPATION.

community school *See* COMMUNITY COLLEGE.

compensation The process whereby a candidate's poor performance in one aspect of an *examination or other *assessment procedure may be made up for by their high level of performance in one or more aspects. This is sometimes applied, within university regulations, in the classification of degrees.

C

competence The ability to perform to a specified standard. The introduction of competence-based vocational qualifications, which was signalled in the 1981 *White Paper *A New Training Initiative*, brought with it a number of changes in the way training and assessment were understood and applied. Where previously gaining a qualification might have been based on time served, or courses attended and examinations passed, it was now based firmly on what the candidate could do; and so the emphasis moved from teaching skills to assessing them. Thus, a candidate for a vocational qualification might be assessed at the point of enrolment, found to be already competent, and awarded their qualification. The introduction in 1986 of *National Vocational Qualifications (NVQs) and the national framework of vocational qualifications established competence-based assessment as the dominant model in vocational education and training. This gave rise to a number of debates, which can be summarized as follows: How does the competent/not competent model of assessment allow for a differentiation to be made between the candidate who is barely competent and the candidate who is very competent indeed? What part do experience and theoretical understanding play, if any, in the competence model? How many times should the candidate be required to demonstrate competence before the assessor can be sure that an assessment of 'competent' is reliable?

An occupational, competence-based qualification is made up of units, each of which contain a number of statements of competence, each with performance criteria defined in terms of standard and range. They describe the skills and knowledge that a candidate must be able to demonstrate in order to be judged competent. The teaching profession has resisted the introduction of competence-based teacher training programmes, arguing that many of the areas of skills, knowledge, and understanding necessary in an effective teacher cannot be described in terms of observable behaviours and require a developmental rather than *instrumental model of learning and assessment. However, the professional standards for teachers in the *lifelong learning sector introduced by *Lifelong Learning UK in 2007 bear a close resemblance to a competence model.

comprehensive school A non-selective model of secondary school which began to replace the former system of secondary moderns and selective *grammar schools in the 1970s. The *Education Act 1976 required *local authorities to make all secondary provision comprehensive; but this was repealed by the Education Act 1979, leaving pockets of selective secondary education in some local authority areas in England. The term 'comprehensive' was used originally to indicate that such schools would provide a secondary education for all pupils in their area.

In Scotland the majority of state schools are comprehensive and are referred to as **high schools** or *academies. Selective education is provided through the independent schools system. In Wales, too, almost all schools were comprehensive by the end of the 1980s. In Northern Ireland, however, selection lingered longer and became the focus of the Burns Report.

computer-assisted learning (CAL) A mode of teaching and learning in which learning material is presented via a computer, and the learner is able to interact with them. *See also* E-LEARNING; INFORMATION COMMUNICATION TECHNOLOGY.

conditional offer An offer of a place made to an applicant by a *university which is conditional on their achieving specified grades, for example in the *General Certificate of Education *Advanced Levels.

Connexions An English service conceived in 2001 to provide universal advice to all 13–19-year-olds and to young people up to the age of 25 with learning difficulties or disabilities; and to support the development of those considered at risk. Every young person has a named Connexions personal adviser, who is able to provide information, advice, and practical help. There are some 47 Connexions partnerships throughout the country. The partnerships enable schools and colleges to work collaboratively with youth welfare services, counselling provision, and careers advisers to offer appropriate advice and support.

SEE WEB LINKS

- Provides links to the specific services and guidance the organization offers.

V.C., K.A.

constructivist A view of education which challenges the belief that learning is something which can be delivered by means of a teacher transmitting facts or knowledge to a class of passive recipient learners; but rather that knowledge, meaning, and understanding are actively constructed by learners by a process of development, which builds on what they already know, causing them to change and adapt and invent ideas. In practical terms, in a classroom where teaching is informed by constructivist theory, the teacher's role is not to *deliver facts, but to provide learners with the stimulus and experience which then allows them to pose their own questions, hypothesize, explore, predict, and investigate knowledge for themselves. The **cognitive constructivist** view is that meaningful learning requires an active construction of meaning, in which we make sense of new information by testing it against, and assimilating it into, what we already know, often thereby achieving a higher level of thinking and understanding. Notable proponents of this view are *Dewey, sometimes referred to as the originator of this approach, *Bruner, and *Piaget. **Social constructivists**, notably *Vygotsky, argue that key elements for successful learning are participation in social interaction, and the processes of thought facilitated through language and dialogue; and that the construction of learning is influenced by the historico-social context in which the learner lives. There are a number of schools of constructivist thought, but all share an emphasis upon the active role of the learner in constructing his or her own reality.

continuing education Education which continues throughout life, both through formal institutions and by other means, as a continuous process of personal development. It is often linked with *adult education in the phrase 'adult and continuing education'. *See also* LIFELONG LEARNING.

continuing professional development (CPD) The continuation of a teacher's professional development beyond their initial training, qualification, and *induction. This may take many forms, including attendance on short courses for updating skills or knowledge; longer programmes of study such as *diplomas and postgraduate degrees in education; staff development events held within the teacher's own institution; conferences; *mentoring; and peer assessment. CPD is now a requirement of teachers in schools who wish to apply for promotion; and a requirement for all those teaching in *further education colleges. Many universities offer CPD courses and qualifications for teachers.

continuous assessment *Assessment of student's work which takes place throughout the duration of their course, usually through *assignments or other *coursework. It involves no terminal *examination, and is sometimes accused of lack of rigour for this reason. However, continuous assessment may also involve some element of external *testing and externally marked assessment, as was the case with *General National Vocational Qualifications in the later stages of their development. Continuous assessment may be *formative, as well as providing a *summative assessment of the student's *attainment.

controlled schools A specific kind of school in Northern Ireland, owned and funded by the *Education and Library Boards. Boards of governors are now taking more control. These are mainly Protestant schools and the Church is represented on the board of governors. J.H.

core skills *See* KEY SKILLS.

core subject A subject which is central to the *curriculum and must be studied by everyone. In the *national curriculum, three of the *foundation subjects are core subjects: English, mathematics, and science; Welsh also is a core subject in Welsh-speaking schools. In contexts other than the national curriculum, too, core subjects, as opposed to optional subjects, are usually those which are mandatory.

corporal punishment Abolished under the *Education (No. 2) Act 1986. Teachers may still use reasonable force to restrain a pupil in order to prevent injury or damage to others or to property, but may not use force as a form of punishment. *See also* BEHAVIOUR.

correspondence course A *programme of study undertaken through written correspondence, where the learner and tutor communicate solely through means of the postal service. This type of *distance learning, typified by the early days of the *National Extension College, has been largely overtaken by technology and *e-learning, although *Open University programmes and others still retain some features of this type of provision. Correspondence courses are still to be seen advertised commercially by private individuals or companies offering specialized skills, such as writing for children or memory enhancement.

Council for Catholic Maintained Schools (CCMS) The Council for Catholic Maintained Schools promotes and directs Catholic education in Northern Ireland. It is funded by the *Department of Education, Northern Ireland. It is responsible for the employment of teachers in *Catholic maintained schools and acts in an advisory capacity. J.H.

Council for Irish-Medium Education (Comhairle na Gaelscolaíochta) This body was set up in 2000 by the *Department of Education, Northern Ireland, to promote and develop Irish-medium education and schools in the province.

SEE WEB LINKS

- Explains the aims and function of the Council.

J.H.

course a discrete *programme of study which follows a predetermined *syllabus or specification, and may lead to a qualification or some other form of certification. Courses of study vary in duration, short courses lasting only days, while a degree course may take three or four years to complete. From a usage point of view there is a lack of clarity about the distinction between 'course' and 'programme', some institutions using the two interchangeably, while others use the term 'course' to refer to a subdivision of a lengthier programme of study, such as that leading to a degree.

coursework Assessed work which is completed by the student during the process of their course of study. It is usually the case that the *assessment outcomes for their coursework will count towards the student's final mark or grade. If the course involves no terminal *examination or end test, the coursework alone will form the basis of the final assessment outcome. This model is known as *continuous assessment, and is often employed for the assessment of *modular *programmes of study. Where an end examination or test is also used, the student's performance in their assessed coursework will constitute a fixed proportion of their final and overall mark or grade. Coursework may be set at regular intervals during the course of study, often, although not always, in the form of written *assignments; or it may take the form of an ongoing project on which the student works for part or all of the duration of their course. It may be *internally assessed by the student's own teachers or institution, or externally assessed by an *awarding body; or the process may involve a combination of both of these, with specified pieces of coursework, or a representative sample of all coursework, being scrutinized by the awarding body, while the remainder is assessed internally. This latter is the type of model which operates, for example, in the assessment of *General Certificate of Secondary Education (GCSE) coursework. As well as providing a means of *summative assessment by contributing to the student's final and overall mark or grade, coursework has the advantage of providing the student with *formative assessment, since it is a means of giving feedback on their current level of attainment and of identifying areas of weakness which need to be addressed. Detractors of coursework-based assessment, on the other hand, accuse it of lack of rigour and of being open to *plagiarism and other forms of inequity which render it unreliable in comparison to invigilated and time-constrained examinations. Nevertheless, it constitutes part of the assessment process in key qualifications throughout secondary and tertiary education, from GCSEs, *Advanced Levels, and *diplomas, to *master's degrees.

crammer The colloquial term for a private college which prepares students aged 16+ for public *examinations and other entry qualifications though short courses, often in school holidays. Such colleges are so called because of the relative shortness and intensive nature of the courses they provide.

creativity An area of proficiency not currently measured in schools by existing methods of testing or measures of progress, but which might manifest itself in abilities and skills such as self-confidence, risk-taking, resilience, teamwork, questioning, and challenging. These are sometimes referred to as **soft skills**, which some employers are eager to see acknowledged as part of pupil assessment, and which the *Department for Children, Schools, and Families is investigating as a possible area of development in terms of testing and standards. Finding a way to measure these aspects of creativity without extinguishing them, however, clearly presents more substantial problems than the testing of academic ability and understanding.

credit 1. Recognition of achievement. In *further and *higher education, a student may accumulate credit, for example in the form of a number of *modules successfully completed, each of which carry a number of credit 'points'. The accumulated credits may be used to gain a recognized qualification, such as a certificate, diploma, or degree. This is sometimes colloquially termed as 'cashing in credits'. A candidate may also transfer credits from one institution to another, adding those gained in one institution to those gained in the next. This is known as 'credit transfer'. **Credit accumulation and transfer (CAT)** is the term used for both parts of this process. S.W.

2. A *grade awarded for successful achievement in an *examination or other *assessment, indicating attainment beyond the minimum level of a pass. It is the highest level of *Standard Grade qualification in the exam taken by students aged 15 or 16 in Scotland. The three levels are Credit, General, and Foundation. Students will usually sit two levels at the same time; hence Credit students will also sit General papers and those taking General level will sit Foundation papers.

SEE WEB LINKS

- The Teaching and Learning Scotland site gives a clear overview of the levels awarded at Standard Grade.

S.M.

Credit and Qualifications Framework for Wales (CQFW) A structure developed from a joint project initiated in 2001 by the *Higher Education Funding Council for Wales and the Further Education Funding Council for Wales (since merged with the Assembly Department of Education) to cover all post-16 learning. From 2005 all accredited learning, including mainstream qualifications offered in Wales, has gradually been brought into a single unifying structure, the CQFW. The Framework merges the concepts of volume of learning achievements (credit) and the demands made by the learning on the learner (level) to create a system that is able to embrace all types and styles of learning. Major objectives are to assist in removing barriers to progression, to allow the accumulation of credits to meet the needs of individuals, and to offer parity in the recognition of achievement for learners of all ages, whether they are learning in the workplace, in the community, or at school, college, or university. *See also* WALES, EDUCATION IN. H.G.

criterion-referenced Describes methods of *assessment which assess the candidate against a fixed set of criteria, rather than by comparison with the performance of others (*norm-referenced) or by comparison with their own earlier performance (*ipsative). (*Competence-based assessment is an example of the straightforward use of criterion-referencing.

cross-curricular If a topic, activity, skill, responsibility, or initiative is applied not just to one subject but across the *curriculum as a whole, it is described as 'cross-curricular'. For example, in schools, *literacy is a cross-curricular issue, relevant to, and embedded in, every subject. A *literacy coordinator, therefore, has a cross-curricular responsibility.

cultural studies An area of study and research which emerged across Europe and America during the 1960s. The Frankfurt Institute for Social Research, founded in the 1920s, became highly influential in the development of the subject. In Britain cultural studies first emerged as a discipline within education at the Centre for Contemporary Cultural Studies (CCCS) at the University of Birmingham in 1964. Richard Hoggart (b. 1918) was the first director. Other notable directors and academics associated with the centre include Raymond Williams (1921–88), E. P. Thompson (1924–93), Stuart Hall (b. 1932), and Dick Hebdige (b. 1951).

In the early years of the CCCS, the modus operandi of these theorists was to acknowledge the growing significance of popular culture and the media in people's lives. Initially, figures like Hoggart, Williams, and Thompson espoused what was to become known later as culturalism, which, as much as anything, was a changing attitude to what was deemed worthy of study. In 1948 F. R. Leavis had written *The Great Tradition*, outlining a series of classic texts which would form the canon of literary texts that encapsulated what was valuable in British culture. By the 1960s Hoggart et al. began to use the same analytical tools of English literature, but, instead of the classics, applied them to the study of ordinary, everyday people. From this moment on, just as much cultural significance could be attributed to a pop song by Petula Clarke as to a poem by W. H. Auden.

Although the earlier members of the CCCS, especially Hoggart, largely viewed the mass media as something which polluted ordinary working-class culture, later theorists such as Hall, Hebdige, and McRobbie, having been influenced by the lessons of the Frankfurt School, structuralism, and Marxism, began to see popular culture as an area of conflict and resistance. The media, and culture in general, could be viewed as a site for the unequal distribution of power of producers and consumers, but also where subcultures like punk could emerge and form identities from the detritus of consumer culture.

Although cultural studies remains a successful area of study and research in global higher education, after nearly 30 years of research, study, and left-wing radicalism, the CCCS was shut down in 2002. C.H.

currency 1. A qualification, or credits towards a qualification, are said to have currency if they are generally recognized and accepted.

2. In *assessment, and particularly the assessment of skills, the currency of a candidate's achievement or level of competence is an important factor. For example, they may possess experience or a qualification in *information technology which they gained many years before, and which does not therefore attest to their ability to work with current systems.

curriculum The content and specifications of a *course or *programme of study (as in 'the history curriculum'); or, in a wider sense, the totality of the specified learning opportunities available in one educational institution (as in 'the school curriculum'); or, in its very widest sense, the programme of learning applying to all pupils in the nation (as in 'the national curriculum'). It has been observed, with some irony, that the word is the Latin term for a track around which competitors race for the entertainment of others. This metaphor is an interesting one in that it suggests a Darwinian view of formal education as a competition in which there are winners and losers. This is a construct at odds with the thinking of educators such as *Freire and *Rogers.

curriculum, common A *curriculum which applies to all learners in a school, or to all learners in all schools in a region or country. Commonality lies in the fact that all learners will have the same learning experiences and have covered the same topics in common. The *national curriculum is an example of a common curriculum in that it applies in all *maintained schools and ensures that pupils share a common experience of learning and assessment at each stage of their education.

curriculum, compulsory A *curriculum which every learner is required to follow. A curriculum may be compulsory within an institution, or may be a statutory requirement for all pupils. The *national curriculum is an example of a compulsory curriculum since it must be applied in all appropriate *maintained schools.

curriculum, core The parts of a *curriculum which are compulsory and common to all. The term is generally used when other parts of the curriculum are optional, so as to identify the central, or 'core', curriculum content which must apply to every learner.

curriculum, entitlement A term used to describe a *curriculum of worthwhile knowledge, understanding, and experience to which every pupil should be entitled. It was coined by *Her Majesty's Inspectorate of Schools in the 1980s and was predicated on a model of education which was *liberal rather than *instrumental.

curriculum, hidden Learners may, in the course of their exposure to the formal curriculum, also learn or acquire knowledge, skills, or attitudes which were not part of the formal intended learning outcomes. This incidental or accidental learning is referred to as the hidden curriculum, since its processes are not apparent and its outcomes are unplanned. It may be positive, as in the case of pupils acquiring the social skills modelled by their teacher; or it may be negative, as when they 'learn' that arriving late can effectively delay the start of the lesson. The term is also used by some to describe the extracurricular activities provided by the school.

curriculum, national *See* NATIONAL CURRICULUM.

curriculum, negotiated Used to refer to the content, coverage, and outcomes of a course of study which has been agreed through consultation between the teacher or institution and the learners themselves. Curriculum content specified by legislation (for example, the *national curriculum) or by an *awarding body is not open to negotiation in this way. However, within those formal restrictions, there may be some narrow scope for negotiation in terms of choice when, for example, selecting a text to be studied from a list of options. This, however, does not, strictly speaking, constitute a negotiated curriculum, since the term implies a wider degree of learner choice over what is to be covered and achieved. Thus, a negotiated curriculum is usually associated with *learner-centred education, where the curriculum is constructed around the expressed needs and interests of the learners themselves.

curriculum, spiral A curriculum whose structure allows for topics or skills to be revisited and repeated, each time in more detail or depth as the learner gains in knowledge, skills, and confidence. This curriculum model is consistent with an *ipsative approach to learning.

curriculum development The review of a whole *curriculum or of specific subjects or *cross-curricular themes for the purpose of revising or improving, or even replacing, it. In its widest sense, curriculum development encompasses all those professional activities which teachers, researchers, and other educationalists undertake in order to improve and support the curriculum, from the development of innovative teaching materials or methods, to the formulation of new learning outcomes or syllabuses.

Curriculum for Excellence* (*CfE*)** Published in November 2004, this document sets out the values, purposes, and principles for education in *Scotland for pupils aged 3–18. It describes the characteristics which education should aspire to encourage, suggesting that schools should produce successful learners who are also confident individuals, effective contributors to society, and responsible citizens. The *Curriculum for Excellence* was drawn up as the result of a review of the Scottish education system begun in 2003, following the 2002 report ***Educating for Excellence, which cited the need for a review of the *curriculum and the need to create a single, coherent curriculum for age 3–18 'with space for children to achieve and teachers to teach'. It also sets out a timetable for engaging with the teaching profession and reviewing the curriculum.

SEE WEB LINKS

- Details of the CfE process, progress, and objectives.

S.M.

Curriculum Online Set up in 2002 to enhance *online education, both in schools and for individual pupils, by improving access to *multimedia resources, which are accessed online through its web site. Schools buy into the resources using funding provided by the *Department for Children, Schools, and Families in form of electronic learning credits. In addition, some resources are provided free.

SEE WEB LINKS

- Provides details of resources.

curriculum planning Creating, designing, and organizing a curriculum, either for one institution or on a national level, for example in the case of the curriculum for a nationally available qualification.

C

Curriculum 2000 (C2K) A broadening of the post-16 curriculum based partly on the recommendations in the 1996 **Dearing Review of Qualifications for 16–19 Year Olds*. Implemented in 2000, it revised the traditional structure of *General Certificate of Education (GCE) *Advanced Level provision, by introducing the requirement for students to choose four or five subjects at *Advanced Subsidiary Level in their first year of studies, preferably spanning a range of arts and science subjects; and only in their second year to narrow their focus, dropping some of their AS subjects and continuing with the rest at A2 level. Curriculum 2000 also introduced *key skills across the post-16 curriculum, for those studying GCEs as well as those on *vocationally related courses. During the pilot year 2000/01 difficulties were reported by both students and teachers over the volume of *assessment. Assessment procedures were subsequently reviewed and simplified, and the inclusion of key skills made optional.

day nursery A facility providing care and education for children aged 0–5, either full-time or part-time. They are usually open from 8 a.m. to 7 p.m., all year round. The day nursery has to be registered with *Ofsted and is inspected every year. At least half the staff must be qualified to level 3 on the *National Qualifications Framework and there must be a qualified teacher either in the nursery, or supported by *local authority peripatetic *early years teachers who work within a family of settings. Day nurseries vary in size, but most take 25–40 children who are grouped together according to age; children aged 0–5 in England follow the *Early Years Foundation Stage curriculum. There are different types of day nursery including those with private, community, voluntary, work-based, and local authority status. Some day nurseries take children up to age 8 as part of 'wraparound care' for school age children. For children under 2, there is a staff ratio of one adult to three children; for those aged 2–3, one adult to four children; and for 3–5-year-olds, one adult to eight children. Most day nurseries operate a key worker system, which supports a child's attachment to a significant adult.

SEE WEB LINKS

- Provides information on the range of childcare provision.
- Gives information for parents about early learning and development, and the range of day care services.

A.W.

day release Used widely in the past in the *further education sector to describe the arrangement whereby trainees in employment attend a *college or similar training organization for one day a week to develop their *vocational skills and gain an appropriate qualification. The employer releases them from work for that day, on the condition that they attend such training, and, in addition, the employer normally pays their fees. The term is now less frequently used, having been replaced by the expression **off-the-job** training. This change of terminology followed the introduction of *National Vocational Qualifications (NVQs), which provided greater opportunities for what was referred to as **on-the-job** training and assessment. Prior to the introduction of NVQs, the curriculum for day release students often included a lesson of *liberal studies as well as training in the vocational knowledge and skills relevant to their employment.

dean A title which has two distinct meanings in *higher education. It may be used to confer status on a head of department or *faculty, in which case the full title will indicate this, as in 'dean of faculty'; or it may indicate a senior member of a *university who is responsible for matters of student discipline.

Dearing Report on Higher Education (1997) Entitled *Higher Education in the Learning Society: The National Committee of Inquiry into Higher Education*, the Report followed a comprehensive review of *higher education and presented 93 recommendations. These included the introduction of student contributions towards their tuition *fees of up to 25 per cent; the introduction of a new national framework of higher education qualifications, to be monitored by the *Quality Assurance Agency for Higher Education; and the setting up of an *Institute for Learning and Teaching in higher education to accredit the professional development of teachers and lecturers in the sector. It also suggested, as one of the nine underlying principles on which the Report was based, that learning should be responsive to the needs of employment and should develop those skills which are valued in the world of work. In this sense the 1997 Dearing Report contributed heavily to the debate about the purposes of higher education. *See also* VOCATIONAL.

Dearing Review of Qualifications for 16–19-Year-Olds (1996) The government brief for this Review was that Sir Ron Dearing and his team should advise on how the existing system of post-16 qualifications might be revised in order to encourage greater *parity of esteem between *General Certificate of Education (GCE) *Advanced Level (A level) and parallel *vocational and pre-vocational routes. The brief included a government admonishment that A levels should not be discarded or undermined. The Secretary of State for Education, Gillian Shephard, writing to Dearing on 10 April 1995, instructed him that 'Our key priorities remain to ensure that the rigour and standards of GCE A levels are maintained.' This proviso made any radical overhaul, such as the introduction of a *baccalaureate system, out of the question. The Committee was also tasked with suggesting ways to build on development in *National Vocational Qualifications (NVQs) and *General National Vocational Qualifications (GNVQs); to increase participation and achievement; to prepare young people better for work and for higher education; and to ensure value for money. Dearing himself described the purpose of the Review as being one of breaking down barriers between academic and vocational courses and thereby promoting parity of esteem between the two.

Describing the scale of the task, Dearing pointed out on page 1 of the Review's published report that, 'In spite of action taken by the government to bring clarity into the structure of vocational qualifications, the world of education and training between the ages of 16 and 19 remains intelligible only to specialists.' The proposals which emerged from the Review included the following:

- a common framework across NVQ, GNVQ, *General Certificate of Secondary Education (GCSE), and A level, comprising four levels: entry, foundation, intermediate, and advanced;
- the renaming of Advanced GNVQs as 'Applied A levels';
- a National Advanced Certificate which would comprise two A levels, or an Advanced GNVQ, or a level 3 NVQ;
- a National Advanced Diploma, comprising the same qualifications as the Certificate, but awarded to pupils who have also covered four general areas of study, such as science, languages, arts, and 'community' studies, such as business or psychology;

- able pupils to be offered units of degree courses while still at school;
- *key skills to be offered across the framework;
- *awarding bodies to make joint arrangements for awards of GCSE, A level, and GNVQ;
- a marrying of the roles of the *Schools Curriculum and Assessment Authority (SCAA) and the *National Council for Vocational Qualifications (NCVQ).

It is clear that many of these proposals were aimed at encouraging a broadening of the curriculum and parity between the different routes through the post-16 education system. Many of the Review's recommendations, including the new Diploma and Certificate, and the renaming of GNVQs, were not implemented. The reorganization of the awarding bodies and the merger of the NCVQ and SCAA did go ahead, however, as did the introduction of key skills across the curriculum. Critics of the report from the academic community argued that Dearing's proposals did not go far enough, while the press criticized the same proposals for their possibly detrimental effect on the status of A levels, claiming that they were too radical.

SEE WEB LINKS

- A critical evaluation of the Dearing Review (subscription).

deficit model A perspective which attributes failures such as lack of achievement, learning, or success in gaining employment to a personal lack of effort or deficiency in the individual, rather than to failures or limitations of the education and training system or to prevalent socio-economic trends. For example, the argument for the introduction of youth and adult training schemes in the 1981 *White Paper **A New Training Initiative* included the suggestion that because people lacked skills there were no jobs for them, and that therefore this deficit must be addressed by appropriate training. The implication here was that unemployment arose from a deficiency in the unemployed themselves, rather than from economic trends. The deficit model of teaching, in which the teacher provides the learning to make good a deficit, stands in direct contrast to the belief that the teacher's role is to draw out learners' *tacit knowledge and understanding through questioning and facilitation.

The deficit model perspective is also apparent in the view expressed in some discourses about learner *attainment and *behaviour which suggest that it is a deficit of some kind in the teacher's performance which leads to such problems, and that learner attainment and behaviour can therefore be improved simply by changing the teacher's behaviour or by enhancing their skills through professional development. An application of the deficit model, as can be seen from these examples, is often indicative of an oversimplified view of the issue in question.

degree A qualification awarded by a *university or other institution of *higher education to candidates who have successfully completed a course of studies. Degrees are awarded at foundation level (*foundation degree), undergraduate level (*bachelor's degree), postgraduate level (*master's degree), and *doctorate level. In Scotland most undergraduate university students embark on a four-year degree, at the end of which they will achieve a master's degree of

MA or M.Sc. Students also have the option to complete their studies at the end of the third year, however; in which case successful candidates will receive a bachelor's degree (BA or B.Sc.) or may be awarded an ordinary or general degree.

degree classification *See* BACHELOR'S DEGREE.

deliver Commonly and increasingly used as an alternative to 'teach' to describe what *teachers do. It is not, however, quite synonymous with 'teach' since its metaphorical roots suggest a process in which something—in this case learning—is simply handed over intact from teacher to student. To 'teach', on the other hand, usually implies a more complex activity, which may involve strategies such as *Socratic questioning, group facilitation, the *motivating and management of learners, *assessment, *evaluation, and so on. The metaphor of 'delivery' also suggests that the lesson itself originates from a source outside the teacher, who simply presents it to the learners; whereas in most cases teaching also involves the teacher in the preparatory planning and *research, as well as in interaction and dialogue with learners. 'Deliver' is also used in the sense of to 'deliver' a lecture, which implies the presentation to an audience of a pre-prepared text, slides, or other material, and again suggests a process of one-way communication from lecturer to learners.

demand-led The provision of education or training courses on the basis of what is currently most in demand, either locally or nationally. In the *lifelong learning sector, where this term is most commonly found, *further education colleges and other providers must respond to the training demands of local employers and businesses, since their funding from the *Learning and Skills Council is dependent on their ability to do this. The curriculum of universities and other institutions of *higher education may also be demand-led, in the sense that courses which show a consistent pattern of under-recruitment may be discontinued and new courses created in response to perceived *market trends. The concept of demand-related funding in this context is closely bound up with the market model of education and training.

Demos A think-tank founded in 1992 whose recommendations sometimes include those on matters relating to education, and particularly in the curriculum area of *citizenship. Its political philosophy is situated to the left of centre.

denomination Most English, Welsh, and Scottish schools tend to be non-denominational, and thus religious observance and study are not a compulsory part of the curriculum. In Scotland those which are denominational tend to be Roman Catholic. These denominational schools follow the same curriculum as non-denominational schools and must accept students who do not follow the religion of the school. *See also* RELIGIOUS EDUCATION; SCOTLAND, EDUCATION IN.

S.M.

Department for Children, Schools, and Families Created in June 2007, and responsible for education in schools and the work of children's services. It succeeded the *Department for Education and Skills, but took over only part of its remit, the responsibility for *higher education and skills training going to another newly created department, the *Department for Innovation, Universities, and Skills. The linking of responsibilities for matters relating to children's health and child poverty to those for education in schools signalled a more coordinated approach to social provision for children in line with the aims expressed in the document **Every Child Matters*.

Department for Education, Culture, and the Welsh Language The Department of the Welsh Assembly which is now responsible for policy and funding for all areas of education, training, and *lifelong learning with the exception of *higher education, which remains with the *Higher Education Funding Council for Wales. The Department operates through five groups: Children and Schools; Qualifications and Curriculum; Lifelong Learning and Skills; Higher Learning; and Culture, Welsh Language, and Sport. From April 2006 an expanded Department has included the work of the Further Education Funding Council for Wales and the responsibilities previously held by the Qualifications, Curriculum, and Assessment Authority for Wales. H.G.

Department for Education and Skills (DfES) The department of state responsible for education and training between 2001 (before which it was known as the Department for Education and Employment) and 2007, when it was replaced as a result of the reorganization of governmental departments. Two new departments took over its remit: the *Department for Children, Schools, and Families and the *Department for Innovation, Universities, and Skills. The title of the DfES was significant in that it brought together general education and skills training under one remit.

Department for Innovation, Universities, and Skills (DIUS) Created in June 2007, and responsible for *higher education, *further education and skills training, and science. It succeeded the *Department for Education and Skills, but took over only part of its remit, the responsibility for education in the schools sector going to another newly created department, the *Department for Children, Schools, and Families. The creation of a department for matters relating to *post-compulsory education and training separate from that concerned with compulsory schooling reflects policy targets to establish *parity of esteem between academic and skills routes, since it signals a differentiation by sector, rather than by whether the provision is general or vocational.

Department of Education, Northern Ireland (DENI) The DENI manages and directs the central administration of education in Northern Ireland. It is responsible for the strategic planning and management of education, the content and delivery of the curriculum, the allocation of funding to the Education and *Library Boards, and the capital costs for most schools. The DENI is headed by the Minister for Education, whose principal adviser is the Permanent Secretary. Two Deputy Secretaries and the Chief Inspector of the Education and Training Inspectorate support the Permanent Secretary. J.H.

Department of Education's Education and Training Inspectorate (DEETI) This body carries out school inspections in Northern Ireland, reporting to the *Department of Education, Northern Ireland. It is responsible for monitoring standards of learning and teaching. J.H.

deputy head A senior member of school staff whose role is normally to act as second in command to the *head teacher, and to stand in for them in their absence. The precise duties and detail of the post will differ from school to school, but will often involve liaison between the head teacher and the teaching staff as well as acting as a member of the senior management team of the school. In larger schools there may be two or more deputy heads, each with a specific whole-school responsibility, such as *curriculum management or pupil *achievement and *behaviour. Increasingly, deputy head posts are being replaced by that of *assistant head, usually at a lower salary.

Derrida, Jacques (1930–2004) Jacques Derrida was a highly influential Algerian-born French philosopher who came to prominence in the late 1960s and early 1970s with the publication of *Of Grammatology* (1967), *Writing and Difference* (1967), and *Margins of Philosophy* (1972). He came to be one of the most controversial thinkers of the 20th century owing to his wide-ranging theories regarding the instability of language and the consequent impossibility of truth claims. Responding to structuralist thought, which had been based on the differential *semiotic theory of Ferdinand de Saussure, Derrida introduced a neologism, *différance*, which brought together 'difference' and 'deferral'. Meaning, according to Derrida, is constantly deferred as ever-changing discursive contexts unravel a never-ending chain of signifiers.

The term that he is widely associated with is 'deconstruction'. Derrida was always keen to stress that deconstruction was not something that was used as a method to 'take apart' that which is studied; for him deconstruction is something that already happens within texts. For Derrida, institutions such as *schools, *colleges, and *universities were contexts where various and competing discourses could be observed, and it was in the space where these discourses clashed that one could observe dissonances that questioned the naturalness of the underlying presuppositions that informed educational policy and practice. For instance, it could be argued that the importance of increasingly commercial value placed on education could be at odds with the search for 'truth' in the various disciplines.

Latterly, Derrida discussed the future role of the humanities in *The Future of the Profession, or, The University Without Condition* (2003). Here, Derrida likened the university to a kind of supplementary body which, although increasingly a part of the commercial world, could still carry out the critical pursuit of truth. Although Derrida, in much of his work, had rejected the concept of ultimate and universal truths (something which fired animosity among his contemporaries), he did not reject, and indeed advocated, a more critically reflective search for truth; the focus on critical reflection must be continuous, as truths, according to Derrida, tend to exclude. C.H.

deschooling A term coined by Ivan Illich (1926–2002) in his book *Deschooling Society* (1971), in which he argues that schooling and education are by no means necessarily synonymous. He suggests that the function of schools is as much about social control as it is about learning; and that most of what is valuable in our learning takes place outside such institutions. He further argues that schools are not only an inefficient means of providing education in that they generate excessive bureaucracy and expense, but that they are also socially divisive.

descriptor *See* GRADE; LEVEL.

descriptor of need *Special educational needs are categorized into four main areas. These are:

- cognition and learning, which is about specific or moderate learning difficulties, severe, and profound and multiple learning difficulties;
- behavioural, emotional, and social development needs;
- communication and interaction needs, which refer to speech and language and communication needs as well as autistic spectrum disorders;
- sensory and/or physical needs, which include visual, hearing, and physical impairment and also multi-sensory impairment.

These categories are used to identify a student's main areas of need. They are set out in detail in chapter 7 of the Code of Practice for Special Educational Needs (revised), DfES/581/2001. *See also* ASPERGER'S SYNDROME; AUTISM; LEARNING DIFFICULTIES. T.B., L.E.

detention A strategy for behaviour management used by schools, which takes the form of keeping pupils 'detained' under the supervision of a teacher in a classroom at break, lunchtime, or after school. Its purpose is to impress upon pupils the negative consequences of unacceptable behaviour, in this case the forfeiting of their free time. If pupils are to be detained after school, the school is obliged to give parents or carers a day's notice of the fact. In the past, pupils were often required to undertake some punitive activity during their detention, such as the writing of 'lines', a sanction famously satirized and subverted in the opening sequence of the cartoon series *The Simpsons*. These days it is more usual for schools to use detention time constructively; for example, by taking the opportunity to provide pupils with support for completing coursework. Detention is one of the few sanctions, short of *exclusion, open to schools for the management of pupil behaviour.

Determined to Succeed (DtS) A Scottish policy designed to develop enterprise in education. DtS aims to promote young people's self-confidence, self-reliance, and ambition to achieve goals in work and in life.

SEE WEB LINKS

- An overview of the aims of DtS and the policies which have been introduced to promote it.

S.M.

Developmental Coordination Disorder (DCD) A disorder in which a child has poor motor control and core stability. The ability to carry out fine and gross motor skills with fluency and accuracy is lacking and the child appears clumsy. The condition can be greatly ameliorated by practising a skill repeatedly (skill practice). The term DCD is often closely linked and incorrectly used interchangeably with *dyspraxia, causing confusion. T.B., L.E.

Dewey, John (1859–1952) An American educational philosopher who was a major influence in *progressive education and was recognized for developing an approach based on practical experiences which he called **instrumentalism**. Focusing on intellectual and social issues in education, he believed that schools should enable problem-solving skills in students rather than providing an instructive menu of *rote learning. He believed that students should be autonomous decision makers and individuals able and prepared to make judgements, and should become citizens, although this in no way represented a denial of the rights and academic status of teachers. He encouraged teachers to develop a learning cycle: to plan, implement, and review through observation and reflection; to watch for social change; and then to support their students in active citizenship.

As Director of the University of Chicago's Laboratory School, he developed the notion of educational *ideology as an experimental science, and, through observations of the teaching–learning dynamic, wrote his most important texts: *The School in Society* (1899) and *Democracy and Education* (1916). Dewey espoused the concept of learning by doing, which was never really integrated into American public (i.e. state) schools even though his ideas were popular at the time. It is interesting to note that his philosophy underpinned the child-centred *pedagogy of the *Plowden Report (1969) and has been embraced more recently by *early years educators in the UK, New Zealand, Australia, Scandinavia, and Italy, where ideological beliefs conceive the child to be an active, competent, and social learner—one who, through social interaction and experiential education, constructs their own understanding of the world.

Dewey proposed that the role of teachers was to harness the interest shown by students and plan for an emergent curriculum to exploit their natural drive to learn. *See also* LEARNER-CENTRED. A.W.

diagnostic test A test whose purpose is to evaluate a learner's strengths and areas for development. It is not a test in the sense of a *formative or *summative *assessment of the learner's attainment, but rather a means of discovering what level of support or challenge the learner will need. A diagnostic test is often a first step in developing an *individual learning plan. It is usually carried out when the learner enters their course of study, and its results are sometimes referred to as the learner's 'entry behaviour', or starting point.

dialogic teaching Teaching, usually in primary education, through dialogue between teacher and pupils and between pupils themselves, which thereby places an emphasis on speaking and listening as well as on thinking skills, clear lines of enquiry, and pupil engagement. In operational terms this may mean teachers encouraging pupils to give extended, rather than brief, answers and to pose their own questions. It may involve allowing pupils the time to reflect upon questions and answers before responding, and calling upon named individuals for answers, rather than encouraging the classroom 'bidding' process of raised hands. However, the dialogic approach is more than the sum of these sorts of strategy. It demands that there be a balance in the pupil–teacher dialogue so that the teacher's input does not dominate; and it relies upon a positive teacher–pupil relationship, which may be reflected in a number of ways, including the utilization and arrangement of classroom space. In these ways and more, dialogic teaching recognizes and builds upon the cognitive potential of classroom talk.

The pedagogy underpinning this approach to teaching places an emphasis on five principles: reciprocity, or the sharing of ideas between teacher and pupils; cumulation, or the careful building of arguments or lines of enquiry by linking the ideas of all those contributing to the dialogue; cooperation and collectivity, with pupils working together with the teacher or in groups; supportiveness, which encourages all to feel accepted and included; and purpose, in that the dialogue is intended to achieve specific educational goals.

Evidence from pilot projects in London and Yorkshire suggests that dialogic teaching supports inclusive learning, in that it encourages quieter or less able learners to contribute with confidence. It forms part of the UK government's *Primary National Strategy and the strategy for *Key Stage 3.

Further Reading: R. J. Alexander *Education as Dialogue: Moral and Pedagogical Choices for a Runaway World* (Dialogos, 2006).

differentiation The practice of acknowledging and allowing for different levels of *attainment in a group of learners. This may be done through differentiation by activity, which involves the teacher in planning and providing different activities for learners who may be working at a higher or lower level of attainment than the majority. These are known as **differentiated activities**. It may also be applied to the assessment of learners, through differentiation by outcome, where multi-level assessment tasks are set which allow learners to respond at a level appropriate to their ability or attainment. Another means of differentiated assessment is to set different tasks or questions for different ability groups, as is the practice in the examination of some *General Certificate of Secondary Education subjects. Two terms associated with differentiation in schools are 'enrichment', which is the provision for more capable learners to study a subject or topic in more depth; and 'extension', which is the provision for accelerated progress through all or part of the curriculum. *See also* TIERING.

diploma An award conferred on successful students at the end of their course of study. These may be at any level of the qualification framework, from *postgraduate diplomas to diplomas of completion for non-academic courses. The term is also used to refer to the document itself which the candidate receives, attesting to their achievement. *See also* 14–19 DIPLOMA.

directed time Time on the learners' *timetable during which they are required to study but without input from a teacher and, usually in the case of older learners, without supervision. It is 'directed' time in that clear instructions are provided by the teacher beforehand about the specific task or tasks to be undertaken as well as the total study time required. A typical period of directed study might involve the learner in carrying out a library task, such as research; or in reading and analysing a given text or texts. It is a strategy often used in *further and *higher education where the age of the learners does not require that they be closely supervised.

director of studies Used to describe a variety of roles in schools, colleges, and universities, so that the precise definition will depend upon the institution and the context concerned. In a large school this title may denote the senior member of staff responsible for coordinating the teaching and learning. In some institutions it might be used to indicate responsibility for a particular *curriculum area and involve duties of the sort associated with a departmental head. In *higher education it is often used as a term for the principal supervisor of a doctoral research student, to distinguish them from other members of the supervisory team. The title may therefore, according to context, indicate a whole-institution responsibility, a departmental leadership role, or small-team academic leadership.

disadvantaged A learner may be disadvantaged by their social, economic, physical, or family circumstances. Where any one (or more) of these is the case, there are implications for the learner's specific educational needs, and how they can best be met. The concept of disadvantage is linked to that of deprivation, in the sense that social or economic deprivation can result in individuals or sections of society being disadvantaged educationally and therefore in terms of their life chances in general. *See also* SOCIAL CLASS; SOCIAL JUSTICE.

disapplication Used to describe instances where an exception is made to the statutory requirement to apply the *national curriculum to the education of all pupils. For example, in the case of 14-year-olds undertaking a *vocational course which replaces a part of their *national curriculum *Key Stage 4 studies, that part of the national curriculum is said to have been **disapplied**.

discipline 1. A field of academic study, such as chemistry or English, which constitutes an area of teaching and research within *higher education and in the academic community as a whole.

2. The control exerted by a teacher over the *behaviour of the learners. 'Discipline' in this sense is less frequently used now than the alternative expressions: **classroom control** and behaviour management, perhaps partly because of associations with *Foucault's usage of the term to denote social and political manipulation.

discovery learning An approach to learning in which the learner is allowed to explore and become actively engaged with concepts, objects, or the physical environment in order to develop their understanding of it. In this process, the teacher is a facilitator rather than an instructor, and it is their role to organize a rich or appropriately resourced learning environment and to encourage the learner's self-directed curiosity and problem-solving skills, rather than to demonstrate or provide 'correct' answers or procedures. Discovery learning is a *learner-centred approach, theoretically underpinned by a *humanist philosophy of education, according to which the planning and teaching of lessons should take into account the learners' needs in relation to their social, emotional, and personal development, and should take as their starting point those topics which are of direct interest and relevance to the learners. The principles of discovery learning for the education of young children were set out by *Piaget, who, while stressing the need for the teacher to adopt a non-directive and relatively non-didactic role, nevertheless emphasized the importance of peer interaction in the process of such learning as a means of encouraging the child to engage with and consider viewpoints which perhaps conflicted with their own (a process known as **socio-cognitive conflict**) in order to develop their ability to review and revise their own understanding. Piaget argued that, while children might refine and evaluate their own ideas as a result of socio-cognitive conflict with peers, they would tend to adopt uncritically and too easily the ideas of teachers and other adults where these conflicted with their own. In the latter case the result would be conventional instructional learning rather than learning constructed by the child through their own discoveries.

discrimination *See* EQUAL OPPORTUNITIES ACT 2006; SOCIAL JUSTICE.

disruptive Children and young people who have difficulty forming relationships owing to persistent antisocial *behaviours such as lying, breaking of rules, aggression, stealing, defiance of authority, and cruelty may have **disruptive behaviour disorder**. Many children will show some of these behaviours occasionally but it is the pattern of consistency which suggests a mental health disorder. 'Disruptive behaviour disorder' is an overarching label for a range of conditions including **oppositional defiant disorder** and **conduct disorder**. A coordinated approach to dealing with the disorder involving the child or young person's school, family, and other professionals is necessary, via a combination of treatments embracing therapy (see *child and adolescent mental health services), specialist parent training, and possibly medication. *See also* PUPIL REFERRAL UNIT. T.B., L.E.

dissemination Sometimes referred to as the **sharing of good practice**, dissemination is an integral part both of *curriculum development and of teachers' own professional development. Ideas and examples of good practice may be disseminated through conferences, web sites, academic papers and other publications, national bodies and committees, local authority advisory services, or in-service professional development programmes. Dissemination may take place within a school, college, or university, or between institutions on a local or national level.

dissertation A lengthy piece of academic writing based on research undertaken by the candidate and submitted by them in partial fulfilment of the requirement for an award, usually as postgraduate level, such as that of a *master's degree. It is a term sometimes used interchangeably with *thesis, although in most universities it is used to assess candidates at a level lower than that of *doctorate.

distance learning A mode of learning designed to be undertaken without frequent or regular direct face-to-face contact between student and teacher. It is also sometimes referred to as *distributed learning. It usually involves the production and distribution of learning materials by the supporting institution to the student, either in hard copy or, as is more normal today, by electronic means. Students are provided with tutorial support, which takes place by telephone, email, or other electronic means, possibly with occasional face-to-face meetings and short periods of attendance, such as a weekend or summer school. The *Open University and the *University for Industry are perhaps the best-known providers of this mode of learning in the United Kingdom, although many universities and colleges also run their own programmes. In Scotland the University of the Highlands and Islands (UHI) Millennium Institute provides access to graduate level study through a partnership of colleges and research institutions for students in the highlands and islands. *See also* E-LEARNING.

SEE WEB LINKS

- Describes the operation of the UHI and the courses it offers.

distributed learning A mode of study in which students are following the same programme of learning but do not come together as a group in the same location. It is a term which is now applied to *distance learning. The rapid growth of information communication technology to support learning and teaching has facilitated the development of distributed learning through electronic networks and web sites. *See also* ASYNCHRONOUS LEARNING.

divergent thinking A process which seeks a number of possible solutions to a question, rather than assuming, as is the case in **convergent thinking**, that there can be only one correct answer and only one way to arrive at it. Some educationalists have suggested that the ability to apply divergent thinking indicates a predisposition towards success in arts subjects rather than in sciences, since it is regarded as a creative, rather than an analytical, skill. *See also* LATERAL THINKING.

doctorate The highest *postgraduate degree award made by a university or other institution of *higher education. The degree of Doctor of Philosophy (Ph.D. or D.Phil.) is awarded following the candidate's successful completion of a *thesis, which they must also successfully defend at a *viva voce examination. Higher doctorates such as Doctor of Literature (D.Litt.) are awarded in acknowledgement of the recipient's body of published works. Once awarded the doctorate, the successful candidate is entitled to be called 'doctor' if he or she so wishes.

don A colloquial term for university lecturers or teachers. It was originally applied only to those who were Fellows of an Oxford or Cambridge college, and indicated a person of rank. It has since entered the colloquial Australian vocabulary as a synonym for 'expert'.

Down syndrome A genetic condition caused by the presence of an additional copy of chromosome 21 at conception, affecting about 600 babies in the United Kingdom a year. Why an additional copy of the chromosome is present is unknown, although the incidence increases with maternal age, especially over 35. The average life expectancy is approximately 60. Physically, people with Down syndrome typically have almond-shaped eyes and a flat facial profile. They tend to be shorter than average, have low muscle tone (hypontonia), and a large proportion will have a congenital heart deformity. A number of medical conditions such as thyroid gland problems and cataracts are also common. Developmentally, a degree of *learning difficulty is associated with the syndrome, although the severity of this can differ considerably from individual to individual. Most children with Down syndrome will encounter delay in speech and language acquisition and reach motor milestones at a later age than the norm. Frequently children of school age will be in receipt of a *statement of special educational need, but increasingly they are being educated in mainstream schools. Children with Down syndrome are usually very affectionate and happy. T.B., L.E.

Dunning Report (1977) The Report sets out the findings of the Dunning Committee, which recommended that all pupils should be given the opportunity to take courses leading to the *Scottish Certificate of Education and that both examinations and internal assessment by teachers should play a part in determining awards. It also advised that all pupils should be assessed in a way which would enable them to demonstrate positive achievement. Together with the *Munn Report, this document was the basis of the focus on equality of access to education in the Scottish education system after 1977. *See also* SCOTLAND, EDUCATION IN; SCOTTISH LEAVING CERTIFICATE. S.M.

dyscalculia A specific learning difficulty in mathematics. Many of the characteristics found in *dyslexics are also found in people with dyscalculia. Errors will be made when writing and reading numbers. The position and reversal of digits is common, so that, for example, 127 can be written as 721. Difficulties in sequencing creates problems with turn-taking. Spatial problems such as confusing left and right may be present. People with dyscalculia will also struggle with life skills such as understanding time and money and personal organization. Seemingly straightforward mathematical processes are often beyond a person with dyscalculia and present tremendous obstacles to them. T.B., L.E.

dyslexia A disorder which causes difficulty with reading and writing particularly. People with dyslexia can find it hard to keep their place when reading, as print seems to be shifting on the page. They have problems with phonological processes, which makes blending and sequencing a strain. Spelling is erratic, with letters of a similar shape such as *b* and *d* being mixed up. Words and letters may be written back to front. As grammar and punctuation are usually weak, writing can become altogether messy. The condition is also associated with poor short-term memory, a lack of concentration skills, and difficulties with mathematics. Not all those who have difficulty reading are dyslexic. *See also* DYSCALCULIA. T.B., L.E.

dyspraxia A coordination disorder causing specific difficulty in planning an action or movement (fine or gross motor), sequencing the movements required, and performing the action in a smooth and controlled way. A child with dyspraxia is likely to have difficulty with planning movements in physical education, undertaking basic motor skills such as catching a ball and climbing, recording their knowledge on paper, and organizing themselves. They are likely to have an average or higher than average IQ and good general knowledge, but this is not reflected in their school work owing to difficulties with organization and handwriting. Dyspraxia is often linked with *developmental coordination disorder and with *dyslexia. T.B., L.E.

early excellence centres A government initiative started in 1997 to move towards the delivery of integrated services for young children and families within England. Existing provisions already encompassing high-quality services for *early years became designated early excellence centres and were used as models for research and dissemination across England. A parallel development in *Sure Start centres alongside the *Every Child Matters agenda has joined up these three initiatives and created the current *children's centre model in England.

A.W.

early intervention is about professional agencies working together to respond to the additional needs of pre-school or school age children without delay. These needs may be due factors within the child, e.g. disability, or situations surrounding the child and their family, e.g. social issues. For every child identified as requiring multi-agency support, a lead professional should be allocated to take responsibility for co-coordination. Early intervention may be directly focused on the child in the form, for example, of support from a specialist pre-school teacher, or it may involve professionals working together to address issues surrounding the child. Early intervention is firmly routed in the *Every Child Matters agenda. *See also* COMMON ASSESSMENT FRAMEWORK.

T.B., L.E.

early years A crucial stage of life in terms of children's physical, intellectual, emotional, and social development and well-being, internationally recognized as the years 0–8, when growth is both rapid and differential. A significantly high proportion of learning takes place between the ages of 0 and 6, and it is a period of time when children need particularly high-quality care and learning experiences from attuned adults and an appropriate environment. *See also* EARLY YEARS FOUNDATION STAGE.

A.W.

Early Years Foundation Stage (EYFS) A framework setting out the national standards for the learning, care, and development of children from birth to the age of 5 which was launched in 2007 and became a requirement for all schools and *early years providers from September 2008. It superseded previous statutory guidance for the *Foundation Stage, as well as the *Birth to Three Matters framework and the previously existing frameworks applying to day care and childminding for under-8s. The framework makes it a requirement for all providers to teach *literacy and *numeracy skills to under-5s, so that, by the age of 5, children have acquired sufficient knowledge of *phonics to write simple words, and to begin to form simple sentences in writing. Under the terms of the framework, children should also be taught to understand simple concepts of addition and subtraction. In addition, it requires carers to base their planning of learning activities on their structured observations and assessments of children's learning, play, and behaviour in order to ensure that such activities are appropriate to the child's stage of development. These assessments can then be shared with parents, carers, and appropriate professionals. The *summative assessment, known as the Early Years Foundation Stage Profile, is included in the *local authority attainment data which are submitted annually for publication to the *Department for Children, Schools, and Families.

The introduction of this framework gave rise to some controversy and earned it the nickname 'the nappy curriculum'. Opponents include many teachers and academics, particularly those engaged with the *Montessori or *Steiner approaches to early years education, who express fears that its introduction of formal literacy and numeracy instruction to very young children runs counter to the developmental needs of this age group. Opposition was also expressed at the failure of the framework to make opportunities for outdoor play a mandatory requirement, and at its raising the pupil–adult ratio limit in some cases from the previously required 8:1 to 13:1. Supporters of the framework, on the other hand, argue that it allows flexibility and encourages providers to employ more qualified specialist staff.

Economic and Social Research Council (ESRC) A body to which educational researchers in universities and other institutions of *higher education may apply for funding for *research projects. This is because, in an academic context, education is included as one of the social sciences. Applications for funding are considered not only against criteria relating to research design and originality, but also according to whether they focus on issues which have been identified as being of priority concern in the field.

Edexcel *See* AWARDING BODY.

educability The extent to which an individual or group is considered able to benefit from a programme of education. It is a term laden with assumptions, and is used with caution by educationalists, many of whom prefer to take the approach that almost everyone is capable of learning if the learner's level of capability, rather than the requirements of the *syllabus or *curriculum, is taken as a starting point.

EDUCATION ACT

Legislation relating to innovation and reform of the education system, its provisions, funding, inspection, curriculum, and assessment is agreed by Parliament in the form of Education Acts. These are normally preceded by a *White Paper, which sets out the arguments for the policy to be enacted; or by a *Green Paper, which calls for consultation over some aspect of the policy prior to legislation. Over the past century or so there have been a number of landmark Acts which have signalled significant changes in key aspects of the education system. Examples of these may be summarized as follows:

Education Act 1902	Made the Board of Education centrally responsible for educational provision; created *local education authorities
Education Act 1918	Raised the school-leaving age to 14
Education (*Butler) Act 1944	Reorganized education into three sectors we recognize today as primary, secondary, and further education
Education Act 1979	Made the development of a comprehensive system of secondary education by local authorities optional rather than mandatory (by repealing an earlier Act of 1976), thus enabling some authorities to retain a selective system
Education Act 1980	Gave parents the right of representation on schools' governing bodies; required local authorities and governing bodies to demonstrate transparency in relation to examination results and admissions policies; introduced the concept of parental *choice
Education Act 1986	Abolished corporal punishment in schools; required every local authority school to have a governing body, and gave added responsibilities to governors
*Education Reform Act 1988	Introduced the *national curriculum and the option for schools to apply for *grant maintained status
Education (Schools) Act 1992	Introduced the requirement for schools and local authorities to publish *league tables based on examination performance; instigated four-yearly inspections of schools by *Ofsted
*Further and Higher Education Act 1992	Enabled polytechnics to adopt university status
Education Act 1996	Section 19 of this Act requires local authorities to provide appropriate education for children of compulsory school age either at school or otherwise than at school; forms of alternative provision are now known as *Education Otherwise (than at School)
Education Act 1997	Brought together general and vocational qualifications under one regulating authority by replacing the *School Curriculum and Assessment Authority and *National Council for Vocational Qualifications with the unitary *Qualifications and Curriculum Authority

School Standards and Framework Act 1998	Created *education action zones; empowered local authorities and the Secretary of State to intervene in the case of *failing schools; replaced the *grant maintained schools initiative with *foundation schools
Education Act 2002	Was amended at a late stage to include a specific duty on state schools and local authorities to have arrangements in place for safeguarding children. This amendment is contained in section 175, and came into force later (June 2004)
*Education (Scotland) Act 2004	Addressed the issue of educational support in Scotland's schools
Children Act 2004	Superseded the *Children Act 1989 and set out a legislative spine for the government's wider strategy in England and Wales, for improving children's lives, covering universal and parental responsibility, the *Every Child Matters agenda, services accessed by children, and the targeted services for those with additional needs
Education Act 2005	One of the longest Education Acts since that of 1944. Introduced a system of shorter, sharper inspections, with small Ofsted inspection teams visiting schools for no more than two days; schools to be judged not only by quality of teaching but also against the outcomes of the *Children Act 2004 and how they promote pupils' well-being; replaced the Teacher Training Agency with the *Training and Development Agency; encouraged local authorities to exert local leadership, but with effectively less funding
Education and Inspections Act 2006	Enabled schools to become trust schools; local authorities regained some of their strategic role; introduced specialized *diplomas for 14–19-year-olds; merged inspectorates to become the Office for Standards in Education, Children's Services, and Skills; extended the power of the *Learning and Skills Council to providing support for under-16s
Child Care Act 2006	Legislated for the duties, regulations, and inspection arrangements in England and Wales for childcare providers, simplifying the Ofsted Child Care Register Standards

See also Equal Opportunities Act 2006.

education action zone (EAZ) A partnership between a group of schools which also involves local businesses, parents, and the *local authority for the purpose of raising educational standards in areas where such standards are cause for concern, and particularly in areas of social deprivation. Each zone consists of around 15–25 schools and receives about £1 million extra funding each year, 75 per cent of which comes from central government; the remainder of the funding is raised by the zone itself from its business and commercial partners in the private sector. Each zone is managed by a project director and run by an action forum of local partners. EAZs were introduced under the provisions of the Schools Standards and Framework Act 1998, and each is supported for a maximum of five years, after which it becomes an *Excellence in Cities action zone or an **Excellence Cluster**.

Educational Institute of Scotland (EIS) Founded in 1847, the EIS is the oldest teaching union in UK. It has over 59 000 members and represents around 80 per cent of teachers in Scotland, working in nursery, primary, secondary, and special education, right through to further and higher education.
See also TEACHERS' UNIONS. S.M.

educational psychologist Psychologists often employed by the local authority who specialize in the psychology of children, particularly as it relates to motivation and learning. They provide diagnoses of emotional or behavioural difficulties and of specific learning needs and disabilities. Training for educational psychology usually requires that the applicant hold a first degree or equivalent in psychology, or, in the case of graduates in other disciplines, have attended a bridging course in psychology before commencing their formal educational psychology training. It is also normally expected that an applicant to the profession will be a qualified teacher with at least two years' teaching experience.

Education Maintenance Allowance (EMA) A regular weekly payment of up to £30 made to young people over the age of compulsory education who go on to some form of further education or training. Introduced as a pilot scheme in a limited number of local authorities in 1998, the EMA was originally conceived as a means of encouraging 16-year-olds from low-income families to stay on in education or training. After the initial three years of the scheme it was widely adopted. Payment is made directly into the student's bank account. Because payment of the allowance is contingent on the student's regular attendance, some teachers in further education have found it an effective source of motivation for students, although others claim that, while it encourages attendance, it does not necessarily improve students' motivation to engage with their learning when they are there.

An EMA was also launched in Scotland in August 2005, following a pilot phase, again in order to provide financial support to young people from low-income families. EMA in Scotland functions in the same form as its English counterpart.

SEE WEB LINKS

- Has details of eligibility and of the results of Scottish pilots such as that in East Ayrshire in 2002.

education otherwise than at school (EOTAS) Section 19 of the Education Act 1996 states that *local authorities must provide appropriate education for children of compulsory school age either at school or otherwise than at school. Placements must be appropriate to the needs and ability of the child (including any special educational need), in line with local authority policy and their requirement to use public resources efficiently, and agreed with the child's parents. Education Otherwise, also referred to as 'alternative provision', encompasses a range of provision including *pupil referral units, hospital schools, home tuition, further education *colleges, *work experience, private or voluntary sector schools, teenage pregnancy units, and *National Vocational Qualifications. Parents may also take the decision to educate their child otherwise than at school by electing to pay for an independent school place or by providing education at home. *See also* HOME EDUCATION. T.B., L.E.

Education Reform Act 1988 (ERA) Introduced originally as the Great Education Reform Bill (colloquially referred to at the time as Gerbil), this Act marked a major milestone in education provision, introducing for the first time a *national curriculum with core subjects (English, science, mathematics, and religious education) taught to all pupils. It also introduced the need to promote the cultural, moral, and spiritual development both of pupils and in wider society as a whole; and it began the process of delegating responsibility for school finance away from local authorities to the schools themselves, introducing the concept of *grant maintained schools. *Further education colleges were removed from local authority control, and their governing bodies were required to have less local authority representation but to ensure representation by local employers. In this way the Act illustrates two major themes which were to continue through education policy for the next two decades: the diminishing of local authority control over educational funding, policy, and practice, and the introduction of *market values into educational provision. *See also* EDUCATION ACT.

Education (Scotland) Act 2004 This replaced sections of the Education (Scotland) Act 1980, which dealt with additional support for learning. The Education (Additional Support for Learning) Scotland Act 2004 sought to change the way in which children and young people's educational support was identified, planned, and recorded. Key changes included the replacement of *special educational needs with additional support needs; the introduction of new duties on education authorities and other agencies; measures to improve integrated working; greater rights for parents and young people along with provisions for avoiding and resolving disputes; and the introduction of a coordinated support plan. S.M.

Education Welfare Service (EWS) A service which acts on behalf of the *local authority to ensure that parents fulfil their legal obligation to provide their child with an appropriate education. Its officers, known as education welfare officers (EWOs), education social workers, or attendance advisers, work with families and with schools to address cases of persistent *truancy and other problems of non-attendance. Parents or carers can be served with a notice or school attendance order if EWOs discover a child is not receiving an education.

EWOs also support families of pupils who have encountered difficulties at school, or where home circumstances are causing disruption to the child's education.

educator Used as an alternative word for 'teacher', particularly in the context of adult and community education, where the emphasis is upon facilitative rather than didactic teaching. The relationship implied between educator and learner (or 'educatee') is a more equal or egalitarian one than that between teacher and pupil; and one through which both parties expect to learn and to develop their understanding. This is particularly the case where education is aimed at bringing about economic change or social justice, as, for example, in the work of Paulo *Freire. The term may also be used in order to distinguish the concept of a teacher as one who encourages individual development and a spirit of enquiry from that of one who delivers standardized training or a prescribed curriculum in line with the *objectivist model of teaching. Thus, an educator has come to mean more than simply a transmitter of knowledge or skills.

e-learning Learning facilitated by the use of computers, using the Internet, an institution's intranet, or material on disks. The term is an abbreviation of 'electronic learning', and is an aspect of *information communication technology. As a form of *distance learning, it is often described as 'distributed, *asynchronous learning'—distributed in the sense that learners are not all in one location, and asynchronous in that they are not learning at the same time. Although this mode of learning has a number of advantages, such as allowing large groups of learners anywhere in the world to network through chat rooms or to discuss issues between themselves and their tutor through online discussions, it also presents some potential barriers to learning. For example, it requires learners to have functional levels of literacy in both the traditional sense and with regard to *information technology; and it does not provide face-to-face contact with the tutor or teacher (except perhaps through a webcam), or between the learners themselves. The removal of this social aspect of the educational experience does not appeal to all learners. The dynamics of e-learning have led to the development of a slightly different terminology for this mode of teaching and learning. E-learners are often referred to as 'participants' rather than students; and the teacher managing the learning programme may be referred to as the 'e-moderator', facilitator, or tutor. Group discussions in e-learning, which allow the thread of each participant's contribution to be reviewed and summarized, are known as **threaded discussions**. Salmon (2004) presents a model of e-learning which consists of five steps in the course of which the tutor or e-moderator progresses from being proactive and directive to being responsive and supportive, while the learner progresses from being dependent and reactive to independent and proactive. Where an e-learning approach is used as only part of a programme of learning, combined with provision for face-to-face contact with tutor and other students in a conventional attendance mode, this is known as *blended learning.

Further Reading: G. Salmon *E-Moderating: The Key to Teaching and Learning Online* (Kogan Page, 2004).

element In *National Vocational Qualifications (NVQs) statements of *competence are broken down into their constituent parts, the smallest of which is an element of competence. It is against these elements of competence that the NVQ candidate is assessed. A number of elements make up a *unit of competence. Units, but not their constituent elements, may be awarded separately as part of a process of credit accumulation.

elementary school Prior to the 1944 Education Act (*Butler Act), elementary schools were the standard educational provision for pupils aged 5–14. They were replaced by the system of primary and secondary schools with which we are more familiar today.

Eleven Plus A *test or *examination once commonly taken by pupils at the age of 11 to determine their progression route into secondary education. Administered by *local authorities, the Eleven Plus could take the form of an examination in English, mathematics, and general knowledge, or of a test which aimed to measure the *intelligence quotient (IQ) of pupils. Those who achieved highest scores gained entry to *grammar school or grammar technical school; the rest were destined for technical or secondary modern schools. When this system of *selection at the age of 11 gave way in most authorities to a system of non-selective, *comprehensive education following the *Education Act 1976, the Eleven Plus was largely discontinued, except within those authorities with a strong Conservative council, such as Lincolnshire and Kent, where the policy of retaining their grammar and secondary modern schools was enabled to continue by the Education Act 1979, which made the abolition of selection optional rather than mandatory, and meant that the testing for selection at the age of 11 continued to be used in some authorities into the 21st century.

The accuracy of the Eleven Plus as a predictor of future achievement has been widely questioned. In addition, it is now argued that two key factors cast doubt on its validity and reliability as a method of assessment. One concerns doubts raised over the use of blanket IQ testing, with its assumptions of implicit cultural and ethnic norms. Another arises from the recognition that testing for selection tended to favour boys, since their scores were often adjusted in cohorts where fewer boys than girls achieved a 'pass', in order to balance the numbers of boys and girls progressing to grammar schools. *See also* BUTLER ACT; INTELLIGENCE TEST.

emeritus A title given to *professors, and sometimes to *readers, on their retirement. They then become known as 'emeritus professor' or 'emeritus reader' of whatever is their specialist field.

emotional intelligence A theory developed in the 1970s and 1980s by Howard Gardner (b. 1943) and others, and popularized by Daniel Goleman (2005), which suggests that the ability to think and act from a position of awareness of one's own emotions and with sensitivity to the emotions of others is a form of intelligence which is undervalued in comparison to cognitive or intellectual *intelligence, as measured by traditional *intelligence tests. Purely cognitive intelligence, argues Goleman, is of limited use in forming and sustaining relationships, and in conducting most social interactions, where our feelings—emotions or intuitions—need to come into play. This idea can usefully be applied to the teacher–learner relationship. The emotionally intelligent teacher would typically have a knowledge of their own strengths and weaknesses; be able to exert control over their own emotions; recognize the emotional needs of others; and demonstrate honesty and integrity. In this sense, emotional intelligence could be said to be integral to the *humanist ideal of the teacher, as presented by, for example, Carl *Rogers. This form of intelligence is also increasingly regarded as a subject which may be taught in schools, as witnessed by publications such as Maurice Elias and Harriett Arnold's *Educator's Guide to Emotional Intelligence and Academic Achievement: Social–Emotional Learning in the Classroom* (Sage, 2006). The complex set of skills and qualities described by proponents of the emotional intelligence theory goes far beyond the common misunderstanding of emotional intelligence simply as a willingness to display one's emotions, and emphasizes the central role which self-knowledge plays in our personal development and social interactions.

Further Reading: D. Goleman *Emotional Intelligence* (Bantam Books, 2005).

SEE WEB LINKS

- Provides details of the emotional intelligence theory and links to critical analyses.

employability The extent to which an individual possesses the skills and qualities required by employers in a suitable employee. These will usually include the *key skills of communication and *numeracy, and qualities such as willingness and an ability to interact appropriately with others, as well as *vocationally specific skills. In an era when much education and training policy is driven by the imperative to build a more highly skilled workforce, the notion of employability has become increasingly relevant to the prevalent understanding of education's purpose.

employer engagement (employer links) A catch-all term for the initiatives, particularly in *vocational *further education and training, aimed at involving local employers in the planning, development, delivery, and evaluation of learning programmes. It is closely associated with the first theme of the *White Paper **Success for All* (2002), 'meeting needs, improving choice', which acknowledged that existing provision at that time did not uniformly meet the requirements of local employers, and that ways to improve collaboration and communication between employers and education and training providers should be developed.

Many further and *higher education institutions have responded to this challenge by creating business units to centralize responsibility for employer links and engagement, and to separate this aspect of provision from that funded by the *Learning and Skills Council (LSC); others devolve it to individual departments, a strategy which may enable them to avoid internal competition or potential communication problems. Typically, local partnerships are formed with Business Links, chambers of commerce, and **JobCentre Plus**, as well as Regional Boards of the LSC. The *governing bodies of education providers offer a universally used forum for engagement, in addition to other formal opportunities. *See also* CENTRES OF VOCATIONAL EXCELLENCE; ENTRY TO EMPLOYMENT; NEET; WORK-BASED LEARNING; YOUNG APPRENTICESHIPS. V.C., K.A.

employer-led A phrase used to describe the origins of national occupational standards in many spheres of work; and also to identify the influence which has shaped some aspects of education and training policy. Standards which are employer-led are those which are identified by employers through common agreement as being necessary for carrying out skilled work in their vocational area, and are then set as the national standard at a number of levels of skill. Policies which are said to be employer-led are those which are drawn up in response to needs expressed by employers in terms of the skills required of potential employees. At a national level an employer-led approach could be said to include the introduction of a *National Vocational Qualification framework in 1986, and the setting up of the *Learning and Skills Council in 2001.

employer training pilot (ETP) These pilots sought to assess the effectiveness of the training of low-skilled employees by evaluating its impact on the operation of the employing organization. It offered free or low-cost training for *vocational qualifications at level 2 on the *National Qualifications Framework, and entry to level 2 qualifications in *literacy and *numeracy. The first ETPs were carried out in local *Learning and Skills Councils (LSCs) in 2002, and the provision was expanded to the remaining local LSCs after a positive evaluation. As well as providing both employers and employees with information, advice, and guidance on a variety of training provisions, the pilots offered wage compensation to employers who gave employees paid time off in which to train. The initiative came to a close in 2005.

SEE WEB LINKS

- Presents an evaluation of the second year of the initiative.

V.C., K.A.

ENGLAND, EDUCATION IN

Responsibility for education and *training is divided between two specialized governments departments, each headed by a *Secretary of State: the *Department for Children, Schools, and Families, with a remit for *compulsory education and children's services; and the *Department for Innovation, Universities, and Skills, with a remit for science, *further and *higher education, and skills training.

Education in school is compulsory between the ages of 5 and 16, although more than 50 per cent of under-5s attend some form of *pre-school provision, and the *Early Years Foundation Stage sets out a curriculum for children aged 0–5. The majority of 16-year-olds remain in some form of education or training at least until the age of 18, and there are plans to require all young people to stay in school, training, or workplace training until the age of 18 by 2013.

In most *local authorities there is a system of *primary schools and secondary schools, with transfer to secondary school being made at the age of 11. In some authorities, however, a system of *first, *middle, and secondary schools operates, with middle schools providing for 8–12-year-olds. Most secondary provision is in the form of *comprehensive schools, although a small minority of local authorities have retained a system of *selection at 11 through the *Eleven Plus examination, according to the results of which pupils are allocated a place at either a *grammar school or a non-selective school in their local authority area.

A *national curriculum was introduced in 1998, consisting of four *key stages, for ages 5–7, 8–11, 11–14, and 14–16, at the end of each of which pupils are assessed. At the end of Key Stage 4 the *assessment for most pupils takes the form of the *General Certificate of Secondary Education, which was originally conceived of as a school-leaving examination, but is now seen more as a means of selection to determine the next stage in pupils' progression. This may be into a school sixth form or a *sixth form college to study for *General Certificate of Education *Advanced Levels (A levels) or *Vocational A levels or a diploma, or to a *college of further education for a more vocationally focused education or training. Some pupils may take the option to begin studying for a 14–19 Diploma at the beginning of Key Stage 4 in place of some of national curriculum subjects.

At 18 many students use their A level, diploma, or equivalent qualification to progress to *university or some other form of *higher education. The current government target is that 50 per cent of all 18–30-year-olds should at some point be participating in higher education by 2010. Others may proceed to employment or further *skills training. The creation of a more highly skilled workforce has been the goal of successive governments since the last quarter of the 20th century. Adult and *continuing education may take the form of reskilling or up-skilling for work, of personal development, or of learning for leisure. Only the first of these qualifies for subsidized funding. Providers of *adult education include the *Workers' Educational Association, local authorities, and further education colleges. *Ofsted is responsible for the inspection of primary, secondary, and further education provision, and of teacher training provision in higher education. Other higher education provision is subject to inspection by the *Quality Assurance Agency.

English as a Foreign Language (EFL) Taught both overseas and in the United Kingdom to learners for whom English is not their first language, and whose permanent place of residence is not the UK. It is this latter fact that distinguishes it from *English for Speakers of Other Languages, which is intended for those who have made their home in the UK. The *British Council takes a leading role in the provision of EFL overseas. *See also* ENGLISH FOR SPEAKERS OF OTHER LANGUAGES.

English as an Additional Language (EAL) *See* ENGLISH FOR SPEAKERS OF OTHER LANGUAGES.

English for Speakers of Other Languages (ESOL) The provision of English language learning for those with other first languages who have settled in the UK. The *Adult ESOL Core Curriculum* of 2001 outlines the skills, knowledge, and understanding that non-native English speakers need to demonstrate as set out in the National Standards drawn up by the *Basic Skills Agency. The adult ESOL curriculum, which relates to **Adult Literacy Standards** and *English as a Foreign Language, separates the skills of speaking and listening, to reflect the tendency for ESOL students to understand more than they can speak. ESOL learners constitute a diverse group of students in terms of the disparity in their cultural, educational, linguistic, and economic backgrounds. ESOL practitioners are therefore required to meet the challenge of planning and delivering differentiated but inclusive teaching and learning sessions. Teachers of ESOL have, since 2004, been required to gain specialized practitioner qualifications at level 4 on the *National Qualifications Framework. *See also* BASIC SKILLS. V.C., K.A.

enhanced resources school A mainstream school which receives additional funding to meet the needs of pupils with a particular *special educational need or disability. A typical example of enhanced resource provision would be for pupils with hearing impairment. Schools in any key stage could have enhanced resourced status. Funding is received from the *local authority to be managed by the school to enhance staffing, teaching, and learning resources, the learning environment, and access to the curriculum. Pupils are generally taught with peers in lessons with additional adult support and appropriate equipment, but may receive specialist teaching in small groups or one-to-one within the resource base. T.B., L.E.

enrichment programme A programme of activities designed to provide additional stimulus for more able pupils, or to give additional support to pupils from areas of social and cultural deprivation by providing some of the activities, resources, and stimuli not available to them in their home environment.

Enterprise Strategy Set out initially in the document *A Smart, Successful Scotland* (January 2001; revised November 2004) to provide the Enterprise Networks (Scottish Enterprise and Highlands and Islands Enterprise) with a clear strategic direction for economic development in Scotland. The document highlights priority areas which Scotland must develop in order to achieve medium- to long-term economic development. These are grouped as three strategic themes of Growing Businesses, Global Connections, and Skills and Learning. It is a significant driver in the provision of *vocational education and skills training in Scotland. S.M.

entitlement All students have a right or entitlement to a broad and balanced curriculum. Prior to the Education Act 1970, children with severe learning difficulties or disabilities were the responsibility of the Health Service and often labelled as ineducable. They had no access to school or qualified teachers. Schools can use the flexibility they now have to develop a curriculum which responds to the strengths and needs of all students. This would include award-bearing vocational and entry level courses at Key Stage 4. For younger children it requires appropriate differentiation of the *national curriculum to ensure they receive their entitlement to learn at their own level alongside their peers. Students should be given the opportunity to express their own hopes and aspirations for their future. T.B., L.E.

entry level The lowest level of the *National Qualifications Framework, and based on a level of achievement below that of *General Certificate of Secondary Education. Foundation level qualifications are available in a range of subjects from the vocational, such as that in hairdressing, and the vocationally related, such as life skills, to national curriculum subjects such as science.

Entry to Employment (e2e) A programme which was conceived in the Report of the **Modern Apprenticeship Advisory Committee**, *Modern Apprenticeships: The Way to Work* (October 2001), as a new programme of high-quality learning for young people at the pre-apprenticeship stage. Individual local programmes are delivered by a range of training providers, and funded by the *Learning and Skills Council. It typically attracts those young people who would not normally be working, training, or learning, and targets 16–19-year-olds with lower attainment in education, who have a high risk of dropping out. For this group it is the personal and social factors that often present some of the most difficult barriers to learning. Tackling the barriers and helping learners to make progress is crucial to the e2e programme. The approaches used are specifically designed to remotivate and to appeal to the e2e group, in terms of relevance both to the individual's own context and to real employment opportunities. The programme is used also to prepare learners for entering *Young Apprenticeship schemes. V.C., K.A.

epistemology The study and understanding of knowledge. Teaching and learning depend on an often implicit understanding of what knowledge is. So does educational *research. Epistemology addresses the issue of what counts as knowledge. Theories of knowledge draw distinctions between knowledge understood as being, for instance, implicit or explicit; practical or theoretical; of things or of people; and of skills or of facts. Further distinctions are drawn between human wisdom and understanding as opposed to information. Only the latter can be stored or coded as facts and symbols. Some epistemologies take it that knowledge is independent of power and ethics, while others (for example, **postmodern, poststructural, feminist,** and social epistemologies) take these to be central. How these distinctions are articulated affects how questions are posed and answered about: how knowledge is recognized *as* knowledge, ways of getting it (methodology), and its relation to reality, truth, certainty, and cultural differences. All of these questions, including what counts as knowledge, are themselves dependent on *ontology, which addresses the issue of what exists. If the real is taken to be articulated as propositions that something is the case ('knowledge that'), then knowledge is held to be justified true belief. However, this formulation is inadequate if knowledge is held to include skills ('knowledge how') or to include understanding of social meanings which vary with social–cultural context **(relativism).** M.G.

equal opportunities *See* SOCIAL JUSTICE.

Equal Opportunities Act 2006 This Act replaced the Equal Opportunities Commission, the Commission for Racial Equality, and the Disability Rights Commission with a unitary **Commission for Equality and Human Rights**. The Act requires public authorities to promote equality between men and women, and between girls and boys, and to explicitly prohibit sexual harassment. It also makes it unlawful for any individual, collective body, or organization to discriminate on the grounds of religion and belief; and it enables provision for the prohibition of discrimination on the grounds of sexual orientation. The Act represents an important step in anti-discrimination, and is of direct relevance not only to classroom practices, but also to the regulations and policies of all educational institutions. In semantic terms it is significant as a move away from the concept of 'equal opportunity' in favour of an emphasis on the *social justice constructions of 'equality' and rights. *See also* EDUCATION ACT.

Erikson, Erik (1902–94) A developmental psychologist and psychoanalyst known for his theory on the social development of human beings. Through his association with Anna Freud, and his study for a certificate in *Montessori education, he became interested in the influence of culture and society on child development, and his book *Childhood and Society* (1950) is considered a classic text by educators, psychologists, and sociologists. For those professionals working with the *early years, Erikson's theory of the **eight ages of man** shows how children develop the foundation for emotional and social development and mental strength through social interactions with significant adults, and thus are able to assimilate the culture of their own community. The attachments made with adults help to internalize culture, essentially when the child is supported to 'pass through' each of the developmental stages which define each individual child's personality. The stages, therefore, are based on psychosocial development rather than, as *Piaget's are, on *cognitive stages, which Erikson might argue are dependent on a child's well-being. Erikson's theory, based on attachment to adults, suggests that it is essential for a child to develop trust and empathy in order to be able to achieve higher levels of social functioning. This reflects a similar notion to *Maslow's *hierarchy of needs. Erikson further states that these stages are epigenetic; that is, they are predetermined and sequential. The confidence and self-esteem gained through the success of the child overcoming each stage of psychosocial 'crisis', Erikson suggests, should not be rushed, but can be revisited. In the early years, it is critical for significant adults to help children develop trust, autonomy, and initiative by offering real and practical tasks that the child will be able to accomplish and which will therefore enable them to develop confidence. Requiring children to learn, work, or carry out tasks beyond their stage of personality development, Erikson argues, could have the effect of denying the child an opportunity for their needs to be met, and may result in negative outcomes for the child, their schooling, and their later successful participation as adults in society. Erikson was Danish by parentage but became an American citizen. He is thought to have coined the term 'identity crisis'. A.W.

Estyn [Welsh *verb* 'to extend'] The office of Her Majesty's Inspectorate for Education and Training in Wales, funded by the National Assembly for Wales but independent from it. For Wales it is the equivalent body to *Ofsted in England. Estyn is responsible for school inspections and for reporting on school achievement for all levels of compulsory education, as well as for pre-schools, government-funded training programmes, and colleges of further education, including adult education. Stated objectives are to deliver high-quality inspection of individual education and training providers, and related services, and to provide advice, based on inspection evidence, to inform the Welsh Assembly in the formulation and evaluation of education and training policy.

H.G.

European Social Fund (ESF) The ESF's main purpose is to support the annual UK **Employment Action Plan**, which is intrinsically linked with the **European Employment Strategy**. It aims to help unemployed and inactive people enter work; provide opportunities for people at a disadvantage in the labour market; promote *lifelong learning; develop the skills of employed people; and improve women's participation in the labour market. In the period 2000–06 the ESF provided about £4.5 billion in Great Britain to organizations which submitted successful bids. This was distributed to projects through the *Learning and Skills Councils, **Jobcentre Plus**, and other organizations which are responsible for finding the 'match funding' (that is, for raising an equivalent sum in order to match the funding received). This system is known as 'co-financing' and it enables successful applicants to receive 100 per cent funding for their projects.

SEE WEB LINKS

- Provides links to information on the application process and specific projects.

V.C., K.A.

evaluation The measuring of the effectiveness of a lesson, course, or *programme of study, often based upon, among other sources of evidence, the views and responses of the learners concerned, which constitutes qualitative evidence, as well as upon a quantitative assessment of the impact the course or lesson has had on learners' levels of *attainment. As well as participating in formal evaluations carried out for institutional purposes of quality assurance, teachers are encouraged to evaluate their own performance in planning, teaching, assessing, and supporting learning through a process of reflection on their professional practice. Evaluation is a process quite distinct from *assessment. While student attainment may be assessed, it is the effectiveness of the processes which have contributed to their learning which are the focus of evaluation, although this may include using assessment data on attainment as one source of evidence.

evening class Traditionally, a *lesson, or course of lessons, in the *post-compulsory sector, conducted after 5 p.m., and sometimes associated with leisure or cultural activities, such as yoga, holiday Spanish, local history, or the study of literature. Such classes are aimed primarily at adults, and are often held in colleges of *further education or on school premises. Although at one time subsidized by *local authorities, students are now required to pay the full cost of fees for attending such non-vocational provision. As a result, evening classes are currently declining in number, and are recruiting a narrower demographic, largely confined to those who can afford the increased fees. Vocationally related courses which are scheduled for evenings are usually run at this time because they are aimed at adult learners in employment who cannot attend during standard 9–5 working hours. The vocational content of such courses makes them eligible for funding, usually through the local *Learning and Skills Council. *See also* ADULT EDUCATION; WORKERS' EDUCATIONAL ASSOCIATION.

Every Child Matters This policy strategy is a shared programme of change to improve outcomes for all children and young people. It takes forward the UK government's 'vision of radical reform' for children, young people, and families. This programme was set out in response to an inquiry regarding the death of **Victoria Climbié** in 2000. She was a child murder victim whose death led to major changes in child protection policies as a result of the **Laming Report** (2003) and shared working agreements between the professional agencies (health, education, social services, probation) who may support children and their families. Every Child Matters affects all children from 0 to 19. It aims to improve educational achievement and reduce the levels of ill health, teenage pregnancy, abuse and neglect, crime, and antisocial behaviour. The shared outcomes—being healthy; staying safe; enjoying and achieving; making a positive contribution; and achieving economic well-being—are embedded in legislation (the *Children Act 2004), shared across all government services, and underpinned by an integrated inspection framework (*Common Assessment Framework) to ensure all services work together effectively and share information.

SEE WEB LINKS

- Explains the strategy and planned outcomes.
- Provides further information about Every Child Matters.

A.W.

examination A means of formal *summative assessment, usually involving time-constrained tasks, which assesses the *knowledge, *skills, or understanding of the candidate. Conduct of candidates and the regulation of start and finish times are usually monitored and enforced by one or more **invigilators**. The major national examinations in England, Northern Ireland, and Wales are the *General Certificate of Secondary Education and the *General Certificate of Education (GCE) *Advanced Level (A level). In Scotland they are the *Standard Grades, the *Highers, and the *Advanced Highers. These public examinations are externally assessed by *external examiners, although schools and other institutions may set their own examinations, for example when presenting pupils with mock A levels, in which case the examination is internally assessed by the candidates' teachers. Proponents of the examination system claim that it has advantages over *continuous assessment in that it is a more reliable, objective, and stringent means of *assessment. Opponents, on the other hand, argue that examinations impose anxieties and false constraints which may adversely affect candidates' performance, and that such restraints, being unrealistic, undermine the examination's validity. Some researchers claim that examinations disadvantage female candidates while *continuous assessment disadvantages male candidates. Whatever the facts of the matter, recent policy developments have shown a resurgence of emphasis on assessment by examination and a reduction in continuous assessment by coursework in, for example, the GCE A level.

examination board 1. *See* AWARDING BODY.

2. A formal board convened at a *university or *college to consider students' assessment results and approve the mark, grade, or qualification awarded. Such boards consist of course leaders and their teams, external examiners, administrative staff, and a senior member of the institution in the role of chair.

In most cases, all assessment decisions on *undergraduate and *postgraduate courses are subject to the approval of the examination board.

examination terminology Traditionally termed '**rubric**', *examination terminology refers to the instructions to candidates found in examination papers. An ability to understand and comply with these instructions is obviously essential to the candidate's successful performance, and a failure to notice or comprehend them could seriously disadvantage the candidate involved. For this reason, many secondary schools now include guidance on examination terminology in their preparation of pupils for the public examinations such as the *General Certificate of Secondary Education and the *General Certificate of Education *Advanced Level.

e

examiner, external 1. In schools and colleges, the assessor responsible for marking external examinations and other assessments. They are external in that they represent the *awarding body and not the institution in which the candidate has been taught.

2. In *higher education the external examiner's role is to ensure that standards of achievement are being maintained in line with those in other institutions, and to this end an academic from another higher education institution is usually chosen for this role. In the examination of candidates for a *doctorate, the external examiner is selected in their capacity as an authority in the candidate's field.

examiner, internal An examiner who assesses an internally set examination or piece of coursework, who teaches in the school, college, or university attended by the candidate, and may even be one of the candidate's teachers.

Excellence in Cities An initiative launched in 1999 to raise standards of pupil achievement in schools situated in large cities. It provided funding to support *learning mentors, the development of *pupils deemed to be *gifted and talented, *Learning Support Units, and the formation of *education action zones. The initiative was subsequently extended through the establishment of **Excellence Clusters**.

Excellent Teacher Scheme (ETS) A scheme designed to recognize the achievements and skills of excellent teachers by drawing upon their expertise to help other teachers to improve their effectiveness. Excellent teacher status was introduced in April 2006 as a means of rewarding teachers who wish to pursue their careers further without going into a management role in schools. In order to apply externally for an ET post, teachers must meet prescribed ET standards which are part of the government **framework of professional standards for teachers**. The government estimated that 5 000 teachers would apply for this route in the first year; in fact, by 2008 fewer than 40 teachers in all had qualified for excellent teacher status. Several reasons have been suggested for this, including the level of the fixed salary offered, the reluctance of teachers to put themselves forward as 'excellent', and the alternative route of *advanced skills teacher, which offers a higher salary and the opportunity to carry out professional development work in other schools. As a consequence, in 2008 the Secretary of State for Children, Schools, and Families accepted a recommendation by the **School Teachers' Review Body** to review the pay scale for excellent teachers with a view to raising the upper pay limit.

SEE WEB LINKS

- Provides information and guidance about the ETS.

exclusion The barring of a pupil from attending school, either temporarily (up to fifteen school days) or permanently. *Behaviour for which pupils may be permanently excluded includes *bullying, carrying weapons, acts of violence, supplying drugs, sexual misconduct, and persistent non-compliance. Pupils who have been excluded from secondary schools may be provided by their local authority with a place in a *pupil referral unit, where they can continue full-time with their education, although this will not necessarily include full coverage of the *national curriculum.

experiential learning Sometimes called 'learning by doing', this type of learning allows the pupil or student to learn through practical experience rather than through formal instruction by the teacher. The emphasis is on practice rather than on theory. To some extent a belief in the efficacy of experiential learning underpins the provision of *teaching practice for trainee teachers and of *work experience for trainees on vocational programmes.

external verifier *See* VERIFICATION.

extracurricular Organized activities which fall outside the formal school, college, or university *curriculum may be described as extracurricular. This would include, but would not be restricted to, such things as whole-school drama productions, sports matches with other schools, hobby clubs, and theatre visits.

extramural department A university department which provides courses, usually in *adult education, for members of the local or wider community, often outside the university *campus. Its literal meaning is 'outside the wall'. Such provision has declined since the withdrawal of public funding from *liberal (non-vocational) adult education.

extrinsic motivation *See* MOTIVATION.

faculty A subdivision of a *university or *college according to subject or field. For example, a university might consist of a number of faculties, including perhaps faculties of science, humanities, education, and so on. The term itself refers both to the academics—the teaching and research staff—working within that subdivision, and to the organizational subdivision itself. Thus, it may be used either as a collective noun, or to indicate a part of the institution's organizational structure, usually managed by a head—or dean—of faculty.

Fade or Flourish Subtitled *How Primary Schools Can Build on Children's Early Progress*, this report, funded by the Esmée Fairbairn Foundation in 2006, presents evidence to suggest that the educational and social benefits of an *early years, *pre-school education can be lost if not consolidated in the *primary phase.

SEE WEB LINKS

- Presents the full text of the Report.

failing school A secondary school whose *General Certificate of Secondary Education results fail to reach nationally set minimum *targets based on the proportion of pupils achieving five passes at grade C or above. Such a school is deemed to be failing, and is required to improve its results in order to meet the minimum target within two years. Under the 1998 School Standards and Framework Act, those schools which are unable to do this face closure by their local authority, or renaming and reopening under the *Fresh Start scheme with a new head teacher. The minimum percentage target used to identify failing schools has been raised several times from its original level of 15 per cent.

faith schools Schools, both *primary and secondary, which are provided under the aegis of a recognized religious faith. Although the most common faith schools are those supported by the Church of England and the Roman Catholic Church, the range of such provision reflects a multi-*denominational, multicultural society and includes a rapidly growing number of Muslim schools. All newly established faith schools are required to liaise closely with other schools, including other faith schools, in their geographical area. The 2001 *White Paper *Schools: Achieving Success* recommended that, in order to avoid insularity or inter-faith conflict, the interests and sensibilities of the whole community be taken into consideration by those establishing a faith-specific school.

falling rolls A decline in the number of pupils entering a school. Although this can be a problem for individual schools, it has also been seen as a national trend since the final quarter of the 20th century. Some of its consequences can be seen in the closure or amalgamation of schools. The introduction of a quasi-*market in education following the *Education Reform Act 1988 required schools to compete for pupils by introducing the concept of parental *choice to replace the system of local authorities allocating school places on the basis of *catchment areas. This proved an effective strategy for reducing school places overall in the face of falling rolls, since it led to failure and closure of less popular or more isolated schools.

family grouping *See* VERTICAL GROUPING.

f

family pack A pack published by the *Department for Education and Skills for use by parents and carers of young children with additional needs and disabilities. The pack is designed to facilitate the coordination of professional support and assist partnership working while keeping the family fully involved and at the centre of their child's support. The pack contains a family file, in which parents can write about their family, list the professionals involved with their child, and keep a record of professional contacts. Parents can make this file available to professionals, thus ensuring that the team involved in the care and education of the child is kept informed of the support given by fellow professionals from all agencies, and that information and processes are not duplicated. Also contained in the pack is a background file containing useful information about available services and routes of access. There is also a history file, in which parents can store paperwork that is no longer current but may be useful for reference purposes in the future.

SEE WEB LINKS

- Gives details of the pack.

T.B., L.E.

Fast Track An accelerated professional development programme for teachers which prepares them to progress to positions of leadership in school within four years. Such a position may involve school management, such as that of *head or *deputy head, or may be concerned with leadership in professional development, such as an *advanced skills teacher post. The Fast Track training lasts up to five years and is aimed at teachers in the early years of their career who demonstrate the potential to benefit from such a programme. They must hold *qualified teacher status, be teaching in a *maintained school in England, be registered with the *General Teaching Council for England, and not yet have reached the threshold on the teachers' *pay scale. Applications are considered on a case-by-case basis by the *National College for School Leadership. The programme, which began in 1999, was first announced in the 1998 *Green Paper *Teachers: Meeting the Challenge of Change.*

SEE WEB LINKS

- Detailed information about the Fast Track programme.

feedback A technical term taken from communication theory which, when applied in an educational context, refers to a formal response from teacher to learner about their work or progress; or from learner to teacher in answer to a question, problem, or task which has been set. In the first case, a teacher's feedback to the learner can take the form of either a spoken or a written appraisal of the learner's performance, including advice on what areas need to be improved and which should be regarded as strengths. This may be referred to as *formative assessment. In the second case, learners who have been set a task, individually or in groups, may be asked to 'feed back' their findings or conclusions to the teacher and the rest of the class, for the purposes both of providing the teacher with an opportunity for the *assessment of students' learning, and also of providing an opportunity for peer learning, where students learn from one another. This process is also known as **debriefing**. If learners are asked to evaluate a lesson or module or course, their spoken or written responses are again referred to as 'student (or learner, or pupil) feedback'.

feeder course A programme of study which prepares the learner, directly or indirectly, for entry to a specific and more advanced course. For example, a *further education college may enrol students onto intermediate or advanced level vocational courses with a view to encouraging them to progress onto a *foundation degree taught in the same college.

fees Payment charged by a university, college, or non-maintained school for tuition and, in some cases, accommodation. Schools which charge fees are sometimes referred to as 'fee-paying'. In England tuition fees for undergraduate students in *higher education were at one time normally paid by the student's *local authority, but are now charged to the student themselves. Although government *loans are available to ease the immediate financial burden on the student, many find it necessary to take on part-time employment to meet the cost of their higher education, and as a consequence have less time to spend on their studies. It was partly for this reason that tuition fees for Scottish students in higher education in Scotland were abolished in 2000. Instead, Scottish graduates pay a **graduate endowment**—a one-off payment at the end of their course. English students studying in Scotland pay a fixed-rate tuition fee, while Scottish students studying in England are required to pay the standard tuition fee demanded by their institution.

In Wales students may receive a **fee remission grant**. This is a tuition fee grant of up to £1 800 a year payable to all students normally resident in Wales who study at a Welsh higher education institution. It is non-means tested and covers the additional expense resulting from the introduction of variable fees. All students, as elsewhere, are eligible for the £1 200 fee loan. Unlike the arrangements in England, variable fees were not introduced in Wales until autumn 2007.

fellow In a general educational context this most often refers to someone who holds a funded *research post in an institution of *higher education, and is known in full as a *research fellow. These are usually fixed-term contract posts created for the furtherance of specific research projects. The funding may come from within the university or college itself, or from an external partner organization or sponsor, which may give its name to the fellowship. The term may also be used to indicate membership of a professional or academic group, as in 'Fellow of the Royal Institute of British Architects' (FRIBA). It is also a title given to senior members of Oxford or Cambridge colleges who, as well as their teaching duties, contribute to decision-making on academic and administrative matters relating to their college.

Ferl A web-based information and resource service which is managed by the *British Educational Communications and Technology Agency (Becta). When it was formed in 1988, the acronym stood for 'Further Education Resources for Learning'. However, the role and focus later widened to include management, technology, and teaching and learning approaches. Ferl supports the effective use of *information communications technology and *e-learning for the *post-compulsory education sector. This support is provided through a series of networks, conferences, publications, skills teams, and e-resources, which are managed by Becta. Support is available for organizations as well as for individual practitioners within the sector.

SEE WEB LINKS

- Provides links to resources and strategies for traditional and online teaching and learning.

V.C., K.A.

Fforum The body representing colleges of further education, sixth form, and specialist colleges in Wales as an associate of the *Association of Colleges (AoC). The AoC was established in 1996 by the colleges themselves to provide a voice for further education at national and regional levels, working closely with government and other key agencies to assist policy development. H.G.

field study A project, investigation, or activity carried out 'in the field', outside or away from the learner's school, college, or university. Its purpose is to allow learners to investigate questions or subjects which cannot be fully or satisfactorily studied in a classroom or workshop. Subjects such as geography, archaeology, and architecture can be taught more effectively by providing learners with access to a wider environment where the focus of study may be examined in context.

field trip An organized visit for pupils or students under teacher supervision for the purpose of carrying out a *field study or some activity relevant to their curriculum. Such trips might take the form of a visit to a museum or art gallery, or of activities such as abseiling or canoeing. In the case of younger learners, parental permission must be formally given, and expectations about standards of learner behaviour clearly articulated. For all field trips, observance of health and safety measures are of central importance. The responsibility of teachers for pupils' safety and behaviour on such trips means that *pupil–teacher ratios must reflect the need for close supervision. In recent years there has been a growing reluctance among some teachers to take part in out-of-school visits such as field trips for fear of litigation.

first The highest classification of a *bachelor's degree, the others being an upper second (2.1), lower second (2.2), and third class. Possession of a first class degree has traditionally been one of the prerequisites for progression to postgraduate-level study, although 2.1s are now also widely accepted for this purpose. Published figures are open to the interpretation that a first class degree may be more readily attainable at some institutions and in some subjects than others, based on a comparison between candidates' *General Certificate of Education *Advanced Level scores and subsequent degree classification attained.

first degree A degree taken at the end of *undergraduate studies. It is described as a 'first' degree in order to distinguish it from higher degrees such as those at *master's and *doctorate levels, which may be taken subsequently. First degrees are awarded by universities and some other institutions of higher education. *See also* BACHELOR'S DEGREE.

first school Provides education for pupils aged 5–8, who go on to continue their education in a *middle school. The first and middle school system operates within some local authorities in place of the more commonly found infant and junior provision, and was introduced following recommendations in the *Plowden Report (1967). The system is claimed by some professionals in education to ease the difficulties of *transition experienced by some pupils in moving from one stage of their education to the next.

Flying Start A programme for 0–3-year-olds in Wales launched in 2006, targeted at families in some of the most disadvantaged areas, defined as those where over 45 per cent of children in local primary schools are entitled to free school meals. The range of services provided under the programme includes centre-based childcare for all 2–3-year-olds on a part-time basis, health visitor support, and programmes designed to improve parenting skills. Integrated centres provide a base for the professionals working in the programme and serve as information points for families. Flying Start targets the language and the cognitive, social, and emotional development of the children involved, as well as their physical health. H.G.

folio A piece of extended work completed during a Scottish *Standard Grade or *Higher course which is marked externally but counts as a *National Unit in a National Qualification. *See also* SCOTLAND, EDUCATION IN. S.M.

foreign language assistant (FLA) Native speakers of the appropriate language employed in the language departments of schools, colleges, and universities to assist in the teaching of a modern foreign language, particularly by providing a model of practical language skills and accurate pronunciation. FLAs are often recruited from students studying English at a university in the country of origin, in which case their experience in a British school is expected to aid the development of their own English language skills. Their status and terms of employment within schools and other institutions is not equivalent to that of qualified teachers, and they are paid on a different scale. In United Kingdom schools they are organized through the Education and Training Group.

formative assessment *Assessment which is designed to provide feedback to the learner in order that they may improve their performance. In this sense it helps to 'form' the learner. Its very purpose demands that formative assessment be part of the learning process rather than a terminal assessment event which takes place at the end of the course of study. *Continuous assessment, for example through *assignment work, is formative, as are week-by-week teacher assessments of class work and *homework. The key feature of effective formative assessment is that it provides the learner with clear constructive feedback. The distinction between formative and *summative, or end, assessment was pointed out by Scriven in 1967. *See also* ASSESSMENT FOR LEARNING.

Further Reading: M. Scriven 'The Methodology of Evaluation' in R. W. Tyler, R. M. Gagné, and M. Scriven (eds) *Perspectives of Curriculum Evaluation* (Rand McNally, 1967).

form 7 The census form completed by *primary, *middle, and secondary schools operating under *local authority control, which has given its name to school census returns. The *Education Act 1996 required governing bodies of all local authority maintained schools (and the executives of independent schools) to provide information on the school as required by the *Secretary of State for Education. Data from this census were used in the calculation and allocation of funding for schools. The final such census was conducted by the Department for Education and Employment in 2001, after which it was replaced by the **Pupil Level Annual Schools Census (PLASC)**, most of the data for which is generated from schools' management information systems. The name 'form 7', however, is still commonly used as a generic term for the current annual census.

Foster Report (2005) The publication of the findings of the **Foster Review of Further Education**, the full title of which is ***Realising the Potential: A Review of the Future Role of Further Education Colleges***. It represents a significant landmark in the history of *further education (FE) since it offers the definition of the purpose of the sector, which was to inform the 2006 *White Paper *Further Education: Raising Skills, Improving Life Chances*. The vision it puts forward is of FE as the cornerstone of skills training. In paragraph 57 of the Report this is set out clearly as follows: 'A focus on vocational skills building is not a residual choice, but a vital building block in the UK's platform for future prosperity. It gives FE colleges an unequivocal mission and the basis of a renewed and powerful brand image.' This 'unequivocal mission' was not welcomed unanimously by educationalists within FE, some of whom retained a vision of the sector which included its role as provider of the 'second chance' for those seeking to re-engage with a general, rather than an instrumental, education. The Report is notable for its employment of a *market-related vocabulary in a context of education and training, as illustrated in the extract above; and also for its introduction of a new metaphor for FE, describing it as a 'middle child' occupying a position between the schools sector and *higher education, and sometimes suffering neglect as a consequence.

Foucault, Michel (1926–84) A French social theorist, philosopher, and historian, and one of the most influential poststructuralist thinkers of the 20th century. Like *Derrida, Foucault's ideas caused controversy as they questioned long-held opinions regarding the nature of identity, truth, and how power operates. As a historian, Foucault challenged the received methods of historical investigation, proposing the idea that the dominant method of narrating a linear story of Western development was one of exclusion, which tended to silence those thus marginalized. But, arguably, the most important aspect to Foucault's work, as it relates to education, was his focus on the concept of **discourse** and its role in the formation of identity.

Throughout Foucault's major works, including *Madness and Civilization* (1961), *The Birth of the Clinic* (1963), *Sex and Sexuality* (3 vols, 1984), and especially *Discipline and Punish* (1975), he concentrated on showing how the concept of the individual is a political subject, one that is formed in the very particular discourses of certain, usually institutional, contexts. Here, the term 'discourse' is used to mean language in context. According to Foucault, power flows in a complex web which defines what we can know and how we can express knowledge of our 'selves' and the world around us. In educational institutions, whether as students or teachers, we are constituted as subjects; the discourses available in that context define what can be said and known, and what is excluded or rendered 'invisible'. In the modern world, suggests Foucault, it is no longer possible to have a unified theoretical concept of power as in Marxism. Power is localized and particular.

f

Foucault's ideas, and particularly the emphasis he places on the function of **surveillance**, have proven influential in educational theory. In contemporary culture surveillance does not simply refer to the ubiquitous surveillance camera, but also to the way we are in various ways encouraged to observe and discipline ourselves and others. Many have linked these ideas to the cultural significance placed on achieving educational qualifications, the importance of measuring success, the emphasis on self-assessment, and the compilation of *portfolios of evidence and learning journals, as well as the stigmatization and consequences of not gaining qualifications. *See also* IDEOLOGY. C.H.

foundation course An introductory course, or one at a basic level, designed for beginners who are unfamiliar with, and lack the 'foundations' of, a subject. Students may take a foundation course as a first step in their progression to more advanced qualifications. In the vocabulary of the *National Qualifications Framework, 'foundation' has a measurable meaning in terms of level, and refers to the most elementary, or 'entry', level of *National Vocational Qualification, a level below that at which most trainees will commence their training. In the context of the *Open University, too, 'foundation course' has a very specific meaning, in this case referring to the first, more general, stage of studies which some students undertake before going on to focus on their chosen degree subject.

foundation degree A two-year degree course, usually taught in *university or a *college of further or higher education, and focusing on a vocationally related area of study. Introduced in 2001, this degree can be awarded in the arts (Foundation Degree Arts, FDA), the Sciences (Fd.Sc.), or in specific vocational fields such as law (FDL) or engineering (FDE). Further education providers offer foundation degrees in partnership with a university or other institution of *higher education; and successful students can go on to 'top up' their qualification by additional study in higher education to achieve an *honours degree. The foundation degree was introduced primarily as an additional means of building a more highly skilled workforce, and its implementation has involved cooperation between employers, trainers, and professional bodies, as well as colleges and higher education institutions. It was designed to recruit primarily from those in the 20–30 age group of the population who have not engaged with higher education through more traditional routes.

Foundation Phase A rolling implementation programme to introduce a new and uniquely Welsh foundation phase for 3–7-year-olds with the emphasis on learning through well-structured play, practical activity, and investigation. Pilot schemes were conducted in 42 maintained and non-maintained settings across Wales, with piloting and evaluation to be completed before September 2010.

H.G.

foundation school A school which has ownership over its own premises. Foundation status became an option for schools from 2001. For some schools it presented an alternative route to some degree of independence from *local authority control at a time when *grant maintained status became discontinued since it enables schools to operate with a high degree of autonomy in the implementation of admissions procedures and the recruitment and appointment of teaching staff. *See also* CITY ACADEMY.

Foundation Stage Superseded in September 2008 by the revised *Early Years Foundation Stage for 0–5-year-olds, the original Foundation Stage of education in England began when children reached the age of 3 and continued until they left their *reception class at age 5+. The last year of the Foundation Stage is often described as the reception year, since most children in England are admitted to the reception class of an *infant or *primary school at some point during that year. Like its successor, the Foundation Stage was a distinct *curriculum stage, important in its own right, operating in close partnership with parents and carers, and guided by a set of pedagogic principles appropriate to the age of the children. It prepared children for learning in *Key Stage 1 (5–7-year-olds) and was consistent with the *national curriculum areas of study. Again like its successor, the original Foundation Stage aimed to develop key learning skills such as listening, speaking, concentration, persistence, and learning to work with other children. The QCA's *Curriculum Guidance for the Foundation Stage* described stepping stones to show the knowledge, skills, understanding, and attitudes that children needed to learn during this period to meet the early learning goals which they should achieve by the end of the Foundation Stage. Documentation supported teachers to plan for and teach an appropriate curriculum for six learning areas: personal and social education; communication, language, and literacy; mathematical development; knowledge and understanding of the world; physical development; and creative development. Teachers monitored and recorded achievement on a child's *Foundation Stage profile.

Its replacement, the Early Years Foundation Stage, incorporating the *Sure Start *Birth to Three Matters guidance, now presents a seamless 0–5 curriculum for young children in England, and continues the Foundation Stage's emphasis on a partnership with parents or carers as children's first and most enduring educators.

Further Reading: QCA *Curriculum Guidance for the Foundation Stage* (London, May 2000).

SEE WEB LINKS

- Sets out changes to curriculum guidance.

A.W.

Foundation Stage profile A record of children's development across the six areas of learning in the *Early Years Foundation Stage which is completed at the end of the *reception year in English *primary schools, or in any government-funded setting where children complete the 0–5 stage of their education.

Achievement is recorded on thirteen assessment scales derived from the stepping stones and early learning goals.

SEE WEB LINKS

- Checklists for assessment.

A.W.

foundation subjects *National curriculum subjects which are compulsory and form the core of the curriculum. In all *key stages these include English, mathematics, and science; in Key Stages 3–4 they also include technology, physical education, and a modern foreign language; and in Key Stages 1–3, history, geography, art, and music. In Wales, Welsh is an additional foundation subject in all *maintained schools.

14–19 agenda The focus on the development and implementation of education provision for 14–19-year-olds in the UK in the first decade of the 21st century. Following the final report in 2004 of the committee chaired by Mike *Tomlinson, which proposed a radical reform of qualifications for students at *Key Stage 4 and in 16–19 education, the government published the *White Paper *14–19 Education and Skills* in February 2005. This White Paper, and its accompanying implementation plan, identified several proposals aimed at 'improving choice, improving chances', with the accent on enhancing employability. These included a commitment to raising the levels of skills in English and mathematics; the development and ensured local provision of vocational *diplomas which would replace the hundreds of individual qualifications offered by *awarding bodies and would—alongside *General Certificate of Education *Advanced Levels—allow progression to *higher education as well as to employment; the ability for candidates to achieve qualifications at the appropriate level for their ability rather than their age, with the intention of encouraging providers to challenge individual students; and a more robustly supported approach to disengaged students. The goal is that, by 2015, 90 per cent of 17-year-olds will still be working towards qualifications at levels 2 and 3 on the *National Qualifications Framework, in comparison with 76 per cent in 2006.

A distinctive Welsh programme is in place in Wales to provide structured learning pathways tailored to individuals, designed to motivate and enthuse young people, balanced by real-life learning experiences and opportunities to develop essential skills. This programme is linked with the *Welsh Baccalaureate qualification and began as a pilot in September 2004. The programme is supported by the **Learning Coaches Scheme**, whereby students are given guidance by adults trained to help with the development of study skills and to make choices which reflect the aptitude and potential of the individual learners. *See also* ENTRY TO EMPLOYMENT; FUNCTIONAL SKILLS; SKILLS AGENDA; YOUNG APPRENTICESHIP.

SEE WEB LINKS

- Provides a list setting out the timetable for 14–19 reforms.

V.C., K.A.

14–19 Curriculum and Qualifications Reform *See* TOMLINSON REPORT (2004).

14–19 Diploma A qualification for 14–19-year-olds, introduced in 2008, to run alongside the *General Certificate of Secondary Education and the *General

Certificate of Education *Advanced Level. The Diploma combines theoretical and practical learning, and is aimed at young people of all ability levels. It consists of four main components: 'principal learning' with a focus on a specific sector of employment; 'generic learning', which includes functional skills in literacy, mathematics, and information technology; 'additional or specialist learning', which offers either breadth or depth of study in a particular topic; and *work experience, which relates to their 'principal learning' focus. The first Diplomas to be introduced (2008/11) are in engineering, construction, and the built environment; information technology; society, health, and development; and creative media. They constitute part of a wider reform of education for 14–19-year-olds discussed in the 2005 *White Paper *14–19 Education and Skills*, which sets the target that all young people should possess functional skills in English and mathematics by the time they leave school. It is interesting to compare the purpose and role of the Diploma with those attributed to the *General National Vocational Qualification when it was introduced in 1992.

SEE WEB LINKS

- Gives the full text of the White Paper which introduced the Diploma.

Freire, Paulo (1921–97) An international educationalist based in Brazil, Paulo Freire's philosophy grew from his experiences of teaching adult literacy to the underprivileged poor of Latin America. Freire called for a change from more formal, teacher-controlled education to that constructed by the learners themselves. In his seminal work *Pedagogy of the Oppressed* (1970) he used the phrase 'the banking concept' to describe formal education, which he felt restricted teachers to delivering a curriculum highly prescribed by those with governmental power. In contrast, Freire sought to develop an awareness among underprivileged learners that they should consider their social and cultural backgrounds as the starting point for their literacy learning, with the intended outcome that they would recognize ways they could transform their learning and their lives for themselves. Although his original focus was on adults and the oppressed, the outcomes of his writing and the subsequent influence have extended well beyond this. Because of the political implications of his approach he is classed as a *radical educator.

Further Reading: P. Freire *The Pedagogy of the Oppressed* (1970; Penguin, 1972). V.C., K.A.

Fresh Start Schools judged by *Ofsted to be *failing schools, and which subsequently fail to meet their two-year targets, may, as an alternative to permanent closure, be permitted a Fresh Start under a new name and a new *head teacher. The Fresh Start schools programme was initiated in the academic year 1998/9. Despite initial positive publicity about *'superheads' achieving notable results in terms of pupil motivation and behaviour, the Fresh Start strategy was, in the longer term, judged by some heads to have raised unrealistic expectations of what could be achieved by a change of school leadership, particularly in those schools which drew their pupils from areas of social deprivation.

Froebel, Friedrich (1782–1852) A German educator and originator of the *kindergarten, who argued that young pupils should not be constrained by a formal, regimented curriculum structured according to specific age groups. Instead, he advocated that pupils be provided with the opportunity to develop as individuals, and not be subjected to *rote learning. His philosophy of teaching and learning underpinned provision in **Froebel schools**, of which the first in England was established in 1851; and in 1892 the **Froebel Educational Institution** for the training of teachers was opened in London. Froebel's approach to education continues to inform much of *pre-school and *early years provision in Great Britain.

full-time equivalent (FTE) A measurement used in the calculation of teaching-related resource needs in *further and *higher education, where a proportion of students are enrolled on a part-time basis. For example, two part-time students attending for 50 per cent of a full-time timetable may be deemed to be the equivalent of one full-time student in terms of teacher contact hours, or in terms of their required attendance in hours or days. This makes it possible to calculate the total number of students enrolled in terms of full-time places or their equivalent, an important calculation in terms of institutions' levels of external funding.

functional literacy The level of literacy necessary to cope with the demands of everyday adult life, and to function effectively both socially and in the workplace. While difficult to define in absolute or universal terms, national levels of functional literacy have been a subject of concern in a number of *White Papers, which have raised the issue of pupils leaving compulsory education without having acquired the literacy skills necessary to secure employment or to contribute fully to society and to the economy. Part of the reason for the introduction of *key skills across the 16–19 curriculum in 2000 was to address this problem by providing continued support in literacy skills beyond the age of 16. *See also* BASIC SKILLS.

functional skills Qualifications in English, mathematics, and *information communications technology (ICT) in the UK, which are available from entry level to level 2 on the *National Qualifications Framework. The introduction of the new **Functional Skills awards** was announced as part of the *14–19 Education and Skills* White Paper of 2005. They are being developed for all learners aged 14+ to strengthen the practical skills necessary for employment, and for access to further and higher education. They will build on the *literacy and *numeracy strategies at primary schools as well as the secondary school *Key Stage 3 strategy, and will be a mandatory component of all learning programmes at *Key Stage 4 and beyond. It is expected that functional skills will replace *key skills and *Skills for Life qualifications. Following national trials, English and ICT functional skills awards will be available in 2009, and mathematics in 2010. V.C., K.A.

Further and Higher Education Act 1992 Approved by Parliament in March 1992, this piece of legislation marked a turning point in the provision of *post-compulsory education. It was an enactment of the proposals set out in the 1991 *White Paper *Education and Training for the 21st Century*, one of the most far-reaching of which was that colleges of *further education, *sixth form colleges, and *tertiary colleges were to be removed from the control of *local education authorities (LEAs). The colleges were now to be funded through the *Further Education Funding Councils, of which there was one for England and one for Wales. This transformation of the further education colleges into corporate bodies became known as incorporation, and brought about major changes in the employment conditions of lecturers in further education, which had hitherto been set out in the *Silver Book. Existing lecturers were required to sign new contracts involving them in longer hours and shorter holidays in return for progression in pay. Those who were unwilling to relinquish their original conditions of service remained on the old pay scale with their salaries frozen. All new appointments were made under the revised terms and conditions. This matter of contracts caused widespread discontent among lecturers in the sector, and a deterioration in the relationship between lecturers and senior management. Incorporation also marked the real beginning of a quasi-*market in further education, as colleges whose provision had previously been managed and agreed strategically under the aegis of the LEAs began to operate as individual corporate organizations. Competition for students often involved offering courses and qualifications which duplicated provision in neighbouring colleges and sixth forms. The necessity to compete in a crowded market created a situation in which stronger (larger, better resourced, or more entrepreneurial) colleges thrived at the expense of others which were less favoured by the market, which inevitably led to some college closures and mergers in the years following this legislation. Moreover, by allowing schools to bring an element of *vocational education into the *post-16 curriculum with the introduction of *General National Vocational Qualifications (GNVQs), the Act was also responsible for creating further competition between schools and colleges for attracting or retaining pupils at 16. Many 11–16 schools used the introduction of GNVQs as an opportunity to open vocational sixth forms, thereby enabling them to retain pupils after *Key Stage 4 who would otherwise have gone on to further education college or joined the sixth form of a neighbouring 11–18 school. In a number of ways, therefore, the Act was responsible for pushing the secondary and tertiary sectors of education firmly into the world of competition and market forces, with the declared purpose of raising standards of provision. In a similar vein, it also brought about a reform of the careers advisory service by requiring *local authorities to put this service out to tender.

In terms of higher education, the Act abolished the *binary system (or binary divide), allowing *polytechnics to assume the title of 'university', and introducing the *Higher Education Funding Council, with separate councils to fund higher education in Scotland and Wales. The Act encouraged the implementation of an alternative, vocational route at 16—a route described as having *parity of esteem with *General Certificate of Education *Advanced Levels—and at the same time an expansion in higher education provision. In this way it ensured a *progression route for students wishing to use their GNVQs to gain entry to university.

Further and Higher Education (Scotland) Act 1992 This Act reviewed Scottish Further and Higher Education. Its main proposal was the creation of a new funding agency, the **Scottish Higher and Further Education Funding Council**, thus creating a single body to oversee strategic developments at both higher and further education levels. S.M.

further education (FE) A sector which encompasses all *post-compulsory education and training, with the exception of *higher education. Although a semantic distinction is made between further and *adult education, FE in its broadest terms encompasses this, too. The terminology for the sector has been subject to a number of recent developments, particularly in government policy documents, which refer to it variously as the skills sector, the *lifelong learning sector, the learning and skills sector (although this does not apply in Scotland), and the post-compulsory education sector. It is associated with *vocational education and skills training, which, following the *Foster Report (2005), has been confirmed as the primary focus of further education *colleges. Traditionally, however, it has been widely regarded as the 'sector of the second chance', providing an opportunity for learners who have not succeeded within the school system to re-engage with their education, including preparing for public examinations such as the *General Certificate of Education *Advanced Level at colleges of further education. Referred to as the 'Cinderella sector' by Kenneth Baker when Secretary of State for Education in the 1980s, it has often been regarded as a relatively low-status provision in comparison with sixth forms on the one hand and *higher education on the other, largely because of its association with vocational skills training. Three decades later, in the Foster Report, it is referred to as a 'middle child', a metaphor which suggests that as a sector it still remains to some extent undervalued.

Further Education Development Agency (FEDA) Established in 1994 as a result of the amalgamation between the *Further Education Unit and the Further Education Staff College, FEDA's role was to support research into further education and to provide advice on curriculum, management, and pedagogic matters. It was renamed the *Learning and Skills Development Agency in 2001 when the *Learning and Skills Council took over the management of funding for *further education.

Further Education Funding Council (FEFC) Established under the 1992 *Further and Higher Education Act to take over responsibility for the funding and inspection of further education colleges from *local authorities. *Colleges and other training organizations in the skills sector were required to submit bids to the FEFC for the funding of vocationally related courses. Although some *adult education remained under the financial control of the local authorities, the FEFC managed funding for all other provision in the sector, and specifically that related to vocational education and training. It operated its own inspectorate, responsible for carrying out full inspections of further education colleges. In 2001 the *Learning and Skills Council took over many of the responsibilities of the FEFC, and the inspection of non-adult provision became part of the remit of *Ofsted.

Further Education National Training Organization (FENTO) A national training organization set up to develop national standards for the initial and in-service training and qualification of teachers in the *further education sector. The standards reflected the targets set in the 1998 *Green Paper *The Learning Age*, that all those teaching full-time or substantial part-time hours in *colleges of further education should undertake a professional teaching qualification, as a means of improving standards of provision and student attainment in the sector. Funded initially for three years by the Department of Employment, FENTO subsequently became self-financing. The standards developed were known as the **FENTO Standards** and were published in 1999. From 2001 all teacher training programmes and awards for the sector, provided by universities, colleges, and national awarding bodies, were required to be endorsed by FENTO as conforming to the standards. The model of professional development presented by the standards consisted of three stages: Introductory, Intermediate, and Certification, which related not to the length but to the breadth of the teacher's professional experience. The work of FENTO was taken over in 2005 by *Lifelong Learning UK and its verification arm, *Standards and Verification UK, and revised professional standards were developed for the sector. *See also* QUALIFIED TEACHER LEARNING AND SKILLS.

Further Education Unit (FEU) Between 1977 and 1994 the FEU advised on, and supported research into, *curriculum and pedagogical matters relating to *further education. Funded by, and originally located within, the Department of Education and Science, it became an independent agency in 1992, shortly before being renamed and redefined as the Further Education Development Agency in 1994.

Gaelic schools Education in Gaelic is available in around 60 Scottish primary schools, the majority of which are located in the Highlands and Islands of Scotland. As Scotland's longest-established language, Gaelic features in both primary and secondary schools to a varying degree, both as a subject and as a teaching language in class, and there are separate qualifications and examination courses available in this language. *See also* SCOTLAND, EDUCATION IN. S.M.

games 1. An alternative terminology for physical education which forms part of the curriculum of compulsory education, and is sometimes referred to as 'organized games'.

2. A *method of teaching which involves an element of simulation or competition, and which may be used to encourage learners to engage more actively with the area of study. These learner activities can take simple form such as word games, or may be complex and extend over several lessons or periods of study if they take the form of simulations with learners playing allotted roles. Computer games, too, can be used as learning tools. Although they have the advantage of making learning vivid and engaging, games can have the disadvantage of being time-consuming when compared to more traditional teaching methods such as exposition. They tend, therefore to be used rather less frequently than alternative methods, particularly when the curriculum is full and time-constrained. A further disadvantage is the danger that learners will view such activities as entertainment and fail to recognize the *objective or intended learning outcome. When incorporating games into their *lesson plan, therefore, teachers have to ensure that the purpose of the activity is explained clearly to the learners and is followed by a discussion or plenary in which the learning outcomes are discussed and clarified.

SEE WEB LINKS

- Provides details of computer games used for learning.

Gardner, Howard *See* MULTIPLE INTELLIGENCE.

gender A term used to differentiate between males and females resulting from social and cultural influences as opposed to purely biological ones. Increasingly the use of the term is taken to be inclusive of issues that relate especially to boys and men as well as to those which relate mostly to girls and women. Theories of gender range through those which: emphasize cultural conditioning (liberal feminism), take a psychoanalytic stance, stress large-scale power relations in society (socialist or Marxist feminism), or draw attention to discursive relations (postmodern and poststructuralist approaches). The phrase 'doing gender' is becoming more common. It refers to a conception of gender as learned through performance and which helps to constitute personal identity. Since the 1980s the realization that gender always intersects with race, religion, *social class, and so on has led to an understanding that it is more appropriate to talk of femininities and masculinities rather than a unitary femininity or masculinity. However, there remain dominant conceptions of both, which are reinforced in educational institutions, partly through the elision of sex, gender, and sexuality. This is one function of playground insults which refer to sexuality. For many young people, 'gay', for instance, is widely perceived as a term of abuse, even by those who have no particular prejudice against lesbian, gay, or bisexual people.

There is a wide range of issues in education which are gender-related. They apply not only to students, but also to everyone else involved, including teachers, governors, and policy-makers. Furthermore, they apply to the structures of education, within and outwith schools, universities, and colleges. They also apply to policy at local and national level. Policy has an influence on educational structures and gender relations. Some policy is intended to influence gender reform directly. Finally, informal as well as formal education is accessed and experienced differently by males and females.

Gender is a special case of *social justice and so is directly related to equality of outcome, equality of opportunity, and the formation of identity in education. Gender is often specifically addressed in equal opportunities policies to be found in schools, colleges, and universities. Areas where issues of equality of opportunity arise include those of *curriculum, *pedagogy, and *assessment.

It has become rare for girls or boys to be formally excluded from particular areas of the curriculum. However, subject choice at school and later is still strongly correlated with gender. Post-16, males predominate in physics, technology, and sport, while females are over-represented in biology, languages, and the humanities. As students are increasingly expected to make choices earlier in their educational careers, these differences are intensifying and have consequences for available employment. Currently 60 per cent of working women are clustered in 10 per cent of occupations. The hidden curriculum is also inflected by gender. Attitudes and aspirations are differentiated by gender, with girls generally expecting to work harder but having fewer career aspirations—but, of course, this is strongly mediated by social class.

Pedagogies appear to be gender-differentiated, although, as with everything else, they also depend on other markers of difference such as social class and ethnic heritage. For instance, research shows that boys tend to prefer more competitive and individualist ways of learning while girls tend to prefer more collaborative, cooperative methods. The difference in preferred pedagogy is particularly evident for some subject areas. There is evidence that girls prefer science to be related to the everyday and that the role of speaking and listening is highly significant in raising boys' literacy. Assessment strategies are similarly gender-differentiated, with boys excelling in end-of-session *examinations and girls shining in *coursework and *continuing assessment. It must be emphasized that these are generalizations which hide large variations. Many middle-class boys excel in every area and by every means, and many working-class girls underachieve whatever the subject and however assessed.

Equality of outcome has become a hot issue for schools. Both boys and girls continue to improve in their performance as measured by national tests.

However, the girls, in general, now outperform the boys at all levels, especially in literacy, although less so in physics and chemistry. This underachievement of boys has caused widespread concern in the press and in policy circles.

Gender issues affect teachers as strongly as students. There has been much concern expressed about the alleged feminization of teaching, even though the proportion of women teachers has changed only slowly over decades. Men are still over-represented in senior positions in schools, colleges, and universities. Even where there are senior women, management styles are increasingly masculine as a result of the intensification of work and the stress on *performativity found in all sectors of the education system.

Educational *research has identified a number of underlying gender issues, especially those related to personal identity. The significance of motherhood and the ways it intersects with teaching is one such issue. Another is citizenship, where the traditional model of a good citizen has been male. The current emphasis on the significance of parental involvement in schools is another area where there are gender issues, since the 'parent' is often tacitly assumed to be a mother. *See also* INCLUSION. M.G.

General Certificate of Education (GCE) In 1951 two levels of public examinations were introduced: the GCE *Ordinary Level and the GCE *Advanced Level (A level). The former was designed as a school-leaving examination to replace the *School Certificate. It remained in place through the *raising of the school-leaving age to 16, until it was replaced in turn by the *General Certificate of Secondary Education in 1988. The GCE A level, however, remains the 'gold standard' examination for 18-year-old school-leavers, and still fulfils its original purpose as a preparation, and a means of selection, for university and other types of *higher education, although it now constitutes one of several routes into higher education for 18- and 19-year-olds since the introduction of *Vocational A Levels and *diplomas.

General Certificate of Secondary Education (GCSE) Introduced in 1988 to replace both the *General Certificate of Education *Ordinary Level and the *Certificate of Secondary Education with one unified examination syllabus. Nevertheless, the GCSE still offered the opportunity for *differentiation by task through the introduction of *tiering. The regulations also allowed for GCSE candidates to be assessed in all subjects through a combination of *coursework and end *examination. Pupils' assessment at GCSE marks the culmination of their *Key Stage 4 studies. The grading criteria and syllabus now conform with *national curriculum level descriptors and *programmes of study in each subject area. There are eight pass grades awarded, from A* to G, each carrying a number of points which are used in the presentation of secondary schools' performance tables. GCSE short courses cover 50 per cent of the syllabus content and carry 50 per cent of the points. For pupils studying a combination of full and short GCSEs and Applied GCSEs, or *14–19 Diplomas in Key Stage 4, the common points system can be used to calculate their accumulated points score.

SEE WEB LINKS

- Provides tables showing how points are calculated for GCSE attainment and equivalent.

general education An education designed to support the development of the learner as an individual, rather than to equip him or her with specific, vocationally related skills. In this sense, a general education may be defined as developmental rather than instrumental. It is a term which is often used in differentiating an academic route, such as that represented by *General Certificate of Secondary Education and *Advanced Level, from a *vocational route, for example through the various levels of *National Vocational Qualifications. A general education may be described as 'broad', in contrast with the acquisition of narrowly focused skills for work. For historical reasons, a general education still tends to be accorded a higher status in some quarters than a vocational education or training. The *14–19 Diploma and the Applied GCSE, while designed to have a broad vocational focus, are nevertheless often presented as consistent with a general education curriculum, perhaps in the same sense that led to the choice of name for the *General National Vocational Qualification (1992–2007), suggesting that, while the contexts used are vocational, the skills and understanding developed, such as *literacy, *numeracy, analysis, and synthesis, are transferable and general. *See also* LIBERAL EDUCATION; PARITY OF ESTEEM; TAUNTON REPORT.

General National Vocational Qualification (GNVQ) Introduced in 1992 to provide a third qualification route which bridged the gap between the *academic or *general education provided by the *General Certificate of Secondary Education (GCSE) and *General Certificate of Education *Advanced Level route in schools, and the vocationally specific training provided by *National Vocational Qualifications (NVQs) in *further education. Introduced initially in the 1991 *White Paper *Education and Training for the 21st Century*, GNVQs were intended to be taught in schools and to cover 'broad occupational areas'. Their introduction, according to the White Paper, had a number of purposes. They were to provide an alternative route to both employment and *higher education; to allow progression to and from NVQs; and to 'be of equal status with academic qualifications'. This last point proved difficult to achieve, despite repeated government claims about *parity of esteem. Nevertheless, within two years of its introduction the GNVQ was being offered at *Foundation, Intermediate, and Advanced Level in five broad occupational areas in many schools and colleges. Intermediate Level was taken to be broadly equivalent to four good GCSEs, while the Advanced Level was, for the purposes of progression to higher education, accorded equivalence with two A Levels. At all levels *assessment was initially by *continuous assessment. This in itself created some difficulties in establishing the status of the Advanced award; and over time the assessment regime was developed to include more rigorous external assessment and testing. Candidates succeeded in gaining university places through the GNVQ route, and one of the strengths of its curriculum—the inclusion of *key skills—was later (2000) extended to all 16–19 provision. In 1999–2000 Advanced GNVQs were restructured to increase their compatibility with modular A Levels and, as part of the *Curriculum 2000 reforms, became known as *Vocational Advanced Levels. Foundation and Intermediate GNVQs remained an optional component of the Key Stage 4 curriculum in schools, and were included in the calculation of pupil attainment points. Their withdrawal was announced by the *Qualifications and Curriculum Authority in November 2003, and they were phased out between 2005 and 2007, to be replaced by successor qualifications, again with a broad vocational focus, such as National Certificates, National Diplomas, and Applied GCSEs, developed and regulated by the same unitary *awarding bodies which were previously responsible for awarding GNVQs.

general studies 1. A *General Certificate of Education *Advanced Level (A level) and *Advanced Subsidiary Level subject which was originally designed to introduce breadth into A level studies, particularly for candidates taking exclusively science subjects. It requires the candidate to demonstrate an appropriate level of literacy and fluency in their written English as well as an ability to give informed consideration to a range of topics, including current affairs.

2. An alternative title for the programme of *liberal studies which formed part of the curriculum for vocational students in *further education in the 1960s and 1970s.

General Teaching Council (GTC) There are separate Councils for the four principalities of the United Kingdom. The purpose of each Council is to monitor professional standards of teachers, and to establish a code of conduct, to be enforced through a disciplinary committee. The Council for Scotland (GTCS) has been in existence since 1965, and was one of the first teaching councils in the world. It has wider powers than the other three, including the power of approval for programmes of teacher education and training. Its 50 members including elected teachers, appointed representatives of *local authorities, and those nominated by Scottish government ministers to represent the interests of parents, employers, and teachers of children with special educational needs. The Council for England (GTCE) was founded in 1999 following the **Teaching and Higher Education Act 1998**, and has been active since 2000. Of its 64 members, nine are teachers appointed by and representing teaching unions; sixteen are appointees from other relevant bodies; thirteen are nominees of the *Secretary of State for Education and Skills; and one is appointed by the Commission for Equality and Human Rights. In addition, there is a chair of council.

A Council for Wales (GTCW) was set up in the same year, with 25 members and a chair. In Wales teacher representation is proportionately higher than in England, with twelve elected teachers, nine nominees of teaching unions appointed by the National Assembly for Wales, and four direct appointees of the Assembly. All qualified teachers in the state sector must be registered with the Council, which is responsible for investigating and hearing cases of misconduct or incompetence. The Council advises the Assembly on policy in relation to teaching issues such as *continuing professional development, recruitment, retention, and supply. It also administers funding programmes for the Welsh Assembly to meet the professional development needs of teachers.

A Council for Northern Ireland (GTCNI) was set up in 2002. It has 33 members, of whom fourteen are teachers elected by the profession. Five members are nominated by the Northern Ireland Teaching Council, ten by other stakeholders such as employers and *higher education, and four are appointed by the *Department of Education for Northern Ireland.

SEE WEB LINKS

- A detailed description of the GTCE's role and function.
- A detailed description of the GTCS's origins and purpose.
- A summary of the GTCNI's activities.
- A summary of the GTCW's purpose and functions.

generic criteria Criteria for *assessment which apply across a range of subjects, topics, or assignments, and which are related to the level of study rather than to its content. For example, students' work which is being assessed at *master's level will be assessed against criteria specific to their focus of study, but also against the generic criteria which are applicable to all master's level study, such as the ability to cite and reference sources correctly.

Gestalt A theory of learning based on the idea that the teacher should view the student's experience of learning as a whole, rather than as the sum of a series of stimuli; and that the learner achieves understanding by a process of reorganization of their existing ideas, thereby discovering how one fact might relate to another, or how gaps in their pattern of understanding might be filled. The word itself is German, and means a perceptual pattern or configuration which cannot adequately be described in terms of its component parts but must be perceived as a whole. Gestalt psychology was to some extent a reaction against the *behaviourists and neo-behaviourist definitions of learning. A key figure was Kurt Koffka (1886–1941), who taught for most of his career in the United States of America. Like other Gestaltists, he argued that during learning the human mind goes through a process of drawing on previous experience in order to reorganize its perceptions, a process which is infinitely more complicated than a series of stimulus–response interactions. The idea of wholeness is implicit both in the way the learning process is construed and as a significant event when learning leads to insight and the learner suddenly perceives 'the whole picture'. This theory of learning reminds teachers to encourage learners to make their own connections and discoveries in order to find solutions to the questions they are exploring. In this sense it contrasts sharply with approaches based on *rote learning.

Further Reading: K. Koffka *The Growth of the Mind* (Transaction, 1980) presents the Gestaltist argument against a behaviourist approach to child psychology and the process of learning.

gifted and talented A term applied to pupils who have abilities which are developed to a level significantly above that of their year group, or who are judged to have the potential to develop such abilities. It is recognized that such pupils need to be taught in a way and at a level that challenges them; and to be presented with tasks which stretch and motivate them. This understanding has been reflected in government education policy. A **Gifted and Talented Programme** was introduced in 2000 as part of the *Excellence in Cities initiative; and was applied initially in 495 secondary schools and with older children in 400 primary schools. In 2002 a National Academy for Gifted and Talented Youth was established for 11–16-year-old pupils. Based at Warwick University, it follows a similar model to that used in provision for talented children in America. In 2005 the *White Paper *Higher Standards: Better Schools for All* set out the aim that every pupil should have the right to a *personalized curriculum designed to enable them to reach the full potential of their ability. In the case of gifted and talented pupils, this implies not only greater challenge within the classroom, but also the provision of opportunities to develop their abilities and talents further outside school at a local and national level. The same 2005 White Paper also required that every secondary school and every cluster of primary schools has a trained leading teacher for gifted and talented education; and was instrumental in the setting up of a National Register to improve the identification and tracking of gifted and talented pupils' attainment and performance. Regional Partnerships work collaboratively with schools to improve overall provision for gifted and talented learners through self-evaluation. Schools are able to evaluate their own provision for gifted and talented pupils by measuring their provision and practices against the **National Quality Standards in Gifted and Talented Education**. I.F.W.

Gittins Report (1967) Published under the title *Primary Education in Wales*, the Report presented the findings of an examination into *primary education in Wales and of the *transition of pupils to the secondary phase. Like the *Plowden Report, it argued for a system of *first and *middle schools to help ease the difficulties of transition. It also argued for the inclusion of Welsh into the curriculum of all Welsh schools as either a first or second language. *See also* WALES, EDUCATION IN.

governors Since the *Education Act 1980 the law has required that all *maintained schools have a board of governors which represents parents and teachers as well as drawing membership from the local community and volunteers with appropriate management skills. The Education Act 1944 (*Butler Act) made it mandatory for the duties and responsibilities of schools' governing bodies to be defined in an instrument of government, and their role to be set out unequivocally in their articles of government. This was a means of clarifying the respective responsibilities and roles of the *head teacher, the *local authority, and the governing body itself. Training for governors is not compulsory, but governors are strongly encouraged to take advantage of the **National Strategy for Training and Support**, which provides a national training programme for new governors, as well as training for chairs and clerks to the board. Governing bodies are encouraged to provide induction training for new members.

Governors are responsible for ensuring that the school provides an adequate quality of education and that standards of attainment within the school are maintained and, if necessary, raised. They are responsible for the selection of the *head teacher, together with whom they define the school's aims and policies. They are responsible to parents, to the wider community, and to funding bodies for the school's performance; they make decisions about the school's budget and staffing; they are responsible for ensuring that the *national curriculum is taught, and for deciding ways in which the school will encourage pupils' spiritual, moral, and social development.

The number of governors on a school's governing body varies according to the size of the school. Membership may include representation from community and business interests, the Church, and charitable trusts, as well as from parents and from teachers at the school. Membership is normally for four years. In the case of *special schools, the governing body may include representation from health authorities and from relevant voluntary or charitable organizations.

SEE WEB LINKS

- Provides details of governor training.

grade The category of mark awarded in the *assessment of a candidate's performance. This may constitute part of a *continuous assessment or represent the result of a final assessment such as an *examination. Grade categories may be descriptors, such as pass, *credit, or distinction; or they may be referred to by letter, as in the *General Certificate of Secondary Education (GCSE) grading system; or by numerical category, as in the case of *bachelor's degrees. Normally, each grade occupies a range of percentage marks, and therefore the grade awarded is based on the percentage mark achieved. It is usual for the assessor to refer to *grading criteria, in the form of **grade descriptors**, for guidance in coming to an assessment decision.

Often, and particularly in GCSEs and *General Certificate of Education *Advanced Level, the grade achieved may be crucial to the candidate's progression to the next stage of their education. In some cases, where the grade awarded in these public examinations falls significantly below that predicted by the candidate's school or college, a **grade review** may be requested, which involves the double-checking of the examination result in question.

grading criteria Descriptors setting out in detail what a candidate must achieve in order to be awarded a specific *grade. These are drawn up for the benefit both of the candidate themselves, who is thereby provided with a clear guidance on what must be achieved in order to attain the required grade, and of the assessor, for whom they provide a means of making an accurate and reliable *assessment decision.

graduate The term may be used as a noun, indicating someone who has successfully completed their *undergraduate studies and been awarded a *bachelor's degree; or as a verb, indicating the achievement of that graduate status, as in 'She graduated last week'. It may also be used as an adjective, in describing the level of study undertaken, as in 'Since she graduated she has enrolled on a graduate course in education studies'. *See also* GRADUATION.

graduated approach Students who do not make adequate progress may be identified as having *special educational needs (SEN). The student is placed on the school SEN register. This should be done with the knowledge and agreement of parents and the child. There are varying levels of intervention which can be implemented. A graduated approach to intervention enables a wide range of strategies to be applied to the diverse needs on the SEN continuum. School-based interventions are known as School Action and School Action Plus. At School Action teachers identify students who need support that is different from, and in addition to, the normal strategies for differentiation and support already in place. A lack of adequate progress might trigger the input from other professionals, and at this stage the student moves to School Action Plus on the register. If students still do not make adequate progress after having had interventions at both these stages, it may be necessary to request a statutory assessment, which may or may not result in a *statement of special educational needs being issued.

Further Reading: Department for Education and Skills *Code of Practice for Special Educational Needs (Revised)* DfES/581/2001 (DfES, 2001). T.B., L.E.

Graduate Teacher Programme (GTP) A programme of teacher training which allows *graduate trainee teachers to gain their teaching qualification while working in schools. Although originally aimed at mature entrants to the profession, age discrimination legislation prevents recruitment on this criterion alone. The training takes between three months and a full academic year to complete. The programme can be undertaken in any *maintained school in England or Wales (other than schools in *special measures and *pupil referral units) which is prepared to employ the trainee as an unqualified teacher. Applicants are required to hold *General Certificate of Secondary Education qualifications in English and mathematics at grade C or above (or the equivalent), as well as a recognized degree. *See also* QUALIFIED TEACHER STATUS.

SEE WEB LINKS

- Provides details of conditions and entry procedures.

Graduate Teacher Training Registry (GTTR) Graduate applicants for initial teacher training, and those in the final year of their undergraduate studies, register with the GTTR as part of their application process for a place on a *Professional Graduate Certificate of Education programme. They list in order of preference a choice of higher education institutions where they wish to undertake their training, and these applications are then processed by the GTTR, just as the *Universities and Colleges Admissions Service (UCAS) processes applications for undergraduate courses. Indeed, the GTTR is now a part of UCAS, but continues to operate separately as a vehicle for *initial teacher training applications.

graduation The gaining of *graduate status through successful completion of undergraduate studies. This is usually marked by a **graduation ceremony**, attended by dignitaries of the awarding institution as well as by the graduates and their families and friends. This provides a formal occasion for the awarding of certificates and other honours, and the event itself is often referred to in brief as a 'graduation'. The term has been taken up and used in a wider context, so that now we may speak of pupils 'graduating' from school, or from one phase of schooling to another. In all contexts it indicates the progression from one grade to a higher one.

grammar school Originally, a school which focused on an education in the classics, and specifically upon the grammar of Latin and Greek. Following the *Education Act 1944 (*Butler Act), *local authorities were empowered to set up secondary schools inspired by this model, and the name became attached to the selective schools in the *tripartite secondary system designed to cater for the needs of the most academic pupils. Selection of pupils was carried out at the end of *primary schooling through the *Eleven Plus examination, which was believed to identify the type of schooling most appropriate to each child. Those not selected for grammar schools were allocated places at a secondary modern school or, in some local authorities, a technical school. Following the

*Education Act 1976, the Eleven Plus was largely discontinued, except within those authorities with a strong Conservative council, such as Lincolnshire and Kent, where the policy of retaining their grammar and secondary modern schools was enabled to continue by the Education Act 1979, which made the abolition of selection optional rather than mandatory. In most of England, however, the selective system was gradually replaced by *comprehensive schools in the 1970s and 1980s; and by the early 1990s there were few grammar schools remaining. These do continue to exist, however, alongside secondary modern schools, in some local authorities, such as Lincolnshire.

grant maintained school (GMS) Schools which were allowed to opt out of *local authority control, under the provision of the *Education Reform Act 1988, and receive their funding directly from the Department for Education and Employment. They were part of a move by the government of the time to introduce *market forces into educational provision. As a result of the School Standards and Framework Act 1998, the option of **grant maintained status** was discontinued, and was replaced by the *foundation schools initiative in 2000.

Great Debate The ongoing debate about standards in education, which is widely held to have been launched in 1976 by James Callaghan, then Prime Minister, in a speech at Ruskin College, Oxford. In the speech, calling for a public debate on education, he drew attention to the need for school-leavers to possess the appropriate levels of literacy and numeracy required of them by employers. One of the consequences of the Ruskin speech was the publication of the *Green Paper *Education in Schools: A Consultative Document*, which was published later that same year. The eventual introduction of *key skills into the post-16 curriculum is often attributed in part to the concerns raised in the process of the Great Debate.

SEE WEB LINKS

- Review of the Great Debate and its developments since 1976.

Greats The title given to an undergraduate course of study in classical history, philosophy, and languages at Oxford University.

Green Paper A consultative or discussion document in which the government sets out its proposals for future policy for debate and discussion before a final policy decision is made. Like *White Papers, Green Papers are a type of command paper and may be the subject of statements or debates in the House of Commons. Following the consultation triggered by the Green Paper, the government normally publishes a White Paper setting out firmer recommendations.

Examples of recent key Green Papers relevant to education and children's welfare include the following:

1998 *The Learning Age* set out the proposal that all teachers in the further education sector should have, or be working towards, a recognized teaching qualification, and invited responses to this suggestion from relevant stakeholders

Meeting the Childcare Challenge

2001 *Schools: Building on Success*

2002	*14–19: Opportunity and Excellence*
2003	**Every Child Matters*
2005	*Parental Separation*
	Youth Matters
	Offender Learning
2006	*Care Matters*
2007	*Raising Expectations: Staying in Education and Training Post-16.*

group discussion A method of teaching and learning where learners discuss a given topic. This may be done as a whole group, led by the teacher; or may take the form of small-group discussion at the conclusion of which each group feeds back its ideas to the class as a whole.

g

group size *See* CLASS SIZE; PUPIL–TEACHER RATIO.

guidance In Scottish schools this is the term given to the personal support available to students set out in the **National Review of Guidance** (2004). All education authority secondary schools in Scotland have at least one principal teacher with responsibility for guidance. In primary and special schools this is a designated member of senior staff or management. This role may also encompass responsibility for *personal and social development. S.M.

half-term A holiday for *pupils, usually of a week's duration, in the middle of each *term of the school year. The summer half-term holiday usually coincides with the Whitsun bank holiday; the autumn half-term falls at the end of October; and the date of the spring half-term depends upon the length of that term and when Easter falls, but is usually sometime in February. While most schools have half-term holidays, they are less commonly found in further education, and not at all in universities.

hall of residence Living accommodation for students on or near the *campus of a university or college. A hall will usually contain a number of single or double rooms furnished to provide both sleeping accommodation and a desk at which to study. There is also normally a kitchen facility, although many halls also include a common dining room in which student meals are provided.

halo effect The tendency of *assessors to be influenced by their previous evaluation of a learner's standard of work when arriving at an assessment decision. Therefore, if a teacher has already come to the conclusion that a learner produces good (or poor) work, so the halo effect theory goes, the mark or grade they award, even though it might be in an unrelated subject, may be in danger of reflecting this prejudgement, rather than being based entirely on the standard of the actual work being assessed. This effect can also apply to their perception of learner behaviour, in line with the old saying 'Give a dog a bad name …'.

Hawthorne effect The tendency of learners to perform better when being closely observed by the teacher. The effect is so called because it derives from research into the performance of workers in an American factory bearing that name. Close observation by the teacher is clearly easier in some circumstances than others; for example, when *class sizes are smaller. In such a case, a question is inevitably raised for educational researchers about whether it is the close observation or in fact the *pupil–teacher ratio, or a combination of both, which accounts for the improvement in performance. *See also* MOTIVATION.

head of house A pastoral role in those secondary schools which operate a 'house' system. The teacher who is appointed head of house has pastoral responsibility for all pupils in that house, much as a *head of year has in schools which do not operate a house system. Perhaps the most famous heads of house currently are the fictional ones responsible for the pupils in the four houses at Hogwarts School in the *Harry Potter* books.

head of year In most secondary schools this is a pastoral role which also involves leading a team of year tutors and monitoring the progress of pupils within that year group. The head of year normally also has responsibility for liaising with parents and carers, and with other agencies, over issues relating to the welfare of pupils under their care. The post carries responsibility points which are reflected in the calculation of the post-holder's salary. *See also* HEAD OF HOUSE.

headship development The *National College for School Leadership took over responsibility for the professional development of *head teachers and aspiring head teachers from the Department of Education and Skills in 2001. For teachers aspiring to headship, such as *deputy heads and *assistant heads, it offers four programmes: The *National Professional Qualification for Headship (NPQH), the **Future Leaders Programme**, the **Trainee Headteacher Programme**, and the **Development Programme for Consultant Leadership**. For newly appointed head teachers in their first headship role there is a range of five programmes of professional development on various aspects of the head's role: **Early Headship Provision**, **New Visions, Safer Recruitment, Strategic Leadership of ICT**, and **London Leadership Strategy**. All of these are available also to experienced head teachers, in addition to programmes on school improvement and building schools for the future. Some universities and other higher education institutions accept evidence of successful completion of programmes such as the NPQH as grounds for accelerated entry onto *postgraduate programmes in education.

SEE WEB LINKS

- Provides access to details of all headship development programmes.

head teacher The senior leadership role in primary and secondary schools. Together with the governing body, the head teacher has responsibility for much of the management of the school, including, since the *Education Reform Act 1988, management of the school's budget. The role of head teacher has developed over the past quarter of a century from one largely concerned with leadership and curriculum issues, to one which focuses also on management, finance, and marketing. This development has been reflected and supported by the extensive provision of professional development programmes for headship. *See also* HEADSHIP DEVELOPMENT.

Her Majesty's Inspectorate (HMI) The Inspectorate was founded in the 19th century and its role was gradually expanded from its early function of overseeing public spending on the education of the poor to its late 20th-century remit of inspecting the standards of teaching and learning in all maintained schools and local authority funded colleges, and providing professional development courses for teachers. The Education (Schools) Act 1992 established a new inspection regime under *Ofsted. Thereafter the number of HMI inspectors was reduced, and their role became one of training, monitoring, and advising Ofsted inspectors, and sometimes acting as lead inspectors. *See also* HER MAJESTY'S INSPECTORATE OF EDUCATION.

Her Majesty's Inspectorate of Education (HMIE) In Scotland HMIE operates as an executive agency of Scottish government ministers under the terms of the Scotland Act 1998. The Inspectorate operates independently and impartially while remaining directly accountable to ministers. The core business of HMIE is inspection and review in order to improve the quality of education and raise attainment. The HMIE inspects and evaluates pre-school education, primary and secondary schools, teacher education, community learning and development, further education, and the education functions of local authorities in Scotland. Schools are rated on a scale of one to six, from unsatisfactory to excellent. These inspections are the equivalent of *Ofsted inspections in England and Wales. *See also* HER MAJESTY'S INSPECTORATE. S.M.

heuristic play Heuristic learning encompasses the notion of exploratory play which is self-directed by the infant and young child. Eleanor Goldschmied uses the specific term 'heuristic play with objects' to explore 'a large number of different objects and receptacles with which [children] play without adult intervention' (Goldschmied and Jackson 1994: 128). Commonly, the objects are placed in a **treasure basket** within reach of where very young infants are seated, and high levels of concentration, engagement, and persistence are observed as the children explore the nature of the presented objects. The adult acts as observer, having first selected a range of natural, everyday objects or combinations of objects, to stimulate particularly the child's senses and their development of *schema.

Further Reading: E. Goldschmied and S. Jackson *People under Three: Young Children in Day Care* (Routledge, 1994) gives a clear overview of heuristic play. A.W.

hidden curriculum *See* CURRICULUM.

Higher Equivalent to *Scottish Credit and Qualifications Framework level 6, this is a qualification taken by students in Scotland who have achieved passes in *Standard Grades at *Credit level or completed a course at Intermediate level 2. Highers are required for entry into *further or *higher education study, and therefore their level is roughly equivalent to that of *Advanced Levels (A levels) elsewhere in the United Kingdom. For the purpose of university entry, three Highers are usually taken to be the equivalent of two A levels in terms of coverage and entry points. Students will normally complete an average of five Highers over a year. *See also* ADVANCED HIGHER. S.M.

higher degree An award at a higher level than a *bachelor's or *first degree. This includes *master's degrees and *doctorates. An applicant to study for a higher degree will normally be required to hold a good first degree at either first class or upper second class level for entry to a master's programme; and usually to have successfully completed a master's degree for entry to doctorate level. Higher degrees are awarded by *universities and some other institutions of *higher education.

higher education Programmes of study which lead to advanced qualifications such as those at *National Qualifications Framework (NQF) level 5 or 6 and above, such as *degrees and diplomas. These are usually offered in **higher education institutions** (HEIs) such as *universities, but may also form part of the provision of *further education (FE) colleges, as in the case of *foundation degrees. The higher education sector is largely comprised of universities and *university colleges, and is distinct from the further education sector in terms of funding and purpose. The *provision* of higher education, however, is an area in which there is some overlap, since HEIs may accredit FE colleges to deliver some higher-level, vocationally related courses.

In Scotland higher education institutions include thirteen universities, the Open University in Scotland, one university college, two colleges of higher education, two art schools, one conservatoire, and the Scottish Agricultural College. The universities developed in three stages: the ancient universities (St Andrews, Glasgow, Aberdeen, Edinburgh) date from the 15th and 16th centuries; four others (Dundee, Strathclyde, Heriot-Watt, Stirling) achieved university status in the 1960s; and the newest group (Glasgow Caledonian, Napier, Paisley, Robert Gordon, Abertay) achieved university status in the 1990s. Students can be accepted to university on completion of their Higher examinations at the end of Year S5; however, Scottish students wishing to attend an English university may often go on to complete Advanced Highers in Year S6.

Higher Education Funding Council for England (HEFCE) The body which distributes funding for teaching and research to support *higher education provision in colleges and universities. HEFCE was set up as a non-departmental body in 1992, following the *Further and Higher Education Act of that year which awarded polytechnics university status. Separate councils were established for Wales (*Higher Education Funding Council for Wales) and Scotland (the *Scottish Funding Council). Although the HEFCE does not form part of the *Department for Innovation, Universities, and Skills, it operates within the framework of policies set out by the *Secretary of State for that department.

SEE WEB LINKS

- Summarizes the work of the Scottish Funding Council.
- Explains HEFCE's role in supporting research.

Higher Education Funding Council for Wales (HEFCW) An Assembly-sponsored body established in May 1992 under the *Further and Higher Education Act, responsible for funding the higher education sector throughout Wales; it also has the power to fund higher education in *colleges of further education. Its key strategic aims are widening participation; encouraging excellent student learning and support; delivering improved research performance in the sector; encouraging more productive links between higher education and the public and private sectors; supporting high-quality *initial teacher training provision; and developing a strong emphasis on collaboration and reconfiguration in higher education in Wales. H.G.

Higher Education Wales (HEW) The national council in Wales of Universities UK, established in 1996 to represent the *higher education sector in Wales. Membership includes all the heads of universities and higher education institutions in Wales, and the Welsh director of the *Open University. HEW promotes and supports higher education in Wales, representing the interests of its members to the National Assembly, to Parliament, to political parties, and to European institutions and bodies, with whom it negotiates on behalf of Welsh higher education. It also provides an expert resource on all aspects of higher education to stakeholders, including Assembly Members and Welsh MPs, the Welsh and UK media, business leaders, and industrial entrepreneurs. H.G.

higher-level teaching assistant (HLTA) One who works in a classroom support role but with a high degree of autonomy and responsibility. HLTAs work under the direction of a *qualified teacher to support individual children and small groups of pupils; and they are also expected to assist in planning lessons and monitoring the progress of pupils. Some will line-manage or be responsible for supervising, others will support staff. HLTAs are qualified to deliver individual, group, and whole-class learning activities without the presence of a qualified teacher. HLTA status is achieved when the person has successfully demonstrated they have met professional standards set by the *Training and Development Agency for Schools in professional values and practice, knowledge and understanding, and teaching and learning activities. *See also* TEACHING ASSISTANTS. T.B., L.E.

Higher National Certificate (HNC) A vocationally related national qualification, usually offered by colleges of *further education as a part-time programme of study for those already in employment who wish to gain further qualifications. It is available in a wide range of subjects, from business and finance to engineering. Applicants are usually required to have five *General Certificate of Secondary Education passes at grade C or above, including English and mathematics, and at least one pass at *General Certificate of Education *Advanced Level. *Assessment is by *assignment, and the award is accredited in England and Wales at *National Qualifications Framework level 4. In Scotland an HNC is equivalent to level 7 on the *Scottish Credit and Qualifications Framework.

Higher National Diploma (HND) A vocationally related national qualification, usually offered by colleges of *further education as a two-year full-time programme of study, available in subjects such as business and finance and computing. Applicants are usually required to have *General Certificate of Secondary Education passes at grade C or above in English and mathematics, or the equivalent *key skills, as well as a total of around 80 *Universities and Colleges Admissions Service (UCAS) points. HNDs can be 'topped up' by additional study by those students wishing to gain a relevant *honours degree. The award is accredited in England and Wales at *National Qualifications Framework level 4. HNDs now form part of the *foundation degree framework. In Scotland an HND is equivalent to level 8 on the *Scottish Credit and Qualifications Framework.

Higher Still An alternative name for the Scottish *Advanced Higher. S.M.

Highlands and Islands Enterprise *See* SCOTTISH ENTERPRISE, HIGHLANDS AND ISLANDS ENTERPRISE.

high school At one time used as a title by some grammar schools (as in 'girls' high school'), non-selective schools, and independent schools, it is still used in Scotland in the term **junior high school**, a school which offers both primary and secondary provision. Pupils may also associate the term with the American secondary schooling system, with which they have become familiar through popular television series.

home education Some parents exercise their statutory right to give their child of compulsory school age (5–16) full-time education within the home. In the United Kingdom it is education that is compulsory and not attendance at school. Any home education programme of work, however, must be relevant to the age, needs (including any special needs), ability, and aptitude of the child, but is not required to conform absolutely to the *national curriculum. There is no financial support available to home educators, and the education they provide is subject to *local authority monitoring and inspection. *See also* EDUCATION OTHERWISE THAN AT SCHOOL. T.B., L.E.

home–school agreement An agreement drawn up by the school's *governing body, in consultation with parents and the head teacher, setting out a statement of the school's values and aims, and the role and responsibility of parents and carers in supporting these by ensuring that their child meets the required standards in respect to *behaviour, attendance, and the completion of homework. Parents and carers are requested and encouraged to sign the agreement, although doing so is not a mandatory requirement. The main purpose of the agreement is to improve standards of behaviour and *attainment, and to encourage and enhance cooperation between school and home. The agreement became a requirement for all schools under the provision of the School Standards and Framework Act 1998. There is so far insufficient evidence to confirm whether the introduction of the agreement has had any direct impact on the level of parental cooperation.

SEE WEB LINKS

- Explains the purpose of home–school agreements, and provides links to case studies.

home tuition Sometimes referred to as 'private tuition', it is the provision of additional support for learning, outside school hours, usually engaged and paid for by the parents or carers in the case of young learners, or by the learners themselves if adults. Home tuition may be sought in subjects in which the learner is having difficulties at school or college, and is often designed to supplement and reinforce the teaching they are receiving elsewhere. It is particularly sought by parents to prepare their children for public examinations, such as the *General Certificate of Secondary Education in core subjects such as English and mathematics. *See also* EDUCATION OTHERWISE THAN AT SCHOOL.

home tutor A teacher employed by a *local authority to teach pupils who cannot, for whatever reason, attend school. Instead, the pupils are taught in the home. *See also* EDUCATION OTHERWISE THAN AT SCHOOL.

homework Tasks related to their school studies which pupils are expected to complete outside school hours. All schools are required to have a homework policy, which is drawn up to promote the partnership between school and home and to extend and build upon learning undertaken in school. Many schools post their homework policy on their web site. In 1998 the government published guidance on the type and extent of homework that pupils could be reasonably expected to undertake at each stage of their education. According to this, pupils in *primary schools may be expected to spend 10–30 minutes a day on homework, which should focus on literacy and numeracy skills. For secondary pupils the coverage extends across the curriculum and the recommended duration is 90 minutes a day in *Key Stage 3, rising to a maximum of two and a half hours a day in Key Stage 4. *See also* HOME–SCHOOL AGREEMENT.

SEE WEB LINKS

- Guidelines on homework for primary and secondary schools.
- A summary of good practice in the setting of homework.

homework club Run after school hours in local libraries, and sometimes in schools, *homework clubs are intended to provide pupils with a safe environment conducive to study, which may also offer support for computer and Internet access. They are available to pupils aged 7 years and over. Schools and *local authorities provide parents and carers with information about the location of their nearest homework club.

h

honorary degree A *degree awarded by a *university or other higher education institution to individuals who are not students of that institution, but who have gained wide recognition for their achievements in a worthwhile field. The award is usually made formally at a *graduation awards ceremony by the chancellor, vice-chancellor, or some other dignitary of the institution.

honours degree A degree which indicates a higher level of achievement than a *foundation degree or a pass degree, and may require the student to study to a greater a depth or breadth. A candidate who has achieved an honours degree may indicate this by the inclusion of the abbreviation '(Hons)' after their qualification; for example, Mohammed McPherson BA (Hons). Unlike a pass degree, an honours degree award is divided into different classes which are used as grading indicators of the level of achievement the student has attained in their undergraduate studies. These classes are **first** class, **upper second** class (sometimes referred to as a **2.1**), **lower second** class (sometimes referred to as a **2.2**), and **third** class, the first class degree being the highest awarded. Most honours degrees awarded fall into the second class category. *See also* BACHELOR'S DEGREE.

humanist A philosophy which views the individual and their potential for development as the essential starting point for theorizing about, or implementing, systems of teaching and learning. A humanist approach to education focuses on the learner as an individual, taking their interests, enthusiasms, and goals as the basis upon which to organize or facilitate their learning experiences. Learning is not seen as an end in itself, but rather as a means towards enabling the individual to realize their full potential, referred to by some humanist theorists such as Abraham *Maslow and Carl *Rogers as achieving **self-actualization**. In the education of young children the philosophy and activities of the *Reggio Emilia schools or of the *Montessori method are examples of this approach, encouraging children to develop their curiosity by facilitating their exploration of their current interests and their creativity, rather than imposing a mandatory and uniform curriculum. A. S. *Neill's *Summerhill School, too, provides an example of a humanistic approach in its creation of a democratic community of learning where pupils and *teachers have equal status, and pupils are empowered to exercise choice over whether and what they will learn. What these approaches have in common is that they are *learner-centred, the learner acknowledged not only as the starting point of the education process, but also as taking responsibility for their own learning. The teacher or *educator is regarded, according to this model, as a facilitator of learning, rather than as a dispenser of knowledge or skills; and the learning process itself takes into account not only the academic needs of the learner, but also their emotional, creative, psychological, and developmental needs.

A humanistic model of education operates on the belief that achievement is its own reward and that personal satisfaction at having learned or understood or created something will motivate the learner more effectively than the *extrinsic rewards and sanctions favoured by *behaviourists. For this reason even the 'reward' of praise is treated cautiously, since it could lead to a craving for teacher approval, displacing the learner's *intrinsic enjoyment of learning. The humanistic approach places an emphasis upon recognizing and valuing the dignity and self-worth of every individual learner, and upon developing the self-concept of the learner. It starts from the assumption that the learner must feel positive about themselves and about their ability to improve and progress towards the realization of their full potential; and that, in order to do this, they must have a clear and accurate understanding of their own strengths and weaknesses.

In practice, a humanistic method of education is one in which an emphasis is placed on *discovery learning and the learner's right to self-determination. It places little or no emphasis on externally imposed attainment standards, targets, and testing, and may indeed be seen as antithetical to a rigid, mandatory, standardized curriculum. The teaching is student-centred, and takes into account the learners' social, emotional, and personal development. The curriculum takes as its starting point topics which are of central interest to the learners, and allows for learner control over the learning activities employed. Learners are encouraged to monitor and evaluate their own progress.

There are clear difficulties in operating such a model on a whole-school basis in the UK, not least because of the demands of the *national curriculum. A humanistic approach, however, may be applied to individual lessons, or may constitute the preferred teaching style of individual teachers. When the terms 'humanist' or 'humanistic' are used in this microcosmic sense, they imply a limited application of this approach, and one which is consistent with, and accommodated within, the statutory requirements of the national curriculum framework.

humanities A collective term for a range of academic disciplines or fields, all of which draw upon a knowledge of the development, achievements, behaviour, organization, or distribution of humanity. These include literature, history, philosophy, and some aspects of geography. In its widest sense it is used to draw a distinction between 'hard' sciences and other subjects. When this is the case, education and the social sciences may also be included in the category of humanities.

ideology One of the most important and widely used conceptual categories, not just in education, but also in other areas such as the media, politics, economics, and other arenas of cultural activity. There are many competing definitions of the term as its use has been determined by various contexts. At its most basic level, it can be used to refer to a set of beliefs and ideas which inform the practices of a profession such as teaching. These ideas will inform all aspects of the training of a teacher and reflect the values placed on education in any particular context. Ideologies represent what appear to be 'common-sense' ideas—ideas which are taken for granted and rarely questioned or analysed critically—such as acceptance of the power relationship inherent in interactions between teacher and pupils. It is in addressing assumptions such as these where an understanding of the concept of ideology gains a more critical edge, particularly in relation to ideas or practices which are taken for granted but which may function to exclude, or render 'invisible', certain groups or types of learners.

Ideology was originally exclusively a Marxist term, and was used to imply a body of ideas and attitudes which not only bound a society together but were used to mask or conceal the material reality of people's lives. In the 19th century, Karl Marx (1818–83) conceived a theory which offered a historical account of how society and culture replicated unequal distributions of power and wealth. It offered a base–superstructure model of how capitalism reinforced class distinctions. The most significant part of this model was the base, which comprised the mode of production (technology) as well as the relations of production (the difference between workers and those who own the means of production). The superstructure comprised all the other aspects of life such as education, the arts, politics, religion, and the family. It was through areas such as education that an ideology (or a body of ideas which supported capitalism) would communicate, for Marx, a 'false consciousness'. In classical Marxian thought, people are understood to be born into a pre-existing ideology and to live in a condition of conflict between their material lives and the ideologies which determined their identity.

One of the most influential definitions of ideology since the 1960s came from the Marxist academic Louis Althusser (1918–90). Althusser developed Marx's concept of ideology by arguing that it was through the way language functioned as a structure that ideology gained its significance. Like many other contemporary theorists, Althusser benefited from Ferdinand de Saussure's (1857–1913) concept of *semiotics, and the structuralism that was its outcome, by suggesting that people gained their identity from pre-existing structures that dominated every aspect of their lives. He called these structures **ideological state apparatuses**, one of which was education. According to Althusser, ideology was not just a set of ideas which bound people together; it also represented the everyday material practices of our experiences. Meaning and identity were communicated at the level of the sign, and any object or gesture—not just verbal or written language—could operate as a sign. Thus, although the architectural features of a school building may at first seem neutral and value-free, they carry with them ideological assumptions built into the structure of its design. Similarly, the way *lecture theatres and classrooms are designed can tell us about the hierarchical relationship between teacher and pupil; the teacher's position at the front might hint at the unidirectional flow of knowledge. In the same way, the categorization of knowledge into the arts, sciences, business, and other fields is reflected in the faculty system, which houses separate disciplines in different buildings. According to this theory, all 'texts' speak to an implied reader: in a school situation, all the texts in the institution, including the building, the textbooks, the posters on the wall, and the teacher, address the pupil and 'hail them into being'; the moment the student reads these texts, they adopt a particular identity which comes with an associated set of ideological attitudes and values. This process is called **interpellation**.

Although poststructuralist ideas in the late 1960s about the instability of language led theorists such as Michel *Foucault to doubt the possibility of a unified, stable set of beliefs which bound people together, ideology still has its Marxist connotations today. It became a central concept for those academics working at the Centre for Contemporary *Cultural Studies. Referring to ideology and the related concept of hegemony (the resolution of conflict by power through rhetoric or persuasion), theorists such as Stuart Hall and Dick Hebdige studied practices of production and consumption in the media, proposing that oppositional ideologies could exist which countered more dominant ideologies.

Ideology is a concept which has been used to refer to power relations outside the issue of class: the various feminisms have used the term when discussing the inequalities that are a consequence of a patriarchal systems and beliefs. Similarly, postcolonial theorists analyse the consequences of colonial ideologies. The term today permeates all subject areas in the arts, humanities, and social sciences, and has become an important critical tool in higher education.

C.H.

Illich, Ivan *See* DESCHOOLING.

inaugural lecture When an academic is promoted or appointed to the post of *professor, and occasionally *reader, in *higher education, they are usually expected to deliver an initial lecture which is open to all and which allows them to introduce and expound upon their existing body of work or their current research in their specialist field. This event is known as their inaugural lecture.

inclusion A term used to describe and promote policies, strategies, and practices which aim to enable all learners to participate fully in education. As widely conceived, inclusion is closely connected with *social justice concerns for equality and rights for all. In this conception it often refers to **social inclusion**, which is concerned with reducing inequalities between the relatively disadvantaged sectors of society and the relatively advantaged. In this sense it may refer to race, *gender, *social class, disability, learning difficulties, religious belief, or some other category or group. It is contrasted with exclusion. *Exclusion may be imposed. It may also take the form of self-exclusion, as in *truancy, or as in the self-exclusion of the middle classes from mainstream educational institutions. More narrowly conceived, the term 'inclusion' can refer especially to pupils and young people with *special educational needs. Such pupils have traditionally been excluded—or excluded themselves—from classrooms, mainstream institutions (schools, colleges, and universities), and the curriculum. The 1994 Salamanca Statement is widely credited with promoting a view of special education as an equality or social justice issue rather than as a response to a *deficit in individuals. Consequently, 'inclusion' rather than 'integration' has become the preferred term, implying that the school must change to 'fit' the pupil rather than the pupil to fit the school. However, the concept of inclusion continues to be contested. Tensions arise because there are contradictory educational policy imperatives both for inclusive education and for competition and selection. Moreover, policy approaches to inclusion may prioritize the supporting of individual children, making schools inclusive at a systems level or, more politically, challenging discrimination. Underlying these tensions are different kinds of explanatory framework within special education: individual pathology, social theory, critical theory, and social justice perspectives.

SEE WEB LINKS

- Presents the Salamanca Statement.

M.G.

inclusive learning *See* INCLUSIVITY; TOMLINSON REPORT (1996).

inclusivity This term, when used within the *learning and skills sector, denotes open access for students with learning difficulties or disabilities, and opportunities for progression. Inclusivity is a goal which aims for a situation where all students—regardless of their learning difficulty or disability—can take part in education or training to enhance their quality of life. In terms of purpose, it is argued that this will lead to their improved integration into communities. The *Tomlinson Report (1996) set out suggestions of ways in which to improve the organizational culture of learning and training institutions in order to ensure that they respond positively to applications from students with difficulties and disabilities, and are able to acknowledge and address their needs. In recent years the terms 'inclusivity' and *'widening participation' have, to some extent, been used interchangeably to encompass the improvement of learning opportunities for all. However, 'widening participation' derived originally from the main theme driving the *Kennedy Report (1997), which aimed to ensure that *all* UK citizens over the age of 16 would have equal access to further and higher education. V.C., K.A.

independent schools Sometimes referred to as **public schools**, these include both preparatory, or 'prep', schools, which prepare pupils for the *Common Entrance Examination at 13 or for the *Eleven Plus in those areas where it still exists; and private secondary schools. They are fee-paying.

In Scotland, too, independent schools are fee-paying, and provide education for the age of 3–18. Again they are known as private or 'public' schools although they do not receive any public funding. All are registered with the Scottish

Education Department and receive regular inspections from HM Inspectorate of Education. As they are not managed by the education authority, these schools are not required to teach the Scottish national curriculum although in practice nearly all pupils are entered for the same public examinations as in state schools. However, after standard grade examinations, some schools choose to follow the English *Advanced Level system as opposed to Scottish *Highers.

index for inclusion A document produced by the **Centre for Studies in Inclusive Education (CSIE)**. It outlines a series of indicators of *inclusion which form guidance for developing policy, practice, and culture. The CSIE promotes a move away from segregated education. The index for inclusion describes how good education and good social sense uphold human rights. There is a **Charter for Inclusion** which was first written in 1989 and was rewritten in 2002. Typically, schools will use the index to support self-review and to identify *barriers to learning. It contains comprehensive definitions for inclusion. The index upholds the rights of all individuals to be educated locally and recommends the training of staff to support the development of an *inclusive ethos and practice. T.B., L.E.

individual learning 1. The practice of allowing students to learn at their own pace and according to their own preferred *learning style, and to cover those areas of the *syllabus or lesson which are necessary to their learning. It is an approach which necessitates the teacher having a clear understanding of the starting point and learning needs of each student, and is part of the wider practice of *differentiation. In this approach, which is widely used in the teaching of *basic skills, for example, students may have their own **individual action plans** and learning *objectives.

2. The practice of encouraging pupils to work separately on individual tasks, for example using *work cards, rather than working as a group or class. This alternative meaning does not necessarily imply the practice of differentiation. *See also* INDIVIDUAL LEARNING PLAN; PERSONALIZED LEARNING.

Individual Learning Account (ILA) Under the terms of the Education and Training (Scotland) Bill, ILAs were presented as a strategy to promote *lifelong learning. Introduced in October 2000, they were designed to encourage people to invest in their own learning and development by registering through a card membership scheme. Account holders would receive a grant to encourage them to undertake a range of learning opportunities such as basic *information technology skills, *numeracy and communication, *Standard and *Higher grades, *vocational qualifications, and part-time *higher education. The accounts were discontinued in December 2001.

SEE WEB LINKS

- An evaluation of ILAs undertaken in June 2002. S.M.

individual learning plan (ILP) First outlined in the 2003 *Green Paper *14–19: Opportunity and Excellence*, ILPs are intended to map individual 14-year-olds' routes through the *Key Stage 4 curriculum and allow the monitoring of individual progress. The plan records the learner's achievements at the age of 14; identifies their choices for Key Stage 4, which may include *vocational options as well as entitlement subjects, and may also incorporate some element of *work experience. It establishes career goals; and provides a means of transferring information about the learner from the compulsory to the *post-compulsory stage of their education. ILPs are revised each year. The growing complexity and flexibility of the 14–19 curriculum signalled in the 2005 *White Paper *14–19 Education and Skills* has made the use of ILPs a necessity in this phase of education and training. *See also* 14–19 AGENDA.

induction 1. The process by which pupils or students are introduced to their educational institution, their *course, or their subject. This may take a variety of forms, from a simple welcome and an introductory lecture, to a full week or more of organized activities. A thorough induction will be designed to ensure that learners are able to find their way about the school or *campus; that they have met key members of teaching staff; have been introduced to the *aims and structure of their course; have been made aware of the institution's rules and regulations; and have been informed about the learner support services available. In many universities the induction of new students takes place in the week before other students return to resume their studies after the summer break. This is known as **freshers' week**.

2. The process by which a newly appointed teacher is introduced to their school. This particularly applies to *newly qualified teachers (NQTs) in their first year of teaching, for whom the induction period is set as a full three *terms; that is, an entire school year. This induction replaces what was known formerly as the 'probationary year'. During this time, the NQT's timetable should allow them at least 10 per cent non-class-contact time in order to focus on their professional development. During this process they will normally have the support of an induction *mentor. At the end of the three terms a decision will be taken by the local authority, based on evidence from the induction tutor and *head teacher, as to whether the teacher has met the required **induction standards**.

induction mentor *See* INDUCTION; MENTOR.

induction standards *See* INDUCTION.

infant school A school for children aged 5–7 which teaches *Key Stage 1 of the *national curriculum. It may form part of a larger *primary school or operate as a separate institution. Some infant schools have *pre-school facilities attached for children below the age of compulsory schooling.

information learning technology (ILT) The term used in *post-compulsory education, particularly in *colleges of further education, to refer to the use and applications of technology by teachers to support students' learning. It includes *e-learning and *blended learning programmes. *See also* BRITISH EDUCATIONAL COMMUNICATIONS AND TECHNOLOGY AGENCY.

SEE WEB LINKS

- Examples of ILT policies and strategies in colleges of further education.

information communication technology (ICT) 1. An area of the *curriculum concerned with the uses of technology. Although it is sometimes used interchangeably in schools with the term *information technology, ICT is widely recognized as denoting the study of the applications and use of the technology, for example through the exploration and creation of electronic toys and models, and through the production of electronic music. Since the introduction of the *national curriculum, ICT has been a compulsory subject for all pupils.

2. Also used to refer to resources for supporting learning, such as computers, televisions, or audio equipment.

3. The title given to one of the three externally assessed areas of *key skills, and thus constituting part of the 14–19 curriculum.

SEE WEB LINKS

- Provides guidance on ICT resources for teachers at all key stages.
- Gives access to the detailed list of the ICT key skills.

information technology (IT) The study of computing, microelectronics, and the storage and transmission of data. Once a generic term for all aspects of this field of study, its most common usage now is in referring to the study of the software and hardware which computer technology employs, for example in subjects such as computer studies, rather than to the use or application of that technology, which now comes under the curriculum area of *information communication technology. Both have become an important part of the school curriculum following the publication of the Stevenson Report in 1997, which argued for a greater emphasis on IT in schools in order to hasten the development of an IT-literate workforce. *See also* British Educational Communications and Technology Agency.

SEE WEB LINKS

- Describes educational uses and implications of IT.

initial teacher training (ITT) Courses of training which lead to *qualified teacher status (QTS) or *qualified teacher learning and skills (QTLS). Those courses of teacher training which lead to QTS are regulated by the *Training and Development Agency, and those which lead to QTLS are regulated by *Lifelong Learning UK. Teacher training combines a course of academic and professional study in institutions of *higher education (HE), such as *universities, with periods of practical experience in schools or colleges. Some ITT programmes, such as the *Graduate Teacher Programme, have a larger weighting of 'on-the-job' training in schools than other, full-time university- or HE-based provision. Historically, teacher training for schoolteachers took place in teacher training colleges, which were renamed **colleges of education** following the recommendations of the 1963 *Robbins Report. Now, however, the majority of those entering the profession do so as *graduates through the *Professional Graduate Certificate of Education or the *Postgraduate Certificate of Education route, while non-graduates can undertake a *Bachelor of Education degree. In Scotland, ITT takes the same form as in England but is referred to as initial teacher education. *See also* newly qualified teacher.

in-service education of teachers (INSET) Now often referred to as *continuing professional development, INSET is the provision of professional education, training, and updating for teachers already employed in schools or colleges. It takes a wide range of forms, from formal provision such as part-time study for a postgraduate degree in education, to development days in school run by the teachers themselves. Such days are sometimes still referred to colloquially as 'Baker days' after Kenneth Baker, who, as *Secretary of State for Education under the 1980s Thatcher administration, instigated the inclusion of five non-contact days (days when teachers are in school but pupils do not attend) each academic year for the purposes of INSET. Professional development is also provided by *advanced skills teachers, by *local authority advisory services, through attendance at conferences, and at short courses run by or on behalf of the *Department for Children, Schools, and Families.

inspection For schools and colleges these are carried out by *Ofsted, which is also responsible for the inspection and regulation of the provision of care for children and young people under the Education and Inspections Act 2006. The **New Inspection Framework** reflects the statutory duty of inspectors, as set out in the *Education Act 2005, section 28(5), to report not only on the quality of education provided to pupils in the school, but also on how effectively it meets the needs of the whole range of those pupils; the *standards achieved; the quality of school leadership and management, including the management of financial resources; and the school's provision for the spiritual, moral, social, and cultural development of its pupils. At the same time, the inspection gives consideration to the contribution of the school to the five outcomes for children and young people set out in the Children Act 2004, which includes reporting on the contribution made by the school to the well-being of its pupils. Teams of inspectors carry out inspections and regulatory visits, and publish their inspection reports on the Ofsted web site, where recommendations and statistical information is also posted. Prior to an inspection, schools were required to provide statistical and other information about the school. Before the New Inspection Framework was implemented, this information was submitted by the school using Forms S1–S4. These forms have now been replaced by one document known as the self-evaluation form, or **SEF**. Inspectors use this as the key document when planning the inspection of the school, together with the school's previous Ofsted report and the school's documentation of its Performance Assessment National Data, known as **PANDA**. The introduction of self-evaluation for schools has meant that inspections can proceed with what has been termed 'a lighter touch', with inspection visits lasting a shorter time and involving a smaller team of inspectors than previously. The external check on schools provided by Ofsted inspections is nevertheless still an essential part of the evaluation process, and will involve such activities as the inspection team considers necessary for clarification of uncertainties or contradictions apparent in the SEF. This may include the scrutiny of pupils' work and other documentation, the observation of teaching, interviews with teachers and pupils, or scrutiny of evidence relating to leadership and management.

For the inspection of *further education and teacher training provision the same procedures apply. Where institutions or aspects of their provision are deemed unsatisfactory but capable of improvement, they will receive follow-up monitoring and inspection visits. *See also* HER MAJESTY'S INSPECTORATE; NOTICE TO IMPROVE; SELF-ASSESSMENT; SPECIAL MEASURES.

Institute for Learning (IfL) Formed in 2002, the Institute provides a professional body for teachers in further, adult, and work-based learning and training in the UK. Its aims are to support the professional needs of practitioners and to raise their status across the *learning and skills sector. The 2004 *Department for Education and Skills reform proposals *Equipping Our Teachers for the Future* named the IfL as the body responsible for awarding certification of *qualified teacher learning and skills (QTLS) status to all new teachers entering the *lifelong learning sector from September 2007. As a result of the reforms in teacher training within the sector leading to QTLS, the IfL will have an extended role, which will include registering those who undertake and complete teacher training; monitoring and recording *continuing professional development; and liaising with the *General Teaching Council and the Higher Education Academy (an organization whose purpose is to support the quality of provision and research in institutions of higher education) to ensure cross-sector professional recognition.

SEE WEB LINKS

- Links to information on continuing professional development.

V.C., K.A.

Institute for Learning and Teaching (ILT) A professional body for teachers in *higher education. It was founded in 1998 with the aim of supporting standards of practice in universities and other higher education institutions. Teachers can join the Institute at one of two levels: full members must be academics with a minimum of five years' teaching experience or completion of an ILT-accredited programme of professional development; while associate members must have completed at least one year's teaching *and* an ILT-accredited programme of professional development. The latter may take the form of, for example, a Postgraduate Certificate in Higher Education (PHE) or similar professional development qualification.

instructor Someone who works as a trainer or teacher but does not hold a recognized teaching qualification and does not have *qualified teacher status or *qualified teacher training and skills. The term is more closely associated with skills training than with education, and may carry its own qualifications, as, for example, in the case of a driving instructor. It is a term also used to refer to those with a formal teaching or training role in the police and armed forces.

instrumental Describes learning which is undertaken not for its own sake but for some other purpose. For example, all vocational education is instrumental in that its purpose is to prepare the learner for a specific line of work and to improve their chances of employment. The increasing emphasis on skills for work in the 14–19 curriculum indicates a general trend towards the instrumental, as opposed to **developmental** or *liberal, model of education, as does the concept of *employer-led education and training.

instrument of government Under the terms of the Education Act 1944 (*Butler Act), every secondary school is required to have an instrument of government which clearly records the name of the school and the constitution of its *governing body. Since 1980 *primary schools have also been included in this requirement.

integrated community school (ICS) The pilot programme was launched by the Scottish Office in 1998 with the aim of promoting social *inclusion and raising education *standards by developing schools with increased support for vulnerable children. These schools were to be focused in disadvantaged areas and to undertake close liaison between community and social agencies as well as with parents. Full development of this policy began in 2002 with the aim that by 2007 all schools would be using an integrated community schooling approach to education.

SEE WEB LINKS

- Contains the full report on ICS.

S.M.

integration As described in the *Warnock Report (1978), integration was the original concept of educating children with special needs alongside their peers in mainstream schools. The Report detailed three types of integration: locational, social, and functional. Where a *special school or unit shared their campus with a mainstream school, it was seen as locational integration; social integration was where pupils with special needs were taught separately but joined each other at social times of the day; and functional integration was where children with special needs joined their peers for the full educational experience. The terms 'integration' and *'inclusion' are not to be confused as they describe entirely different philosophies. Integration is a situation in which children with special needs are deemed to benefit from fitting into a largely unaltered routine and procedure of a mainstream school, whereas inclusion is a process benefiting the whole school community. *See also* INCLUSIVITY. T.B., L.E.

INTELLIGENCE

Usually defined as a measure of cognitive skill and the ability to solve problems, intelligence has been a topic of debate precisely because it has been open to a range of definitions and has fuelled theories of a contentious nature about the question of genetic inheritance. The theory that there exists a general intelligence factor, or 'factor g', was first proposed in 1904 by the British psychologist Charles Spearman (1863–1945), who based his claim on statistical analysis. The concept of a factor g has underpinned all subsequent psychometric models of intelligence, and has been used to fuel the controversial argument that genetic inheritance plays a major role in determining an individual's intelligence. Traditional understandings of intelligence were brought into question in the 1980s by Howard Gardner's (b. 1943) theory of *multiple intelligences. Nevertheless, the assessment of 'intelligence' continues to play an important role in some areas of educational and psychological measurement and testing.

The origins of such testing is generally accredited to the work of the French psychologists Alfred Binet (1857–1911) and Théodore Simon (1873–1961), published in 1905, which was designed to identify pupils aged 3–12 who would find learning difficult and would therefore need a different teaching approach or additional support. This led to the development of the Stamford–Binet intelligence scale (1916), which remains in use today, when psychologists from Stamford University in the United States translated and revised the assessment tasks designed by the two French psychologists. Building on this work, the American psychologist David Wechsler (1896–1981) developed what became known as the Wechsler scale for the psychometric measurement of intelligence. Like the Stamford–Binet model, Wechsler's approach was to use *standardized testing, individually administered and assessed by professional psychologists, to arrive at a score referred to as the individual's intelligence quotient (IQ). This led to the development of tests designed for ease of administration to large groups, both in educational contexts and in the armed services, often for the purposes of *selection, such as the *Eleven Plus test.

The contentious and fiercely argued debate over the extent to which intelligence is an inherited or an acquired factor is yet to be resolved. There are claims that psychometric intelligence tests have been misused or misinterpreted to substantiate erroneous claims that specific ethnic and racial groups are inherently less intelligent than others. This theory of genetic determinism has been used, particularly in the United States, to support the argument against government programmes of intervention designed to compensate for the social and environmental deprivation of some groups of the population. There are also fears that it could be used to argue the case for eugenics, the process of human genetic selection. The genetic determinism model of human intelligence was encapsulated in a controversial book entitled *The Bell Curve* (1994) by the Americans Richard Herrnstein and Charles Murray, who further argued that there was a correlation between low intelligence scores and antisocial behaviour. The title of their work refers to the shape of norm group scores, which, when entered on a graph, create a shape which is sometimes referred to as a bell-shaped curve, widest in the middle since most scores fall into the average range, with relatively few very high or very low. The first British educational psychologist, Sir Cyril Burt (1883–1971), also made claims that intelligence was an inherited factor. Following his death, accusations were made that some of the data on which he had based these claims may have been fabricated. Recent research, however, has cast doubt on these accusations.

Also vigorously debated is the question of whether birth order affects intelligence levels. Research evidence on the whole has suggested that it may do in some cases and that the number of siblings, as well as birth order, may have some effect on intelligence levels. An early researcher, statistician, and psychologist, Francis Galton (1822–1911), in his book *English Men of Science: Their Nature and Nurture* (1874), claimed to have discovered a correlation between birth order and high achievement, first-born sons tending to achieve eminence in their field. However, his results did not take account of female children, so that a first-born son might in fact be one of the last of his siblings, provided those born earlier were all girls. Further studies appear to confirm Galton's thesis, first-born children being disproportionately represented among psychologists, composers,

Nobel Prize winners, and other eminent personalities. In 1973 Lillian Belmont and Francis Marolla published research findings which suggested that first-born children score best in an intelligence test, with performance declining in line with children's place in the birth order; and that children with many siblings tend to score less well, regardless of social class, although still exhibiting differences according to birth order.

However, controversy still surrounds the validity of intelligence testing; that is, whether they indeed measure what they purport to measure. Some current researchers, such as Howard Gardner, suggest that such tests measure only a small part of intellectual performance, and do not make allowance for the cultural or social contexts in which those tested find themselves. Test questions can be based on assumptions about cultural or social norms which those being tested may not recognize or share. This factor alone can provide an explanation for why some ethnic or cultural groups consistently score less well in standardized intelligence tests. Moreover, Gardner suggests that we should understand intelligence as a multiple array of responses to our multifaceted environment, rather than as a singular cognitive or intellectual skill; and researchers such as Daniel Goleman also currently argue that our concept of intelligence should be expanded to embrace other facets, such as *emotional intelligence. The concept of multiple intelligences is also known as **MI theory**, and encompasses the idea that we possess moral intelligence (the ability to distinguish between right and wrong), and social or interpersonal intelligence (the ability to understand other people and how best to work with them). A further broad definition of intelligence was posited by Robert Sternberg in *Beyond IQ: A Triarchic Theory of Human Intelligence* (1985), who defines it as the set of abilities we use in order to attain our life goals, including practical and creative abilities as well as the capacity for analytical thinking.

Interesting claims have been made recently about the possibility of increasing children's intelligence scores by playing them recordings of music by Mozart. This idea is based on work published in 1993 by researchers at the University of California, who found that students' IQ scores temporarily rose by 8 or 9 points and their performance in spatial–temporal tests improved after listening for ten minutes to a Mozart sonata. This has become known as the 'Mozart effect', and has been treated with caution in scientific circles. One explanation which has been offered for this phenomenon is that listening to the music may result in raised levels of intellectual arousal, and therefore in increased readiness to respond to testing.

intelligence test (IQ test) A test designed to measure someone's level of *intelligence in terms of their intelligence quotient (IQ). This may be administered to individuals as part of an assessment of their learning potential, or to whole groups, often for the purpose of identifying and selecting those with the highest scores, as was the case in the implementation of *Eleven Plus testing. Testing may, for example, take the form of a requirement to complete such statements as *Finger is to hand as —— is to foot*, or of the requirement to identify matching shapes. There is evidence to suggest that such tests are generally accurate predictors of an individual's future educational achievement, although not all would agree with this contention, citing cases of individuals who have scored badly in IQ tests but have gone on to become high achievers, scholastically or in some other field.

Most IQ tests are standardized in that they require the examiner and the candidate to follow a clear set of criteria in the way the test is administered, worded, and assessed. The purpose of this is to try to ensure that the only variable will be the responses of the candidate. However, critics of this means of testing argue that such standardization does not resolve the issue of cultural and ideological differences in candidates' backgrounds, which may lead some groups to interpret the content or context of questions differently from others. Tests are usually *norm-referenced in order that the results will show how an individual has performed in relation to other members of the same group. In the case of the Eleven Plus, for example, a child's performance was measured against that of other 11-year-olds. Standardized measures are designed so that the norm group scores, when drawn on a graph, are distributed in a curve, which is sometimes referred to as a bell-shaped curve, which is widest in the middle because most candidates' performance will be average, with relatively fewer scoring very high or very low. IQ tests use the number 100 to denote an average score. Thus, if a child scores higher than 100, they are said to be of above average intelligence; and if they score below 100, they are deemed to be performing at below average intelligence.

IQ testing can be traced back to the work of Alfred Binet and Théodore Simon published in 1905, who were tasked by the French government of the time to discover a means of identifying pupils with learning difficulties. This led to the development in 1916 at Stamford University of the Stamford–Binet intelligence scale, still in use today, building on the work of the two French psychologists. Later, the Wechsler scale for the psychometric measurement of intelligence was developed by David Wechsler (1896–1981). Like the Stamford–Binet model, this used *standardized testing which was individually administered and assessed by professional psychologists. This led to the development of tests which were designed specifically for ease of administration to large groups, both in educational contexts and in the armed services, often for the purposes of *selection.

Intensifying Support Programme (ISP) A government-led programme aimed at school improvement, introduced as a pilot in 2002 and extended for wider use by local authorities and schools in 2004. The four key themes of the ISP relate to developing the school as a learning community, improving conditions for learning within the school, improving student progress and achievement, and raising standards of teaching and learning through a process of collaboration between the school and local authority involving an audit, target-setting, implementation, and review. The initial pilot programme was focused on low-attaining schools in thirteen local authorities.

interdisciplinary Describes a course of study which draws on more than one academic *discipline to create a structured perspective on topics which are common to both. Thus, one might draw on the disciplines of education and sociology to examine the topic of cultural deprivation, for example.

internal assessment The formal *assessment of learners' work or performance which is carried out by teachers within the learners' institution, who are referred to for this purpose as **internal assessors**. It is used in courses which have some element of *continuous assessment, and is normally subject to a process of *moderation. If the assessment contributes towards a national or externally validated award, it will also normally be subjected to *verification by the relevant *awarding body. Proponents of externally set and marked *examinations often claim that internal assessment is insufficiently robust and possibly unreliable; while its proponents argue that it can provide a more accurate evaluation of a candidate's abilities and *achievement, measured over time and removed from the artificial pressures of the examination room. *See also* ASSESSMENT.

internal assessor *See* INTERNAL ASSESSMENT.

internal verification *See* VERIFICATION.

International Baccalaureate (IB) A qualification for pupils aged 18, available at some schools in the United Kingdom and overseas, successful completion of which qualifies pupils for entry to higher education in the UK and in other countries which recognize the qualification. Referred to colloquially as the 'International Bac', it covers a broad curriculum of six subjects which include languages, mathematics, and a science. It may be offered at some schools as an alternative to *General Certificate of Education *Advanced Levels. *See also* BACCALAURÉAT.

interpretivist *See* RESEARCH.

intervention **1.** Following the assessment and identification of *special educational needs (SEN) it is necessary to implement intervention strategies for support which enable students to make progress. Intervention must make full use of SEN provision and match the needs of the student. There are varying levels of intervention. Regular reviews are required to measure progress and plan the next stage of intervention, or indeed to reduce the level of additional support where adequate progress has been made. There are criteria or triggers for intervention at the various stages set out in the SEN Code of Practice 2001. Some establishments will use the guidance in its entirety while others will use it as a framework for establishing their own criteria. *See also* GRADUATED APPROACH.

Further reading: *Code of Practice for Special Educational Needs (Revised)* DfES/581/2001 (Department for Education and Skills, 2001). T.B., L.E.

2. A term used in action *research to indicate the point at which the teacher–researcher implements a change of approach or practice in order to evaluate the subsequent effect on an identified aspect of teaching and learning.

intrinsic motivation *See* MOTIVATION.

invigilate To supervise during an *examination in order to ensure that no cheating takes place and that candidates are supplied with the necessary writing materials. An invigilator will also keep track of time for the candidates, and notify them when the time allowed for the examination has elapsed and they must cease their efforts. They are often also responsible for distributing examination papers and collecting completed scripts.

ipsative A type of *assessment in which the learner's current level of achievement, skill, knowledge, or understanding is assessed against their own previous level, rather than against fixed criteria or a norm. It can also describe a process of learning in which the same content is covered more than once, but at an increasingly challenging level, as happens within a *spiral curriculum model. This is known as an **ipsative process**.

IQ *See* INTELLIGENCE.

Isaacs, Susan (1885–1948) An English *early years educator who ran an experimental school in Cambridge called the Malting House from 1924 to 1927. One of Isaacs's enduring legacies for teachers of very young children is the key skill of narrative observation to document the learning responses of children to environmental and cognitive encounters within an emergent curriculum, through both indoor and outdoor activity. Using observation, Isaacs noted the interests and inquiries of children and allowed experiential learning to further children's quests for constructing their own knowledge and understanding. She claimed that children should be able to express their feelings openly and needed the freedom to explore, take risks, and learn through play. Following the educational theories of John *Dewey, she valued the joy of discovery. This led to one of the better-known stories about her approach to *discovery learning, which involved her response to a group of young children wanting to find out whether a pet rabbit had gone to 'heaven' after burying it. Her answer was to allow the exhumation of the rabbit's remains in order, she explained, to satisfy the children's thirst for knowledge. This incident is often cited as testimony to the progressive nature of her headship and her approach to learning. Isaacs claimed that any testing or assessment of achievement would not demonstrate a child's true ability; and she was one of the first critics of *Piaget's theory of developmental stages. The guidance for the original *Foundation Stage of the national curriculum supported Isaacs's philosophy that parents are the most important educators in a child's life, establishing the importance of significant adults in child development; and this philosophy is equally reflected in the pedagogic principles underpinning the subsequent (2007) *Early Years Foundation Stage. After establishing the Malting House, Isaacs went on to lecture in early childhood education at the Institute of Education at the University of London.

Further Reading: S. Isaacs *Intellectual Growth in Young Children* (Routledge, 1930) sets out Isaacs's educational philosophy and principles. A.W.

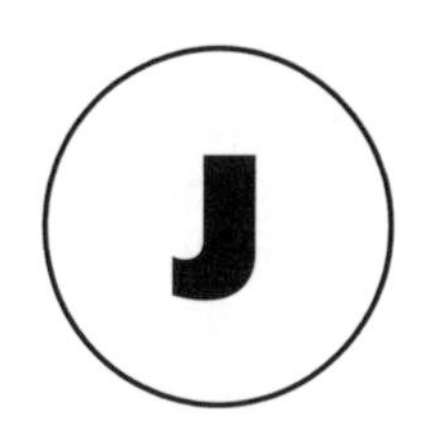

Joint Council for General Qualifications (JCGQ) Established in 1999 to provide a forum for discussion and decisions on joint strategy between the *awarding bodies responsible for the awards of *General Certificate of Secondary Education, *Advanced Level, *Vocational Advanced Level, *key skills, *Advanced Extension Awards, and certification of a range of other achievements and skills. The Joint Council's membership is made up of the **unitary awarding bodies**, which are the *Assessment and Qualifications Alliance, *Edexcel, and *OCR, as well as the Welsh Joint Education Committee and the Northern Ireland Council for Curriculum, Examinations, and Assessment. Its purpose is also to facilitate discussion and consultation with educational professionals and other stakeholders; and its web site, which is accessible to teachers and others, contains data on national examination results.

SEE WEB LINKS

- Provides access to publications on awarding bodies' assessment strategies and procedures.

Joint Council for National Vocational Qualifications (JCNVQ) Formed in 1992 to facilitate collaboration over the development of *General National Vocational Qualifications, the Joint Council consisted of the three major national *awarding bodies for vocational qualifications at that time: the *Business and Technology Education Council, the City and Guilds of London Institute, and the Royal Society of Arts. The Council was merged with the Joint Council for GCSE to become the Joint Council for General Qualifications, which operated from 1998 to 2003. In January 2004 it was superseded by the Joint Council for Qualifications to become the Joint Forum of Awarding Bodies. This, in turn, was superseded in 1999, when mergers between awarding bodies of vocational qualifications with those of general qualifications led to the formation of the *Joint Council for General Qualifications.

Joint Information Systems Committee (JISC) The purpose of this committee is to promote and facilitate the use of *information and communication technology (ICT) in education and research. It manages research and development programmes, funds ICT-related development projects in institutions of *further and *higher education, encourages innovation, and provides resources and advice to support ICT and *e-learning across *post-compulsory education and training.

SEE WEB LINKS

- Provides access to publications on awarding bodies' assessment strategies and procedures.

journal, academic A discipline-specific publication through which academics and other researchers can publish and disseminate their work, the academic journal normally takes the form of a collection of articles, research papers, or reviews which have been submitted to the journal's editorial board. In most cases papers being considered for publication are submitted for scrutiny and appraisal by recognized academics or authorities in the appropriate field, who may recommend that the paper be accepted as it stands, or that specific revisions be made, or that the paper be rejected for publication. This process of refereeing is known as **peer review**. Publication in refereed journals is one of the **outputs** encouraged by the *Research Assessment Exercise (RAE), and is therefore a goal for many teachers in *higher education. For academics wishing to publish their research, a clear hierarchy of journals exists, with international refereed journals being considered the most prestigious. This hierarchy is reinforced by the assessment framework applied by the RAE. There is, therefore, considerable competition to place papers for publication, particularly in high-profile international journals, as an RAE approaches. For teachers and other academics in the field of education, a key publication is the ***British Educational Research Journal***, which is the journal of the *British Educational Research Association.

journal, reflective Teachers, and particularly student teachers, often find it useful to keep a journal or diary in which to reflect critically and analytically on their teaching in order to see what they have learned from it and how they could use this to inform future planning and to contribute to their *continuing professional development. The keeping of such a journal might involve daily reflections, but more usually the journal will be used to record and reflect on **critical incidents**, which are situations or events of particular professional significance. In order to contribute effectively to a teacher's professional development, journal entries would be expected to do more than simply describe events, and should involve some element of action planning for future practice. The keeping of a reflective journal is particularly encouraged in programmes of teacher training, and it is used extensively within the *action research model of education research.

junior school The name usually given in England to schools catering for pupils aged 7–11, delivering *Key Stage 2 of the *national curriculum. In some cases these are combined with an *infant school under the leadership of one *head teacher to provide continuous primary education through Key Stages 1 and 2 until pupils progress to secondary school at the age of 11. *See also* ENGLAND, EDUCATION IN.

Kennedy Report (1997) The Kennedy Report *Learning Works*, published by the *Further Education Funding Council, represents the findings of the committee chaired by Dame Helena Kennedy which investigated patterns of participation in, and access to, *further education, and is a significant document which helped to drive the *widening participation agenda. As a result of the Report, a national strategy was implemented which aimed to ensure that all UK citizens over the age of 16 would have equal access to further and *higher education. The main themes of the Report were that learning was central to national and individual economic prosperity and social cohesion, and that equity dictated that all should have the opportunity to succeed. Furthermore, it was suggested that a dramatic shift in policy was needed to widen participation in post-16 learning, and to foster a culture in which continuing learning was considered a natural facet of adult life. Dame Helena's task was to reach under-represented groups and non-traditional learners and to define the critical role of the further education sector in the process. The Report defined further education as 'everything that does not happen in schools or universities'. The notion of widening participation has been superseded to a great extent by that of *lifelong learning, which continues to address common barriers that adults have in accessing education, such as pressure of work; family and social life; financial constraints; and cultural and language issues.

The issue of *widening participation specifically for learners with learning difficulties or disabilities was explored by the *Tomlinson Report (1996).

V.C., K.A.

key skills These are defined as communication, application of number, information technology (IT), working with others, improving own learning and performance, and problem-solving. They form a part of the post-16 curriculum. Recognition is given to all six, but only the first three are externally assessed. Their inception can be traced back to a document entitled *A Basis for Choice*, produced by the *Further Education Unit in 1979, which advocated a core entitlement for all students in *further education which should include communication, numeracy, and personal skills, arguing that these were the **core skills** demanded by employers. In 1990 the *National Curriculum Council listed six core skills, the development of which should form a part of the post-16 vocational curriculum. These were communication, numeracy, IT, problem-solving, personal skills, and a modern foreign language, and corresponded to the core skills being promoted at that time by the *Technical and Vocational Education Initiative. In the same year there was a recommendation from the **Schools Examination and Assessment Council** that core skills should also become a part of the *Advanced Level curriculum. This recommendation was repeated in the *Dearing *Review of Qualifications for 16–19-Year-Olds* (1996), in which core skills were identified as one of the strengths of the *General National Vocational Qualification curriculum. The skills were referred to in this document as 'key' skills, and this terminology continues to be used, while the skills areas referred to remain the same. *See also* FUNCTIONAL SKILLS.

SEE WEB LINKS

- Provides the detailed list and links to all levels.

key stage (KS) The four chronological stages into which the *national curriculum programmes of study are divided. These are: Key Stage 1 for ages 5–7; Key Stage 2 for ages 8–11; Key Stage 3 for ages 11–14; and Key Stage 4 for ages 14–16. Within the schools sector, education for 16–19-year-olds is sometimes referred to unofficially as 'Key Stage 5', although in reality schooling for this age group falls outside the bounds of the national curriculum.

kinaesthetic *See* LEARNING STYLES.

kindergarten Although widely used to describe any school or class for the youngest of school age children, this term originates in a system of provision aimed specifically at very young children and based on the educational theories of Friedrich *Froebel, who believed that children will best develop holistically through the medium of play. In German the term translates literally as 'children's garden'; in other words, a place of play.

Kingman Report (1988) The *Report of the Committee of Inquiry into the Teaching of English Language*, chaired by Sir John Kingman. It failed to conclude, as some expected it to, that the teaching of English should place more emphasis on the formal rules of grammar. The Report did argue, however, that 'the working of a democracy depends on the discriminating use of language on the part of all its people'.

knowledge What is known. According to *Bloom's Taxonomy, education engages with three domains of knowledge. One is the *cognitive domain, concerned with what students know and understand. The other two are the *affective, which is concerned with the development of attitudes and feelings; and the *psychomotor, which focuses on the development of physical skill, and is concerned with students' knowing how to perform a task. The term 'knowledge' in its broadest sense can be used to encompass all three of these. In its narrowest sense it can be taken to mean a body of information in the form of bare facts, such as that possessed by someone who is able to name capital cities correctly or cite the dates and sequence of monarchs. A fictional exponent of this latter interpretation of knowledge is Mr Gradgrind from Charles Dickens's novel *Hard Times* (1854), who claims that education is all about 'Facts, facts, facts', and whose name is now synonymous with this point of view. Knowledge in this limited sense is about recall and *rote learning. Most educators today would argue that, in many contexts, the acquisition of facts alone is of limited value without the development of some level of understanding. In simple terms, this would involve moving beyond the 'who', 'what', and 'when' to the 'how' and the 'why'.

The contrast between rote learning and understanding is not confined to the cognitive domain. In the psychomotor domain, too, a learner may gain the ability to undertake a task (that is, know how to perform it), without necessarily developing an understanding of why it should be done that way. So, for example, a student may be taught to assemble the ingredients for a loaf of bread, and to knead and bake an edible loaf, without understanding the purpose of including yeast, or how a raising agent works. With the addition of that understanding, their knowledge of how to bake bread would be of a different order. A further question concerning the psychomotor domain, widely debated during the growth of *competence-based training, was that of *sufficiency: how many times must a student perform a task correctly before we can reliably judge that they have succeeded not by chance but that they genuinely know how to do it?

More problematic still is the measurement of a student's knowledge in the affective domain. The question raised here is about the relationship between the acquisition of knowledge and the development of 'right' attitudes or feelings. In the education of health or care workers, for example, it remains unclear whether such curriculum requirements as empathy or *emotional intelligence can be taught or accurately assessed; or, indeed, in what sense such attributes can be construed as a form of knowledge.

For educators, an abiding question has been that of how knowledge is acquired. For example, much of *Piaget's work was concerned with how children move through different stages of learning. Theories of *learning which are currently used to explain knowledge acquisition also draw heavily on the work of psychologists of the *behaviourist, cognitivist, and *humanist schools.

Underlying all this is the philosophical question which asks how we can reliably know anything at all, and what the distinction is between knowledge and belief. The relativism associated with postmodernism suggests that all knowledge is culturally, socially, and politically constructed, rather than absolute. This is most clearly illustrated by the teaching of history, where the distinction between knowledge and interpretation can be problematic, and may be influenced or decided according to current hegemonies. This leads us to wider ideological questions such as who decides what is legitimate or worthwhile knowledge and how *curriculum content is chosen. Teaching and learning depend on an often implicit understanding of what knowledge is. *Epistemology—the theory of knowledge—addresses the issue of what we count as valid knowledge, and what types of 'knowing' we marginalize or reject, and why.

knowledge about language (KAL) An understanding of, and ability to employ correctly, the rules which govern language, such as phonetic rules, spelling, syntax, and grammar. In the context of the *national curriculum, KAL is normally integrated into the pupil's learning experience across all subjects, rather than formally taught through structured exercises in English grammar, as used to be the practice up to the middle of the 20th century. To facilitate this integrated approach, KAL is now an integral part of the *National Literacy Strategy. The theory is that a learner will draw upon the knowledge they have gained about their first language when they begin to learn a new one. Their ability to name the parts of speech, such as nouns and verbs, for example, will

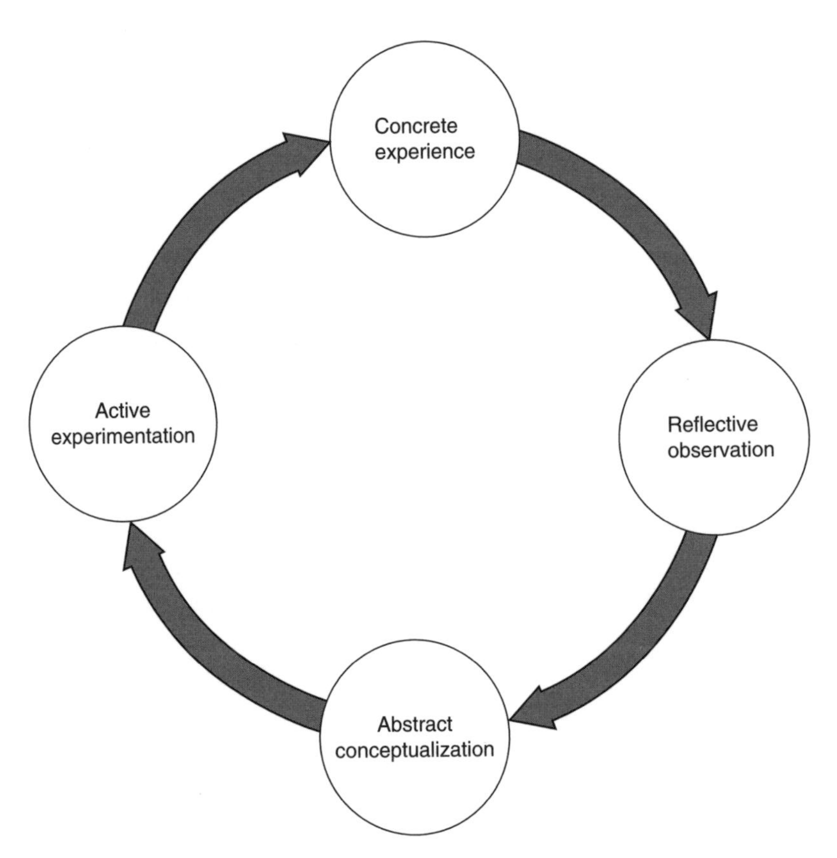

Kolb and Fry's 'learning cycle'

Kolb and Fry's four learning styles

Learning style	Preferences
Converger	Abstract conceptualization and active experimentation: practical, unemotional, rational
Diverger	Concrete experience and reflective observation: imaginative and aesthetic, interested in people and the ideas of others
Assimilator	Abstract conceptualization and reflective observation: theoretical, interested in abstract connections and ideas
Accommodator	Concrete experience and active experimentation: practical, adventurous, intuitive

facilitate their study of a second language by providing a frame of reference and a set of underlying grammatical rules.

SEE WEB LINKS

- A list of ways in which KAL can be applied to the learning of a second language in Key Stage 2.

Kolb, David (b. 1939) An American educator specializing in the field of organizational behaviour as well as education. His name is, perhaps, synonymous with the experiential learning model he developed in collaboration with Roger Fry in the 1970s, which is discussed in his book *Experiential Learning: Experience as the Source of Learning and Development* (1984). This concept had already been the subject of much discussion, and Kolb acknowledges the work of influential educationalists of the 20th century, such as *Piaget, *Dewey, and *Rogers. Kolb and Fry's 'learning cycle', which draws on the work of Kurt Lewin (1890–1947), presents a model of the relationships between 'concrete experience, reflective observation, abstract conceptualization, and active experimentation' in the learning process. They postulate that the cycle can begin at any of the four stages, and, as it is rarely completed in one tour, would be more properly represented as a spiral. They argue that it follows from this premiss that the most effective learning will take place where individuals have an equal and balanced response to each of the stages, but acknowledge that most people have preferences for certain aspects of the cycle. This leads to the recognition of *learning styles; in Kolb and Fry's model, each of the four styles they identify is based on a preference for two of the stages, as shown in the table.

Kolb's work has attracted much attention; it was, for instance, the basis for the commonly used learning styles inventory launched in the UK by Peter Honey and Alan Mumford in 1982. Like the Honey and Mumford inventory, it has been criticized as failing to take sufficient account of reflection, cultural influences, and the acquisition of knowledge. However, Kolb's strenuous argument that individuals differ in the ways that they learn has ensured that his work continues to have influence.

SEE WEB LINKS

- Provides discussion of experiential learning critiques of David Kolb's theory. V.C., K.A.

language across the curriculum A forerunner of the *National Literacy Strategy (NLS), and based on the premiss that, as advocated in the Bullock Report of 1975, all teachers, whatever their subject, should also see themselves as sharing the responsibility for helping pupils to develop English language skills across the curriculum, either directly or by modelling good practice. The introduction of the NLS in 1997 represented a formalizing of this approach. *See also* LITERACY HOUR.

language deficit A lack of skills in spoken and written English which may have a detrimental effect on a pupil's ability to learn. The concept of language deficit has been used to explain underachievement particularly in those pupils whose home circumstances might tend to leave their language skills underdeveloped. In this sense it is an explanation closely linked to theories of cultural and social deprivation and to the concept of *social class. *See also* LITERACY HOUR; NATIONAL LITERACY STRATEGY.

language laboratory A specialized room, equipped with electronic audio resources, for the teaching and learning of spoken languages. Each student is provided with headphones and can listen to, repeat, and assimilate the language at their own pace, from tapes, CDs, or online recordings. The teacher facilitates and supports learning by interacting with individual students through a central control which allows them to instruct, correct, and encourage students, and to monitor their progress. Such facilities are found in further and higher education, but rarely in schools. Developments in *information communication technology have made possible increasingly sophisticated applications for language laboratory use. The language laboratory is classed as a teaching resource, rather than a *method of instruction.

language school A school which recruits mainly overseas students of all ages, and offers courses at various levels in written and spoken English as a second language. Such schools are usually privately owned and employ teachers, often on short, fixed-term contracts, who have a qualification in Teaching English as a Second Language, but do not need to have *qualified teacher status. *See also* ENGLISH AS A FOREIGN LANGUAGE.

languages in primary schools *See* NATIONAL LANGUAGES STRATEGY.

lateral thinking A concept and technique popularized by Edward de Bono (b. 1933), which approaches problem-solving by considering the question from a number of angles other than the obvious one. In that it avoids convergent thinking, it may sometimes be equated with its opposite, divergent thinking, and is best described as a form of reasoning which does not proceed in the usual series of logical steps, but requires creativity on the part of the thinker. The following is a typical question which has been used to encourage lateral thinking in order to arrive at an answer. *John and Mary lie dead on the floor. Part of the carpet has been soaked by water and there are pieces of a broken glass bowl lying beside the bodies. The room is locked and its only living occupant is a cat. How did John and Mary die?* The answer, of course, is that they are goldfish! This sort of puzzle requires the thinker to recognize the automatic assumptions about 'the way things are' (for example, that human names must denote humans) which deflect us from considering other possible interpretations. Thus, lateral thinking is regarded as an aspect of creative thinking, and is often included in the teaching of *thinking skills.

Further Reading: E. de Bono *Lateral Thinking: Creativity Step by Step* (Harper Paperbacks, 1973).

later life learning As *lifelong learning has become associated increasingly with retraining and with learning for employment, those people concerned with learning for its intrinsic satisfactions and sheer joy have searched for a term which makes a distinction. Members of the *University of the Third Age in particular, since they are by definition out of the labour market, have emphasized the value to individuals and the community of continued learning throughout life, including learning undertaken during retirement. To this end, they have coined the term 'later life learning' to refer not only to learning for and by older people but to learning which is usually shared and pursued for its own value to human beings, for example in terms of personal growth and development. In doing so they reject what they see as the reductive view of *instrumental education aimed at preparation for employment which is often the focus of contemporary government policy and funding. In this sense, later life learning is a concept which draws upon the theory of *liberal education.

Launchpad schools An initiative announced in 2002 in which 30 schools drawn from the primary and secondary sectors were chosen to pioneer government strategies to reduce the workload of teachers. The initiative received £4 million in government funding; provided every teacher in the chosen schools with a networked laptop computer and Internet access; gave head teachers professional support in devising strategies to reduce workloads; and enabled schools to appoint extra support staff, including classroom assistants, and technicians to support the teaching of *information technology.

lead inspector The inspector responsible for leading the team formed to carry out an *Ofsted *inspection. Their leadership responsibility includes compiling the pre-inspection briefing, which is based on scrutiny of the school's self-evaluation and will identify possible issues for inspection. It may also include a pre-inspection visit to the school; meeting parents and governors; attending frequent meetings with the head teacher and other members of the *senior leadership team to discuss the progress of the inspection; meeting all staff where possible, briefly, at the start of the inspection; coordinating the inspection; collating the report; and giving feedback on the inspection finding to the head teacher. *See also* SELF-ASSESSMENT REPORT.

league tables (performance tables) Data measuring the performance of educational institutions against established criteria, and against other education providers of the same type. The purpose of league tables, according to the UK government, is to allow parents and carers to make informed choices about the most appropriate schools for their children. The first tables comparing secondary schools' *examination results were published in 1992, followed by the publication of tables for *post-compulsory provision in 1993, and subsequently by *primary in 1997. There was considerable opposition to their introduction from many stakeholders, who felt that the reputation of institutions might be damaged without good reason, particularly because examination results on their own cannot indicate how much progress has been made by students during their time in the institution. To address this, a measurement of the *value added to students' attainment was introduced to the tables in 2003, though the debate over the validity of such published data still continues. V.C., K.A.

Learndirect An *e-learning network which delivers three types of service: careers advice, courses aimed at improving *key skills, and work-based e-learning programmes for businesses. It is operated by the *University for Industry in England, Wales, and Northern Ireland. Learndirect Scotland is funded by the Scottish government, and provides information about access to educational and training courses in Scotland.

SEE WEB LINKS

- Explains the function and remit of Learndirect.
- Explains the purpose of Learndirect Scotland.

learner-centred An approach to teaching and learning in which the learner, their interests, enthusiasms, and aspirations are taken as the starting point of the education process, and the learner is credited with taking responsibility for their own learning. The *teacher or *educator is regarded, according to this model, as a facilitator of learning, rather than as a dispenser of knowledge or skills; and the learning process itself takes into account not only the academic needs of the learner, but also their emotional, creative, psychological, and developmental needs. Based on a *humanistic model of education, the learner-centred (or pupil-centred) approach owes much of its underlying philosophy to theorists such as *Rogers and educators such as *Malaguzzi. The lesson planning and teaching takes into account the learners' needs in relation to their social, emotional, and personal development, and allows for learner control over the learning activities employed; and the curriculum takes as its starting point those topics which are of direct interest and relevance to the learners. In a learner-centred approach, learners are encouraged to take some responsibility for monitoring and evaluating their own progress.

In its most radical form it implies a democratic community of learning where learners and teachers have equal status, and learners exercise a choice over whether and what they will learn. It is an approach to education which emphasizes *discovery learning and the learner's right to self-determination. From a philosophical point of view it sits uneasily with externally imposed targets and testing and with a standardized curriculum. It is commonly (and to some extent inaccurately) used, however, simply to describe a style of teaching in which the learners are actively engaged with their learning rather than adopting the role of passive recipients of knowledge. In this sense it is construed as the opposite of teacher-centred learning, in which the teacher takes the active role and the learners are required merely to be receptive.

learning Learning, rather than teaching, is the central purpose of education. It is usually defined as a change in someone's behaviour, *knowledge, level of skill, or understanding which is long-lasting or permanent and is acquired through experiences rather than through the process of growth or ageing. In this sense it is difficult to draw a clear distinction between what is learned through education or training and what is acquired through conditioning or exposure to propaganda. Some educationalists, therefore, would prefer to link definitions of learning to the concept of self-actualization or personal development, situating the process in a *humanist context rather than a purely *behaviourist one. *See also* MOTIVATION.

Learning and Skills Council (LSC) In 2001 the LSC took over the functions of the *Further Education Funding Council and the *Training and Enterprise Councils (TECs) with a government remit to improve post-16 education and training provision in England, other than that provided by universities, in order to produce a world-class skilled workforce by 2010. As well as a central council, there were 47 local LSCs, each of which was managed by a board of executive directors, whose boundaries of operation roughly coincided with those of *local authorities. Their responsibility included the strategic planning of further education and skills provision within their area, as well as the distribution of funding for such provision. This put them in a position of considerable power in relation to *further education colleges and other providers. Each local LSC board consisted largely of local employers, with some representation from unions and the local authority. When the LSCs took over from the TECs, they also took on many of the TECs' operational staff, such as trainers and administrators, so that some continuity of networks was maintained. From 2008 the local LSCs were replaced by Regional Boards, which took over many of their functions and are responsible to the national Learning and Skills Council.

SEE WEB LINKS

- Details of the LSC's role and aims.

Learning and Skills Development Agency (LSDA) Successor to the *Further Education Development Agency, the LSDA provided advice and curriculum support for post-16 education and training, and resources to support research into post-compulsory education and training. Its function was taken over by the *Quality Improvement Agency in 2006.

Learning and Skills Network (LSN) A national UK organization that was formed in 2006 following the demise of the *Learning and Skills Development Agency. It is a non-profit organization which provides practical support by delivering quality improvement and staff development programmes for the *learning and skills sector. Such programmes are provided directly to schools, colleges, and training organizations, practitioners, and policy-makers. The programmes are offered to support current government quality improvement initiatives in education and training through research, staff training events, or on a consultancy basis.

SEE WEB LINKS

- Provides information on projects and resources.

V.C., K.A.

learning and skills sector One of several terms used to describe the *post-compulsory sector of education and training which covers all provision except that offered by *universities and other institutions of *higher education. The sector is best defined as that covered by the remit of the *Learning and Skills Council, and is therefore wider than that traditionally covered by the term 'further education', since it also includes sixth form provision and *adult education. It is a terminology not in use in Scotland.

Learning and Teaching Scotland (LTS) Established in 2000, LTS is based in Glasgow and Dundee and is the key organization for curriculum development in Scotland, providing support and guidance to teachers and other professionals in education, particularly in the use of *information communication technology for learning. It was formed from the merger of two bodies: the Scottish Council for Educational Technology and the Scottish Consultative Council on the Curriculum. It consists of four directorates, each with a specialized remit.

SEE WEB LINKS

- Provides links to information about the functions and funding of LTS.

learning difficulties Most types of learning difficulty can be categorized as either specific or non-specific. Specific learning difficulties most commonly include conditions such as *dyslexia and *attention deficit hyperactivity disorder; *dyscalculia, verbal *dyspraxia, and dysphasia also belong to this category. Specific learning difficulties affect a particular aspect of learning rather than the overall abilities of students. A dyslexic student, while experiencing significant difficulties with reading and writing, may also enjoy high levels of academic achievement in a range of subjects. It is important not to assume that a student with a specific learning difficulty is less able than others. There are those students who underachieve and are simply classed as less able and as having special needs. These are the students whose learning difficulties might be classed as non-specific or general. The impact on development and progress can result in social immaturity, which impedes the ability to develop age-appropriate friendships, problems with written and spoken language, difficulty in grasping new concepts, poor concentration, which makes listening and acquiring new skills difficult, and poor organizational skills. Whether specific or non-specific, learning difficulties are also described as being moderate (MLD) or severe (SLD). A generalization of thought concerning the distinctions used to be that students with MLD cope well at school, with low levels of intervention needed, and will acquire some level of qualifications, while those with SLD will be educated in special schools without ever having achieved the most basic skills. The latter description is applied to students who are unlikely to achieve level 2 of the *national curriculum by the end of Key Stage 4.

Further categorization applies to students whose *cognitive development is significantly behind that of students of the same age, and who may also have additional sensory or motor disabilities. These are students with profound and multiple learning difficulties (PMLD). Students with PMLD may also have communication difficulties. It is more usual for students with PMLD to be educated in *special school settings. The needs of students with PMLD are complex and require high levels of support and intervention. Schools will engage with other outside agencies such as physiotherapists, speech and language therapists, and medical professionals.

Whatever category of learning difficulty applies, it is essential that reasonable adjustments are made in order to afford the students maximum access to an appropriate curriculum so that they achieve their full potential by setting realistic expectations which challenge and stimulate the students. T.B., L.E.

learning mentor Introduced in 1999 as part of the **Excellence in Cities (EiC)** initiative, learning *mentors are employed to work with learners in schools and colleges in order to help them to overcome barriers to learning and engage more fully with the learning process. This may involve anything from building motivation to giving practical assistance with literacy issues or note-taking skills. They are a recognized occupational group required to work to the national occupational standards for **Learning Development and Support Services (LDSS)**. A 2003 report from *Ofsted, *Excellence in Cities and Education Action Zones: Management and Impact*, concluded that in 95 per cent of the schools surveyed, the mentoring programme had had a positive impact on the school as a whole, as well as on the behaviour and learning of individual pupils. The initiative now falls under the aegis of the Department for Children, Schools, and Families.

SEE WEB LINKS

- Maps the functions of the learning mentor.

learning objective *See* OBJECTIVE, LEARNING.

learning organization An organization in which its members, whatever their level or status, are working continuously as individuals or teams to increase their effectiveness and to achieve outcomes about which they hold a set of shared values. This theory, originally applied in the context of large companies, suggests that if the personnel within an organization are each themselves committed to learning, then that organization will be the better equipped to adapt in response to constant demands for change. This idea is clearly of particular relevance to educational organizations such as schools, colleges, and universities which operate in an environment of rapid and continuous policy-driven change. The concept of the learning organization also involves the idea of continuous improvement, a policy goal which is urged upon educational institutions through, for example, *Ofsted and the *Quality Improvement Agency. One aim of the learning organization, therefore, is that each individual within it also continues to learn and develop. To this end, it will adopt a model of continuing professional development (CPD). We can see this reflected in national policy in, for example, the key areas of reform set out in the 2006 *White Paper *Further Education: Raising Skills, Improving Life Chances*, which include a regulatory CPD provision for all teachers in the further education sector.

Further Reading: P. Senge *The Fifth Discipline: The Art and Practice of the Learning Organisation* (Doubleday, 1990).

learning styles Some students learn in a different way from others and so need to be taught in a way that makes it easy for them to learn. Where their preferred learning opportunities are not provided, students may perform less well and therefore mistakenly be assumed to be underachieving through lack of ability. The three most widely recognized categories of learning styles are visual, auditory, and kinaesthetic. The majority of people are **visual learners**, who use mainly their sight to gather information. They cope well in lessons with lots of written, pictorial, and diagrammatic styles of presentation. Visual learners struggle where there is an emphasis on giving information orally. **Auditory learners** prefer spoken explanations to expand any graphical information presented to them. The use of technological aids such as voice recorders can be as effective as the teacher's voice. **Kinaesthetic learners** prefer to learn through activity. They enjoy movement and space. A great benefit to kinaesthetic learners is to be able to watch another person demonstrate what they need to do before trying themselves. Kinaesthetic learners enjoy hands-on activities. Most people possess elements of all three learning styles. This makes a *multi-sensory approach to teaching the most likely to engage all students most of the time. *See also* KOLB. T.B., L.E.

learning support assistant *See* TEACHING ASSISTANT.

Learning Support Unit (LSU) An integral part of a school's approach to supporting pupils who have become disengaged, and who have challenging *behaviour. LSUs provide individual support programmes which may include one-to-one or small-group teaching for pupils identified as having emotional and social difficulties. Ideally pupils will follow their usual curriculum programmes of study within the support unit. Some pupils may need a support package to be put in place which enables them to carry on studying while they address their behaviour issues. Though the support is carried out away from mainstream lessons, best practice exists where all staff are aware of the ethos of the LSU and work in partnership with support staff to reintegrate pupils as quickly as possible. Some LSUs are not on the same site as the school. It is preferable that a unit is part of a school's *inclusion faculty.

Pupils who are typically supported in an LSU will be those who find it difficult to accept sanctions and who challenge authority. They may be aggressive or possess poor social communication skills. Difficult family circumstances resulting in low self-esteem and poor confidence levels are common among pupils supported in LSUs. Such pupils are quite often victims of bullying or other forms of abuse and have very poor attendance levels. LSUs are often a 'safe haven' where pupil can rebuild their confidence. There should be clear exit and entry criteria and procedures for referrals to LSUs. The units must not be seen as 'sin bins' or 'dumping grounds' for *disruptive pupils. Support in LSUs should be short-term and planned. The work of LSU staff will be closely linked with parents and carers and with professionals from other agencies, particularly with social care workers and behaviour support services. *Child and adolescent mental health workers are often involved with pupils in LSUs. T.B., L.E.

learning theory Sometimes referred to as 'the psychology of learning', the body of theory about how and why learning takes place draws heavily on the work of schools of psychology as diverse as the *behaviourists, on the one hand, and the *humanists, on the other. It underpins much of the professional practice of teachers in all sectors of education since it may be drawn upon to answer the key question, How do learners learn best? Of course, there is no definitive answer to this, but rather a range of theories, any one of which will be more applicable in some situations than in others. For the teacher, the application of a theory is only useful if it works. As professionals, they are encouraged to formulate their own theoretical grounding based on their experience of professional practice and their accumulated propositional knowledge. This may be formalized through the process of *action research or other forms of continuing professional development. *See also* COGNITIVE; GESTALT; MASLOW.

lecture A *method of teaching used mainly in higher education, where students are taught in large groups, often in specially designed **lecture theatres**, which are tiered so that all students have a view of the teacher (or *lecturer) and whatever resources or visual aids are being used. The advantage of the lecture is that it allows a large number of students to be taught in a relatively short length of time. It is therefore cost-effective in terms of human resources. From an educational point of view, however, it does have some disadvantages, including the fact that the lecture format does not easily allow for student–teacher dialogue, and that it requires students to possess sophisticated note-taking skills if they are to benefit fully from the process. The very term 'lecture theatre' itself goes some way towards setting expectations of the respective roles of lecturer and students, since it implies that the lecture will be a performance on the part of the lecturer, thereby casting students simply as an audience. The model of learning implicit in this scenario is a very restrictive one, predicated on the student as the passive recipient of learning. Moreover, the lecture, as a method which lends itself well to teaching in the *cognitive domain, is less effective for other types of learning such as the acquisition of practical skills. It could also be argued that anything capable of being said in a lecture could as easily be presented in written form for students to read at their leisure, thereby dispensing with the teacher–student contact altogether. On the other hand, an interesting lecture, well delivered, may both inspire and motivate its audience.

The term is also used in a less precise way in both *further and *higher education to mean any type of *lesson, as in the sentence 'Lectures begin at nine o'clock', where the 'lectures' in question may, in fact, be seminars, practical laboratory sessions, or lessons in a normal classroom.

lecturer 1. A generic term for a teacher in *further or *higher education. In further education there are three lecturer grades: lecturer, senior lecturer, and principal lecturer. In *universities the grading continues to *reader and *professor. Post-1992 universities and *colleges of higher education usually conflate the lecturer and senior lecturer grades into one, which is the equivalent on the pay scale to the standard lecturer grade in the older universities. Although further education colleges still refer to their teaching staff as lecturers, the national standards for *qualified teacher status in the sector produced by *Lifelong Learning UK refer to them throughout as 'teachers'.

2. One who delivers a *lecture. *See also* PAY, TEACHERS'.

Leitch Report (2006) Lord Sandy Leitch was tasked by the UK government in 2004 to review the UK's long-term skills needs. The final Leitch Report, *Prosperity for All in the Global Economy: World Class Skills*, was published by Her Majesty's Stationery Office for Her Majesty's Treasury in December 2006. Apart from its aim to advise on ways to restore the UK's position as a major leader in the skills needed to compete globally, the Report also presents suggestions for strategies designed to help increase productivity and employment rates in the UK, with the effect of reducing poverty and inequality. The Report recommended that the UK strive to become a global leader in skills by 2020, benchmarked against the most economically developed countries of the Organization for Economic Cooperation and Development. To achieve this, the Report set out a number of 'stretching objectives' which would double education and training attainment levels required by 2020. These include: increasing the achievement of *basic skills to 95 per cent of the adult population for functional *literacy and *numeracy; exceeding 90 per cent of adults vocationally qualified to at least level 2 on the *National Qualifications Framework (NQF); shifting the balance from NQF level 2 to level 3 and increasing the number of those on apprenticeship schemes to 500 000 a year; and raising the number of adults who will be qualified to level 4 and above to 40 per cent, with 29 per cent committed to further progression.

SEE WEB LINKS

- The full text of the Report.

V.C., K.A.

lesson A means of dividing up both the school or college day and also the steps or components of the learning process. In schools and colleges, lessons are usually between 40 and 60 minutes long, and may sometimes run end to end in a 'double lesson' for those subjects where lengthy activities are essential, such as art, *games, and practical sciences. A summary of what lessons are being taught where and when is set out in the *timetable. For the teacher, the lesson represents a unit of planning and preparation. For each lesson a *lesson plan is drawn up which sets out the aims, the learning *objectives, the topic or topics to be covered, the activities and *methods to be used, the methods of *assessment, the resources required, and the arrangements made for *differentiation by task or by assessment. Each lesson constitutes a subsection of the *scheme of work which is drawn up from the programme of study, *syllabus, or course specification, so that, taken together, the complete sequence of lessons for the duration of the course of study in one subject is a process of translating these into learning activities and tasks in order for the specified learning outcomes to be achieved and assessed.

lesson plan A detailed plan, usually drawn up by the teacher, encapsulating the content and sequence of the *lesson. A typical lesson plan sets out the aims, the learning *objectives, the topic or topics to be covered, the activities and *methods to be used, the methods of *assessment, the resources required, the arrangements made for *differentiation by task or by assessment, and the ways in which the lesson will cover generic aspects of the curriculum, such as literacy or social, moral, and spiritual development.

The lesson plan has a number of functions. Primarily it serves to formalize the planning process, which in turn provides a means of ensuring that the curriculum is fully covered. In a practical way it serves as a prompt or reminder for the teacher in terms of how activities will be sequenced, what resources will be required, and so on. Lesson planning is also a developmental process, helping the teacher to think through issues such as the balance between teacher and learner activity; the learning needs of specific individuals and small groups; the provision of a sufficient variety of activities to ensure learner engagement; the most effective ways of presenting unfamiliar topics; and so on. It also contributes to the professional process of reflection and evaluation, in that the teacher is able to review how well the plan succeeded in its implementation, and which aspects they might wish to review and revise when the lesson is taught again. The plan also plays an essential part in quality assurance, and is regarded as an essential piece of documentation for the purpose of inspections and internal quality reviews.

Many schools and colleges require teachers to use a standardized lesson plan format. This usually takes the form of a grid, and is designed to ensure that all components of the lesson, such as inclusion, differentiation, and mandatory curriculum requirements are included.

level Refers both to the standard of achievement within a specific curriculum, and to the status of qualifications in a national framework. Thus, a pupil will be assessed as having attained a specific level as defined by the *national curriculum; and the same pupil may eventually go on to gain a degree, which is a qualification at level 6 of the *National Qualifications Framework. As well as applying to these curricular and national levels, the term may also be used within an individual institution to refer to stages in an education programme, where, for example, students going into their second year of a programme of study may be said to be progressing from level 1 to level 2.

level descriptor A definition of specified outcomes in terms of what the learner should be able to do, know, and understand at each *level of an attainment or qualification framework. Such descriptors are used for each level of *attainment in the *national curriculum.

level of attainment The descriptions of what a pupil who is working successfully at that level is achieving in each subject of the *national curriculum. *Standard Tasks are used to assess pupils at the end of each *key stage in order to ascertain the level of attainment at which each is working. There are seven levels, level 7 indicating the highest attainment and level 1 the lowest. Exceptionally, pupils may be awarded a level 8 for outstanding attainment. There are subdivisions within the levels themselves, indicated, for example, thus: 5a, 5b, 5c, where 'a' represents a higher level of achievement than b, and so on. These subdivisions allow the teacher to report with greater precision and accuracy on a pupil's attainment, as well as enabling a pupil's progress (or otherwise) within an attainment level to be monitored more easily. Attainment levels do not apply at *Foundation Stage. At Key Stage 1 pupils are expected to work at between levels 1 and 3 and to have attained level 2 by the end of that stage. At Key Stage 2 they are expected to work at between levels 2 and 5, and to have attained level 4 by the end of that stage. At Key Stage 3 they are expected to be working between levels 3 and 7, and to have attained level 5 or 6 at the age of 14. *See also* LEVEL DESCRIPTOR.

SEE WEB LINKS

- Provides a summary for parents on levels of attainment.

liberal education Originally, and literally, an education which *liberates* the pupil or student from errors in their thinking by encouraging the acquisition of genuine knowledge through a process of rational thought and reflection. The liberal knowledge thus gained is seen as quite distinct from the types of learning which are acquired through practice or whose purpose is to equip the learner with the ability to carry out particular tasks or activities. This distinction, which draws on Plato's theories of education and the acquisition of knowledge, may be expressed in today's terms as the difference between the acquisition of 'knowledge for its own sake' and the acquisition of instrumental knowledge designed for a specific end such as skills for employment. A liberal education, then, is one which is not designed to equip the learner for a job or the means to earn a living, but one which presents education as a 'good' in itself. The current differentiation in status between *academic and *vocational provision and qualifications, sometimes referred to as the 'academic–vocational divide', has its roots in this historical idea that the most valuable and genuine knowledge is liberal—or *liberating*—knowledge, gained purely for its own sake. The educational ideal formed the basis of school and university provision for the sons of 'gentry' in the 18th and early 19th centuries. The curriculum was made up largely of Latin and ancient Greek, its only purpose being to produce 'gentlemen of culture'. A curriculum which diverged from this liberal model, for example by introducing an element of instrumentalism, such as science or modern languages, which might better equip the learner with skills needed to earn a living, was considered suitable only for classes below the level of gentry, whose circumstances meant they might have to take paid employment. This class distinction between the provision of liberal and instrumental knowledge reinforced the idea that a liberal education was inherently of higher status. Instrumental, or useful, knowledge became closely associated with 'trade' and the artisan classes and with narrowness of purpose, while liberal education maintained its elite status and later became associated with a broad and life-enhancing curriculum and with the principles of *learner-centred education which aims to support the development of individual potential. This distinction was illustrated clearly in the 1960s and 1970s by the provision of an additional and eponymous *liberal studies curriculum for students on skills training courses in technical colleges (now *colleges of further education), designed to broaden their minds and enhance their experience of learning.

A liberal education is associated with the acquisition of knowledge which is theoretical rather than practical, reflective rather than instrumental, and valued for its own sake rather than acquired for some use. It is often understood today to be synonymous with a **general education** or **academic education**, inasmuch as these terms, too, are used to express the opposite of 'vocational' in the context of educational provision. It is, however, as much an ideal or a philosophical construct as it is a type of curriculum. To describe a model of education as 'liberal' is not only to state something about its purpose and curriculum content, but is also implicitly, and unavoidably, to ascribe a value to it.

liberal studies Part of the curriculum of *further education colleges in the 1970s and 1980s intended to contribute breadth to the education of students on *vocational courses by introducing topics such as literature, letter-writing, and sociological debate into their timetable. Its purpose derived from the *liberal education model, which regarded a purely vocational, or skills-based, curriculum as restrictive and mechanistic. It was aimed at developing the 'whole person', and represented the view that education should operate as a means of developing individual potential, aspirations, and enlightenment. By the 1990s liberal studies (or **general studies**, as it was sometimes known in this context) had been widely replaced by the teaching of communication and numeracy skills, later defined as *key skills, with the more instrumental purpose of providing students with the skills demanded by employers and building a more literate and numerate workforce.

Because of the 'bolt-on' nature of much liberal studies provision, it was sometimes viewed both by students and their vocational teachers as irrelevant and even risible. Something of this is captured in Tom Sharpe's comic novel *Wilt* (1976), which famously satirizes the contradictions of liberal studies provision in the 1970s.

library boards As part of the educational system in Northern Ireland there are five education and library boards which are the local education authorities and library authorities for their areas. They are: Belfast Education and Library Board, South Eastern Education and Library Board, Southern Education and Library Board, North Eastern Education and Library Board, and the Western Education and Library Board. Funds are allocated to the boards by the *Department of Education, Northern Ireland, and their responsibilities include: advising on the curriculum, enforcing school attendance, providing milk and meals, free books, and pupil transport, employing teachers in *controlled schools and employing non-teaching staff in controlled and *maintained schools. J.H.

lifelong learning 1. Originally used by educationalists to denote the idea that education is an essential part of life and an ongoing pursuit, rather than something which begins and ends with compulsory education, it has more recently become associated with workforce training. Rapid developments in technology, together with changes in employment patterns, have resulted in a greater demand for retraining and for higher qualifications in order for learners to compete in the job market. As this trend has developed during the 1990s and the early years of the 21st century, so the phrase 'lifelong learning' has become more frequently used, particularly in *White Papers on education and training, to indicate skills training and programmes leading to vocational qualifications.

2. Used to refer to the post-compulsory sector, particularly work-based training and further education, which are known collectively as the 'lifelong learning sector'. *See also* FURTHER EDUCATION; LATER LIFE LEARNING; LEARNING AND SKILLS SECTOR.

Lifelong Learning UK (LLUK) The sector skills council for the professional development of all those working in *further education, *higher education, work-based learning, and community learning and development. Established in January 2005, it took over the work of the *Further Education National Training Organization (FENTO) in managing the national standards for teacher training for the further education or *lifelong learning sector. These standards are now known as the **LLUK standards**, and lead to *qualified teacher learning and skills status. All provision of such training must be endorsed by LLUK's standards and verification arm, *Standards and Verification. The change of terminology for the sector from 'further education' to 'lifelong learning' is reflected in the succession from FENTO to LLUK.

SEE WEB LINKS

- Provides details of LLUK's major areas of operation.

link course A programme of study involving the collaboration of two or more institutions, which forms a 'link' in order to provide full coverage of the curriculum. These courses may represent collaboration between a *college of further education and a *university, where the student attends some classes in each institution or the teaching is shared between the two. More usually the link course is one run collaboratively between a secondary school and a further education college for the benefit of pupils who wish to include an element of vocational study into their *Key Stage 4 *curriculum. Since the publication of the 2005 *White Paper *14–19 Education and Skills*, this has become a more widely accepted practice. In colleges such pupils are sometimes referred to as 'link students'. *See also* 14–19 AGENDA.

Lisbon Strategy Aimed at building a competitive European economy with enhanced employment and a cohesive social structure by the year 2010, the Lisbon Strategy was the result of the Lisbon European Council summit of 2000. It is of direct relevance to education since the strategy's goal was recognized by heads of member states to be largely dependent on a review and modernization of the education and training systems of European member states. This process of change and modernization, where necessary, is carried out by the member states themselves and is not therefore an imposition by the European Union (EU) but rather a mutually agreed strategy. The collective element is in the dissemination and sharing of good practice and in the setting of agreed goals. These are closely linked to those set out for higher education in the member states as part of the *Bologna Process, and those adopted for vocational education and training in member states as a result of the *Bruges–Copenhagen Process. The three major goals of the Lisbon Strategy, to be achieved by a target date of 2010, are: an improvement in the effectiveness and quality of education and training systems within the EU; the accessibility of those education and training systems to all within the EU; and the accessibility of those systems to learners and trainees in the rest of the world.

literacy The ability to read and to write at a standard appropriate both to the individual's needs and to society's expectations. Standards of literacy, particularly among school-leavers, have been a matter of concern to educationalists, governments, and employers. At a policy level the problem has been addressed in a number of ways, including the introduction of *key skills across the post-16 curriculum; the introduction of a *National Literacy Strategy for schools; additional resources to support *basic skills provision for adults; and the reintroduction of phonics into the primary curriculum. A number of explanations have been offered for inadequate standards of literacy. These range from criticism of trends in teaching methods to the influence of video games and the semantic short cuts of mobile phone texting. *See also* ADULT LITERACY; FUNCTIONAL LITERACY; LITERACY COORDINATOR; LITERACY HOUR.

literacy coordinator A teacher with whole-school responsibility for ensuring that the *literacy skills of pupils are supported and developed in lessons across the *curriculum. The literacy coordinator plays a significant role in supporting the implementation of *national literacy strategies in a school and monitoring their effectiveness. Coordinators are often responsible for leading sessions of *in-service education for teachers to enable them to become familiar with materials provided by the national strategies; and for supporting the *senior leadership or senior management team in monitoring provision for literacy in all subjects. In a primary school, the literacy coordinator is responsible for overseeing and supporting the delivery of the *literacy hour. I.F.W.

literacy hour Part of the government's *National Literacy Strategy (NLS) introduced in 1998. While the NLS framework explains *what* should be taught, the *literacy hour is the *means* of teaching it. It is a compulsory part of *primary education which requires primary teachers to deliver a daily literacy lesson according to a recommended structure. Pupils are taught for the first half of the lesson as a whole class, and for the second part of the lesson they work in groups or individually, with the teacher focusing on supporting one group. The lesson ends with the pupils sharing and reflecting on what they have learned. What is taught can vary, but the general aim of the literacy hour is to raise the standard of pupils' reading, writing, spelling, grammar, and communication skills. The recommended structure of a literacy hour is as follows:

Section 1 (15 minutes)	Whole-class guided reading
Section 2 (15 minutes)	Whole-class word- or sentence-level work
Section 3 (20 minutes)	Group or individual work while the teacher works with one or more ability group
Section 4 (10 minutes)	Whole-class plenary session

I.F.W.

LLM Master of Laws, a higher degree awarded by a university or other higher education institution at *master's level. The successful candidate is entitled to use the letters LLM after their name.

loan, student Loans for full-time students on non-postgraduate courses were introduced by the 1990 *Education (Student Loans) Act, and were offered at an interest rate level with the rate of inflation, while at the same time student eligibility for financial help through the social security system was withdrawn. Previously, undergraduates' *fees were in most cases met by their *local authority. As this financial support was withdrawn, the proportion of 'top-up' fees necessary was increased, so that students in England without *bursaries or other sources of income are now expected to fund their tuition fees and living expenses through a combination of student loan and parental support or part-time work. In 2000 the loan system was extended to include part-time students on low incomes. The loans are administered through the Student Loans Company (SLC), a public sector organization, which also manages the collection of repayments from students no longer in higher education. The amount of the loan for which the student is eligible depends upon their course and place of study, their individual circumstances, and where they live. The SLC administers loans for tuition fees, for maintenance (living expenses), and for additional support in cases where the student has dependants, a disability, or a learning difficulty. Loans are paid in equal amounts at the start of each academic *term. All students on eligible courses are entitled to 75 per cent of the maximum loan. Eligibility for part or all of the remaining 25 per cent is based on an assessment of income.

Loans are repaid through the income tax system, repayments not beginning until the ex-student is earning over £15 000 per annum. The repayment is scaled to the loan-holder's income, a system known as income-contingent repayment. Nevertheless, opponents of the loans system argue that it discourages young people from lower-income families from applying for higher education, and is therefore socially divisive. In Scotland, where tuition fees were abolished in 1999, student loans are assessed and awarded through the *Student Awards Agency for Scotland. Loans are means-tested in the same way as student loans in England.

local authority (LA) The locally elected governing body of a town, county, or district, whose remit includes the support of *maintained schools. The arm of local government responsible specifically for education was until recently referred to as the **local education authority**; but the erosion of LA powers during the 1980s and 1990s, including the introduction of *grant maintained schools and the removal of further education colleges and polytechnics from their remit, saw a reduction in LAs' role of strategic planning, funding, and *inspection. The introduction of compulsory competitive tendering for LA *advisory and inspection services, introduced by the Local Government Act 1988, further reduced the LAs' power and influence in relation to the schools in their area of operations. This has resulted in a change of terminology which reflects, on the one hand, the recentralization of education policy-making, and, on the other, the delegation of powers such as budgetary control to the schools. Nevertheless, LAs still retain considerable responsibility for supporting schools in their area, particularly in the drive to raise standards of achievement and to implement national policy initiatives such as reform of children's services. In these areas, they are required to work closely with the *Department for Children, Schools, and Families.

Scottish maintained schools are funded by local authorities, of which there are 32. Currently the Scottish government pays an annual grant to LAs, who then decide how much of the grant will be allocated to education. Schools may then spend money as they see fit, within certain guidelines.

SEE WEB LINKS

- Describes the work of LAs in supporting education.

Local Management of Schools (LMS) A reform introduced in 1988 by the *Education Reform Act, which delegated financial responsibility and budgetary control of individual schools from the *local authority to the schools themselves. Part of its purpose was to introduce *market competition between schools in the belief that this would drive up standards of achievement and provision more effectively than the system of strategic planning operated until that time by local authorities. The reform had far-reaching effects, particularly on the role and responsibilities of the *head teacher, who now became responsible for balancing a substantial budget and for developing an effective marketing strategy, as well as for providing leadership on curricular and pedagogic issues.

London allowance An additional payment included in the salaries of teachers who work in London and its immediate area in recognition of the higher living costs associated with the capital. Lecturers in colleges and universities also receive a London allowance, although it is substantially less than that of teachers in schools. *See also* PAY, TEACHERS'.

longitudinal study Often used in educational *research, this type of study involves tracking individuals or groups over a period of time in order to monitor and record developments in their learning, circumstances, or achievement. A famous example of a longitudinal study is the television series *Seven Up!* (1964–), which followed the development of a group of individuals from the age of 7 into adulthood, reporting on developments in their lives at successive seven-year intervals.

looked-after children These are children who are in the care of the *local authority. Children come into care either through a court care order, where the court has satisfied itself that the child is at risk of 'significant harm' (section 31 of the Children Act 1989), or on a voluntary basis, when parents cannot cope for one of any number of reasons, such as extreme complex needs of the child or parental illness (section 20 of the Children Act 1989). Government statistics show that at any one time around 60 000 children are looked after in England, with the highest percentage being children subject to a care order. The local authority must have regard to their education and plan for minimum disruption to the child's life. Children are normally placed with foster parents or put in the care of relatives, although a small number, particularly those with challenging behaviour, are placed in care homes. Many children encounter several placements. Where possible, the care system aims to return children eventually to their families. The educational achievement of looked-after children is behind government expectations for children of the same age, and a government public service target has been set to address this issue, along with the issue of placement instability. T.B., L.E.

lower school Used in a variety of ways to differentiate between age groups of pupils in a secondary school. Schools with sixth forms may use it to refer to the majority of its pupils, those in Years 7–11. Alternatively, it might be used to indicate Years 7 and 8 only, while Years 9, 10, and 11 are referred to as 'middle' and 'upper' school. Its original usage was in public schools, where it was a term used for the younger pupils.

MA *See* MASTER'S DEGREE.

McCrone Committee of Inquiry Undertaken in 2000 and resulting in the McCrone Report, the Committee of Inquiry carried out a comprehensive review of Scottish education. Prompted in part by threats of industrial action by teachers, the Report focused on improvements to the profession. Its recommendations included those relating to teachers' career structure, working conditions, and pay. It also made recommendations about minimum class sizes, the necessity for stable positions for probationary teachers, the effective use of classroom assistants, and the need to monitor teacher workload. The subsequent implementation of the Committee's recommendations has had far-reaching effects on the working conditions of teachers in Scotland. S.M.

McQualifications A nickname given, initially by the press, to qualifications which are awarded by employers and subsequently recognized and accredited by the *Qualifications and Curriculum Authority (QCA). The nickname arises from the publicity given to the first of these cases early in 2008, when a qualification awarded by a chain of fast food restaurants to its managers who had followed a structured in-house training programme was awarded *National Vocational Qualification status at level 3 by the QCA, equivalent to *Advanced Levels. The significance of this development is in its recognition of the contribution which employers can make to the vocational education and training system, which is claimed by some to mark a liberalization in the provision of *vocational training. The sensationalist and in some cases scornful response to this development in the press and elsewhere may be indicative of an enduring view of vocational qualifications as invested with a lower status or value than their academic or general equivalent.

maieutic The *Socratic method of questioning which is designed to elicit the learner's *tacit knowledge. Learners are guided, by careful questioning, to come up with answers they had not consciously known they possessed.

mainstream Used to describe a 'standard' school in the state sector, supported by the *local authority. The majority of schools are mainstream, catering for the local community.

maintained school A school financially supported by the state; that is, maintained from public funds. These are more usually referred to as *'state schools'.

maintenance grant Money awarded to students for the purpose of subsidizing their living costs, such as accommodation, fares, and meals, but not intended for the payment of fees. In the past, *local authorities' education departments would have a discretionary fund from which such awards were made, either in cases of hardship, or where the applicant's case met the necessary criteria. These have been largely replaced by *Education Maintenance Allowances and other forms of subsistence funding, and by the introduction of *loans for students in *higher education. *See also* BURSARY.

major When undergraduates are studying for a degree which combines more than one subject, one of which is their chief field of study, that specialist subject is referred to as their major subject. As well as serving as an adjective, the term can be used as a noun to refer to the subject or to the student themselves, so that, for example, a student studying English literature, with philosophy and history as subsidiary subjects, will be an English major, for whom English is their major. In addition, it can be employed as a verb, as in 'She will major in English'.

Makaton A simple language based on signs for everyday words but incorporating facial expressions, symbols, and gestures as well as speech. Makaton has a core vocabulary consisting of everyday concepts such as 'drink' and 'toilet'; this is supplemented by a resource vocabulary consisting of over 7 000 words grouped in topics. A *national curriculum resource pack is available. Makaton is a universally recognized form of communication used for children and adults with *learning difficulties in the UK. T.B., L.E.

Malaguzzi, Loris (1920–94) An Italian educator whose work is closely associated with the *Reggio Emilia approach to early childhood education. As a middle school teacher in the Reggio Emilia district of Italy in the immediate aftermath of the Second World War, Malaguzzi was instrumental in founding an approach to young children's education which is based on mutual respect and reciprocity between teacher and child, and the philosophy that teaching and learning embodies a relationship of equality and democracy, rather than a power relationship in which the teacher dominates.

Born in Correggio in the province of Reggio Emilia, Malaguzzi was educated at the University of Urbino, where he gained a degree in pedagogy, and at the National Research Centre in Rome, where he was awarded a degree in psychology. Following the Allied liberation of Italy from fascist rule, in 1946 he became involved in the setting up of pre-schools organized and run by parents in Reggio Emilia, and in 1950 he established the Municipal Psycho–Pedagogical Centre in which he practised as a psychologist until the 1970s. In 1980, working as a consultant for the Italian Ministry of Education, he founded the Gruppo Nazionale Nidi-Infanzia (National Early Years Centre) in Reggio Emilia to promote child-centred education, and went on to travel Europe and the United States promoting his approach to *early years education. His travelling exhibition *The Hundred Languages of Children* (originally entitled *If the Eye Jumps Over the Wall*) was instrumental in bringing his educational philosophy to a wider audience of teachers and parents worldwide. Opening with the words 'Il bambino e fatto di cento' (literally, 'The child is made of a hundred'), Malaguzzi's manifesto goes on to say:

'The child has a hundred languages (and then a hundred hundred hundred more) but they steal ninety-nine. The school and the culture separate the head from the body. They tell the child to think without their hands, to do and make without their head, to listen and not to speak, to understand without joy, to feel love and awe only at Easter and Christmas. They tell the child to discover the world that is already there.'

This extract encapsulates several key points of Malaguzzi's beliefs about the education of young children: that children and their viewpoint are to be taken seriously; that education should not be defined in terms of what the state or the teacher decides should be taught; that it should not be subjected to categorization in the form of *curriculum subjects; but that it should arise from a response to the child's creativity and search for meaning. Indeed, asked whether he advocated curriculum planning, Malaguzzi is said to have responded that in his view this, like lesson planning, would simply lead to 'teaching without learning' and to the humiliation of the child. His ideas on education drew upon, and were influenced by, the work of an eclectic range of philosophers, educationalists, artists, and psychologists, who included key educational thinkers such as *Bruner, *Dewey, *Erikson, *Piaget, and *Vygotsky.

In describing his approach, Malaguzzi employs two metaphors which are useful in helping us to understand his educational philosophy. One presents the educative process as the tossing of a ball back and forth between child and teacher, an exchange in which both players are equal and in which they cooperate equally in the play and development of ideas. Another is of teacher and child embarking together on a journey downriver, rather than standing on opposite banks watching the river flow.

In acknowledgement of his contribution to the philosophy of early years education, Malaguzzi was awarded the Ygdrasil-Lego Prize by Denmark in 1992, and the Kohl Award in Chicago in 1993. He died at home in Reggio Emilia in 1994.

managed learning environment (MLE) The information systems and processes of an organization which contribute in any way to the learning of its students, and to the recording of their achievements. These will typically include the monitoring of attendance and student progress towards pre-set goals, and the tracking of support and guidance. An MLE allows any stakeholder in a student's career to access appropriate and necessary information on that student, within the confines of the law, and with appropriate restrictions according to role. An MLE can also include a *virtual learning environment in its framework. V.C., K.A.

management The *Education Reform Act 1988 resulted in a shift of much of the responsibility for the management of schools from the *local authority to the schools themselves. This was known as *Local Management of Schools (LMS). Part of the purpose for this reform was to encourage *market competition between schools. This was considered to be a more effective way of ensuring that standards of provision would rise than the previous system of strategic management by local authorities, which encouraged cooperation and collaboration between schools. Under LMS the management of the school became largely the responsibility of the *head teacher and the *governing body. They were required to manage the school's budget and business strategy as well as academic and curriculum matters. Some commentators (e.g. Ball 1994) suggest that one effect of this was to create a fundamental divergence between the agenda of school managers, concerned with market competition and balancing budgets, and that of teachers in the classroom, whose priorities were centred on *pedagogic issues. The tension between these two agendas would become apparent in situations where, for example, financial constraints imposed by management on staffing levels led to larger class sizes, thus raising concerns among the teachers about the quality of the pupils' learning experience.

A parallel situation arose when the *polytechnics were removed from local authority control following the *Further and Higher Education Act 1992, which also granted them *university status. Managers of these new universities were required to take control of multi-million-pound budgets and to enable the new university to compete, as a business, within the *higher education 'market'. Here again, this raised questions about the purpose of the organization and the potential contradictions inherent in, on the one hand, ensuring financial growth and, on the other, providing a public service.

Subsequent funding policy and continuing emphasis on market competition has had an impact on the role of management across all educational sectors. One notable consequence has been a growth in the use of business and management terminology within the education sector. Another has been the creation of new roles and titles, such as 'school manager', 'senior management team', 'finance director', and 'human resource manager'. Thus, the overall trend since the 1980s has been for head teachers, *principals, vice-chancellors, and their respective governing bodies to become increasingly involved in the management of business strategy and financial growth as well as the management of education in its pedagogic sense.

All this has been reflected in the range of professional development programmes and qualifications in the field of management which are now available to leaders and aspiring leaders of educational institutions. The acquisition of management skills as a route to promotion within the teaching profession has become widely recognized and acknowledged, and is reflected in the increasing numbers of classroom teachers from all sectors choosing to enrol for continuing professional development qualifications such as a postgraduate diploma or *master's degree in **Education Management**. *See also* MANAGERIALISM.

Further Reading: S. Ball *Education Reform: A Critical and Post-Structural Approach* (Open University Press, 1994).

managerialism The operation of an organization for the benefit of its managers, or in such a way that its activities and development are prescribed by managerial concerns and financial constraints. The word originates from the world of business and commerce, and is one example of the business terminology which has colonized the vocabulary of education since the 1980s. Associated with managerialism, particularly in *colleges and *universities, is the practice of addressing issues of human resourcing as purely business or financial, and the emphasis on *performance indicators, which takes precedence over individual scholarly activity or learning for its own sake. Within an educational context the term is most often used in a pejorative sense, and managerialism has been described by critics as the misapplication of private sector strategies to address public sector issues. *See also* MANAGEMENT.

mandatory award Before the introduction of the *student *loans system, *local authorities were required to award grants to eligible *higher education students in order to pay their university or college fees. Eligibility depended on the type of course being undertaken. The award was mandatory for some forms of higher education, for example for *initial teacher training and first degrees, where this was the student's first experience of this course of study. In some cases the award would also include some funding towards the student's maintenance costs. Eligibility for this was ascertained through means-testing, either of the student's parents or, in the case of adult students, of the students themselves. With the introduction of student loans, mandatory awards began to be phased out. *See also* MAINTENANCE GRANT.

Manpower Services Commission (MSC) A national body set up in 1974 to coordinate *vocational training and with responsibility to manage and expand the government's vocational training schemes, such as the *Youth Opportunities Programme and the Training Opportunities Scheme, which offered retraining and skills development to adults intending to re-enter the workforce. As a result of the *White Paper *A New Training Initiative* (1981), its work came to include coordination and management of the *Youth Training Scheme and the *Technical and Vocational Education Initiative. Its role involved dispensing funding to training providers, who included further education colleges, employers providing work-based training, and private training organizations. This control over funding, and the MSC's policy of funding a range of training providers, was resented in some quarters of the further education sector, which had hitherto seen itself as the main, if not sole, provider of 'off-the-job' training. The MSC was absorbed into the Department of Employment in 1988 and renamed, first as the Training Commission and then as the Training Agency. In 1991 most of its functions were taken over by the *Training and Enterprise Councils.

market Perhaps more properly 'quasi-market' as applied to education, this term refers to a political, social, and economic context in which competition is encouraged between schools, between colleges, and between universities for student numbers, excellence of results, and a reputation for delivering 'value for money'. The ideology of the free market as expounded by Friedrich Hayek (1889–1992) began to shape Conservative thinking radically in the mid-1970s. Hayek argued against socialist ideals of collective planning—a role which, in educational terms, could at that time be said to be embedded as a function of the local education authorities—claiming that such measures are doomed to failure in the face of the complexity and unpredictability of society and human nature. The market mechanism, it was argued, would lead to survival of the fittest through competition. In terms of education, a free market ideology is based on three propositions: that provision must reflect the public will; that schools, colleges, and universities which are responsive to the public are likely to survive; and that unpopular institutions will be forced to change or close. Critics of the free market in education address their arguments to one or more of these propositions, their main criticism being that changes brought about by the market will not necessarily be driven by genuine educational issues. For example, the public might be less concerned with educational excellence than with *league tables, tradition, or conformity of behaviour. Critics also argue that the market creates a situation in which favoured schools are able to exercise choice over the pupils they accept, thus reinstating *selection by the back door and subverting the claim that a free market in education will increase parental choice. Proponents of the application of a market model to educational provision argue that it functions to drive up performance standards, including cost-effectiveness and academic achievement.

marking The process of *assessing and grading learners' written work, usually carried out by a teacher or examiner as a part of their duties. It is a means whereby both teacher and learner can ascertain whether, and to what level, learning has taken place. At a minimum, the marker will indicate whether an answer is correct or incorrect. A more detailed form of marking will award points for each answer out of a possible total set out in a **marking scheme** and based on the stipulated *assessment criteria. The marking of *examinations does not normally involve providing the candidate with any direct *feedback on their work, apart from an overall score or grade. For non-examination work and coursework, however, it is normally expected that the marker will communicate clearly to the learner the strengths and weaknesses of their work, and what they need to do to improve it. Sometimes a process of **double marking** is implemented, whereby the learner's work is assessed separately by two markers. Instances when this might be used include when the initial marking results in a *borderline mark or grade, or the work to be marked is worth a large proportion of the overall *assessment (as in a dissertation, for example), or where the first marker is undecided about the mark to be awarded. Alternatively, a process of **blind double marking** may be undertaken, where the second marker does not know what mark the first marker has awarded. Marking is usually, and of necessity, carried out by teachers and lecturers outside lesson times, and can constitute a substantial part of their workload. *See also* MODERATION.

Maslow, Abraham (1908–70) An American psychologist whose theory of a hierarchy of needs leading to self-actualization is often used to illustrate and explain issues relating to learners' *motivation. It suggests that individuals' basic needs for safety, food and drink, and a sense of belonging and self-worth must be met before they will begin to address their higher-order needs, such as the desire to learn and to fulfil their potential for achievement. Translated into practical terms, Maslow's theory suggests that teachers will find it useful to pay close attention to such issues as whether their students are comfortable and whether their anxieties have been addressed, since any obstacle to their well-being may also prove to be an obstacle to their learning. Maslow is a major figure in the *humanist school of psychology, sometimes referred to as the Third Force, to distinguish it from the schools of *behaviourist and Freudian psychology, which have also contributed to our understanding of learner motivation.

Further Reading: A. Maslow *Motivation and Personality* (Harper and Row, 1987) provides a detailed account of Maslow's ideas on motivation.

master's degree A higher degree, which occupies the next level beyond the *bachelor's degree and sits at level 7 in the *National Qualifications Framework. A master's degree in education is abbreviated as M.Ed.; in science as M.Sc.; and in the arts as MA. To gain entry to master's level study, an applicant will usually be expected to have a good first degree, awarded at either first or upper second class. The master's curriculum often involves the candidate in acquiring research skills, and is normally assessed by *dissertation or *examination, or both of these. Exceptional students may progress from an M.Ed., M.Sc., or MA to the more demanding and far more specialized Master of Philosophy (M.Phil.) or Doctor of Philosophy (Ph.D. or D.Phil.). *See also* DOCTORATE.

matriculation 1. An examination taken in the first half of the 20th century by candidates wishing to gain a *university place. It also came to be used to describe the achievement of candidates who passed five subjects across a required range with a credit grade in their *School Certificate examination, since this achievement exempted them from the matriculation examination at most universities. When School Certificate was replaced by *General Certificate of Education (GCE) *Ordinary Levels in 1951, candidates were required instead to pass two GCE *Advanced Levels to achieve matriculation.

2. The name given to the ceremony at which new students are entered into the university register at the universities of Oxford, Cambridge, and Durham.

Matriculation Diploma This was planned as a generic award covering achievement in a range of existing qualifications including *General Certificate in Secondary Education, *General National Vocational Qualifications, *National Vocational Qualifications, and *General Certificate of Education *Advanced Levels, as well as citizenship and other broader interests. This qualification was proposed in the 2002 *Green Paper *14–19: Extending Opportunities, Raising Standards* as a new, overarching award. The intention was to encourage a breadth of *curriculum across general, *pre-vocational and *vocational routes, and to establish some measure of *parity of esteem between these. Like similar proposals before it—for example, the **General Education Diploma** (1995)—it failed to find acceptance and remained simply a proposal.

mature student In further and higher education, as defined by the *Universities and Colleges Applications Service (UCAS) and for the purposes of government initiatives such as *Aimhigher, a student over the age of 21 is referred to as a mature student in order to distinguish them from those who form the majority in that sector; in other words, 16–19-year-olds in further education, and 18–21-year-olds in higher education. 'Mature' in this case is indicative only of the students' relative age and should not necessarily be taken to imply anything about their developmental *stage or general behaviour. Mature students may gain access to further and higher education through specialized routes (for example, *Access courses) and without meeting the same specified entry requirements as younger applicants.

mechanics' institutes Adult educational establishments for working men (and sometimes working women) which were set up in the second quarter of the 19th century. The establishment of the institutes at this juncture in the country's industrial development reflected employers' needs for a skilled workforce at least as much as it served to meet the workers' aspirations to learning and self-improvement. The institutes provided elements of a general education as well as work-related skills. Classes were held in the evenings, and those who attended usually came there straight from a long day's work. This provision was the forerunner of several aspects of today's *post-compulsory provision: the work-related classes combined with studies based on a *liberal education model becoming features of *further and *adult education in the 1960s and 1970s; and the impetus to self-improvement being reflected in the opportunities for academic study such as those provided by the *Workers' Educational Association. The terminology surrounding them lingered long after the mechanics' institutes had ceased to exist. As late as the 1960s, centres which offered *adult education evening classes were often referred to as 'evening institutes'.

The suspicion by some educators and political activists of the time that the original institutes might be a covert means of creating a docile workforce was one of the factors that fuelled the growth of the 19th-century *Radical Education movement. The radical educators were concerned that the education being offered to the artisan was little more than a process of indoctrination designed to stifle enquiry and discourage questioning about the worker's status and conditions. This debate over what constituted 'useful knowledge' was also a debate about the purposes of education and about what it meant to be educated. A hundred and fifty years later the debate continues.

memory The ability to recall information, experiences, and feelings accurately; or to copy or re-enact procedures correctly. As well as enabling formal learning to take place, memory is the means by which the individual creates a coherent story of their life and experiences, and may therefore be said to be part of what constitutes the self. In both its narrow and wider sense, therefore, memory is central to the learning process. An important concern for educators has been the distinction between short- and long-term memory, and the question of how long a lesson should be remembered for it accurately to be said that learning has taken place. This concern can be illustrated, for example, by the case of the candidate 'cramming' for an examination, who retains what they have learned long enough to write it down in the examination room, but then promptly forgets it. Educators who define learning as a process which brings about a permanent change in the individual might argue that this candidate's failure to memorize in the longer term means that he or she has not learned in any real sense. Memory, therefore, may be said to be inextricably bound up with our understanding of what it means to learn. *See also* ROTE LEARNING.

mentor A more experienced colleague who offers support, guidance, and advice, usually to someone new to a role or organization. The word derives from the name of a character in Homer's *Odyssey*, a wise and trusted friend, Mentor, who promises to look after and teach Odysseus' son while Odysseus himself is away at the Trojan wars. This captures very well the dual role of mentoring, which involves elements of both teaching and caring. Student teachers on *teaching practice are usually allocated a mentor; and it is common practice for newly appointed teachers and lecturers to be mentored during their first year at a *school, *college, or *university. Mentoring is also widely used in the professional development of those in managerial roles in all sectors of education. Where institutional mentoring schemes are in place, these are often integral to the policy of operating as a *'learning organization'.

A three-stage mentoring framework has been developed for schools by the *General Teaching Council, designed to encourage continuing professional development through reflective mentoring, for which teachers can gain national accreditation. In *colleges of further education the role of mentoring newly appointed teachers or those with professional development needs is often one of the duties expected of staff who have achieved advanced teacher status.

SEE WEB LINKS

- A discussion of the benefits of mentoring for teachers.

merit A grade awarded for work in an examination or other type of *assessment which denotes achievement at a level greater than that of a simple pass. Other terms used in a similar way are *credit and **distinction**.

meritocracy A society ruled by those chosen not for their wealth or birth, but for their intellect or talents. A term coined by Michael Young (1915–2002) in *The Rise of the Meritocracy, 1870–2033: An Essay on Education and Equality* (1958), it came to be used, not in the satirical or darkly prophetic sense originally intended, but to describe a society worth aspiring to—one which might be achieved through selective education. The idea of creating a meritocracy, therefore, was used as an argument to support developments such as the use of *intelligence tests and the *Eleven Plus examination to separate talented pupils from the less talented in order to enhance their educational opportunities. Young himself, towards the end of his life, expressed some concern over what he saw as a wilful misunderstanding, particularly by policy-makers, of a term originally coined to describe the social structure of a fictional future—a dystopia in which social divisions of wealth and power have become all the more difficult to challenge because the idea of meritocracy not only allows those with power in society to argue that they deserve their position because they have achieved it through merit, but also increasingly assimilates the potential leaders of the underprivileged into the meritocracy itself, leaving the poor as an underclass further disempowered and disfranchised.

meta-narrative The French philosopher Jean-François Lyotard (1934–98) claimed that two major myths, or meta-narratives, have shaped and legitimized Western thinking for two centuries but are now no longer believed. These are the Myth of Liberation—the idea that history is the account of progress towards an achievable state of freedom and equality; and the Myth of Truth—the idea that any 'truth' can be objective, knowable, or verifiable. This claim, which is central to postmodernist philosophy, clearly questions our understanding of the purposes of education. Implicit within the current concept of education is the belief that it is an instrument for progress, not only of individuals but of society as a whole; and that the endeavours of science and the *humanities will result in the discovery of further 'truths' about ourselves and the human condition. In this sense it could be argued that education is still embedded in, and perpetuates, the meta-narratives which postmodernism brings into question.

method A strategy, activity, or procedure for teaching or supporting learning. Some common teaching methods include: *lecture or exposition, *group discussion, *case study, demonstration and practice, role play, simulation, debate, *field trips, and learning through *discovery. A teacher's choice of method will be informed by factors such as the nature of the subject and topic to be taught; the ability of the learners and their level of *motivation; the time available; the need for *inclusion and *differentiation; the degree to which the learners need to be actively involved; and the teacher's own preferred teaching style. A number of different methods may be employed within one lesson to provide learners with changes of activity, or one method may take up the entire lesson, as in the case of a lecture. A skilled teacher will be spoken of as having 'a repertoire of methods', indicating a confident flexibility of approach.

methodology *See* RESEARCH.

Michaelmas Term Also known as the Autumn Term, it is one of the three *terms into which the academic year is traditionally divided, the other two being the Spring Term and the Summer Term. The Michaelmas Term runs from September or October to December. Its duration depends upon the institution in question, but is usually between eight and twelve weeks. It takes its name from the feast of St Michael the Archangel, traditionally known as Michaelmas Day, which falls on 29 September, thus marking (approximately) the beginning of term. It is the traditional name for the Autumn Term at the universities of Oxford and Cambridge (where the Spring Term is known as **Hilary** and the Summer Term as **Trinity**), and has subsequently been adopted by some other institutions.

microteaching A method used in the development and initial training of teachers whereby the teacher or trainee teacher teaches for a very short time, usually only ten or fifteen minutes, under the supervision of a *tutor, to a *'class' of their peers. The micro-lesson is then analysed by teacher, 'class', and tutor, sometimes with the help of a media recording. Its purpose can be to encourage reflective practice, to build confidence, to address specific skills, or to try out unfamiliar strategies, *methods, or material in a safe learning environment.

middle school A school for pupils aged 9–13/14. It is part of an arrangement, recommended in the *Plowden Report and introduced by some *local authorities in the 1960s, in which compulsory schooling begins with a *first school which takes pupils from age 5 up to the age of 8 or 9, at which point they progress to the middle school. Secondary schooling, therefore, begins at 13 or 14 rather than at 11 as is the case in the more usual structured progression of *infant, *junior, and secondary provision. The middle school system was first introduced in the West Riding of Yorkshire in 1963, and became more widespread partly as a measure to address a school accommodation crisis brought about by the introduction of comprehensive education. The middle schools themselves were seen as a way of introducing a comprehensive model, since they avoided the traditional change of school at the age of 11 and the *selection process it entailed. Because of changing demographics and the reforms of post-16 education which have resulted in more pupils staying on at school in Years 12 and 13, the number of middle schools is currently in decline.

Middle Years Information System (MidYIS) Provides tests which are used nationally by secondary schools to gauge the potential of their *Key Stage 3 pupils. Schools choose whether or not to participate in this type of standardized assessment. Tests results can be used by secondary schools as a baseline for *value added measures. They are also used to predict *General Certificate of Secondary Education grades. MidYIS tests provide an alternative baseline to Key Stage 2 *Standard Task results, which are the outcome of specific learning and instruction rather than innate potential. In addition, MidYIS produces baseline tests for Years 7, 8, and 9. These tests are assessed externally by MidYIS and results are returned to the school shortly afterwards. *See also* COGNITIVE ABILITIES TEST; YEAR 11 INFORMATION SYSTEM. I.F.W.

mind *See* EPISTEMOLOGY; KNOWLEDGE; MEMORY.

minimum core A set of skills and underlying theory, initially in *literacy, language, and *numeracy, and later with the addition of *information communication technology, introduced by the *Further Education National Training Organization in August 2003, and fully implemented as part of the National Standards for further education teacher training programmes from September 2004. The introduction of the core was part of a strategy to ensure that all qualified teachers in the *learning and skills sector have the skills, knowledge, and understanding necessary to support their own learners' development of the communication and numeracy *key skills. The minimum core and its implementation now comes under the aegis of *Lifelong Learning UK. *See also* QUALIFIED TEACHER LEARNING AND SKILLS; STANDARDS AND VERIFICATION UK.

SEE WEB LINKS

- Provides further details of the minimum core requirements.

ministers of state for education In 2007 the reorganization of government departments created two Secretaries of State with responsibility for aspects of education. The Secretary of State for Children, Schools, and Families heads the department of that name (DCSF), and is responsible for matters of policy and other matters relating to compulsory education. The Secretary of State for Innovation, Universities, and Skills at the department of that name (DIUS) is responsible for policy and other matters relating to *further education, *higher education, science education, and training in the *skills sector. Within each department there are other ministerial posts with specific responsibility for schools and learners. In the DCSF the Minister for Schools and Learners has a remit whose policy areas include the raising of standards of attainment in schools, including performances in public examinations and national tests; application of, and matters relating to, the *national curriculum; education for 14–19-year-olds, including the *14–19 Diplomas; school funding; and issues relating to the school workforce. Working within the same departmental team is the Parliamentary Under Secretary of State for Schools and Learners, whose remit covers policy areas relating to the formation of schools, including trust schools, academies, and specialist schools; *primary education, including the teaching of *phonics; and *special educational needs. There is also a Minister of State for Children, Young People, and Families, responsible for policy matters relating to children's well-being and care, *Sure Start, *early years and childcare, and the *Every Child Matters agenda; and with joint responsibility with other departments for policies relating to youth justice and child poverty. Also a member of the ministerial team is the Parliamentary Under Secretary of State for Children, Young People, and Families, responsible for policies relating to, among others, pupil behaviour and attendance, anti-bullying strategies, the Respect agenda, and issues to do with pupils' health, including school meals and child obesity.

Working with the Secretary of State within the DIUS are the Minister of State for Lifelong Learning, Further and Higher Education; the Parliamentary Under Secretary of State for Skills; the Minister of State for Science and Innovation; and the Parliamentary Under Secretary of State for Intellectual Property and Quality.

minority **1.** A group of pupils or students identified as different from the majority by reason of their learning needs, their cultural background, their religious beliefs, or any other factor which might have an impact on how or what they learn and their requirements in terms of educational provision and support. *See also* INCLUSION; SOCIAL JUSTICE.

2. A *curriculum subject which is studied by relatively few. For example, ancient Greek is now considered a minority subject.

mission statement A public statement of institutional purpose, aims, and strategy required of schools, colleges, and universities, and usually disseminated through their web site, prospectus, or other promotional literature. *See also* VISION.

mixed ability An approach to teaching in which pupils are not segregated according to their ability, but rather, each class within a year group contains pupils who represent the full ability range. This is in contrast to the use of *selection, *sets, or *streams, and special provision for the *gifted and talented; and was once thought to represent the *comprehensive ideal. On the whole, however, mixed-ability grouping has not met with great success, and its use has declined. As early as 1978, the report by *Her Majesty's Inspectorate *Mixed Ability Work in Comprehensive Schools* claimed that such grouping prevented most pupils from working at a pace and level appropriate to their ability.

mnemonics A strategy used for aiding the *memory, particularly useful when memorizing specific sequences or lists. Widely known mnemonics include *Every Good Boy Deserves Favour*, used by beginners at the piano to recall the sequence of lines in the treble clef: EGBDF; and *one collar, two socks*, as a reminder of the correct spelling of *necessary*. Teachers often find it useful to provide learners with mnemonics of this kind, or to encourage them to devise their own when *rote learning is necessary.

mock examination An *examination, usually internally set and marked, which is designed to give candidates experience of the examination process, as well as to identify areas of weakness in their knowledge and understanding which they need to improve before sitting the examination proper. It is commonly used in schools to prepare pupils for public examinations such as the *General Certificate of Secondary Education and *General Certificate of Education *Advanced Level examinations. It can also be used in *higher education, from first degree right up to *doctorate level, where it is not uncommon for a candidate to be given a mock *viva in preparation for the real event. Such examinations are often referred to simply as 'mocks'.

moderation The process of ensuring that standards of *assessment are consistent between *assessors in the same institution (internal moderation) or between institutions nationally (external moderation). This work is carried out by moderators. It is distinct from *second marking in that it usually involves the scrutiny of samples of assessed work across a range of marks to ensure reliability of assessment, and provides feedback to the assessor(s) rather than to the learner. Neither should it be confused with *verification, which is concerned with monitoring assessment procedures rather than assessment decisions.

Modern Apprenticeship Introduced in 1995 following the *White Paper *Competitiveness—Forging Ahead*, the Modern Apprenticeship was designed to attract the more able school-leavers into *work-based training, where they could gain a *National Vocational Qualification (NVQ) level 3 within three years through a combination of learning on the job and *day release study, often at a *college of further education. For older entrants who might already, at 18 or 19, have gained general or *vocational Advanced Levels, there was an accelerated route to NVQ level 3 in eighteen months. As Modern Apprenticeships evolved, they became more inclusive, expanding to offer a Foundation Modern Apprenticeship for those aiming at an NVQ level 2 qualification, and an Advanced Modern Apprenticeship for those working towards an NVQ level 3 qualification. In 2004 these two routes were renamed 'Apprenticeships' and 'Advanced Apprenticeships' respectively.

Although the term 'Modern Apprenticeship' was originally designed to distinguish this training route from the original *apprenticeships abolished by the New Training Initiative in 1981, the simpler, one-word form is now increasingly adopted, although the training route it describes is very different from what was meant by 'apprenticeships' prior to 1981.

Modern Apprenticeships in Scotland follow the same format as those in England but are run by Scottish Enterprise and Highlands and Islands Enterprise. *See also* YOUNG APPRENTICESHIP.

modular This term describes a course or *programme of study which is made up of a number of *modules, each of which is taught and assessed as a separate *unit of the whole. Normally, students may, if they choose, gain accreditation for one or more module without necessarily going on to complete the full course at that time. An advantage of modular courses is that they can allow students to accumulate modules over time, allowing them, if necessary, to take breaks (intercalate) between modules and to accumulate sufficient for the full qualification within a designated time period. *See also* CREDIT; MODULE; MODULE SPECIFICATION.

module A self-contained subdivision of a programme of study which is taught and assessed as a discrete *unit. Courses or programmes which are made up of modules are known as 'modular'. The modules may run sequentially or concurrently. Some may be chosen from a number of options; others may be mandatory, or **core**, modules. In some cases, students may gain accreditation for one or more modules without completing the entire course; or may take breaks (intercalate) between modules, building up to the full qualification over a designated maximum period time. In *higher education, credit for modules may also be transferred between institutions, so that a student who has gained modules at *master's level at one *university, for example, can transfer the credit for those modules towards their master's qualification at another university. Thus, the modular system provides both flexibility in the pattern of attendance and the content covered, and an alternative to the situation where assessment relies solely on one set of examinations at the course's end. *See also* CREDIT; MODULE SPECIFICATION.

module specification The details of a *module, including its aims, learning *objectives, content, mode of study, and *assessment methods. Both the total number of hours of study expected, and the total hours of teacher–student contact, will normally also be specified. The module specification is usually the format in which modules are put forward for *validation and approval, and the basis on which the teacher or lecturer will produce their *lesson plans and *assessment instruments.

monitor A pupil who is given special responsibility for a classroom or playground task, usually as a reward for good or responsible behaviour. For example, a pupil given the job of cleaning the board for the teacher would be known as the 'board monitor'. In the days of school milk, a much-sought-after role among pupils was that of 'milk monitor', which involved the dispensing of milk to the rest of the class. The term is regarded now as somewhat old-fashioned, and has largely fallen out of use in state schools.

monitoring The systematic scrutiny of levels of performance and achievement, not only of pupils and students, but also of teachers, managers, institutions, and *local authorities. The monitoring of *standards nationally is carried out by bodies such as *Ofsted and the *Quality Assurance Agency. The rise in levels and extent of monitoring has been concurrent with the growing emphasis on *accountability and the application of *performance indicators across all sectors of education.

Montessori, Maria (1870–1952) An Italian doctor of medicine who became interested in educational theory as a result of her early work among children with *learning difficulties. Her clinical observations led her to analyse how children learn from what they construct themselves from manipulating materials, and more specifically what they encounter in the environment. She went on to design specialized equipment, and exercises for children to carry out without the assistance of adults. This conflicted with the large-group instruction of set subjects taught in the same way for all children which was the educational norm at the turn of the 20th century. Her hands-on approach to materials in a rich learning environment, and her recognition that children have knowing and willing dispositions to learn, has had a major influence in *early years education and teacher training in the UK, western Europe, Scandinavia, the United States, and Australasia.

Montessori was nominated for the Nobel Peace Prize in 1949, 1950, and 1951, and founded the Montessori Education Association in Washington DC (1913), the Association Montessori International in Amsterdam (1929), the Montessori Training Centre in the Netherlands (1938), and the Montessori Centre in London (1947). These centres continued to engage with and adhere to her educational theories based on a *child-centred curriculum, a structured environment, and imaginative and well-designed teaching materials, with which children can proceed at their own pace and make mistakes. Controversially, Montessori saw adults, including parents, as a threat to the child's freedom to do things without help. *See also* MONTESSORI SCHOOLS. A.W.

Montessori schools Schools for young pupils which offer an approach to education developed by Maria *Montessori, based on allowing children to develop at their own pace with plenty of opportunity for practical and imaginative play. Montessori established her first school, the Casa dei Bambini, in Rome in 1907. She designed a series of activities and equipment to encourage the *cognitive development of very young children, including scaled-down furniture (chairs, tables, cookers, dressers, prams), which are now a common feature in most *primary schools, for children to teach themselves through imaginative and practical activity, problem-solving, and trial and error. This self-direction, encouraged by real tasks or apparatus, is not defined as play by Montessori, but rather geared to practical life—perhaps a reflection of her work alongside children with *learning difficulties, whom she encouraged to become independent through the provision of a structured and tranquil environment.

Montessori believed that, through observation, the teacher—or, to use Montessori's term, 'directress'—can provide a range of sequential activities or materials for the child to develop more complex concepts in the progressive development of cognition.

Moser Report (1999) A document which sets out the findings of the review of **adult basic education** undertaken by Sir Claus Moser and his consultative group in order to inform a new framework for *lifelong learning. The Report appeared with the recommendation that there should be a **National Adult Basic Skills Strategy**, which would include setting national targets, increasing opportunities for learners, developing a new system of qualifications, and introducing changes to teacher training and *inspection.

The Report has had its most noticeable impact on the *further education sector, where, as a result of Moser's recommendations, all teachers of adult basic skills are now required to hold a specialist teaching qualification; and teachers of all other subjects in further education are required to demonstrate mastery of a *minimum core of skills, including language, *literacy, and *numeracy, and *information communication technology before they can gain their teaching qualification. *See also* ADULT LITERACY.

motivation The will or incentive to learn. Students or pupils who lack motivation will be unable to benefit fully from their education, and therefore they present a problem for the teacher as well as themselves. If their lack of motivation manifests itself in *disruptive *behaviour, unmotivated learners may also present a problem for their peers. The issue of motivation, therefore, is of crucial importance to the teacher, who must endeavour to devise ways to engage the learner's interest. There are broadly two sources of motivation upon which the individual might act. One is **intrinsic motivation**, which arises from within and is typified by the satisfaction to be gained by doing something for its own sake. In this sense, most teachers will ideally strive to develop intrinsic motivation in their learners by helping them to discover the pleasure of gaining understanding or skill. This is sometimes referred to as **learning how to learn**. The other source is **extrinsic motivation**, which is exerted upon the learner from the outside. This involves the use of **rewards** or **sanctions**, and includes such interventions by the teacher as praise, disapproval, or the promise or withholding of enjoyable learning activities. The most common barriers to learners' motivation are fear, boredom, previous negative experiences of education, and lack of hope about future prospects. While the first three may be seen as within the teacher's power and remit to address, the fourth often has its origins in the wider socio-economic context and is therefore unlikely to be open to resolution on an individual, or even institutional, level. *See also* BEHAVIOURIST; FURTHER EDUCATION; MASLOW; ROGERS.

multicultural education Coverage in the school *curriculum of topics which will develop in pupils a clearer understanding of the variety of cultures which go to make up a multicultural society. Its purpose is not only to increase knowledge and understanding but also to encourage tolerance and promote *inclusion and *social justice.

multilingual In an educational context, this is most often used to describe a class, group, or cohort of learners for whom there is not a common first language. In a multicultural, multilingual society many pupils starting school at the age of 5 have greatest fluency not in English but in the language which is spoken in their home. This has implications for the content and style of the teaching needed to meet their individual learning needs. *See also* ENGLISH AS AN ADDITIONAL LANGUAGE.

multimedia The use of a range of teaching resources, particularly *information communication technology, to reinforce or support learning. This might include such resources as data projectors, interactive computer programmes, interactive whiteboards, and electronic simulations.

multiple choice A form of *assessment or *examination which presents the candidate with a question followed by a series of answers, only one of which is correct. The candidate must identify the correct answer, usually by placing a cross or a tick in a box, electronically or by hand. The incorrect answers are known as 'distractors'. This form of testing was developed in America following the First World War as a means of screening applicants to the army in order to ensure that recruits met at least the minimum level of *intelligence required for their role. It was later adapted to other uses, one of which was the *intelligence test administered by many *local authorities in the United Kingdom as an *Eleven Plus examination. The major advantage of the multiple-choice test, according to its proponents, was that the format of one correct answer enabled the assessment of large numbers of candidates, mechanically in the early days and, later, electronically. It has two major disadvantages, however. It is suitable for the assessment of factual knowledge and understanding, but does not test a candidate's ability to construct a coherent argument, to theorize, or to analyse. It also has a degree of unreliability, in that the candidate may arrive at the correct answer through guesswork. Research suggests that boys score more highly than girls in multiple-choice testing. The reason for this has not been clearly established, but the commonly held hypothesis is that this is related to gender differences in language acquisition and development, as girls have been found to score better in tests requiring essay-style answers.

multiple intelligence A theory, popularized by the American psychologist Howard Gardner (b. 1943), that *intelligence, traditionally seen as an ability or agility which is purely *cognitive, may be more usefully conceived of not as simply limited to mental activity or thinking, but as encompassing a range of functions and abilities. Gardner suggests that intelligence can be divided into seven subcategories. Two of these which have proved useful in thinking about ways in which people learn are *emotional intelligence and kinaesthetic intelligence. An awareness that intelligence may be manifested through ability or agility other than of a cognitive nature enables teachers and others to adapt their teaching style and plan learning activities that will engage and motivate learners who have become reluctant or disenchanted in the face of traditional approaches to teaching and learning as a purely cognitive process.

m

Further Reading: H. Gardner *Multiple Intelligences* (Basic Books, 1993) gives more detail on this topic.

SEE WEB LINKS

- An account of Howard Gardner's work on multiple intelligences.

multi-sensory Lessons which are planned in a way that suits the teacher's own preferred learning style can leave some pupils unable to understand the point of the lesson. Using an approach which embraces all three *learning styles (visual, auditory, and kinaesthetic) provides opportunities for all pupils to learn. A lesson which has hands-on activities and promotes discussion is one which suits all preferred learning styles. This is known as using a multi-sensory approach to teaching, which encourages the use of a range of senses. It requires the use of more than one teaching strategy, which provides a balanced opportunity for pupils to learn through their own preferred style and for them to develop their ability to respond to other styles in the process. T.B., L.E.

Munn Report (1977) Drawn up to present the findings of the Munn Committee, which recommended a restructuring of the curriculum in Scotland to be followed in Standard 3 and Standard 4 to meet the needs of pupils of all abilities; the introduction of teaching and learning methods which reflected pupils' needs and circumstances; and the development of new courses which crossed traditional subject boundaries. Together with the *Dunning Report, this document was the basis of the focus on equality of access to education in the Scottish education system after 1977. S.M.

Nasen Formerly known as the National Association for Special Educational Needs, this organization's purpose is to facilitate equal opportunities in education and training for learners who need special or additional support. It was founded in 1992 through the amalgamation of two bodies with a similar purpose: the National Association for Remedial Education and the National Council for Special Education. The Association produces several specialist journals, including the *British Journal of Special Education* and the online publication *Journal of Research in Special Educational Needs*. It is governed by a board of trustees, and its membership consists of both schools and individuals such as parents and students.

National Advisory Council for Education and Training Targets (NACETT) The role of this advisory body in setting national targets for education and training was taken over in April 2001 by the *Learning and Skills Council.

National Assessment Bank (NAB) A reserve of National Testing materials which can be used in Scotland by teachers and lecturers. It contains *instruments of assessment, marking guidelines, and other useful information relating to the *internal assessment of national qualifications. Examples from the NAB are often used for the *unit assessment element of the course. S.M.

National Association for Gifted Children (NAgC) A charitable organization founded in 1966 and operating in England, Northern Ireland, and Wales (but not in Scotland). Its aim is to secure educational provision for *gifted and talented children which is appropriate to their individual needs and which facilitates and supports the full development of their individual abilities. It provides a source of advice and support to parents and gifted children, as well as to professionals involved in education, including professional development provision for teachers and a web site for older children.

National Association for Special Educational Needs *See* NASEN.

National Association of Careers Guidance Teachers (NACGT) *See* CAREERS ADVISORY SERVICE.

National Association of Educational Inspectors, Advisers, and Consultants (NAEIAC) The professional organization in England and Wales for *local authority advisers, *advisory teachers, and *inspectors, as well as for independent consultants and inspectors. It operates a web site and national events, through which the views and interests of its members can be shared and represented to the *Department for Children, Schools, and Families, the *Qualifications and Curriculum Authority, and others; and produces briefing papers and bulletins.

National Association of Head Teachers (NAHT) Founded in Nottingham in 1897, the Association acts on behalf of it members in relation to their terms and conditions of employment, and provides a source of professional development, information, guidance, and support. In 1985 its membership was extended to include deputy head teachers; and, from 2000, assistant head teachers have also been entitled to membership. Members are drawn from both primary and secondary sectors, the current membership standing at in excess of 30 000 school leaders.

SEE WEB LINKS

- Summary of the Association's aims.

National Association of Schoolmasters Union of Women Teachers (NASUWT) One of the largest unions of teachers in the United Kingdom, the Association was formed in 1976 when the two formerly separate unions of its title merged. The NASUWT also represents head teachers, and extends membership to student teachers.

National Association of Teachers in Further and Higher Education (NATFHE) *See* UNIVERSITY AND COLLEGE UNION.

National Certificate One of the successor qualifications which were introduced by some unitary *awarding bodies to replace *General National Vocational Qualifications (GNVQs) when these were phased out between 2005 and 2007. It is also the title of the non-advanced post-school *vocational certificate awarded by the *Scottish Qualifications Authority; and of a number of *Business and Technology Education Council level 3 awards in vocational areas which were available before, and concurrently with, GNVQs. S.M.

National Children's Bureau (NCB) A charitable organization whose aim is to improve the lives of children and young people, which includes ensuring their access to a sound education. The Bureau encompasses a multi-agency network of semi-independent organizations concerned with the education, health, and social care of young people. It operates in England and Northern Ireland, and works in partnership with the Scottish and Welsh organizations **Children in Scotland** and **Children in Wales**. Founded in 1963, it now also runs a network for young people themselves, **Young NCB**, which provides a forum for those under 18 to express their views on issues of concern to them, such as drug-taking and bullying.

National College for School Leadership (NCSL) A non-departmental public body of the *Department for Children, Schools, and Families, launched in 2000 by the Department for Education and Employment to develop the leadership skills of existing and aspiring school leaders. It offers a range of professional development programmes for *head teachers, *deputy head teachers, and others with leadership responsibilities, and provides online learning through its *virtual learning environment, the Learning Gateway. It also supports research into effective leadership with a view to influencing policy and practice. *See also* HEADSHIP DEVELOPMENT.

SEE WEB LINKS

- List of NCSL goals and activities.

National Commission on Education (NCE) Following a call from Sir Claus Moser in 1990 for a 'visionary' review of education and training in the United Kingdom, the National Commission was set up in 1991 as an independent body, sponsored by the Paul Hamlyn Foundation and operating under the aegis of the *British Association for the Advancement of Science. Its remit was to consider ways in which the provision and goals of education and training should adapt over the subsequent 25 years in order to meet economic and social requirements and the lifelong learning aspirations of the population. The working records of the Commission were deposited in the Institute of Education Library in June 1995.

Further Reading: NCE *Learning to Succeed: A Radical Look at Education Today and a Strategy for the Future* (1993) provides a full report of the Commission's findings.

National Consortium of Colleges (NCC) An organization whose purpose is to encourage and support employers across all sectors of business and industry in providing *work-based training for their workforce. It works with *colleges of further education to provide a directory of funded work-related provision. Established in 2001, it works closely with the *Learning and Skills Council towards the achievement of *National Targets for Education and Training.

SEE WEB LINKS

- Gives a summary of the resources developed by the NCC, and provides a web link to the NCC course directory.

National Council for Vocational Qualifications (NCVQ) Set up in 1986 to reform and rationalize the system of vocational qualifications by establishing a national vocational qualification framework, the NCVQ introduced and endorsed competence-based qualifications which were awarded by vocational *awarding bodies such as the City and Guilds of London Institute. In 1997 it merged with the *School Curriculum and Assessment Authority to form the *Qualifications and Curriculum Authority. This represented the current policy direction, which was to create stronger links between general and vocational education. *See also* NATIONAL VOCATIONAL QUALIFICATION.

NATIONAL CURRICULUM

A curriculum for all children aged 5–16 in *maintained schools. Introduced following the *Education Reform Act 1988 and revised in 2000, 2002, and again in 2007, its framework sets out what subjects must be taught; the skills, knowledge, and understanding required in each at specified stages or levels, the targets to be achieved in each at each level, and the requirements for assessing and reporting on pupils' achievement.

Within the national curriculum, learning is organized into key stages, which set out the curriculum content for five age groups: Foundation Stage for pre-school children; Key Stage 1 for pupils aged 5–7 in *infant schools; Key Stage 2 for pupils aged 7–11 in *junior schools; Key Stage 3 for pupils aged 11–14, and Key Stage 4 for those aged 14–16 in secondary schools. In *primary schools, encompassing Key Stages 1 and 2, there are ten compulsory national curriculum subjects. They are: English, mathematics, science, design and technology, *information communication technology (ICT), history, geography, art and design, music, and physical education (PE). Schools are also required to teach *religious education (RE), but parents may withdraw their child from part or all of this as, like *personal, social, and health education (PSHE), citizenship, and a modern foreign language, it is not compulsory at this stage. In Key Stage 3 the addition of citizenship and a modern foreign language brings the number of compulsory subjects to 12. At this stage schools must also provide sex and relationship education (SRE), careers education and guidance, and RE. As in Key Stages 1 and 2, pupils may be withdrawn by their parents from RE. They may also be withdrawn from non-statutory elements of SRE. PSHE may also be offered at this stage. At the end of Year 9, at the age of 14, pupils choose which subjects they will study in Key Stage 4. These will be a combination of compulsory and optional subjects, in which they will be examined for their *General Certificate of Secondary Education at the end of Key Stage 4. The subjects which are compulsory at this stage are: English, mathematics, science, ICT, PE, and citizenship. In addition to these, pupils must study careers education and work-related learning. They are also entitled to choose additional subjects from the arts, the humanities, design and technology, and modern foreign languages. These are known as 'entitlement' areas, and schools are required to offer at least one subject from each of them. As at other key stages, RE must be offered, but need not be taken. National tests take place in English and mathematics at the end of Key Stage 1, and in English, mathematics, and science at the end of Key Stages 2 and 3.

In 2007 the *Qualifications and Curriculum Authority published a draft of a revised national curriculum for secondary schools intended to allow schools more flexibility on curriculum issues and more opportunities for *personalized learning and integration across national curriculum subject areas. These include reforms to the 14–19 curriculum and the introduction of a *diploma qualification in five subjects, combining practical skills with theoretical learning, which will provide an alternative to the national curriculum for certain students in that age group. The new *programmes of study were disseminated to secondary schools in 2007 for teaching from September 2008. Schools then have until 2010 to implement these more flexible programmes.

Indeed, a gradual increase in flexibility has been the pattern of development in the national curriculum since the change of policy on Standard Assessment Tasks (SATs) in 1992. The original intention was that all pupils would sit national tests at the end of each key stage, not only in the core subjects of English, maths, and science as now, but in their other national curriculum subjects too. Such a project proved impractical and unwieldy, particularly in terms of the paperwork it required from teachers. This led to a boycott of SATs organized by teachers' unions following the Key Stage 3 tests in 1992. In response to this, and in consultation with teachers, the curriculum content and the testing requirements were streamlined. The revised national curriculum specifications which resulted from this became statutory from August 2000, and were amended again following the 2005 *White Paper *Education and Skills*, which set out the policy of lifting national curriculum restrictions for some young learners to allow them to take *vocational qualifications as part of their Key Stage 4 entitlement. Testing is now known as Standard Tasks, although the original abbreviated term 'SATs' has remained in use.

SEE WEB LINKS

- Details of the national curriculum for Northern Ireland.
- Details of the national curriculum for Scotland.
- Details of the national curriculum for Wales.

National Curriculum Council (NCC) Following the *Education Reform Act 1988, the NCC was established in the same year for the purpose of carrying out consultations on *national curriculum subjects and advising on their implementation. A further part of its remit was to advise the *Secretary of State on curriculum matters. In 1993 the Council merged with the Schools Examination and Assessment Council to become the *School Curriculum and Assessment Authority, which in turn merged with the *National Council for Vocational Qualifications in 1997 to form the *Qualifications and Curriculum Authority.

national curriculum for Wales A new and distinctive curriculum was introduced in all Welsh schools from September 2000. Revised arrangements have since been developed in the light of recommendations made in a report published by the Qualifications, Curriculum, and Assessment Authority for Wales. Programmes of study offer greater flexibility to teachers and aim to prepare young people for the challenges of adult life, to promote an approach that is more *learner-centred, focusing on skills, building on the **Foundation Phase**, and linking with the **14–19 Learning Pathways Programme**. The development of a single framework for a curriculum, assessment, and qualifications system from 3 to 19 is intended to raise standards and widen opportunities. All pupils in maintained schools study Welsh up to *General Certificate of Secondary Education stage, though the examination itself is not compulsory. H.G.

National Education Trust (NET) An independent foundation whose declared aim is to contribute towards improving the quality of education nationally. Founded in 1972 and known originally as the National Council for Educational Standards, the Trust seeks to influence policy and opinion through its bulletins and conferences. To this extent it can be considered a pressure group, with an interest in all sectors of education.

National Extension College (NEC) A provider of *distance learning, *blended learning, and *e-learning, the NEC was founded in 1962 in order to provide educational opportunities for learners who are unable or unwilling to

n

undertake conventional modes of attendance, or who desire a 'second chance' at education. Its *curriculum places it firmly in the tertiary sector, and extends from *General Certificate of Secondary Education courses to professional training and updating in vocational areas such as management and childcare. Operating largely on a basis of *distributed, *asynchronous learning, it is often used by adult learners as a first step towards an *Open University course.

National Foundation for Educational Research (NFER) In existence since 1946, NFER is a registered charity with a wide portfolio of activity in the field of educational research and testing. Its stated aim is to 'improve education and training, nationally and internationally, by undertaking research, development and dissemination activities and by providing information services'. Regarded with respect both nationally and internationally for producing high-quality evidence-based information, NFER has also been instrumental in informing government policy. Although perhaps best known for its national curriculum tests and other school-based tests, the organization has developed ability and attainment tests for wide-ranging application including the driving theory test. NFER's test of *cognitive ability, referred to widely in schools as the *CAT test, assesses numerical, non-verbal, and verbal reasoning, and supplies a forecast of the level of attainment a pupil can expect to achieve in national tests. This information supports the planning of teaching and learning and offers guidance for personalized learning. Commissioned regularly to undertake independent research and evaluation, NFER selects a project methodology that is best suited to the needs of the commissioning client. To facilitate the dissemination of research findings in order that the research can be useful to a wide audience of policy-makers and practitioners, the organization offers services in marketing, media management, and publishing. NFER has a comprehensive and free national and international information service available to members of the public, which sits alongside a dedicated service for local authorities. The organization also produces publications for purchase. *See also* VOLUNTARY ORGANIZATIONS.

SEE WEB LINKS

- Provides further information.

T.B., L.E.

National Grid for Learning (NGfL) Introduced by the government to support the use of *information and communications technology (ICT) in schools, this scheme facilitated schools' access to the Internet and provided professional development opportunities for teachers in the use of ICT as a teaching resource. In April 2006 the portal for the Grid was closed down and its services integrated into the provision and resources offered by the *British Educational Communications and Technology Agency.

National Institute of Adult Continuing Education (NIACE) A non-governmental organization, set up in 1949, whose purpose is to support adult continuing education, both through research and through representation of the interests of adult learners. It is a registered charity with a membership made up of both individuals and organizations, and is financed partly through *local authorities, the *Department for Children, Schools, and Families, and a number of *universities. One of the Institute's key aims is to promote equality of opportunity for adult learners who have gained least from their years in compulsory education. It operates within England and Wales, with a specialist Welsh committee, NIACE Dysgu Cymru, which is involved in the development of continuing education within the Welsh border.

National Languages Strategy A government-led strategy to introduce the learning of a modern foreign language (mfl) for every pupil in *Key Stage 2 by 2010, with the aim that, by the age of 11, pupils' language achievement will be at a level recognized by the *Common European Framework. The National Languages Strategy is one element of the broader *Primary National Strategy, and promotes the vision of languages in use for both business and pleasure, and as a means of encouraging an understanding of other cultures. In order to develop the capacity for language teaching in primary schools, it was necessary to establish new initial primary teacher training courses in languages as well as *continuing professional development courses for existing teachers and teaching assistants.

A key document supporting this strategy is the ***Framework for Languages***, designed to aid primary school teachers in developing language provision, and to guide secondary teachers of mfl who are providing support for primary language teaching in adapting their subject specialism to the needs of primary stage learners. It sets out examples of **language-learning strategies** which pupils should have the opportunity to apply during the four years of their Key Stage 2 schooling. The learning *objectives relating to the National Languages Strategy fall into three main strands: *oracy, *literacy, and intercultural understanding; they are linked to those of other aspects of primary provision, such as the *National Literacy Strategy and the *national curriculum *programmes of study in subjects such as English, *personal, social, and health education, and *information communication technology. *See also* KNOWLEDGE ABOUT LANGUAGE.

Further Reading: Department for Education and Skills *Languages for All: Languages for Life* (DfES, 2005) sets out the government's strategy for language learning in Key Stage 2.

National Learning Targets Introduced in March 1999 as part of a government initiative to raise standards of *achievement in secondary schools, improve pupil attainment in *numeracy and *literacy in *primary schools, and encourage *lifelong learning. The targets were seen as means whereby to measure the progress made by the *Department for Education and Employment, and subsequently the *Department for Education and Skills, towards their aims of increasing participation and raising achievement in both compulsory and workplace learning. The targets included, for example, percentage figures for 16-year-olds gaining five *General Certificates of Secondary Education at grades A–C, and for adults gaining a degree, as well as target figures for organizations gaining recognition as Investors in People. These national targets were subsequently replaced by departmental public service agreement targets.

National Literacy Strategy (NLS) A strategy, first announced in 1996, for teaching the parts of the *national curriculum for English concerned with the skills of *reading and writing. It enlarges upon, and complements, the guidance for *Key Stages 1 and 2 and for the *Early Years Foundation Stage, which applies to children aged 0–5. The NLS Framework sets out recommended approaches to the teaching of English, as well as suggesting how lessons might best be structured and resourced; and provides objectives for the teaching of English from Year 1 to Year 6, term by term. *See also* LITERACY.

National Literacy Trust (NLT) An independent charitable trust founded in 1993 with the aim of raising standards of *literacy among children and adults nationally, in order to create a 'literate nation'. It draws attention to the wider issues which affect standards of literacy, such as social and economic circumstances, rather than simply focusing on the teaching of literacy in schools. Among its initiatives are the National Reading Campaign and Talk to Your Baby.

SEE WEB LINKS

- A list of the Trust's aims and activities.

National Numeracy Strategy (NNS) Launched in 1998 and implemented in schools since 1999, this strategy is designed to facilitate a sound grounding in mathematics for all *primary school pupils. The **Primary Framework** for *numeracy sets out targets aimed at raising standards of achievement in mathematics nationally. The Strategy also provides resources for the effective teaching of mathematics and guidance on planning mathematics lessons, which teachers access through the Strategy web site. The Strategy builds on the National Numeracy Project, which was created by the Department for Education and Employment in 1996.

SEE WEB LINKS

- A list of teaching resources and publications generated by the Strategy.

National Nursery Examination Board (NNEB) *See* NURSERY NURSE.

National Open College Network (NOCN) A credit-based *awarding body whose qualifications are delivered through *further education and *sixth form colleges, *universities and other *higher education institutions, trade unions, employers, *local authorities, private training agencies, and *adult education centres. It is a development of the **Open College Network (OCN)**, which was established in 1975 for the purpose of formally accrediting the education and training undertaken by adults, and its broad purpose is to encourage *wider participation in, and promote access to, *vocationally related *post-compulsory learning and training. It operates as the central body for the eleven OCNs in England, Northern Ireland, and Wales.

National Professional Qualification for Headship (NPQH) A qualification which became mandatory on 1 April 2004 for all new *head teachers in *local authority schools. The qualification is delivered under the aegis of the *National College for School Leadership, and was first introduced by the Department for Education and Employment in 1997. Its focus is on school improvement, and it is also open to senior teachers and those aspiring to a headship position. Initially, the regulations governing the mandatory status of the qualification allowed for newly appointed head teachers to be 'working towards' their NPQH, but from 1 April 2009 successful completion of the qualification is a requirement of appointment. *See also* HEADSHIP DEVELOPMENT.

National Progression Award (NPA) *See* SCOTTISH PROGRESSION AWARD.

National Qualification Group Award (NQGA) *See* SCOTTISH GROUP AWARD.

National Qualifications (NQs) Qualifications for students studying in Scottish secondary schools or in Scottish *colleges of further education. NQs consist of *Standard Grades, National Courses, and *National Units. National Courses and Units are sometimes called 'new' National Qualifications since they replaced previously existing qualifications in 1999.

SEE WEB LINKS

- Details of the format of the NQs.

S.M.

National Qualifications Framework (NQF) A comprehensive framework which categorized all qualifications accredited by the regulatory authorities for England (the *Qualifications and Curriculum Authority), Wales (Department for Education, Lifelong Learning, and Skills), and Northern Ireland (*Council for the Curriculum, Examinations, and Assessment) initially into one of six levels, ranging from entry level to level 5 for postgraduate qualifications and their equivalent. The Framework originally included *vocational or occupational qualifications, such as *National Vocational Qualifications (NVQs); general vocational qualifications, such as *Vocational Advanced Levels; and general academic qualifications, such as *General Certificate of Education *Advanced Levels and the *General Certificate of Secondary Education. One purpose of the Framework was to clarify for learners, employers, and others appropriate progression routes through the qualifications system. It also made apparent the status of each qualification in relation to others in the same category (for example, vocational), as well as illustrating theoretical equivalence between the three categories. In September 2004 the Framework was revised by a subdivision of levels 4 and 5 to create additional categories at the higher end of the Framework, resulting in nine levels, from entry level to level 8. Levels 4–8 were presented as equivalent to *higher education qualifications, ranging from Certificate of Higher Education (level 4) to *doctorate (level 8). However, higher-level NVQs were not included in this revised model, and the four lower levels of the Framework remained unchanged.

In November 2006 trials began of further revisions to the Framework and its renaming as the Qualifications and Credit Framework (QCF) under the aegis of the three regulatory bodies. The purpose of the revised framework is to enable learners to gain, accumulate, and transfer incremental credit for their partial achievement of qualifications in terms of *units, thus allowing for greater flexibility and for recognition to be given to employer-led training. The new QCF is designed to be compatible with frameworks and credit accumulation systems in Scotland and other European nations, thus working towards the goal of making qualifications gained in England, Wales, and Northern Ireland transferable across national borders.

SEE WEB LINKS

- Provides access to a fact sheet that can be downloaded detailing the current levels of the Framework.
- Lists all accredited qualifications included in the national framework.

National Record of Achievement (NRA) Originally introduced in the late 1970s, and becoming mandatory from 1993, the NRA was intended to enable pupils to present formally a record of, and gain recognition for, their non-examination and extracurricular achievements as well as their academic ones. In 1996 the *Dearing *Review of Qualifications for 16–19-Year-Olds* recommended a restructuring of the NRA and suggested renaming it the *Progress File. As a result of this review and restructuring, the NRA is to be phased out by 2009.

national skills academies Employer-driven centres of excellence that will deliver the skills required by each major sector of the economy with the support of its sector skills council. The first four academies, which opened by 2006, are for the construction, financial services, food and drink, and manufacturing industries, with a further eight opening between 2006 and 2008. The academies were conceived as a response to the *Foster Report *Realising the Potential: A Review of the Future Role of Further Education Colleges*, which emphasized the key purpose of further education in improving skills development and achieving the national workforce's requirements for future growth and prosperity. The national skills academies are intended to bring together and lead networks of training providers, including further education colleges, *Centres of Vocational Excellence, private training providers, and higher education institutions. *See also* EMPLOYER ENGAGEMENT. V.C., K.A.

National Steering Group for Special Educational Needs in Wales The body set up to ensure provision for children and young people with *special educational needs (SEN) across Wales and to overcome the difficulties encountered by some of the smaller and more rural local authorities. Wales-only clauses were included in the Education Act 2002 to allow for regional collaboration for goods and services, which included services provided on a peripatetic basis. Financial support for this policy has been made available from the Welsh Assembly's School Building Improvement Grant. The general principle, enshrined in law by the 1993 and 1996 Education Acts, is that children and young people with SEN should—where that accords with the wishes of the parties concerned—normally be educated in mainstream schools. The *Special Educational Needs and Disability Act 2001 strengthened that right, amending the 1996 Act, transforming the statutory framework for inclusion into a positive endorsement for inclusion. Equally, however, where parties concerned want a place in a *special school, their wishes are taken into account. H.G.

National Targets for Education and Training (NTET) Originally promoted by the Confederation of British Industry in 1991, the targets were endorsed by the government following the 1995 *White Paper *Competitiveness: Forging Ahead*. The targets set were that, by 2000:

- 85 per cent of young people would be achieving one of the following: five *General Certificates of Secondary Education at grade C or above, an Intermediate *General National Vocational Qualification (GNVQ), or a *National Vocational Qualification (NVQ) at level 2.
- 75 per cent of young people would achieve level 2 in the *key skills of communication, *numeracy, and *information technology by the age of 19; and level 3 in these skills by the age of 21.

- 60 per cent of young people, by the age of 20, would achieve one of the following: two *Advanced Levels (A levels); an Advanced GNVQ (the equivalent of two *Vocational A levels); or an NVQ at level 3.
- 60 per cent of the workforce would be qualified to NVQ level 3 or equivalent.

Schools were also encouraged to set their individual annual targets for improving pupil achievement in line with these national targets.

The deadline set for the targets to be achieved having passed, the verdict from the *Department for Education and Skills was that 'good progress' had been made in achieving those targets, but that there remained 'more to do' (DfES 2001). *See also* STANDARDS.

Further Reading: Department for Education and Skills *Schools: Building on Success* (HMSO, 2001) reviews early progress against the targets.

national training organization (NTO) Replaced in 2002 by the sector skills councils, the NTOs were publicly funded bodies introduced in 1997 as part of the rationalization of education and training provision. Employer-led, their role was to set occupational standards in their specialist vocational area, identify skills shortages and training needs, and help to promote and create an appropriately qualified workforce. The NTO for teachers in further education and the skills sector was the *Further Education National Training Organization, which developed the first set of national standards for teachers in the sector, and which was subsequently replaced by the sector skills council, *Lifelong Learning UK. *See also* SECTOR SKILLS DEVELOPMENT AGENCY.

National Union of Students (NUS) Originally established in 1922 exclusively for *university students, the NUS currently draws its membership from institutions of both *further and *higher education. Each college or university has its own branch of the union, which sends delegates to the national conferences, which are held twice-yearly. Members elect a national executive committee, which acts to promote the interests of students. *See also* STUDENTS' UNION.

National Union of Teachers (NUT) Founded in 1870 as the National Union of Elementary Teachers, it took its current name in 1889, and is one of the largest of the teachers' unions with a membership which includes both the primary and the secondary sectors of education. Local branches elect delegates to the annual national conference, which debates issues of national educational policy and promotes the interests of teachers.

National Units A unit of *assessment for the Scottish *Highers. Individual National Units may be awarded as qualifications in their own right. Each represents the successful completion of approximately 40 hours of study, assessed by **unit assessments**. Many full-time *National Qualification courses in Scotland's colleges consist of groupings of National Units. S.M.

National Vocational Qualification (NVQ) Competence-based qualifications in work-related skills areas, designed to reflect the needs of employers and to offer clear progression routes. They were introduced in 1986 as part of the government's declared purpose to rationalize *vocational qualifications within a coherent framework. Originally set up under the authority of the *National Council for Vocational Qualifications, and falling now under the aegis of the *Qualifications and Curriculum Authority (QCA), they were intended to remove barriers to access by, for example, allowing for the *accreditation of prior experience and learning, providing accumulative awards consisting of elements and units which could be gained over time, and providing an **outcomes-based** route to qualifications. In this way, candidates who could demonstrate the relevant competencies to a qualified assessor could be accredited with a qualification or part of a qualification without the necessity of attending a programme of study. This accessibility was part of a government drive to create a more highly qualified workforce. NVQs provide qualifications at all levels from *National Qualifications Framework level 1, involving repetitive tasks carried out under supervision, to level 5, which denotes substantial managerial and executive competence corresponding to a postgraduate level of attainment. All NVQs are based on performance criteria drawn up by lead bodies made up largely of representative employers from the appropriate vocational field. The QCA endorses the qualifications, while their assessment and administration are the responsibility of a range of *awarding bodies. The introduction of NVQs saw a shift in emphasis in vocational qualifications from input-driven to assessment-driven training. Assessors of NVQs are themselves required to possess units of an NVQ in assessment, originally known as the **Assessor Award**, or the 'D' units, because of their designation as units D32 and D33 of the Training and Development Lead Body's NVQ in work-based assessment. As well as trainers and assessors in industry and commerce, all teachers in *further education colleges who were involved in the assessment of NVQs were required to gain the assessor qualification. This was usually achieved through the compilation and presentation of a portfolio of evidence.

It was originally intended that NVQs should provide a route both to employment and to *higher education. In the 1991 *White Paper *Education and Training for the 21st Century*, it was suggested that there would be clear equivalence and progression routes between NVQs and general academic qualifications, such as the *General Certificate of Secondary Education. This has not proved to be the case in any generalized sense, and the NVQ remains, on the whole, a route for those seeking specifically to enter employment rather than higher education.

National Youth Agency (NYA) Founded in 1991, the NYA supports organizations and agencies which work with young people to promote their personal and social development, which includes their education. The Agency is funded by the Local Government Association and by those departments of central government with whom it works. It provides support for youth work in a number of forms, including resources, the development of innovation in the delivery of services, and the training of leaders and managers involved.

nature or nurture The debate over whether it is a child's genetic inheritance (nature) or their upbringing and environment (nurture) which will have greatest influence on their personality and *intelligence. Work on the human genome project has reignited this debate, with speculation over the possible discovery of genes which govern specific character traits, predispositions, or attributes. One problem raised by attributing much or all of an individual's characteristics to inherited factors is a philosophical one: if we are entirely programmed by our genes, to what extent can we be said to possess free will? Certain advocates of the genetic, or 'nature', argument have brought their point of view into some disrepute in the past with claims that attributes such as intelligence may be classed as an inherited racial characteristic. Those who support the environmental, or 'nurture', argument, on the other hand, maintain that most observable differences between individuals are due not to inherited factors but to their early experiences, the cultural attitudes to which they are exposed, and their learning. Because they share the same genes, identical twins are often used in studies designed to compare their intelligence, health, and behaviour, and these continue to throw new and useful light on the debate. Although it is often claimed in jest that teachers tend to attribute the intelligence of their own children to nature and the intelligence of their pupils to nurture, it seems that most psychologists, sociologists, teachers, and philosophers take the position that elements of both are clearly apparent in a child's development and attitude to learning.

NEET (not in employment, education, or training) An acronym coined to describe those young people who are not engaged in any form of education, training, or employment when they have left school. Government statistics in 2003 concluded that approximately 9 per cent of 16–18-year-olds could be classified as falling within the NEET category. Research to discover the factors which might predispose young people to non-involvement and underachievement has been carried out extensively as a result of the *widening participation agenda. Data suggest that within the NEET category there are disproportionate numbers of young people from the following groups: young mothers; those with low achievement at *General Certificate of Secondary Education level; those from a low socio-economic group; and those who were regular truants in Year 11 at school. V.C., K.A.

Neill, A. S. (1883–1973) Alexander Sutherland Neill was an exponent of democratic, pupil-centred, or 'free' schooling, and the founder of *Summerhill School. His reaction to his own Calvinist upbringing led him to the conviction that children should not be subjected to the imposition of morals or values by adults in authority over them, and should not be disciplined externally by fear or threat. He argued that the purpose of education was not to control the child or to inculcate a set of values or beliefs, but to 'to find out where a child's interest lies and to help him live it out'. Neill's philosophy and theories of education were not, however, systematic or definitively argued. Rather, it is the application and development of his democratic and *learner-centred approach as manifested in the Summerhill School project, rather than its articulation in a body of philosophical or theoretical writings, for which he is remembered. During his lifetime he was seen as an extremist in terms of educational theory and practice, with his emphasis on children's personal freedom and his insistence on equality of status between teachers and pupils.

One of his early influences was the psychoanalytical work of Sigmund Freud (1856–1939), particularly Freud's work on repression, on which Neill drew when exploring and seeking to resolve pupils' difficulties with life and with learning.

Although his emphasis on using the child's interest as a starting point for the planning of learning has much in common with the work of *Montessori, Neill was nevertheless an opponent of her educational methods, viewing them as unnecessarily 'scientific' and moralizing.

He made his first experiment with democratic, pupil-centred schooling in 1921 in Hellerau, a suburb of Dresden in Germany, but shortly relocated it to Sonntagsberg in Austria, claiming that staff at Hellerau were attempting to impose their own values and morals on the children. In Austria he encountered some local hostility to his ideas, and so moved his school again, this time to Lyme Regis in England, where it opened with five pupils. In 1927 Summerhill School moved finally to its current site, near the Suffolk coast. Considered something of an *enfant terrible* in the 1920s world of education, Neill and his unconventional approach to schooling had fallen into relative obscurity by the 1950s, when the number of pupils at Summerhill declined to 25. However, public interest in his work was rekindled by the publication of his book *Summerhill—a Radical Approach to Childhood*, which appeared in America in 1960 and in the UK in 1962. After his death in 1973 his wife, Ena, whom he had married when she was a member of staff at the school, took over as head teacher. On her mother's retirement in 1985, Neill's daughter Zoë took over the leadership of the school. Neill's reaction to his own constrained upbringing led him to place great emphasis on the importance of creating a happy childhood for the pupils in his care. Indeed, he claimed that 'all outside compulsion is wrong, that inner compulsion is the only value'.

Further Reading: Mark Vaughan *Summerhill and A. S. Neill* (Open University Press, 2006).

SEE WEB LINKS

- Provides a biography of Neill, an evaluation of his contribution to educational theory, and an extended bibliography.

newly qualified teacher (NQT) A teacher in schools who has completed their teaching qualification, has gained *qualified teacher status, and is engaged in their first year of teaching. For teachers in *maintained schools and non-maintained *special schools, this has, since 1999, been a mandatory *induction year, during which teachers must demonstrate that they continue to meet the national standards of *QTS as well as the induction standards. The NQT receives individualized support from a designated induction tutor with whom they engage in a professional review of their performance and progress at the end of each of the three *terms. Their teaching is observed, and they themselves are expected to observe the teaching of more experienced colleagues. During this first year of their career, the NQT does not teach more than 90 per cent of a full timetable, and it is the head teacher's responsibility to make sure that this is the case. It is also the head teacher's duty at the end of the NQT year to make a recommendation to the *local authority, or other appropriate body, such as the Independent Schools Council Teacher Induction panel, as to whether the NQT has successfully completed the induction year. NQTs are required to register with the *General Teaching Council at the start of their training, and their registration is confirmed following successful completion of the induction year.

New Opportunities Fund (NOF) Formed in 1998 to distribute lottery funds, in the form of grants, to projects in education, health, and the environment.

It operates throughout the United Kingdom, and focuses grants particularly on community-based projects to support the disadvantaged. Within the Fund's eleven separate programmes, the **Physical Education and Sport** and the **Green Spaces and Sustainable Communities** programmes are of relevance to sports education. The Fund is administered by a board, and its policy and funding framework is directed by central government.

norm-referencing Where student performance in an *examination or other assessed work is measured by comparing it with the performance of others, rather than against fixed criteria. Thus, in a group of very high-attaining students a candidate might gain a high score, such as 70 per cent, but still be graded as a low pass if most of the group gained 80 per cent or more. Similarly, where the standard of performance was low overall, a candidate who answered very few questions correctly might gain a high grade if the rest of the cohort performed even more badly. This method of assessing and grading is in direct contrast with *criterion-referenced *assessment. *See also* ASSESSMENT CRITERIA.

NORTHERN IRELAND, EDUCATION IN

The education system of Northern Ireland is separate and distinct from that of England and has an extremely complex structure, involving nine non-departmental public bodies. These bodies operate independently, collaborate with the *Department of Education (DENI), and are the responsibility of the Minister of Education, including: Belfast Education and Library Board; South Eastern Education and Library Board; Southern Education and Library Board; North Eastern Education and Library Board; Western Education and Library Board; the Council for Catholic Maintained Schools; the Northern Ireland Council for the Curriculum, Examinations, and Assessments; the Staff Commission for the Education and Library Boards; and the Youth Council for Northern Ireland. Other statutory and voluntary groups contribute to the administration of education in Northern Ireland: Comhairle na Gaelscolaíochta (the Council for Irish-Medium Education), the General Teaching Council for Northern Ireland, and the Northern Ireland Council for Integrated Education.

At the time of writing the Minister for Education and head of the DENI is Caitríona Ruane. She is a member of Sinn Féin and has worked as a human rights and community activist, lobbying the United Nations and the European Union on human rights in Northern Ireland. She was an International Observer for the first free and fair elections in South Africa when Nelson Mandela became President. In 2007 the new Minister for Education faced major challenges over the evolution of a single education authority and the end of the *Eleven Plus. In 2006 the *Bain Review (*Schools for the Future*) was published. The report focused on provision for 14–19-year-olds and recommended an end to academic selection and increased collaboration between schools. The current *Transfer Tests are due to end in autumn 2008 and the Assembly has to create new procedures for pupils transferring in 2010 and future years.

Will Haire is the Permanent Education Secretary and principal adviser to the Minister. His presentation to the Members of the Legislative Assembly in April 2007 gave an overview of the challenges facing education in Northern Ireland. Key issues are strikingly similar to those currently being debated in other parts of the UK (14–19 qualifications, development of 'functional skills', inclusion, special education needs, English as an Additional Language, and falling pupil numbers).

The current education system in Northern Ireland reflects the needs of different community groups (Catholic, state, integrated, and Irish-language), while the new legislation proposes to address the needs of geographical areas. Schools will be expected to share lessons and some will become specialists, offering expertise in specific areas of the curriculum.

At the present time the Department of Education in Northern Ireland is responsible for: strategic planning and management of education, curriculum content and delivery, allocating funding to the education and library boards, and covering capital costs for most schools. The five education and library boards oversee the needs of specific areas, fund *controlled schools and satisfy the running costs of *maintained schools. Other responsibilities include: providing milk and meals, and free books and pupil transport, enforcing school attendance, advising on the school curriculum, providing recreational services, employing teachers in controlled schools, and employing non-teaching staff in controlled and maintained schools.

The *Department for Education's Education and Training Inspectorate conducts school inspections and reports to the Department of Education, and publishes reports for parents with recommendations. In 2001 the Department of Education stopped using league tables, following consultation with teachers, schools, parents, and unions.

Compulsory education in Northern Ireland begins at 4 years of age and ends at 16. There are four key stages: Key Stage 1 (4–8 years), Key Stage 2 (8–11 years), Key Stage 3 (11–14 years), and Key Stage 4 (14–16 years).

The curriculum in Northern Ireland is determined by the *Northern Ireland Council for Curriculum, Examinations, and Assessment. Responsibilities of the Council include: assessment of pupils at Key Stages 1, 2, and 3, conducting public examinations, graded objectives in modern languages for students aged 16–19, the regulation of *General National Vocational Qualifications in Northern Ireland, and administering the Transfer Tests. From 2007 a revised curriculum was applied and included annual assessment. The curriculum includes religious education; pupils must have the opportunity to take part in daily collective worship but parents can choose to withdraw children from both.

The state sector incorporates a range of schools. Nursery education in Northern Ireland has received funding from the European Union Special Support Programme for Peace and Reconciliation to increase pre-school education. At the primary stage of education pupils are assessed at Key Stages 1 and 2; children are selected at 11 years for grammar or secondary schools, but this system is now being reviewed. Secondary schools control their own admissions. Controlled schools are owned and funded by the education and library boards and are mainly Protestant, with the Church represented on the board of governors. *Catholic maintained schools are owned by the Catholic Church through a system of trustees. Other maintained schools are owned by the Protestant Church, also through a system of trustees and managed by a board of governors. Voluntary grammar schools are owned by the school trustees and managed by a board of governors. *Grant maintained integrated schools are usually partially owned by trustees and managed by a board of governors. Special needs education is determined by the Education and Libraries (NI) Order 1986; education and library boards have to provide education for pupils with special needs up to the age of 19. This can take place within either mainstream or separate units.

SEE WEB LINKS

- Public Record Office of Northern Ireland providing a history of the DENI.
- Department of Education in Northern Ireland web site, detailing current developments and policies.
- Explains the system of school administration in Northern Ireland. J.H.

Northern Ireland Council for Integrated Education (NICIE) A voluntary organization established in 1987 in order to promote and facilitate integrated education in Northern Ireland. J.H.

Northern Ireland Council for the Curriculum, Examinations, and Assessment (CCEA) The CCEA determines the curriculum in Northern Ireland and manages the assessment of pupils at *Key Stages 1, 2, and 3. It also oversees the conduct of public examinations such as the *General Certificate of Education, the regulation of *General National Vocational Qualifications in Northern Ireland, and the administration of the *Transfer Tests (Eleven Plus tests). These tests may be curtailed in 2008. A revised curriculum was introduced during the academic year 2006/7, incorporating annual assessment. J.H.

note in lieu A note issued following a statutory assessment of a child or young person's *special educational needs. A statutory assessment usually precedes the issuing of a *statement of needs. Where it has been decided that the criteria for issuing a statement are not met, a note in lieu is issued. The note in lieu document contains a description of the child's particular needs and sets out clear objectives to be worked towards to enable the child to make progress. It also describes the level of provision which the school is expected to put in place. Progress towards the objectives would be reviewed as part of regular provision in line with the practice of the school for pupils with individual needs. T.B., L.E.

Notice to Improve Schools in which *Ofsted has judged the quality of education to be inadequate but capable of improvement are served with a

Notice to Improve. After a period of six to eight months this is followed by a one-day monitoring visit by inspectors, who evaluate the progress being made towards improvement in the specific issues and areas identified as inadequate. The visit is made at short notice, with only two to five days' notice given, so that an accurate evaluation may be made. In a meeting at the end of the visit verbal feedback is given to the school and, if appropriate, the *local authority, and is later confirmed in writing, both to the school and on the Ofsted web site. The feedback is expected to help the school set the agenda for further improvement, which will be assessed at their next Ofsted *inspection.

Nuffield Foundation Projects and curriculum developments in subjects such as science education are initiated and supported by the Nuffield Foundation, a body dedicated to the funding of curriculum research and development. In the 1960s, 1970s, and 1980s the Foundation developed science and mathematics projects and produced science curriculums for use in schools. These included the *syllabus for *General Certificate of Education *Ordinary Level and *Advanced Level examinations in science subjects. Since the introduction of the *national curriculum and its related programme of study for science, the Foundation has focused instead on the funding of science-related and other educational projects.

numeracy The ability to apply and interpret numbers and numerical information. Identified as one of the essential skills needed in the world of work, numeracy became a core skill on training programmes such as the *Youth Training Scheme and on projects such as the *Technical and Vocational Education Initiative in schools. It later became a component of the *key skills which were incorporated into the *General National Vocational Qualification, where it was referred to as *application of number; and later, following the implementation of *Curriculum 2000, it became a key skill applied to all 16–19 qualifications. Teachers themselves must demonstrate an appropriate level of numeracy, both in schools and in the *further education sector; for the former through the *teacher training skills test and for the latter through testing of the *minimum core. An individual who is competent in numeracy is termed 'numerate', while one who is not may be referred to as 'innumerate'. One of the earliest references to the term itself was in the Crowther Report (1959), which argued that numeracy, as well as literacy, was an essential skill and central to a sound education. *See also* NATIONAL NUMERACY STRATEGY.

nursery 1. Until comparatively recently (2000), a nursery was the first classroom setting for 3-year-olds entering school. A nursery is more commonly classified as a *day nursery if it provides full day care for children. Since the establishment of the *Foundation Stage in 2000, and the *Early Years Foundation Stage in 2008, foundation units within schools may incorporate nursery and *reception children aged 3–5 years.

2. A term used by parents, advertisers, estate agents, and magazines to describe a room in a house decorated and equipped with play, nursing, and sleeping furniture for very young children. A.W.

nursery nurse Staff qualified to work with children aged 0–7 in a variety of settings, mainly in *day nurseries and in *nursery, infant, and specialist schools.

These duties cover all aspects of physical care and safety, and the nursery nurse is generally responsible for social and educational development. This involves planning for and supervising activities which they will observe. It has become more common to give nursery nurses the title 'teaching assistant' when they work within the maintained school sector. Qualifications (historically gained through the *National Nursery Examination Board (NNEB) and the Council for Awards in Children's Care and Education) are at levels 2 and 3 of the *National Qualifications Framework, at sub-degree level.

SEE WEB LINKS

- A database of childcare qualifications and the range of training opportunities.
- Information on qualifications, practice, and staff development courses.

A.W.

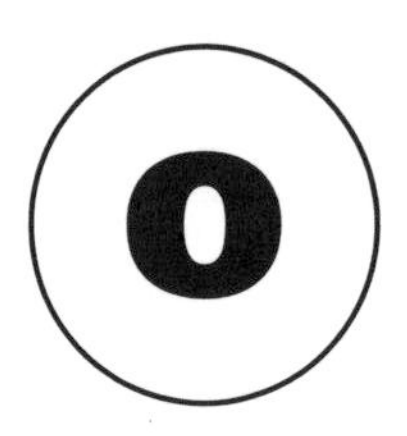

objectives, learning A clear statement of what the student or pupil should have learned by the end of the task, the lesson, the *scheme of work, or the course of study. Learning objectives provide focus and direction, and clarify what must be assessed in order to ascertain whether learning has taken place. They are sometimes referred to as learning **outcomes**. The *programme of study or *syllabus for the course or programme will normally provide a full of list of objectives to be covered, articulated in the form of a list of required learning targets. On the basis of these the teacher will construct a scheme of work, which is then broken down into individual *lesson plans, which, between them, provide coverage of all the learning objectives listed in the syllabus. *See also* BEHAVIOURAL LEARNING OBJECTIVE.

objective test A means of *assessment in which there is no margin for subjectivity, interpretation, or speculation on the part of the assessor or examiner. It involves questions for which there is a clear-cut answer. Simple numerical tests and *multiple choice questions are common examples of objective testing, while assessment requiring a discursive response in the form of an essay, for example, is clearly not. One measure of objectivity is whether the assessment can be carried out by computer.

objectivism The objectivist view of education is that *knowledge is delivered by the teacher to the learner by means of instruction. It assumes that knowledge consists in an accumulation of 'facts' which can be thus passed on unchanged from teacher to learner. Such an approach situates learners as passive recipients of education, and discourages critical analyses and conflicting viewpoints which might arise from individual experience or different contexts. It is a model which necessarily limits learner participation and interaction, emphasizing teacher input rather than teacher–learner dialogue. As a consequence, it encourages learner compliance and places control firmly with the teachers. It is challenged by those with *constructivist views of education on the grounds that it limits the learner by disempowering them and by failing to encourage individuals to test what they are learning against their own experience, and against their own social, political, and economic interactions with others and with the state. Notable critics of the objectivist approach are *Dewey, *Vygotsky, and *Freire.

OCR A unitary *awarding body created by a merger between the *Royal Society of Arts (RSA) and the Oxford and Cambridge examination boards. It is normally referred to by this abbreviated form, made up of the initial letters of Oxford, Cambridge, and RSA. It is one of the three awarding bodies responsible for academic and vocational qualifications for 16–19-year-olds.

Offender Learning and Skills Service (OLASS) The Service was set up regionally in England in July 2006 to help deliver and coordinate the provision of meaningful skills and employment for offenders in custody and in the community. The *Learning and Skills Councils (LSCs), at both regional and national level, oversee the new service, as with all other post-compulsory education and training delivery. As such, the LSC offers a single means of planning, commissioning, and funding the OLASS. The Service focuses on the assessment and planning of learning, the provision of a broader and richer curriculum, developing the mainstreamed delivery of offender learning, workforce development for offender learning, and a refocusing on external inspection arrangements.

SEE WEB LINKS

- Gives access to an archive of press releases.

V.C., K.A.

Office for Standards in Education, Children's Services, and Skills *See* OFSTED.

Office of the Qualifications and Examinations Regulator (Ofqual) A body responsible for the regulation of national qualifications up to those offered by universities and other institutions of *higher education, and including those such as the *General Certificate of Secondary Education (GCSE) and the *General Certificate of Education *Advanced Level (A level), and for monitoring the regime of national testing. Schools which have problems or issues with any aspect of national testing are able to raise these with Ofqual directly. Ofqual began to operate in shadow form in April 2008. Although it works closely with the *Qualifications and Curriculum Authority, it is an independent body with the status of a non-ministerial department, and is responsible for reporting to Parliament in the first instance, rather than direct to government. One of its roles is to determine the terms on which organizations which award their own qualifications may gain national recognition for them. Two of the issues which come under its remit are the question of whether A levels and GCSEs in some subjects are more difficult than those in others, and whether judgements about the relative difficulty of different subjects could result in the setting of differentiated examination grade boundaries.

Ofsted The body responsible for inspecting schools and other educational and training providers, and monitoring and reporting upon their performance. Created following the Education (Schools) Act 1992, it constituted a new system of schools *inspection which replaced that previously carried out by *Her Majesty's Inspectorate (HMI), a body which had been much reduced in size following reorganization. Ofsted is headed by the **Chief Inspector of Schools in England**, who leads an inspectorate made up of HMIs and other inspectors, many of whom take part in inspections on a part-time or consultancy basis.

Initially, inspections were carried out under the *Education Act 1992 (section 9) and then later under the School Inspections Act 1996 (section 10). There have been two major changes to the role and functioning of Ofsted since its introduction. One is the introduction of 'lighter-touch' inspections. In 2003 Ofsted produced a strategic plan for the years 2004–7, which included the proposal that it should engage in a fundamental review of its approach to the

O

inspection of schools. Consultation took place between 10 February and 8 April 2004, which resulted in a reformed inspection framework, published in November 2004 and put into effect from September 2005. These changes to the statutory basis of school inspections, including the introduction of small-team, shorter inspections, were enshrined in the Education Act 2005. The second major change was to the scope and remit of Ofsted. In April 2007, following the Education and Inspections Act 2006, four specialist inspectorates, including the *Adult Learning Inspectorate, became amalgamated with Ofsted to create an expanded inspection service responsible for monitoring and regulating standards of provision in care for children and young people and inspecting the education and training provision for all age groups as well as in schools. Ofsted is now responsible for inspecting the sufficiency of provision to safeguard and promote the welfare of children and young people. This includes reporting on whether systems are in place to protect them from maltreatment and prevent the impairment of their health or development, and to ensure that their circumstances are consistent with the provision of safe and effective care. These multi-disciplinary inspections of local authorities' provision allow Ofsted to make judgements about the overall quality of provision in the geographical area covered by that local authority. This expansion of its remit is reflected in the revised name, which was originally simply the Office for Standards in Education, although its original abbreviation has been retained. *See also* LEAD INSPECTOR.

online learning *See* E-LEARNING.

ontology The study and understanding of what exists, or what there is. Ontology addresses the question of the nature of reality. For instance, reality can be taken to be made up only of facts about the material world, as in physics, or of social constructions (or meanings), such as 'family' or 'democracy', which depend on human understanding, as in sociology. Answers to questions of reality constrain and underpin theories of knowledge (*epistemology) and theories of how knowledge can be gained (methodology), learned, or taught (*pedagogy). In one sense ontology may be described as the study of what it means to be human. *See also* RESEARCH. M.G.

open admission A policy operated by some *universities or other institutions of *higher education allowing students who do not possess the normal entry requirements, such as *General Certificate of Education *Advanced Levels, to gain entry to courses. In the United Kingdom, only the Open University operates an open admissions policy as a norm, although other universities and colleges have admissions regulations for *mature students which are more flexible or open than for applicants who are school-leavers. Sometimes also referred to as **open access**, open admission is more often encountered in American universities. *See also* ACCESS COURSE; NATIONAL OPEN COLLEGE NETWORK.

open-book examination *Examinations where candidates are permitted to take in with them, or are otherwise provided with, copies of the texts on which they are being examined, or of key texts related to the subject in question. In an English literature open-book examination, for example, candidates are able to refer to, and quote from, set texts in order to develop and support the arguments on which their essay-style answers are based. The rationale for allowing books into examinations is based on the belief that the ability of the candidate to memorize, for example, long passages of text or lists of dates is less meaningful educationally than their skills of comprehension and synthesis, and that it is therefore more appropriate to construct and conduct examinations in such a way as to test the latter rather than the former. This concept of higher and lower orders of skills owes much to the categorizations set out in *Bloom's Taxonomy. *See also* ROTE LEARNING.

Open College *See* NATIONAL OPEN COLLEGE NETWORK.

open-ended A form of questioning which requires more than a 'yes' or 'no' answer, and does not restrict the choice of answer to one of a list, as in *multiple-choice testing. It requires students to articulate answers in their own words, and thereby it tests their skills of comprehension and synthesis rather than, or as well as, their memory. Open-ended questioning may be used verbally by teachers in class as part of a question-and-answer session to check student progress and understanding; or it may be used in a written form in tests and exams. In some contexts, for example in questionnaires, such questions are known as **open questions**. The *assessment of answers to open-ended questions is usually open to more subjectivity than that of **closed questions** to which there is an agreed objective answer of the factual or true–false kind. Because an open-ended question may have no one definitive or final answer it has a wider range of uses in teaching than simply that of testing students' knowledge. It may be used to encourage learners to draw upon their own *tacit knowledge; to make connections between previous and current learning; to hypothesize or theorize; or to create and invent. *See also* OBJECTIVE TEST.

open enrolment A policy which may be operated by schools of admitting the maximum number of pupils which their capacity allows if there is demand from parents that they should do so, even in the situation where there are falling rolls, and therefore spare places, in neighbouring schools. The *Education Reform Act 1988 encouraged schools to adopt this practice as a response to the demands of the *market, the assumption being that if excellent schools were fully subscribed to the detriment of others in their area, those less popular schools would be forced to improve their standards of provision in order to compete or even survive. In this way, it was argued, national standards of education could be raised. *See also* CHOICE.

open-plan The design of school accommodation, particularly in *primary schools, which creates open areas for group work and other activities rather than dividing the space into discrete, closed classrooms. The use of open-plan learning environments is associated with *progressive educational methods and a *child-centred approach, and its incorporation into the construction of some new state primary schools in the 1950s signalled a move away from traditional strategies of rank-order seating and *rote learning. One disadvantage reported by teachers is the problem of distraction or disruption by one group of another, particularly when noise levels rise, although the advantages it provides in terms of flexibility are considered by many to outweigh this. About one in ten primary schools in the United Kingdom are of an open-plan design. Some open-plan teaching accommodation exists in other sectors, for example in the art, drama, and textile workshops of further education *colleges.

Open University (OU) A *university which teaches by *distance learning and whose original purpose was to make degree level education accessible to people who have not had the opportunity to attend university in the traditional way. It now, in addition to first degree courses, offers *master's degrees and supervision for *doctorates, as well as short courses in various aspects of professional or personal development. It currently claims to be the largest provider of management education in Europe. In 2007 in total, across all its courses, it had more than 180 000 students enrolled. The students study mainly at home and interact with the university online and through course materials such as books, CDs, videos, and television programmes, as well as local *tutorials and residential or day schools. This style of distance learning is known as **supported open learning**. The support is provided by a tutor and by student services located at regional centres as well as centrally at the university's site in Milton Keynes. Assessment is usually through *examination and tutor-marked *assignments, although some courses use alternative *assessment instruments such as computer-marked assignments, *dissertations, or *project work. The university has thirteen regional centres throughout the United Kingdom.

The concept of the OU has its origins in the 1920s, when the idea of a 'wireless university' was suggested by J. C. Stobard, an educationalist working for the BBC. It was taken up seriously only in the 1960s, when the presence of television in most homes offered interesting possibilities for a 'College' or 'University of the Air'. Harold Wilson (1916–95), elected Prime Minister in 1964, gave the project his support and directed the Minister for the Arts, Jennie Lee (1904–88), after whom the OU's first library was named, to oversee the project's development. The first personnel moved into its site at Milton Keynes in 1969, and the first student applications were taken in 1970. The first OU students began their studies in 1971, and by 1980 enrolment figures had reached 80 000. *See also* ADULT EDUCATION.

options Components of a course or programme over which the student has some choice. Within the *national curriculum, options are introduced at Key Stage 4 and are chosen by the pupil from the **entitlement** areas of arts, design and technology, humanities, and modern foreign languages. Some courses, particularly those which are made up of *modules, require the student to take a number of mandatory, or **core**, components, and, in addition to these, a specified number of additional components which the student will select from the range offered. This type of structure is known as the **core plus options** model, and is often found in *degree courses, both at first degree and at *master's level. Some confusion was introduced into the meaning of 'option' by the original structure of *General National Vocational Qualifications, where 'option' units were selected not necessarily by the student but by the school or college where the course was taught, and were so called in order to differentiate them from the core units, which were assessed differently.

oracy The skill of communicating clearly by speech, and of comprehending the spoken communications of others. It is used to emphasize the importance of spoken language skills, particularly, but not exclusively, in *primary education, and has been coined relatively recently to stand alongside *literacy and *numeracy as an essential component of a child's education. The importance of oracy is reflected in the *National Literacy Strategy and the *literacy hour. Comprehension of the spoken word and the ability to speak articulately and fluently are emphasized in the *national curriculum *attainment targets for speaking and listening. Oracy skills are also a component of the Adult Basic Skills Strategy, designed to raise levels of *adult literacy.

oral examination A method of formal *assessment in which the candidate is questioned face to face by the examiner and is assessed on the quality of their response. The examination of candidates in modern foreign languages usually includes an oral component to enable the student's skill in comprehending and conversing in the spoken language to be assessed. Oral examinations may also be conducted as an alternative where the candidate is unable to sit a written examination. *See also* VIVA.

Ordinary Grade (O grade) A Scottish secondary qualification which was replaced by the modern *Standard Grade qualification in the early 1990s, and which could be considered broadly equivalent to the English *General Certificate of Education *Ordinary Level. S.M.

Ordinary Level (O level) An examination and qualification for pupils of school-leaving age which was in operation from 1951, when it replaced the **School Certificate**, until 1986, when it in turn was replaced by the *General Certificate of Secondary Education. The *General Certificate of Education O level was offered in a range of subjects, pupils usually taking between four and ten, depending on the school's judgement about their level of ability. It was originally intended for the most able pupils as a step on their trajectory towards a *higher education or entry to one of the professions, but became a standard qualification demanded by employers, particularly in English and mathematics. It was partly for this reason that when the *Certificate of Secondary Education (CSE) was introduced in 1965 for pupils whose ability to succeed at O level was in doubt, its highest grade—a grade 1—was announced as equivalent to an O level pass at grade A–C, thus allowing CSE candidates the opportunity to gain a qualification which would enable them to choose from a wider range of employment when leaving school. The O level was offered by eight different *examining boards, each with their own syllabus. It was graded A–E, although only grades A–C were considered as a respectable pass grade by universities, other institutions of higher education, and employers. The grade F indicated a fail, and U indicated the result was so poor as to be unclassified. School-leavers applying for *university entrance were usually expected to have eight or more good O level passes; and, for candidates applying to study some degrees at some universities, specific subjects at O level were required, in addition to the stipulated grades at *Advanced Level. These often included English and mathematics, and sometimes O level Latin for those wishing to study for a degree in English.

organized games Sporting activities, usually involving teams, which take place within school hours as part of the school *curriculum, and are a component of physical education or sports studies.

outcomes *See* OBJECTIVES, LEARNING.

out of hours activity A structured activity which takes place after school hours, during school holidays, at lunchtimes, or at break, and is not directly included in *national curriculum requirements. It is usually organized and supervised by teachers, and takes the form of such activities as sports and sporting competitions, drama rehearsals and productions, chess clubs, orchestra and choir practices and performances, and homework clubs. Engagement in these activities is normally voluntary on the part of pupils and teachers alike. *See also* EXTRACURRICULAR.

out of school hours learning *See* STUDY SUPPORT.

outreach Programmes of education or training which are delivered out in the community rather than on the premises of the provider. The purpose of these is to facilitate access to education for groups who might find it difficult or undesirable to attend an educational institution or who otherwise feel themselves excluded from available provision. Such groups include young people who have disengaged from education and training, and ethnic minority groups who may have specific cultural or language needs. Outreach courses are often referred to as 'projects'. They are increasingly forming part of the *curriculum of *colleges and *universities. They are also a characteristic provision of youth services and *adult education. *See also* WIDENING PARTICIPATION.

Oxbridge An abbreviated colloquial term for the *universities of Oxford and Cambridge, often used as an indicator of high status or esteem in such phrases as 'an Oxbridge education'. It is suggestive of a clear distinction between the two earliest universities and the later universities founded in the 19th and 20th centuries, which are often referred to colloquially as 'red-bricks', and 'new universities' or 'ex-polytechnics' respectively.

pace The rate at which a lesson progresses. This is not about the speed with which the teacher can get through the *lesson plan, but rather the sense of engagement and purpose engendered in the learners by the sequencing and length of each activity. The teacher should aim to pace the lesson according to the learners' needs. If it is too hurried, some learners may get left behind; if too leisurely, some may become bored. The pace of the lesson, therefore, calls for a careful balance and, in some cases, *differentiation of activity for individuals or groups.

para-professional Sometimes used to describe staff who assist with teaching in schools, colleges, and universities, such as *teaching assistants, *instructors, and **technicians**.

PARENTAL PREFERENCE

Under the *Education Act 1980 parents are permitted to state a preference for which school their child will attend, although under that legislation there was no requirement for schools or *local authorities to comply with parents' declared preferences. At this time the allocation of places fell under the remit of local education authorities, which were responsible for strategic planning of provision in their own geographical area. Following the Education Act 1988, however, schools are now obliged to comply with parental preference, as long as there are places available. Taken together, these two Acts have allowed parents to express a preference over their child's schooling, and to expect a positive response if a place is available, even in cases where the preferred school lies at some distance and in a different local authority from that in which the child lives. If parents are unsuccessful in gaining their first *choice of school for their child, they are entitled to lodge an appeal against the school's decision. Such appeals are heard by independent appeal panels, which exclude from membership any representative of the local authority or member of the *governing body of the school in question. The decision of the appeals panel is final.

Inevitably, the expression of parental preference has led to some schools—usually those which are known to perform best in raising and maintaining pupil attainment—becoming a more popular choice than others. This is reflected in the fact that the number of admissions appeals made in England annually continues to rise. Popular schools may quickly become oversubscribed, and as an inevitable result it becomes the school itself which is in the position of exercising a degree of choice over its intake of pupils. Less popular schools which have not succeeded in gaining as good a reputation have less choice over which pupils they enrol. To some extent, therefore, it could be argued that the introduction of parental preference has led to practices of recruitment and enrolment which bear some echoes of a selective model of school place allocation, since schools which are in a position to exert some choice over their intake will tend to recruit pupils whose potential for attainment will reflect well on the school. *See also* SCHOOL ADMISSIONS.

parent council A form of parent representation and a vehicle for parent decision-making and voice in schools. Such councils were introduced in Scotland by the Scottish Schools Act 2006, and from August 2007 these groups replaced school boards. In England the *Children's Plan, a government initiative launched in December 2007 to enhance provision of education, play facilities, and care for children up to 19 years of age, set out as one of its targets the setting up of parents' councils in every secondary school in England.

SEE WEB LINKS

- Gives details of the nature of the new parent councils in Scotland.

S.M.

parent governor A member of a school's *governing body who represents the parents of pupils at that school. Parent governors make up 25 per cent of the governing body and are nominated by parents and elected by secret ballot. Once elected, they normally serve for four years, and are offered formal training to support their role and responsibilities. The requirement for schools to have a governing body on which parents have strong representation is set out in the *Education Act 1986. A small number of **parent governor representatives** in each area are elected by fellow governors to work with their local authority to provide parents with a voice in locally made policy decisions.

parent partnership service An impartial service provided by all *local authorities to discharge in part their responsibility for making information, advice, and support relating to matters of *special educational needs (SEN) available to the parents of children in their area. Authorities may administrate and manage the service themselves, purchase it from an external provider, or offer a mix of the two. Services must be evaluated regularly and organized in such a way as to engender and maintain parents' confidence that they are being offered neutral, accurate, and unbiased information. Authorities have responsibility for publicizing the service to parents, schools, and relevant agencies and bodies. Additionally, their responsibility extends to informing parents about the service in writing when a proposed statement or amended proposed *statement of SEN is issued or when a decision has been taken not to undertake a statutory assessment of SEN. The core functions of the service are to work with parents to empower them to play an active and informed role in their child's education by offering a wide and flexible range of services; to network and collaborate with schools, local authority officers, and other agencies, including voluntary organizations, and to ensure parents' views are represented in the development of local special educational needs policy and practice. T.B., L.A.

parents' evening An event at which parents are invited into their child's school to meet the teachers and discuss their child's progress. It is held after school hours and pupils may or may not be encouraged to attend with their parents. It is usual in larger schools, particularly secondary schools, for a schedule of appointments to be drawn up for each teacher so that a parent can 'book' their allotment of time with each of their child's teachers. In secondary schools, separate events are often held for separate year groups. The frequency of parents' evenings will depend upon the school, but parents will normally be provided with such an opportunity to come into school at least once each academic year. It is often said by teachers that those parents who consistently fail to attend parents' evenings are often precisely those whom the school would most wish to engage with about their child's progress or behaviour.

parent–teacher association (PTA) An association organized on an individual school basis, made up of staff and parents, for the purpose of discussing and acting on a number of school-related issues. These may include anything from organizing events to raise funds for the school, to the debating of educational issues such as those raised in an inspection by *Ofsted. It is often run by a committee to which nominated parents are elected by ballot. The extent of its activities and the robustness of its membership will vary from school to school, and will often be dependent to some extent on how far such an association is encouraged by the *head teacher and *governors. Such an association does not exist at all schools. There is, however, a **National Confederation of Parent–Teacher Associations**, which acts as a platform for the views of its constituent members.

SEE WEB LINKS

- Details from the National Confederation of Parent–Teacher Associations on how and why a PTA may be established.

parity of esteem Used, particularly in political policy discourse, to refer to an equality in status between routes of study, particularly ones where such equality could demonstrably be argued not to exist. It was a phrase used, for example, to describe the relationship between *grammar school and secondary modern provision as implemented by the Education Act 1944 (*Butler Act), suggesting that the two types of provision were, in some undefined sense, of equal value. More recently, it was used as part of the rhetoric surrounding the introduction of *National Vocational Qualifications and *General National Vocational Qualifications (GNVQs), suggesting that these qualification routes would be held in equal regard, by parents, employers, and *higher education institutions, with the *General Certificate of Secondary Education or *General Certificate of Education *Advanced Levels (A levels). In the *White Paper *Education and Training for the 21st Century* (1991), the government of the day declared its intention to 'promote equal esteem for academic and vocational qualifications'. A clearer sense of what such 'parity' might be taken to mean in practice emerges from a City and Guilds of London Institute newsletter of 1992, which claimed that, 'at Level 3, GNVQ will have parity with A levels and thus provide a viable route to Higher Education'. Claims of parity between the general and the *vocational routes appear to have been made largely on a theoretical basis only. For example, on 13 November 1993, before the first cohort of GNVQ students had even completed their qualification, and therefore before this contention had been put to the test, John Patten, then Secretary of State for Education, announced on Radio 4's *Today* programme that the Advanced GNVQ 'has parity of esteem with A levels'. The urgency to establish credentials for alternative, vocational routes into higher education may be explained by the policy goal of higher participation rates in education and *training after 16, and national *targets to create a higher proportion of graduates in the workforce.

Thus, we see that 'parity' in this context tends to be defined in terms of utility. The vocational qualification may be regarded as having 'parity of esteem' in the sense that it will serve the purpose of enabling progression to employment or to higher education just as the general or academic qualification will do. In wider terms of value or status, however, the claims for parity are more difficult to substantiate. It also remains questionable whether parity of esteem is accorded to students on vocational and general education courses within the same institution. One of the initial obstacles to establishing parity for GNVQs was their emphasis on *continuous assessment, which led opponents to argue that, without a rigorous system of *summative and externally assessed *examinations, the new qualification could not realistically be considered as a currency equivalent to a level for progression to higher education. The eventual introduction of more rigorous external assessment did not, however, lead to equality of status. This was not surprising as the lack of parity arose from systemic social, economic, and political causes which rendered it impervious to a simple change of assessment mode.

Evidence suggests that learning providers in the *learning and skills sector, such as *further education colleges, whose *curriculum is largely *vocational, are not considered to have equal status with school sixth forms and *sixth form colleges, partly because they tend to recruit students who have achieved less well in public examinations. Teachers in the learning and skills sector also argue that they themselves do not have parity with their colleagues in schools, basing their argument on the disparity in teachers' pay and conditions of service between the two sectors.

Parity of esteem, therefore, may be used to apply to utility; to value as a currency for progression; to social status; and to pay and conditions. Ironically, it is used most in those contexts where parity is by no means obvious. It has most recently been employed in *Department for Education and Skills discourse, and subsequently that of the *Department for Innovation, Universities, and Skills, in relation to the status of *foundation degrees.

See also TOMLINSON REPORT (1996).

SEE WEB LINKS

- Provides some working definitions of 'parity of esteem' in education and training, and examples of how it may be achieved.

participant research *See* RESEARCH.

part-time education In *further, *adult, and *higher education students may choose, or be obliged for financial or other reasons, to study on a part-time basis, often combining their studies with paid employment. This mode of attendance can apply to a very wide range of provision, ranging from adult education classes in leisure pursuits, to *work-based training, to *postgraduate *research at *doctorate level. Much of teachers', head teachers', and other education professionals' in-service *continuing professional development is undertaken as part-time study in the professionals' own time, usually in the evenings and at weekends while they continue their work during the week. *See also* EVENING CLASS.

pass grade When a candidate's achievement in assessed work is expressed in terms of *grades, a pass grade may refer to any grade above a fail, or, more specifically, just to the category 'pass'. So, for example, where the possible grades are A or distinction (for the highest range of marks), B or credit (for the middle category), C or pass (for a range of marks which are no more than satisfactory), and F or fail, a pass grade may refer to a C or simple pass, or, depending on the context, may be taken to encompass all three of those grades which are indicators that the candidate has passed rather than failed the assessment. *See also* PASS MARK.

passive learning Learning which does not require any activity or active engagement on the part of the learner, other than perhaps taking notes. The learner is not provided with an opportunity to contribute to the lesson in any way, but simply required to take in information from the teacher. Mr Gradgrind, in Dickens's *Hard Times* (1854), refers to his pupils as 'pitchers' whom he will fill up with knowledge. This is a useful metaphor for passive learning as it highlights the issue which this style of teaching inevitably raises, of who has control over what constitutes relevant *knowledge. Where learning is passive, the teacher's input is likely to be treated uncritically as 'fact', thus discouraging analysis and other higher-order types of learning. *See also* BLOOM'S TAXONOMY; FREIRE.

passive vocabulary Words which are understood and recognized by the learner, but which cannot necessarily be easily recalled or correctly used. That is, they are not part of the individual's *active vocabulary. In the learning of languages, both spoken and written, including the individual's first language, the passive vocabulary will be acquired more quickly and will be more extensive than the active one.

pass mark The minimum mark which a candidate must achieve in order to be deemed to have successfully passed the *assessment. It is commonly applied in assessments which are expressed in percentages. In such cases the candidate may need to achieve a mark of, for example, 40 or 50 per cent in order to pass. *See also* BORDERLINE; EXAMINATION; PASS GRADE.

pass rate The proportion of candidates who succeed in passing an examination or other assessment. Pass rates can be used as a quality assurance indicator or *performance indicator by an educational institution when evaluating the quality of teaching and learning or some other aspects of their provision. However, although pass rates may be presented as measures of success—for example, when schools publish their pupils' achievements in public examinations such as the *General Certificate of Secondary Education—such bare numerical data do not necessarily indicate accurately how much learning has taken place, nor how much effort has gone into the teaching, since they cannot reflect disparities in the starting points of individuals or groups of learners. *See also* LEAGUE TABLES; VALUE ADDED.

pastoral care Guidance and support which focuses on the learner's welfare and their social and emotional needs, rather than their purely educational ones. Although to some extent all teachers are expected to provide a degree of pastoral care, in secondary schools it is often the *head of year who, among their other responsibilities, has an additional pastoral role in relation to pupils in their year group. In some schools a member of the senior management or senior teaching team, such as a *deputy head teacher, may be designated as having overall pastoral responsibility in the school, the day-to-day operation of which will be delegated as appropriate, to the heads of year or group tutors, for example. Matters of concern are reported by other teachers to those with pastoral responsibility where there is reason to think that the pupil may need additional support. In *colleges and *universities, specialist pastoral care is provided by student support services. *See also* STUDY SUPPORT.

Pavlov, Ivan *See* BEHAVIOURIST.

pay, teachers' In England and Wales the pay scales for teachers in maintained schools are determined by the *Secretary of State for Children, Schools, and Families, based on recommendations from the School Teachers' Review Body, and are set out in the **School Teachers' Pay and Conditions Document**. There is a six-point **Main Pay Scale** for classroom teachers, for which there are four separate scales which apply according to the geographical location of the school. There is therefore a differentiation in pay scales between teachers in Inner London, Outer London, the London fringes, and the rest of England and Wales, which is intended to allow for the higher costs of accommodation in London and the surrounding area. This is sometimes referred to as the **London allowance**. The six points on the main scale are known as M1–M6. Teachers taking up their first appointment will normally begin on M1, although mature entrants may be given extra points as an acknowledgement of any relevant experience they bring to their post. The six-point scale is also known as the **common pay spine**. Each year of their teaching experience, teachers gain additional points on the spine. They may also be awarded additional allowances for specific responsibilities in roles related to either teaching or management.

Pay for teachers in *colleges of further education is calculated on a different scale from that of teachers in schools, and whereas in some cases a further education teacher and a schoolteacher may be teaching classes of comparable size, subject, and age group, the further education teacher is likely to be earning rather less than their opposite number in school. Most colleges in England are members of the *Association of Colleges, which represents the colleges in their capacity as employers when carrying out negotiations on pay and conditions with teachers' unions such as the *University and College Union (UCU) in the National Joint Forum. In Wales there is an additional negotiating forum, *Fforum.

Pay for teachers and lecturers in *higher education is negotiated between the Universities and Colleges Employers' Association and unions such as the UCU and the Educational Institute of Scotland. Negotiations take place through an academic subcommittee of the Joint National Committee for Higher Education Staff. The local branches of the unions then negotiate with individual universities, the employers, over the implementation of nationally agreed pay scales. *See also* ADVANCED SKILLS TEACHER; EXCELLENT TEACHER SCHEME; PERFORMANCE THRESHOLD.

SEE WEB LINKS

- Links to current details of pay and conditions for teachers and lecturers in further and higher education in England, Wales, and Northern Ireland.
- Current salary details for teachers in maintained schools.
- Details of Soulbury Pay and Conditions.

pedagogy Teaching, as a professional practice and as a field of academic study. It encompasses not only the practical application of teaching, or pedagogic, skills, but also *curriculum issues and the body of theory relating to how and why learning takes place. Because it derives from a Greek expression referring to the education of the young, pedagogy is sometimes taken to be specifically about the education of children and young people, in which case the more recently coined term 'androgogy' is used in relation to the education of adults. 'Pedagogue', once an alternative term for 'teacher', has come to have overtones of pedantry, and is sometimes used now in a pejorative sense. Either 'pedagogic' or 'pedagogical' may be used as an adjective.

performance *See* ACHIEVEMENT.

performance criteria A clear statement of what the candidate must achieve in order to be deemed successful in an assessed task, *assignment, or *examination. The criteria will normally specify what areas of knowledge, skills, and understanding must be demonstrated, and to what level. They are often used as a way of breaking down the learning outcomes or *objectives into more detailed and specific guidance for the student, and may be used by the teacher or *assessor as a checklist when marking or assessing. When assessment feedback is given to the student, either written or spoken, it should be related to the performance criteria in order to convey clearly where these have and have not been met. The use of performance criteria was integral to the original *General National Vocational Qualification, and was seen by some academics and teachers as being very closely related to the use of *statements of competence.

performance indicators (PIs) Levels of performance and achievement of teachers, managers, institutions, and *local authorities are monitored against national *standards and against targets which may be imposed by government policy or by bodies such as *Ofsted and the *Learning and Skills Council, or in some cases by the individual educational institutions themselves. Such targets may be referred to as performance indicators, and they reflect a growing emphasis on the notion of *accountability. PIs are usually expressed as numerical data relating to measurable aspects of, for example, recruitment, retention, attainment, and progression.

p

performance-related pay *See* PERFORMANCE THRESHOLD.

performance tables A means of presenting information on individual school performance, more often referred to as *league tables. In Scotland they were abandoned in 2003 by the *Scottish Executive; instead such information is now accessed through the Scottish government's Parentzone Scotland web site, which provides details on individual schools, such as statistics about their examination performance. S.M.

performance threshold As a move to introduce some form of performance-related *pay for teachers, a measure was introduced by government in 2000 by which teachers could apply for their performance to be appraised against a set of national standards and, if successful, would cross the performance threshold which would take them onto an upper pay range. To be eligible, teachers must be on point M6 of the main pay scale, and are required to submit evidence of their performance over the previous two to three years. The decision on whether their application to cross the threshold is successful rests with the *head teacher. Success is dependent on the effectiveness of the applicant's teaching skills alone, and is not influenced by their performance in any additional duties or responsibilities they may have taken on, such as in a pastoral or management role. This measure was not welcomed by teachers' unions, who feared it would prove divisive; nor by many head teachers, who viewed it as administratively burdensome. It has not been possible to measure accurately its impact on school performance and quality of learning.

SEE WEB LINKS

- Details of threshold accreditation.

performativity A relatively recent term coined to convey the emphasis which current monitoring of education and training provision by government agencies and other regulatory bodies such as *Ofsted place upon the achievement of set targets or *performance indicators. The measurement of performance against indicators or targets is a largely quantitative approach to the evaluation of a school's, or a college's, or a university's effectiveness in terms of the quality of its provision, and does not easily take account of qualitative data such as pupils' or students' views on their own motivation or their responses to inspired teaching, for example. The term 'performativity' is often used when indicating the limitations of this quantitative, target-based approach to the evaluation of an educational process.

peripatetic teacher A teacher who teaches in several schools within a *local authority area and is employed by that authority, rather than being attached to and employed by one particular school. Such an arrangement is most often made in specialist subjects such as music or a modern foreign language where there is insufficient demand within one school alone to employ a full-time specialist teacher.

personal, social, and health education (PSHE) Under the *national curriculum, schools are advised, although not categorically required, to teach a range of topics which will help pupils towards a clearer understanding of society and their role and responsibilities within it, health issues, aspects of personal development, and philosophical and moral questions to do with ethical living. These are classed together as personal, social, and health education. But this is not to say that PSHE is necessarily taught as a discrete subject; aspects of it may be embedded in lessons for other subjects, or covered during tutorial times. There may be areas of overlap between PSHE and two areas of required provision: *citizenship and sex and relationship education, as well as with religious education.

SEE WEB LINKS

- Details of the content and purpose of the PSHE curriculum.

personal education plan (PEP) All *looked-after children must have a PEP as part of an overall care plan. The PEP reviews progress in academic and other areas of development. It sets out short- and long-term targets with strategies for enabling the child to reach their full potential. It is the responsibility of the social worker to instigate the plan and seek contributions from the young person, a relevant family member or carer, the designated teacher in school, and any other involved agencies. The PEP is held in school and must move with the child at any stage of transition. It is updated prior to the care plan review, and forms the body of information for the care plan. Ultimately, the PEP folder is the property of the young person. T.B., L.A.

PERSONALIZED CURRICULUM

A curriculum in which both the teaching and the content, or programme of study, are tailored to the learning needs of each individual child. It presupposes the facility to monitor closely each child's progress on a day-by-day or week-by-week basis, and to provide 'catch-up' programmes for those pupils whose learning is progressing more slowly. Since 2005 government education policy discourse has emphasized the concept of 'personalization' of the school curriculum; and the introduction for teachers, in September 2005, of 10 per cent of their timetabled time free from teaching for the purpose of planning, preparation, and assessment is viewed as one means by which such an approach might be facilitated, since teachers need time free from classroom teaching in order monitor individual pupil progress, devise individual learning plans, and liaise closely with parents and carers over their child's individual action plan.

The implementation of a personalized curriculum requires the adoption of alternative pedagogical approaches, since it cannot be achieved through conventional whole-class teaching. For example, it requires the teacher to act as a facilitator of learning, rather than instructor or director. It also implies some degree of negotiation between teacher and pupil about what is to be learned and how, a model approaching that sometimes described as 'learner-managed' or 'co-constructed' learning. Moreover, the concept of *personalized learning presupposes an approach to pupil progression which is based on the stage they have reached in their learning, rather than upon their chronological age. How these implications can be squared with the requirements of the externally imposed *national curriculum in its current form, with its age-related key stages and mandatory curriculum content, is as yet unclear.

In practical terms, 'personalization' is likely to take the form in schools of greater use of *setting by ability; strategies to stretch the ability and attainment of those pupils classed as *gifted and talented; additional support for pupils who are falling behind in their learning; more small-group teaching; and more one-to-one tuition. It may also involve an increasing deployment of teaching assistants, working under the supervision of the class teacher, to maintain a constant presence in the classroom while the teacher is engaged with individual pupils or small groups. *See also* STAGE NOT AGE.

personalized learning In personalized learning the curriculum and teaching approaches are adapted to meet the unique needs of every child, enabling them to achieve and participate at the highest level. This will involve a range of pedagogical approaches including the use of learning technologies, and should embrace close links between the school and the family. In recent years there has been a strong emphasis on raising standards in individual schools, and the personalized learning agenda moves this forward to focus on raising standards of achievement for individual pupils. Personalized learning should not be confused with individualized learning or differentiation, although it may contain elements of the two. *See also* INDIVIDUAL LEARNING PLAN; PERSONALIZED CURRICULUM.

T.B., L.A.

p

Pestalozzi, Johann Heinrich (1746–1827) The founder of what became known as the 'Pestalozzi Method' for the education of young children, Zurich-born Pestalozzi believed that children should learn through activity and through the handling and use of material objects rather than simply through words. He argued that children should be encouraged to follow their own interests, make their own discoveries, and draw their own conclusions. In this, he was exploring and developing the educational ideas of *Rousseau, and particularly Rousseau's recognition of the potential conflict between the pursuit of individual freedom and the necessity for civic responsibility. His approach emphasizes the importance of allowing children room for spontaneity and the freedom to generate their own ideas and activities, and of allowing them to arrive at their own answers. In order that they may do this, their ability to reason, judge, and perceive for themselves must be nurtured and encouraged. In this sense, his method has much in common with the *Reggio Emilia approach to early childhood education which was developed in Italy over a century later. A key underlying principle of the Pestalozzi approach is that it is not enough to provide children with an education which is purely *cognitive or intellectual; that they should be given a balanced, whole-child approach to learning based upon *psychomotor, *affective, and cognitive development, or, in Pestalozzi's phraseology, 'hands, heart, and head'.

Pestalozzi developed the concept of *Anschauung*, or **object lesson**, which was the principle that no word should be employed until it was thoroughly understood by concrete observation or perception, whether it referred to a material object, an action, or a means of distinguishing one thing from another. From this his proponents have developed principles which inform much of modern-day pedagogic practice at all levels, such as the necessity, in effective teaching, of starting with the concrete before moving to the abstract, and starting with the simple before moving to the complex.

He also placed great emphasis on the personal dignity of the child as learner, and the importance of preserving the integrity of each individual personality. He viewed education as a means of improving conditions for the socially marginalized, and for society generally. This concern with *social justice and with kindness, positive regard, and a mutually respectful teacher–learner relationship also led him to ban flogging in his schools. In seeing each child as the potential, or 'seed', of the adult they will become, Pestalozzi was concerned that no undue pressures or influences should warp the development intended by nature and thereby prevent the child from growing to fulfil their inherent promise. He also emphasized the potential of everyday life as a source of learning experiences, claiming that 'There can be no doubt that within the living room of every household are united the basic elements of all true human education across its whole range.' Nevertheless, he saw the school as a central part of the education process, and in this respect his thinking diverged from that of Rousseau, who was of the view that the one-to-one tutor–pupil relationship was the optimum means of ensuring a meaningful education.

His initial experiments in establishing a method of schooling at Neuhof were based on combining education with productive employment, thus enabling the children to finance their own learning, so that they remained independent of influence or interference by sponsors, stakeholders, employers, or the state. Although this project failed, its basic premiss was later taken up by Gandhi as part of his movement to challenge colonialism and achieve independence for India. In 1801 Pestalozzi published a book entitled *How Gertrude Teaches Her Children*. This encapsulated much of the Pestalozzi Method, and is a major source of his subsequent influence on pedagogical theory and the philosophy of education. His ideas were put into practice with great success in his school at Yverdon, which was set up in 1805.

This emphasis on reflection, experimentation, and action in the development of pedagogic practice and ideas makes Pestalozzi one of the earliest examples of what we now refer to as a *'reflective practitioner'. His work has had a major influence on the ideas of later educators such as *Malaguzzi.

Further Reading: K. Silber *Pestalozzi: The Man and his Work* (2nd edn, Routledge and Kegan Paul, 1965).

phonics The sounds which make up spoken language. Thus, for example, the letter A has a name (which we pronounce 'ay'), but also represents a number of sounds, depending on its use. The sound it makes in the spoken word 'bad', for example, is different from the sound it makes in 'spade', and different again from its sound in 'scarf', and so on. One of the ways in which children may be taught to read is through recognition of these sounds and the way they link together to build up whole words. This is known as the phonics approach to *reading.

Within the teaching of phonics there are two distinct approaches, **synthetic phonics** and **analytic phonics**, and there is continuing debate over which is the more effective. Synthetic phonics is so called because it 'synthesizes', or puts together, groups of sounds. For example, one phoneme (a word which indicates the smallest unit of sound into which language may be broken down) may be represented in a number of different ways in writing, so that the 'o' sound we hear in 'phoneme' may be represented by other combinations of letters, depending upon the word. Thus, 'ow', 'oa', and 'ough' can sound identical when read aloud, even though they are represented on the page by quite different graphemes (ways we express phonemes in writing). When a child is taught to read English using synthetic phonics, they will learn to recognize up to 44 phonemes and the graphemes used to represent them. From this they can progress to sounding out whole words by blending the phonemes together. Where this approach is used, children begin learning early in their first year of *primary school, and will learn, as a whole class, up to six sounds a week. They are shown the grapheme, listen to the sound, repeat it, and perform a related action, such as drawing the grapheme in the air. This multi-sensory 'drilling' is designed to reinforce the learning. A disadvantage, however, is that phonetically irregular words, for which English is notorious, are not so easily decoded using only this approach.

Analytic phonics is an alternative approach to the teaching of reading which encourages the learner to break down each word into its component sounds and spelling patterns. Thus, the initial vowel sound of the word can be merged with the sound that follows, as in 'c-at', and the inherent rhyme utilized to recognize or form other words which conform to the same spelling pattern (for example, 'h-at', 'r-at', 'b-at', and so on). This approach works well in helping learners to recognize phonetically irregular words, such as 'would', 'should', and 'could' as conforming to a common pattern.

In the current debate over the efficacy of teaching methods for reading skills, government policy encourages the synthetic phonics approach.

Further Reading: K. Goouch and A. Lambirth (eds) *Understanding Phonics and the Teaching of Reading* (Open University Press, 2008).

Piaget, Jean (1896–1980) A Swiss biologist, Piaget published his first article on the psychology of *intelligence in 1921, and began research into the reasoning processes of very young children in the same year at the Jean-Jacques *Rousseau Institute in Geneva. His made his own children the focus of intense observation, worked as Professor of Psychology at the University of Geneva from 1929 to 1975, and, having produced over 60 books on children and learning, he was regarded by the time of his death in 1980 as one of the most significant psychologists of the 20th century. Piaget was interested in the nature of thought and the development of thinking, and observed that even young children have skills with regard to objects in their environment. Their explorations—first through sensorimotor activity and at a later stage through formal or hypothetical operations—he described as *schemas. He identified a number of specific age–*stage developmental activities: sensorimotor (0–2);

pre-operational–symbolic (2–7); concrete–logical operations (7–11); and formal abstract operations (12+). Piaget devised a number of laboratory-based experiments to establish children's *cognitive stage of development, and the similarities between children's actions and responses at certain ages. The experiments included those to test children's ideas of **object permanence** (*Do I look for it? Where has it gone?*); **conservation** (*Is the mass the same if I change its shape?*); **seriation** (*Can I group things in order?*); and **egocentrism** (*Do I know what it is like to be someone else?*). The theory of *constructivism, where an individual constructs knowledge through action from within themselves then discards or modifies ideas when faced with new information which has to be **accommodated** to re-establish the learner's **equilibrium**, has been extremely influential in *pedagogy at all levels of education.

However, subsequent research and replication of these experiments have demonstrated the existence of a much greater variation between children, with the result that Piaget's chronological developmental stages are no longer perceived as rigid norms. It is argued that when the experiments are given contextual meaning in a natural (not laboratory) environment, children are able to demonstrate cognitive understanding at an earlier age than Piaget once claimed.

It is also known that Piaget observed children in isolation from peers and supportive adults. However, **social constructivist** approaches, which are currently influential in pedagogical theory, suggest that children working with others construct knowledge above their own individual abilities, through modelling, negotiation, and language. Nonetheless, Piaget's theories about the stages of development have provided a broad overview of how children think in their *early years, and his influence on education, developmental psychology, and the evolution of human intelligence is still highly regarded by many educationalists.

Further Reading: M. Donaldson *Human Minds: An Exploration* (Penguin, 1992). A.W.

p

picture exchange communication system (PECS) A simple communication system involving exchanging pictures for a desired item or activity. It is used extensively with children who have **global developmental delay** and those with *autistic spectrum disorder, who have little or no verbal communication. The system supports the development of functional communication rather than language, starting with single pictures and building up to the use of sentences to make requests. PECS is an aided form of *augmentative and alternative communication. T.B., L.A.

pilot A trial or experimental period during which a new teaching *method, learning technology, *course, or *programme is run for a restricted number of learners in order to evaluate the effectiveness of its structure or content and make revisions, if necessary, before making it widely available. Notable examples of national pilots, or pilot schemes as they are sometimes known, are the *General National Vocational Qualification pilot of 1992, and the *diploma pilot of 2008, during both of which the newly introduced qualification was subjected to a year's initial evaluation using a limited number of students.

placement Time spent in a place of work, normally unpaid, as part of an educational or training experience. Students or trainees whose course of study requires them to spend some time on *work experience will either have a placement organized for them by their school, college, or university, or be expected to organize their own. This also applies to student teachers, all of whom must spend some time on placement in schools or colleges as part of their *initial teacher training. In departments where large numbers of their students undertake work experience as part of their studies, there may be a designated member of staff responsible for coordinating and monitoring placements, sometimes known as a **placement tutor** or **placement coordinator**. *See also* TEACHING PRACTICE.

plagiarism The act of appropriating someone else's idea or work and passing it off as one's own. The growing problem of plagiarism in the secondary and tertiary sectors of education can be attributed to two major causes. One has been the trend away from end examinations towards *continuous assessment of *coursework. This increased reliance on work produced in unsupervised conditions as a basis for assessing learner achievement has created additional opportunities for unscrupulous students to present work written by others as their own. The other major factor has been the advance in technology and the easy availability of Internet access, which allows a dishonest minority of students to 'cut and paste' text from unacknowledged sources and incorporate it into their own work. More serious still is the international Internet market in essays, assignments, coursework, and dissertations, which allows students to buy bespoke or 'off-the-peg' pieces of written work and present them as their own. The ease with which this may be perpetrated, and the seriousness of the issue, particularly for awarding bodies and for institutions of further and higher education in terms of quality control, has resulted in the development of a range of software designed to identify any instances of plagiarism within a piece of written work. Such software is now widely used in universities and colleges, and students are often required to produce evidence that their work has been scanned and found clear of plagiarism by a designated software program.

'Plagiarism' is also the formal term applied to the practice of copying another pupil's work and submitting it without acknowledging the source. Technically, it would also apply as a consequence of the practice of some parents and carers who make substantial contributions to a pupil's homework or project work but allow the pupil to pass the work off as their own. It is also possible for a student to fall into the error of **self-plagiarism**. This is the practice of using text from previously assessed work and including it verbatim in a subsequent essay or assignment without acknowledging its source. The reason why this is considered unacceptable is because the piece of text being used in this way has already been used to gain the student marks or credit. To resubmit it as though it were an entirely different piece of work amounts in effect to trying to claim two marks or sets of credit for one piece of work. If the piece of text is clearly acknowledged as part of the student's earlier work, however, it is permissible to include it, and such an inclusion is not classed as plagiarism.

Students may also fall into plagiarism through carelessness, simply by forgetting or omitting to cite clear sources for extracts of text which they have quoted, or by failing to make quite clear where their own words stop and the source quoted begins. Experienced teachers in all sectors may find it relatively straightforward to recognize parts of a student's work which are clearly not the student's own. They may notice, for example, an abrupt change in written style, or evidence of a vocabulary which is normally outside the student's experience or expertise. They may even recognize the original source of a passage quoted without acknowledgement. At higher levels, however, and particularly at *postgraduate and *doctorate levels, the recognition of plagiarism may become a more complicated and difficult task. Unwitting plagiarism, where the student unknowingly presents as their own an idea, argument, or theory which has already become the intellectual property of another, through patent or publication, is nevertheless treated as a serious error, and one which postgraduate students are advised to avoid by a very careful scrutiny of existing publications on the topic. *See also* AUTHENTICITY.

plan-led funding A funding strategy developed by the *Learning and Skills Council (LSC) in response to **Success for All* (Department for Education and Skills, 2002). Plan-led funding is based on the LSC's current funding formula, which involves the following: programme funding determined by the number of starters, finishers, and continuing students; learner-related factors including achievement, disadvantage, and fee remission; and institutional factors including area costs and specialist status. The plan-led approach, adopted in 2004, is based on three-year development plans negotiated between providers of *post-compulsory education or training and their local LSC, which result in a funding arrangement for the three years covered by the plan. The plans take national, regional, local, and sector-specific factors into account, as well as the LSC *Strategic Area Review. The advantage for providers is that funding for the subsequent year is guaranteed as long as certain 'headline targets' are met. This refers mainly to learner numbers, employment engagement, success rates, and the professional qualifications of staff. V.C., L.A.

playground An outdoor area on the school premises where pupils play, under supervision, at break times and during the lunchtime break. The area may also be used during lesson times for *organized games, physical education, and other activities such as measuring, drawing, or nature observation. Unlike the *playing field, it will usually have a hard surface so as to be usable in all weathers. During outdoor break times the supervision of pupils by teaching staff is known as **playground duty**, and is usually organized on a rota system. In primary schools these breaks are commonly known as **playtime**.

playgroup, pre-school A registered childcare facility that offers sessional care—usually two to three hours, for children between the ages of 2½ and 5. Pre-school playgroups are commonly organized by a committee of parents and staffed by a qualified and experienced supervisor with a team of staff who are additionally supported by parents helping on a voluntary rota basis. Playgroups are required to register with *Ofsted to meet national standards, which specify the suitability of carers, premises, and record-keeping. There is an annual inspection. Playgroups can be in community centres, schools, church halls, leisure centres, or youth and sport facilities, often sharing a building with a range of community groups. The maximum number of children in a group is normally 26, but this will depend on the size of the room and the building facilities. The staff ratio is one adult to four children aged 2 and one adult to eight children aged 3–5. Playgroups provide children with pre-school experiences such as art, craft, and construction activities, music and movement, large physical play, books, and stories. Pre-school playgroups are required to provide teaching and care which complies with the *Early Years Foundation Stage framework for all children aged 1–5. A.W.

playing field A grassed area which is usually, but not always, adjoining the school, and is used for activities such as *organized games and competitive sports. The number of schools with extensive playing fields has fallen for two reasons: successful and popular schools wishing to expand their teaching accommodation may use playing field land for this purpose, while those in need of additional finance may apply through their local authority to sell some or part of their playing fields to raise funds. Such applications for approval are made to the *Department for Children, Schools, and Families. This trend has, however, recently reversed, and some schools are seeking additional space for use as playing fields. *See also* PLAYGROUND.

P Levels *Assessment criteria for use with pupils aged 5–16 who are attaining below *national curriculum level 1. They were introduced by the *Department for Education and Skills in 1998 and were amended in 2001 and 2004. They exist for all national curriculum subjects including religious education, *personal, social, and health education, and *citizenship. There are eight levels for each subject (P1 being the lowest and P8 the highest) with P1–P3 each split into two sub-levels (P1i, P1ii, etc.). They are used by special and mainstream schools to establish pupils' current level of performance, monitor their progress, and set targets. T.B., L.E.

Plowden Report (1967) An advisory report into primary education and progression to the secondary phase, carried out by the Central Advisory Council, chaired by Lady Plowden (1910–2000). Among its recommendations was to replace *infant and *junior schools with a system of *first schools and *middle schools, thus raising the age at which the pupil began their secondary education to at least 12. This was not, however, widely implemented. The Report also advocated more parental involvement with schools, the setting up of educational priority areas where social disadvantage could be specifically addressed, and more flexibility in the age at which children start school. It is perhaps most famous for having advocated putting the child at the centre of the educational process, a recommendation which does not on the face of it appear contentious, but which subsequently led to criticisms from right-wing educators that the Plowden Report had endorsed and encouraged a *progressive approach to education which was ultimately to prove counterproductive. This negative view is challenged, however, by the majority of educationalists, who view the Report as ground-breaking for its time. *See also* BLACK PAPERS.

points *See* UNIVERSITIES AND COLLEGES ADMISSIONS SERVICE.

polytechnic Institutions of *higher education which existed under that name between 1969 and 1992, after which they were redesignated *universities. The first of these were established following the 1966 *White Paper *A Plan for the Polytechnics and Other Colleges* and were intended as a means of providing specialist higher education for those students intending to go on to work in industry and commerce. They operated under the control of their *local authority, which was also responsible for funding them. Their degrees and other awards were validated through the **Council for National Academic Awards (CNAA).** The *Education Reform Act 1988 removed the polytechnics from local authority control and set up the Polytechnics and Colleges Funding Council, through which they were henceforth to be funded. This was soon afterwards merged with the University Funding Council as a result of policy presented in the 1991 White Paper *Higher Education: A New Framework*, which set out the argument for abolishing the distinction between polytechnics and universities. Finally, the *Further and Higher Education Act 1992 awarded polytechnics the power to confer their own degrees, and granted them the right to call themselves universities.

portfolio Candidates for *competence-based qualifications may be required to compile and present evidence of their achievement in the form of a portfolio for the purposes of assessment. This is particularly the case where the candidate is claiming *accreditation for prior experience or learning. The portfolio might contain evidence such as witness statements of the candidate's competence, photographs of completed work or artefacts, and certification of qualifications already gained. In art and design courses a student's portfolio will contain examples of their work.

positivist *See* RESEARCH.

post-compulsory All education undertaken after the age of compulsory schooling, and sometimes referred to also as **post-16 education**. Although in a literal sense it applies to all such provision, including sixth forms, *higher education, and *adult education, it is more usually taken to indicate *further education and training, and the *learning and skills sector in general, as in the expression **post-compulsory education and training (PCET)**.

postgraduate The levels of qualification and study above the first or *bachelor's degree, and designated level 7 and above in the *National Qualifications Framework. Such study includes *master's degrees and *doctorates, which are known as *higher degrees; and also *postgraduate diplomas. The term may also be used to refer to the students themselves, so that a *graduate who undertakes further study is known as a postgraduate.

Postgraduate Certificate of Education (PGCE) The teaching qualification taken by some graduate entrants to the profession. Since this qualification was originally awarded at *higher education level 3, or undergraduate level, its title was deemed to be misleading, making it appear that the term 'postgraduate' applied to the level of the qualification itself, rather than to the entry qualification of the student teachers. As a consequence, higher education institutions who validated the PGCE agreed to introduce instead a differentiated award which would allow student teachers to take the qualification at its original level 3 and gain a Professional Graduate Certificate of Education (PGCE), or, with the agreement of their tutors, to undertake a proportion of the work at master's level in order to gain a Postgraduate Certificate of Education (PGCE). Thus, the postgraduate certificate is now postgraduate in the real sense that it denotes achievement at master's level. The identical initials, while a possible source of confusion, are designed to be non-divisive. *See also* QUALIFIED TEACHER STATUS.

SEE WEB LINKS

- Details from the Training and Development Agency for Schools on content, structure, and necessary entry qualifications.

prefect A pupil in their final year of secondary school who is granted special status and given responsibilities such as monitoring the behaviour of younger pupils. It is a system which originated in *independent schools in the 19th century, where prefects were often given the power to discipline younger pupils. A prefect system still operates in many independent schools and some *maintained schools. Prefects are usually selected by the head teacher and senior staff, and a **head boy** and/or **head girl** is often appointed from among the prefects chosen.

preparatory school An *independent school for day pupils or boarders aged up to 13 years. Its name derives from its role in preparing its pupils for selective examinations: the *Eleven Plus or the *Common Entrance Examination for independent secondary schools. Such schools do not necessarily follow the *national curriculum. For example, they will offer Latin and French for pupils preparing for the Common Entrance Examination. They are often referred to by the abbreviated form '**prep school**'.

pre-school 1. The years of a child's life before compulsory schooling begins, as in 'the pre-school years'.

2. May be used to describe a child who is too young for, but approaching, school age, as in 'a pre-school child'.

3. May be used as a synonym for *playgroup.

4. In Scotland all 3- and 4-year-olds are offered free part-time education, which equates to five sessions of 2½ hours per week. *See also* PRE-SCHOOL LEARNING ALLIANCE.

p

Pre-School Learning Alliance A registered charity, previously known as the Pre-School Playgroup Association, which was established in the 1960s as a response to the growth of community and parent-run groups for children under statutory school age. Parents and employed staff began to establish local committees, known as branches, who then became part of a county, regional, and national structure. National staff and training officers supplied information, support, and training for all volunteers and staff, as well as accreditation of courses, which were delivered at *further education colleges or on site in the *playgroups themselves. There now exists a national centre which supports regional offices and 400 local branches of volunteers who shape the direction of the charity. Through the Alliance, parents and staff in *pre-schools can access a range of training opportunities including *National Vocational Qualifications in childcare, training, and support.

SEE WEB LINKS

- Details on the organization, training, and support of pre-school staff.

A.W.

pre-vocational education A course designed to prepare pupils and students aged 14–19 for eventual entry to a programme of specific *vocational training which will lead to a skills qualification. Such pre-vocational provision—of which the short-lived *Certificate of Pre-Vocational Education, developed in response to an initiative from the Department of Education and Science, and introduced in 1983 for 16–18-year-olds who had left the schooling system with few qualifications, is an instructive example—usually provides the student with some limited experience in a chosen vocational area, together with a curriculum which emphasizes the acquisition of the *key skills: *communication, *numeracy, and *information communication technology. The term is little used now, since the curriculum model and format underpinning it was incorporated first into *General National Vocational Qualifications (1993) and then again into parts of the *14–19 Diploma (2007). As originally conceived, pre-vocational education was targeted at those students who were not expected to progress to *Advanced Level study or to *higher education, but who were expected to leave school at 16 and seek employment. It was intended not only to help them to gain the key transferable skills they would require, but also to make an informed vocational choice. To some extent the role of such courses has become redundant as fewer and fewer school-leavers expect to enter the workforce without first gaining higher qualifications of some kind.

primary education In England and Wales this refers to provision for children aged 5–11. It is usually divided into two phases: the *infant school for 5–7-year-olds, which delivers *Key Stage 1 of the *national curriculum, and the *junior school for 7–11-year-olds, which delivers Key Stage 2. This system operates in all areas except those where first and *middle schools have been introduced. It has been formally in existence since the *Education Act 1944 (*Butler Act), having replaced the system of *elementary schools, which, up until the mid-1920s, took pupils aged 5–14 (constituting, for many, the only schooling they would receive), and later aged 5–11. During the primary phase of their education, pupils take two national tests in the form of *Standard Tasks, one at age 7 and the next at age 11. In Scotland primary education is between the ages of 5 and 12, and follows a national curriculum, although there is no synchronous national testing.

Primary Leadership Programme (PLP) Part of a government-led strategy for school improvement, the PLP was established in 2003 and is aimed at improving leadership capacity within *primary schools in order to raise standards of pupil achievement in *Key Stages 1 and 2. The programme was developed by the *Primary National Strategy in collaboration with the *National College for School Leadership, and is open to all schools in the primary sector, including *nursery schools and *special schools. A key role in the programme is that of primary strategy consultant leaders. These are *head teachers noted for their leadership skills who are recruited by their local authority to work with other schools as well as their own, helping those leadership teams to operate more effectively in improving pupil progress.

SEE WEB LINKS

- Provides statistics on the PLP and links to further information and materials.

Primary National Strategy (PNS) Launched in May 2003, the PNS is a government strategy aimed at enriching pupils' experience of *primary education. It places a particular emphasis on encouraging high standards of *literacy and *numeracy, and to this end encompasses and renews the already established *National Literacy and *National Numeracy Strategies, subsequently jointly referred to as the Primary Framework for literacy and mathematics. The level of support originally given to these two curriculum areas is extended under the Strategy to other subjects, including music, physical education, and modern foreign languages, as well as to the use of *information communication technology to facilitate teaching and learning. The declared goal of the Strategy is that primary schools should be enabled to provide excellent teaching and an enjoyable experience of learning. To this end, it encourages schools to set their own *attainment targets at *Key Stage 2 for *national curriculum levels 4 and 5, with *local authority target-setting following this lead. It also encourages networking between schools for the purpose of disseminating and sharing good practice, as well as closer links with parents and with the local community. In these ways, it is claimed, schools will be enabled to exert more control over their curriculum and to develop their individual characteristics and strengths. Under the Strategy, government provides additional support for the professional development of teachers and for the leadership development of school heads. It also trials an alternative approach to the assessment of pupil attainment at Key Stage 1, using tests to underpin the assessment carried out by teachers, rather than reporting the results of the tests separately.

SEE WEB LINKS

- Provides a history and summary of the Strategy.

primer A textbook, particularly an introductory text which sets out the basics of a subject. For example, a Latin primer would contain tables of conjugations for verbs and declensions for nouns, as well as other details of grammar and lists of vocabulary. It is a term less widely used now than previously, perhaps because of the accessibility of key subject information on the Internet. It derives from Latin *primus*, 'first'.

principal The title given to the chief executive of a *college of further education. It is also used at some *universities instead of the title vice-chancellor. In a small minority of English secondary schools it is a title given to the *head teacher, although this use is the norm in American schools, as many English pupils will be aware through watching the confrontations between Principal Skinner and his nemesis, Bart Simpson.

principal teacher In Scotland the head of a subject area is referred to as a principal teacher; for example, a principal teacher of mathematics. S.M.

prison education Now more usually referred to as **offender learning**. The policy for the education and training of offenders was set out by the *Department for Education and Skills and the national *Learning and Skills Council in the **Offenders Learning and Skills Policy**, which now fall under the remit of the *Department for Innovation, Universities, and Skills. The policy relating to younger offenders, the School Age Offender Policy, is under the aegis of the *Department for Children, Schools, and Families. For both groups of offenders the teaching of *literacy and *numeracy are of primary concern, although education and training at all levels is made available as appropriate to offenders serving custodial sentences. All are entitled to a minimum of 30 hours' education and training, with an emphasis on the acquisition of skills for employment. The curriculum is managed and coordinated by a director of learning and skills within the institution, who is responsible directly to the governor. Some teaching in prisons is done on a voluntary basis, particularly in the area of basic literacy skills.

SEE WEB LINKS

- Provides access to the document *The Offender's Learning Journey: Learning and Skills Provision for Adult Offenders in England.*
- Provides access to the document *The Offender's Learning Journey: Learning and Skills Provision for Juvenile Offenders in England.*

private education *See* INDEPENDENT SCHOOLS.

probationary year *See* QUALIFIED TEACHER STATUS.

problem-solving *See* KEY SKILLS.

Professional Association of Teachers (PAT) A *teachers' union whose members are opposed to strike action by teachers and which promotes the development of a professional code of conduct for the teaching profession. It has a membership in excess of 30 000 teachers.

professional body A body which sets the professional and academic standards for those who wish to practise within the profession concerned. The endorsement of such bodies may be required for awards in *further and *higher education which constitute or incorporate professional qualifications; and in some cases the body itself may be responsible for shaping the *syllabus of courses leading to such awards. The nearest equivalent for the teaching profession is the *General Teaching Council. The standards for the profession, however, are set by government agencies such as the *Training and Development Agency for Schools and *Lifelong Learning UK, and differ according to the sector of education concerned.

professional development *See* CONTINUING PROFESSIONAL DEVELOPMENT.

Professional Graduate Certificate of Education (PGCE) A teaching qualification awarded to non-postgraduate entrants to the profession. Originally, there was a unitary qualification for graduate entrants, known as the *Postgraduate Certificate of Education (PGCE), which was usually awarded at *higher education level 3, which is the equivalent of a first degree. The ambiguous title of the award, which could be taken to suggest that the term 'postgraduate' applied to the level of the qualification itself, rather than to the entry qualification of the student teachers, was eventually judged to be misleading. As a consequence, higher education institutions who validated the postgraduate certificate agreed to introduce instead a differentiated award which would allow student teachers to take the qualification at its original level

3 and gain a Professional Graduate Certificate of Education, or, with the agreement of their tutors, to undertake a proportion of the work at master's level in order to gain a Postgraduate Certificate of Education. Since this may be achieved through a process of differentiation by outcome and assessment, it can allow both groups of student teachers to follow the same programme. The potential divisiveness of this restructuring and renaming is further minimized by the fact that the two qualifications retain the identical abbreviation.

Professional Graduate Diploma in Education (PGDE) A one-year postgraduate qualification required for teaching in Scotland. As with the *Postgraduate Certificate of Education and the *Professional Graduate Certificate of Education, student teachers will have already achieved a degree qualification before embarking on this course. PGDE courses are offered at six universities: Aberdeen, Dundee, Edinburgh, Glasgow, Paisley, and Strathclyde.

S.M.

professionalism A level of behaviour and performance expected of teachers as professionals. This encompasses not only the standard of their teaching, but also the application of an appropriate set of values, and conformity to an accepted code of practice. One factor which sets teachers apart as a profession is their daily close contact with children and young people, and the consequent necessity to act as positive role models. Another is that, unlike other professions, such as medicine and the law, teachers have their standards of practice imposed externally by one of a range of government bodies, depending on the sector, as well as by the *General Teaching Council, which, among its other functions, sets standards of professional conduct. Nevertheless, because of these two factors, an understanding of what we mean by 'professionalism' is of key concern to teachers and their unions.
See also PROFESSIONAL BODY.

professor The title given in institutions of *higher education to the most highly ranked teaching posts, where the teachers in question are an acknowledged authority in their field. It may also, as is the practice in some post-1992 universities, be attached to management posts such as head of department or faculty, where it is often an honorific rather than an indication of the post-holder's academic standing. Where the professorship is a permanent part of the academic structure and requires the post-holder to give academic leadership in a particular subject area or faculty, it is known as a 'chair' in that field or subject concerned. A professorship can also be awarded by an institution as a personal title in acknowledgement of an individual's academic standing in their field, nationally or internationally.

programmed learning *See* COMPUTER-ASSISTED LEARNING.

programme of study (PoS) The subject knowledge, skills, and understanding which are required to be taught in each subject during each *key stage of the *national curriculum. Each national curriculum subject has its own PoSs for each stage. It is upon these that the teacher will base their *schemes of work and *lesson plans. *Further education and *higher education institutions also have PoSs, outside the national curriculum.

Progress File Their Progress File enables students, both adults and those aged 13–19, to present a record of their achievements formally and to set their goals in relation to work as well as learning. The introduction of Progress Files was first recommended in the 1996 *Dearing *Review of Qualifications for 16–19-Year-Olds*, which suggested restructuring the *National Record of Achievement (NRA) which was then in current use, and renaming it the Progress File. The File is in use in all sectors of education and training, and is intended to replace the NRA fully by 2009.

SEE WEB LINKS

- Information on the use of Progress Files in higher education.

progression The transition from one stage of education or training, or one level of qualification, to the next. Thus, a pupil is said to progress from *primary to secondary education, or from one *key stage to another of the *national curriculum. At some points in the student's academic career there will be more than one possible **progression route**. For example, at the end of Key Stage 4 a pupil might be advised to take a *vocational direction rather than an *academic one. One measure of a qualification's worth or currency is how it serves the student in terms of progression. A useful example here is the *General Certificate of Education *Advanced Level, which offers a progression route into *higher education, but is also valued by employers when considering applications for jobs.

progressive A contentious term when applied to education, and taken to mean anything from a principled opposition to corporal punishment to allowing pupils complete freedom to learn as and when they please. It is often employed to indicate the opposite of 'traditional', as in the debate over the relative merits of *comprehensive and selective education, where proponents of *selection refer to comprehensive education, in pejorative terms, as 'progressive'. In this sense it implies a slipping of standards of achievement and a tolerance of inappropriate behaviour. On the other hand, it has been used in a very positive sense by those advocating educational reform, such as the abandoning of *rote learning in favour of discovery and understanding, which was seen as progress against the draconian methods of 19th- and early 20th-century educators. Under the Conservative governments of the 1970s and 1980s, 'progressive education' became a regular target of criticism in *White Papers, where it was blamed for a number of social ills, including youth crime and high levels of unemployment. Because of the extent to which the term has become politicized, it is perhaps now better treated as an example of rhetoric rather than as an educational term with a precise and agreed meaning. *See also* Black Papers; Plowden Report.

project 1. A programme of *research into some aspect of education, undertaken by an individual or team of researchers.

2. A piece of assessed work undertaken by a pupil or group of pupils, which explores or develops a topic, often of their own choice. *See also* assignment.

prospectus A brochure produced by a *school, *college, or *university, whose contents are often replicated on their web site, which sets out information about the institution and the provision it offers. All maintained schools are required by law to produce a prospectus for the benefit of parents and others, and to include in it information on the school's admissions policy and the policy relating to pupils with *special educational needs. The document may also contain the governors' annual report in part or in full, and details of the school's *national curriculum, *General Certificate of Secondary Education, and *General Certificate of Education *Advanced Level results. Universities and other institutions of *higher education may produce separate prospectuses for undergraduate and for postgraduate provision. It is normal practice for larger institutions such as colleges and universities to provide an online prospectus as well as a hard-copy edition.

provision mapping A part of the school self-evaluation process. Provision mapping looks at the levels and types of *special educational needs (SEN) and plans the most effective ways of using resources to make provision for those who need support which is 'different from and in addition to' that which is given to all students. Provision mapping enables the SEN coordinator to keep an overview of support interventions. It clearly identifies individual students and the type of support they receive on a weekly basis and the staff who support them. Provision mapping enables comparisons to be made between methods of intervention in terms of progress and achievement, and cost-effectiveness. Most schools begin by identifying a particular group of students who might be vulnerable or have additional educational needs. Provision mapping is closely linked to schools' *graduated approach to supporting SEN. Head teachers find provision maps useful as a detailed record against which they can plan SEN funding. It is a good indication for outside agencies and local authority officers to gain an overview of SEN provision for individual students. T.B., L.E.

psychomotor One of the three domains of learning identified in 1956 by Benjamin *Bloom (1913–99) and his team of educational psychologists, and used to describe learning which requires the development of some level of physical coordination or practical skill. This could involve learning, at one extreme, a relatively simple, lower-order skill, such as placing a smaller box inside a larger one, to, at the other extreme, a complex procedure requiring skills of the highest order, such as brain surgery or ballet. The teaching and learning of psychomotor skills is usually achieved through a process of **demonstration and practice**, and can normally be assessed through an observation of the learner's performance. Derived from the terms 'psyche' (mind) and 'motor' (movement), the concept of the psychomotor domain is best understood in terms of the learner's development of the ability to coordinate thought and activity in order to perform a task at a required level of skill. In terms of educational values, achievements in the psychomotor domain sometimes appear to be accorded less status than those in the *cognitive domain; a pupil who is skilled at mechanical tasks, for example, may be regarded differently from one who is skilled at mathematics. This distinction can also be seen in prevailing assumptions about the difference in status between *National Vocational Qualifications, which are largely associated with the psychomotor domain, and *General Certificate of Education *Advanced Levels, which are generally regarded as addressing the cognitive domain. Many educationalists would argue, however, that such clear-cut distinctions are misleading, and that the learning of most practical tasks, and particularly those of a higher order, also inevitably involves cognitive learning in terms of the required underpinning *knowledge and understanding.

SEE WEB LINKS

- Provides details of the levels of learning in the psychomotor domain, with examples of level-related key words.

public school *See* INDEPENDENT SCHOOLS.

pupil A child or young person who is enrolled at a school, or a learner of any age who is being given expert tuition in a creative skill; for example, an artist's pupil or a piano pupil. *See also* STUDENT.

pupil-centred *See* LEARNER-CENTRED.

pupil referral unit (PRU) A type of school maintained by the *local authority for children of compulsory school age who require *education otherwise than at school. A high percentage of children attending PRUs have been permanently excluded from mainstream schools, but other groups of learners—such as those at risk of permanent exclusion, pregnant and teenage mothers, pupils with medical needs, pupils in hospital, and those who would benefit from a work-related curriculum—may also access this provision. PRUs are established to meet the specific needs of the relevant local authority's area and policy. Some units will be on a single site while others may have many locations but be under a single management structure. Units may set up to offer education to discrete types of learner, e.g. hospital schools. There is no requirement to follow the *national curriculum, but the curriculum offered must be appropriate to the needs and ability of each individual child (including any *special educational need) placed in the provision, while ensuring that public resources are used efficiently. Pupils permanently excluded from school must receive full-time education amounting to 25 hours per week, whereas pupils with medical needs have a minimum requirement of five hours or more if their condition allows. PRUs are subject to *Ofsted inspections and should have regard to the need to plan for the reintegration of pupils into mainstream education where possible. No child may be placed in a unit without the agreement of the child's parents.

T.B., L.E.

pupil–teacher ratio The number of pupils in a class or school divided by the number of teachers. In a *maintained *primary school the number of teachers employed will be based largely on the number of pupils on the school roll, so that if the number of enrolments falls, teaching posts may be lost rather than *class sizes reduced. In secondary schools the situation is rather more complicated, as specialist teachers must be employed to cover each curriculum subject. A pupil–teacher ratio which creates class sizes of more than 30 pupils will normally raise concerns from parents and teachers, as it is widely believed that pupils will benefit more from being part of a smaller group in which the teacher is able to give more attention to each individual. For example, in *independent schools the pupil–teacher ratio is normally significantly lower than in the maintained sector. However, the relationship between pupil–teacher

p

ratios and the effectiveness of teaching must also take into account the nature of the learning activities. The effectiveness of a teacher-centred *method such as exposition or *lecture may be very little affected by class size, while *learner-centred activities such as discussion or *discovery learning may work much better in group sizes which allow the teacher to give individual attention where it is needed. By the same principle, the pupil–teacher ratio will have an impact on the range of learning activities which the teacher is able to facilitate effectively.

Qualifications and Credit Framework (QCF) *See* NATIONAL QUALIFICATIONS FRAMEWORK.

Qualifications and Curriculum Authority (QCA) Responsible for maintaining and developing the *national curriculum in England, together with all the associated *testing, *assessments, and *examinations, the QCA also monitors and provides *accreditation for qualifications in the *post-compulsory sector of *vocational education and training. Its remit does not, however, include accreditation of qualifications awarded by universities or other institutions of higher education. A non-departmental public body, it was set up in 1997 to take over from the *School Curriculum and Assessment Authority and the *National Council for Vocational Qualifications, thus combining in one body the responsibility for overseeing both general and vocational qualifications. It is sponsored by the *Department for Children, Schools, and Families, and the members of its governing board are appointed by the Secretary of State for that department. Separate and equivalent bodies exist for *Scotland (*Scottish Qualifications Authority), *Northern Ireland (Council for the Curriculum, Examinations, and Assessment) and *Wales (Qualifications, Curriculum, and Assessment Authority for Wales).

qualified teacher learning and skills (QTLS) Since September 2001, and following a recommendation in the 1998 *Green Paper *The Learning Age*, all teachers in *further education and the skills training sector have been required to hold, or to be working towards, a nationally recognized teaching qualification for that sector of education, now known as the *lifelong learning sector or (except in Scotland) as the *learning and skills sector. Initially, the standards for these qualifications were drawn up by the *Further Education National Training Organization (FENTO), which endorsed a range of teaching qualifications awarded by higher education institutions and other *awarding bodies, such as the *City and Guilds of London Institute. These standards were known as the **FENTO standards**. They were replaced in 2007 by a revised set of national standards drawn up, following consultation with the sector, by *Lifelong Learning UK and its standards and verification arm, *Standards and Verification UK (SVUK), which replaced and took over some of the functions of FENTO. The revised standards are known as the **QTLS standards**, and it is a requirement that all newly appointed teachers to the sector must hold a qualification which meets these standards. This could be a specialized SVUK-endorsed *Certificate of Education or *Postgraduate or Professional Certificate of Education, or a teaching qualification at *National Qualifications Framework level 5 or 6 from one of the commercial awarding bodies.

The QTLS standards are made up of six domains, covering key aspects of the further education teacher's role. These are: access and progression, professional values and practice, specialist learning and teaching, planning for learning, learning and teaching, and assessment for learning. There is an emphasis on reflective practice and on promoting equality. To achieve QTLS status, teachers must also perform satisfactorily in a set of communication and numeracy skills known as the *minimum core.

Prior to 2001 the further education sector employed large numbers of teachers with no formal teaching qualification. This was due largely to the focus of the sector on specialized vocational training, which meant that it was the quality of the vocational skills which the teacher would be expected to pass on, for example in catering, mechanical engineering, hairdressing, or electronics, which were seen as of paramount importance, rather than the quality of their teaching. It therefore tended to be skilled craftspeople, specialist instructors, or experts with professional qualifications in their specialist vocational area who were recruited as 'teachers'. This model, of the experts passing on their skills and knowledge, was closely related to the traditional concept of *apprenticeship. Teacher training, if it took place, was usually voluntary, and was normally undertaken on a part-time, in-service basis, either within the college itself, or at a neighbouring higher education institution. When the requirement for a teaching qualification was introduced, all remaining unqualified teachers within the sector were required to undertake in-service training in order to gain their qualification, regardless of the length of their teaching experience.

The introduction of QTLS was presented at government policy level as a means of securing for further education teachers an equal status with teachers in schools. However, there remain two key obstacles to achieving *parity of esteem between the two sectors. Firstly, teachers with QTLS are not deemed qualified to teach in schools, while schoolteachers with *qualified teacher status are qualified to teach in the learning and skills sector; and, secondly, there is no parity in either pay or conditions between the two sectors.

q

Further Reading: Department for Education and Employment *The Learning Age: A Renaissance for a New Britain* (HMSO, 1998) sets out the government argument for requiring all further education teachers to have a teaching qualification.

SEE WEB LINKS

• A full version of the QTLS standards.

qualified teacher status (QTS) All teachers who enter the profession to teach in compulsory state education in England are required to have achieved, or be working towards, a teaching qualification which satisfies the national standards set out by the *Department for Children, Schools, and Families for qualified teacher status. There are several available routes to QTS. The most usual are full-time teacher education programmes offered by *universities and other *higher education institutions, which lead to the award of *Bachelor of Education for non-graduate candidates, or *Postgraduate Certificate of Education or *Professional Graduate Certificate of Education for those already possessing a degree. The formal qualification must be followed by successful completion of a year's work as a *newly qualified teacher (NQT), known as the

NQT year, before the teacher is deemed to be a fully qualified member of the profession under the terms of the *General Teaching Council. There are also routes, such as the *Graduate Teacher Programme, which allow the teaching qualification to be gained while the candidate is teaching in a school. The standards consist of three components: professional values and practice, knowledge and understanding, and practical teaching. To gain QTS, all candidates must also achieve a satisfactory score in a compulsory test of their literacy, numeracy, and *information technology skills, which is undertaken online and administrated by the *Training and Development Agency (TDA). The QTS standards apply specifically to teachers in England. Similar standards, but with specific reference issues in Welsh schools, apply in Wales. Teachers who hold teaching qualifications awarded outside the United Kingdom, but who wish to teach within the UK, may be required to undertake the **overseas trained teacher** route in order to gain QTS, although there is a growing movement towards establishing a system of recognition and equivalence between teaching qualifications awarded within the European Union.

SEE WEB LINKS

- The TDA site dealing with standards.
- Further details about the components of QTS.
- Further information about the QTS skills test.
- Details of QTS as it applies in Wales.

qualitative *See* RESEARCH.

Quality Assurance Agency for Higher Education (QAA) An independent body established in 1997 to oversee standards of provision in *higher education. It carries out audits in individual universities and other higher education institutions, examining the internal systems of quality management, as well as carrying out a review of the standards of teaching and learning in individual subject areas. Thus, the quality of both management and teaching come under scrutiny in a QAA review. This will include, but will not be restricted to, institutional and departmental systems for quality control, including the monitoring and provision of professional development for staff, the processes for ensuring the rigour and accuracy of assessment decisions, the lines of communication and control in relation to quality management, and the effectiveness of teaching provision. Thus, the QAA's overall purpose is to ensure, in the public interest, that internal quality controls are effective and fully operational in higher education. Higher education institutions undertake **internal audits** or **subject reviews** in which the QAA criteria framework is applied in order to arrive at a judgement about the quality of their own provision. The Agency is funded by higher education institutions themselves, through subscriptions, and also by contract to major funding bodies of higher education. An early application of the concept of **quality assurance** to an educational context can be found in the 1991 *White Paper *Higher Education: A New Framework*. It provides an example of the trend for importing the vocabulary of the business world into the vocabulary of education.

SEE WEB LINKS

- Further details of the role of the QAA, and the operation of quality assurance in England, Northern Ireland, Scotland, and Wales.

Quality Improvement Agency (QIA) A non-departmental public body set up in 2006 whose role is to monitor and raise standards of teaching and learning across the *learning and skills sector. It succeeded the *Learning and Skills Development Agency in England, taking over many of its functions and its personnel. In the 2006 *White Paper *Further Education: Raising Skills, Improving Life Chances*, the QIA received its government briefing to lead the National Improvement Strategy for further education. Partners in this Strategy include, among others, the *Learning and Skills Council, the *Adult Learning Inspectorate, *Ofsted, *Lifelong Learning UK, the *Centre for Excellence in Leadership, and the *Department for Education and Skills.

Further Reading: QIA *Pursuing Excellence: The National Improvement Strategy for the Further Education System* (QIA, 2006).

SEE WEB LINKS

- A list of the priority actions which the QIA and partners are undertaking in pursuit of their aims.

quantitative *See* RESEARCH.

q

radical educators From a historical perspective this is a 19th-century movement which arose from concerns that the education being offered to the artisan classes was little more than a process of indoctrination designed to stifle enquiry and discourage questions about the worker's place and meagre rewards. This was a debate over what constituted 'useful knowledge'; and also about what it meant to be educated, and who was empowered to define which knowledge was 'useful' and which was not. The response of the radical educators was to set up an alternative to the existing educational provision for working people. This would offer 'really useful knowledge', which provided a more *liberal education in the sense of being wide and not exclusively instrumental or work-related. Its three main thrusts, as identified by Johnson (1981), were political knowledge aimed at bringing about democratic change; social science, informed by social cooperation, secularism, and feminism; and an exploration of the questions of poverty and exploitation. Such a curriculum might even today be described as radical.

Also sometimes classed as radical educators are those teachers and theorists who take a *progressive, *learner-centred, or unconventional approach to the education of children. This category includes educationalists such as Loris *Malaguzzi, Maria *Montessori, A. S. *Neill, Johann *Pestalozzi, and Rudolph *Steiner. *See also* MECHANICS' INSTITUTES.

Further Reading: R. Johnson 'Really Useful Knowledge: Radical Education and Working Class Culture 1790–1848' in J. Clarke et al. (eds) *Working Class Culture: Studies in History and Theory* (Hutchinson, 1981).

raising of the school-leaving age (Rosla) The statutory minimum school-leaving age was raised from 15 to 16 in 1972, and the first cohort of pupils to be affected were those who reached the age of 15 in the academic year 1972/3. This change had a dramatic impact on secondary schools, and particularly those without sixth forms, who were obliged to provide pupils with a suitable curriculum for the additional year of their schooling. For some years subsequently pupils who would by choice have left school at 15 were widely referred to as 'Rosla pupils'. The idea of raising the minimum leaving age had been discussed as early as 1944 in the Education Act (*Butler Act), and had been recommended in the **Newsom Report** in 1963. Some commentators have seen more recent developments such as the *Youth Training Schemes of the 1980s and the introduction of *General National Vocational Qualifications in the 1990s as government strategies indirectly to raise the leaving age still further with the goal of keeping all young people in full-time education or training until the age of 18. Historically, the minimum school-leaving age has risen steadily, from 10 in 1880, to 11 in 1893, and to 12 in 1899. In 1918 it was raised to 14, and again to 15 in 1947. It currently remains at 16, but there are plans to require all young people to stay in school, training, or workplace training until the age of 18 by

2013. This will not mean that they will have to remain in school or continue with an academic curriculum, but that they will be required to be receiving education or training of some kind. This is not technically, therefore, a raising of the *school*-leaving age, but rather an extending of the period of education and training necessary before young people become eligible to join the workforce.

Raising Skills, Improving Life Chances A landmark *White Paper published in 2006 as part of the government's response to the *Foster Report of 2005 into *further education (FE). It confirmed the judgement, expressed in that Report, that the role and purpose of the further education sector was one of skills training. Among its proposals were four national targets for education and training, and six key areas of reform, which included, in addition to the clarification of FE's role:

- developments to meet the needs of employers and learners;
- the introduction of mandatory *continuing professional development for all teachers in the sector;
- extending the 'market' in skills training to more providers outside FE colleges;
- reforms to the funding for 14–19-year-olds' education to facilitate dual provision in school and college;
- more autonomy for colleges in relation to their local *Learning and Skills Councils, which would take a more strategic, supervisory role.

range The extent and depth of knowledge, skills, or understanding, and the contexts in which the learner must be able to apply these. In this specific sense, it is part of the terminology originally used in the assessment of *General National Vocational Qualifications, where elements of achievement were required to be demonstrated across a range. A **range statement** was a list of contexts in which the elements should or could be demonstrated. Reference to a range, therefore, was a means of refining and clarifying the *objectives or outcomes of the learning in order to aid the *assessor in their task.

reader 1. A title conferred in *universities and some other institutions of *higher education to acknowledge a lecturer's academic standing. In terms of seniority and status it sits between the grade of senior lecturer and the position of *professor. The bearer's full title identifies their specialist field; for example, reader in education.

2. A textbook containing extracts of the work of one author, or of several authors on a common subject or theme. The purpose of such a volume is to provide an overview of a subject or of an author's works as an introduction for students or for a general readership.

readiness The point at which a learner is receptive to what is to be learned. This will differ from learner to learner and be dependent on a number of factors, including level of maturity, prior learning, and motivation. It is most commonly used in relation to teaching *reading, in the phrase **reading readiness**. The concept of readiness includes the notion that it may be counterproductive to coerce a child into learning before they are ready. Teachers and educationalists are by no means unanimous on this point, many arguing that readiness can be achieved through the teaching and learning process and is not a point arrived at passively simply by waiting. The idea that children go through a series of *stages which correspond with their state of readiness for certain types of learning has been underpinned in the past by reference to *Piaget's work on stages. More recently, however, this concept of development in fixed stages has been widely questioned.

reading Reading ability is tested throughout school years and was commonly recorded in terms of reading age, although it is more usual now to express competence in reading in terms of readability levels. The *Rose Report (2006) identifies five competencies in a beginner reader's 'toolkit' which they will need if they are to be able to read:

- recognition of letters (and groups of letters such as digraphs) (*st*);
- the ability to sound out phonemes (*s*);
- the ability to hear and blend phonemes (*str*);
- the reading of phonically regular words (*sat*);
- the reading of some irregular words (*she*).

These competencies, however, are part of the subject of a continuing debate about the teaching of reading and its central importance to successful schooling. Two polarized approaches to the teaching of reading are the **look–say** method, which uses a whole-word approach to recognizing and remembering words when encountered in new text, and the *phonics approach, whereby children are taught to sound out and blend specific phonemes (sounds).

Schools in England have traditionally used a variety of approaches and reading schemes (these included among others Dick and Jane, Janet and John, Initial Teaching Alphabet (ITA), Pirates, and the Oxford Reading Tree) to reinforce word recognition in familiar and sequential texts. More recently this has been succeeded by a 'real books' approach, where children could choose their own books from classified sets, and vocabulary would vary from simple to complex and small number to greater range. The disadvantage of this approach was that children had to learn new vocabulary with each chosen book and this could place some children at a distinct disadvantage if book-reading was not a common activity at home.

With the onset of the *National Literacy Strategy in 1997, a more systematic *literacy hour was adopted in *primary schools, introducing a phonics approach to the learning of reading, together with individual and shared reading, the use of a Big Book for all children to look at, and diverse activities to reinforce phoneme and word recognition.

The Rose Report suggests that 'there is much convincing evidence to show from the practice observed that, as generally understood, *"synthetic" phonics is the form of systematic phonic work that offers the vast majority of beginners the best route to becoming skilled readers' (para. 47). Under current government policy, the use of *synthetic phonics is the preferred approach to the teaching of reading in *Key Stage 1.

Further Reading: Department for Education and Skills *Independent Review of the Teaching of Early Reading* (DfES, 2006).

SEE WEB LINKS

- Full summary of the Rose Report.

A.W.

r

reading age *See* AGE, READING.

received pronunciation (RP) Sometimes called colloquially a 'BBC accent', RP is a standard form of pronunciation rather than a local accent, although it is generally associated with the south-east of England. At one time it was considered the most socially acceptable accent, and was encouraged in schools at the expense of regional pronunciation and dialects. It was usual, and even expected, as late as the 1970s, that television and radio announcers and newsreaders would use RP, theoretically in order to be widely understood. This hegemony is now giving way, with the result that regional accents and dialects are becoming valued for the richness they bring to the language. Now, however, rather than local accents, it is the argot and jargon of youth culture, with its 'innits' and glottal stops, for which RP is seen by some as a corrective.

reception The class into which pupils enter when first starting *primary school at the age of 5. Depending on the size of the intake and the internal organization of the school, there may be more than one reception class. The teachers responsible for these classes are known as **reception teachers**, and the first year of the pupil's schooling is sometimes referred to as their **reception year**. *See also* INFANT SCHOOL.

record of achievement *See* NATIONAL RECORD OF ACHIEVEMENT; PROGRESS FILE.

rector 1. The title given to the *head teacher of a Scottish school.

2. The rector is the third ranked official of *university governance (behind the chancellor and the principal and vice-chancellor) in the four ancient Scottish universities: Aberdeen, St Andrews, Edinburgh, and Glasgow. The post-holder is elected at regular intervals (usually every three years to enable every undergraduate completing a degree to vote at least once), and their role includes the chairing of meetings of the University Court, the governing body of the university. The election of the rector is considered by many students to be integral to their ability to shape the university's agenda and it is one of the main functions of the rector to represent the interests of the students. To some extent the office has evolved into that of a figurehead, with a trend towards celebrities being elected to the role; but there has been a resurgence of interest in recent years in the idea of electing more experienced figures in order to avoid the possibility that the status of the rector as chair of the Court might be discontinued. S.M.

red-brick A descriptor used to differentiate the *universities built in major cities in the 19th and early 20th centuries from the ancient universities of Oxford and Cambridge. The term came into use following the publication of a work entitled *Redbrick University* by Bruce Truscott in 1943, and is thought to have been coined by the author. The reference to 'red bricks' is intended to contrast with the historical stonework of many *Oxbridge colleges.

refereed journal *See* JOURNAL, ACADEMIC.

reflective practice Teachers can learn from their own teaching experience in order to develop their pedagogic skills by reviewing specific incidents in their professional practice and reflecting upon them in order to draw conclusions about how they might improve their own performance as teachers. This is the process known as reflective practice. Although it is closely related, in principle and purpose, to *action research, and employs the same cycle of reflection–action–reflection–planning, it is for teachers a continuing, often daily, process of self-appraisal and action planning. The reflective process might be formulated in a series of questions such as the following:

- What incident or issue in my teaching am I most concerned about?
- What might I wish to change about it, and why?
- How might this be achieved? What theories might I draw on to inform my decision?
- Did it work? If so, why? If not, why not? How does this accord with current theories?
- If it worked, is there a general principle here that I could use again?
- If it did not work, what might I try next, and why?

The ability of the teacher to reflect upon their practice in order to adapt and develop it is described by Gregorc (1973) as the 'fully functioning' phase of their professional development in which they have developed skills of self-evaluation based on self-referenced norms, and are taking responsibility for their own continuing professional development. *See also* JOURNAL, REFLECTIVE.

Further Reading: A. F. Gregorc 'Developing Plans for Professional Growth' *NASSP Bulletin* 57/377 (1973); A. Pollard *Teaching: Evidence-Informed Professional Practice* (Continuum, 2005) examines the reflective practice of teachers in schools.

Reggio Emilia An approach to the education of young children in the *pre-school and *primary phase which is based on the belief that children's learning should be unconstrained by formal *curriculum planning, but rather should allow children themselves a voice in the direction and content of their learning, in order to ensure that they find their learning meaningful. It operates on the principle that learning should involve children using all their senses; that intellectual curiosity should always be rewarded; and that they should be presented with the freedom to express themselves in as many ways as possible. At the heart of the Reggio Emilia philosophy is the belief that the relationships which are built between the child and the *educator, between the child and the world, and between the child and other children are essential to the process of learning. The relationship between the child and the teacher should not be one based on unequal power or status, but rather one in which the child is carefully listened to and respected. The approach itself takes its name from the Reggio Emilia district of Italy, where parents rebuilding village schools in the 1940s after the ravages of the Second World War wished to establish a democratic and child-centred education for their young children which reflected the value which society should place upon its young. The first schools were built by parents and children using bricks and other materials salvaged from bombed buildings.

What began as an experimental approach soon gained momentum as the 1950s brought a migration of workers and their families from the comparative poverty of southern Italy to the more prosperous industrial north, including the district of Reggio Emilia. The care and education of children whose parents were both working outside the home was of major parental concern, and so provided added impetus to the establishment of pre-schools which were run as cooperative ventures with heavy parental involvement. Indeed, the importance of parental involvement is a central element of the Reggio Emilia approach. Parents are accorded respect as the child's initial teacher, and are involved in every aspect of the schools' provision, some acting as volunteer teachers within the school, and many maintaining the same philosophy of education in the child's home activities and general upbringing. This strong sense of continuity between the child's home life and school is a key aspect of the Reggio Emilia approach; and its emphasis on community support for young children and their families reflects the belief, embedded in Italian culture, that the welfare and well-being of its children is a primary responsibility of the state.

The Reggio Emilia approach encourages a high level of teacher autonomy. Although they are provided with extensive opportunities for professional development, teachers' professional practice is not constrained or regimented by *targets, *national curriculum standards, or *attainment tests for pupils. Instead, teachers are encouraged to set their own targets and to base their planning and teaching on the close observation of children's day-to-day individual and group needs. To this end, two teachers routinely work together with the children, one observing and noting—through photographs, video recording, and handwritten notes—children's conversation and play in order that these can be used as the starting point for developing further learning activities. This development and exploration is shared with a specialist teacher known as the *atelierista* (literally, one who works in an 'attic' or studio), who encourages the children to express themselves symbolically through artistic work, which may include drawing, painting, music, puppetry, or some other form of creative expression. Co-teaching is an essential part of Reggio teacher training. There are no professional hierarchies, however, within the school, and no differentiated salary scale. Teachers are given six non-contact hours each week in order to facilitate their tasks of documentation, project development, and liaison with parents. Parents, too, are involved in the planning and evaluation of activities. A *pedagogista* has responsibility for educational leadership of several schools, a role which involves mentoring staff, developing awareness of the theories which support their practice, and leading the collective discussions of teachers and parents from those schools as they explore ways of building upon children's enthusiasms and activities. This reflective, responsive approach, which puts the child at the centre of the educational process, is directly at odds with the concept of an externally imposed national curriculum and the implementation of mandatory and standardized attainment tests.

Since children are considered to be born with the innate ability to explore and discover the world, a typical Reggio Emilia school is designed with the purpose of facilitating the child's exploration of the environment. Indeed, the environment itself is referred to as the child's 'third teacher', the first being the parent and the second the teacher. It includes an *atelier*, or art studio, and usually further small *ateliers*, or art corners, attached to each classroom. The layout of the school is designed to echo that of a town or civic community, with an indoor *piazza*, or town square, for communal activity and socializing, off which the classrooms and eating area are situated, with no long corridors or hallways, hallmarks of an institution, for the child to negotiate. Children, therefore, can become involved with all the activities of the school, including helping with the preparation of meals and keeping the communal spaces clean. Every classroom has access to an outdoor area for exploration and play. There is also a 'welcome area', which marks the intersection between school and the wider world, and where parents and carers are encouraged to linger and to interact with teachers and each other.

A major exponent of the Reggio Emilia approach was Loris *Malaguzzi, who became involved in the building of the first schools, and was instrumental in bringing the Reggio Emilia approach to the notice of the rest of the world. Elements of the approach are applied in Scotland's early years education, and there is a movement to explore how these principles might be used more extensively.

Further Reading: L. Thornton and P. Brunton *Understanding the Reggio Approach* (David Fulton, 2005) gives a full explanation of the philosophy underpinning the Reggio Emilia approach to early years education, and how it is applied in practice; M. Valentine *The Reggio Emilia Approach to Early Years Education* (rev. edn, Learning and Teaching Scotland, 2006) gives a clear explanation of the Reggio Emilia approach to education and explores how elements of this approach might be applied in Scotland's schools.

register 1. A record of *attendance. Teachers in schools are required to keep accurate registers, which include a record of lateness as well as of attendance and absences. These are used as a basis for identifying persistent cases of *truancy or school refusal. In *further and *higher education the keeping of an attendance register is also a requirement. Where this is done by electronic means it is known as a computerized register. This facilitates the processing of attendance, retention, and completion data in colleges, universities, and larger schools where greater numbers of registered enrolments are involved.

2. The use of language appropriate to a specific context or social situation. The uses or contexts may be broad categories, such as formal and informal; or more narrowly defined, such as undergoing an interview or dining with friends. The ability to identify or adopt a vocabulary and style of communication appropriate to the situation and context is one of the requirements implicit within the *National Literacy Strategy. The *minimum core language and literacy skills which teachers preparing for the status of *qualified teacher learning and skills are required to demonstrate include an understanding of the concept of register and its implications for student learning.

Further Reading: R. Hoggart *The Uses of Literacy* (Penguin, 1992).

Registered Teacher Programme (RTP) A route to *qualified teacher status for non-graduates working in school as unqualified teachers. It is aimed specifically as those with some experience of *higher education who have not, however, completed a degree. The RTP allows them to extend their subject knowledge to degree level at the same time as obtaining their teaching qualification and continuing in paid employment. The Programme normally takes two years, and the in-school training is carried out in partnership with a local higher education institution. Schools in *special measures and *pupil referral units are not eligible to take on RTP trainees. The Programme was discontinued in Wales from 2007.

SEE WEB LINKS

- Details of qualifications necessary to enter the RTP, and sources of financial support available.

registrar A senior administrative post in a college or university whose holder is responsible for student enrolment and the administration of records, including those of student completion and achievement, awards and examinations, and the business of institutional committees.

regius professor *Professorships (or **chairs**) at the *universities of Oxford and Cambridge and some Scottish universities, which were funded, or **endowed**, by the Crown and for which the Crown retains the right to nominate appointees. In practice, candidates are chosen on the advice of senior government ministers. The first such chair to be founded was that of Regius Professor of Divinity at Oxford University in the 15th century.

reliability *See* ASSESSMENT.

religious education (RE) This is a non-statutory part of the *national curriculum at all stages, which means that parents can withdraw their child from part or all of the RE offered by their school. Each school's curriculum for RE is drawn up locally, either by the individual school or by a representative body of parents, teachers, and faith groups from a number of local schools. The purpose of this is to ensure that the RE curriculum should reflect the cultural and religious background of the population from which the school draws its pupils. It is usual for RE to provide pupils with the opportunity to investigate a range of faiths and beliefs, and to explore philosophical and practical questions of values and ethics. *See also* DENOMINATION.

remedial Previously used to describe education or special classes provided as a remedy for those whose achievement was significantly below the level expected of their year group. Because it presents a *deficit model of the learner it is now considered by many to be an unacceptable term, and has been largely superseded by the concept of special education. *See also* SPECIAL EDUCATIONAL NEEDS.

remission A reduction in a teacher's hours of class contact made to allow them to undertake some other, non-teaching role. For example, a university teacher responsible for managing the recruitment of large numbers of students to a particular programme of study may have a number of teaching hours remitted from their timetable to allow them to do this.

report Schools are required to send parents or carers at least one report each academic year detailing their child's progress in *national curriculum *core subjects and, where appropriate, the results of their *Standard Tasks (SATs). The report must also make clear how the pupil's SAT score compares with those of others in their age group. Parents are also informed of their child's attendance record, their attitude to learning, and their general progress. Schools may include other information, such as the results of internal examinations, or progress in subjects and activities outside the core subjects. The report forms part of the essential communication between school and home, and often suggests ways in which parents and carers can support the child in improving their performance.

RESEARCH

The systematic search for answers to certain questions, often using empirical evidence but also using logical arguments and reflection on social understandings. The search may aim at discovering facts, putting forward theories, increasing understanding, and/or changing practice. Both the systematic search and the conclusions drawn are then made public and are subject to critical scrutiny. The primary purpose of education research varies from **project** to project and from researcher to researcher. The different purposes are indicated in terminology: 'research on education', 'educational research', and 'educative research'. Research on education includes research carried out for academic purposes, regardless of its impact on the world of education—so-called 'blue skies' research. It may be carried out by researchers who work in *higher education departments of education but also in departments of cultural studies, history, philosophy, psychology, and sociology. Educational research is intended to improve educational practices, though sometimes over the long term. Educative research is intended to enact educative relations—for those engaged in the project and those beyond. These three kinds of research may overlap, especially the second and third. All three may be called education research.

Education research has continuities with research in other disciplines, notably the social sciences and the arts and humanities. It may also take the form of *action research and/or *reflective practice which is also found in other professions such as nursing or town planning. Within all these areas there are controversies about *epistemology and *ontology: about what there is to be known, what can be known and, therefore, what counts as data, evidence, systematic inquiry, and argument—and what kinds of conclusion can properly be drawn from them. Therefore, researchers have to be able to give a rationale for the conduct of their enquiries. This rationale is termed 'methodology'. A distinction is often made between methodology, *methods, and techniques in research. Methodology refers to the overall rationale, and depends on the view taken of ontology and epistemology. Method is the strategy undertaken to fulfil the rationale; and the term 'technique' refers to the specific research tools used, such as large-scale questionnaires, structured interviews, or video tapes.

Methodologies mirror the deep divisions found between different ontological and epistemological positions. These divisions are complex, multiple, and overlapping. They include positivist versus interpretivist, qualitative versus quantitative, and objective versus committed (feminist, social justice, anti-racist, Marxian, etc.). Further distinctions can be made between methodologies aiming at practical wisdom and those seeking theoretical understanding, or between those methodologies seeking an illumination of practice against those which want to evaluate it against criteria. Any of the interpretivist, qualitative, and/or committed methodologies may be postmodern in outlook. In this context, 'postmodernism' is an umbrella term for a number of reflexive, ironic approaches to knowledge which see it as always already imbricated with power and which are sceptical towards any universal 'grand narratives' as accounts of reason, truth, and knowledge.

A positivist approach depends on an epistemology which takes the world as made up of facts and theories which can be falsified or verified through the testing of hypotheses. The interpretivist approach takes the world as made up of social meanings constructed by human beings. These can be interpreted and understood but measurement is relatively insignificant in doing so. Not surprisingly, then, quantitative research is often assumed to be positivist because it depends on measurement and may use statistical techniques. Similarly, qualitative research which uses data such as words and pictures is often assumed to be interpretivist. But this is too simplistic. Hypotheses need not be tested using statistics; meanings can be surveyed and counted. Complicating the picture even further, with the dimension of objective versus committed, research which is feminist, Marxian, or otherwise committed, etc. may also be quantitative or qualitative, positivist or interpretivist. Similarly for research which is aiming at objectivity. Moreover, some of these techniques and methods can be carried using a postmodern approach. Postmodern methodologies are particularly relaxed about combining different methods and techniques, viewing each one as giving only partial and provisional knowledge. The result of such combinations is sometimes called **bricolage**.

Educational research is carried out at all levels of the education system and it serves a number of practical purposes, ranging from investigations of practice in a single classroom, as, for instance, in some action research, to projects intended to inform national policy. At every level, the research may be driven by the educational commitments of individual researchers. They may be self-funded, or funded through their own institution or through **grants** from national research councils, especially the *Economic and Social Research Council. Alternatively, the research may be commissioned or facilitated by institutions including national and local government, charities, unions, and quangos who want to make use of the answers for their own purposes.

The roles of the researchers vary. They may be teachers or academics. They may be independent consultants or employed by local or central government. They may be students working for first degrees, diplomas, masters', or doctorates. Quite often they may be more than one of these at the same time since educational research is typically carried out by people with knowledge and experience of practice and policy, often some time after their initial period of full-time education is over.

Research is made public in different ways depending on its purpose and on its intended audience. Research reports can be found in learned journals aiming at a primarily academic audience. Professional magazines and newspapers publish reports aimed at practitioners, policy-makers, and the general public. Research reports are also presented to commissioning bodies, which sometimes make them available to a wider public. All of these forms of reporting are increasingly found on the World Wide Web. Research is also reported orally at seminars, conferences, in-service days, and public meetings. Occasionally, research is published in creative ways, for instance, using drama or an installation.

Issues of ethics are key in all education research. There are two aspects to this: moral virtue and intellectual virtue. Firstly, education is inescapably concerned with human beings, so researchers are necessarily involved in social relationships in which moral virtues are relevant. An example is found in the ethical requirement to obtain informed consent from participants. However, cases exist where the requirement should be disregarded. Either way, the judgement is an ethical one. Equally, the judgement about what counts as 'informed consent' is an ethical one. Secondly, education is bound up with strongly held opinions, and is used by interested parties to influence policy and practice. So intellectual virtues such as honesty, careful attention to evidence and argument, and open-mindedness are crucial in high-quality education research.

Further Reading: *Revised Ethical Guidelines for Educational Research (2004)* (British Educational Research Association).

SEE WEB LINKS

- British Educational Research Association Guidelines.

M.G.

Research Assessment Exercise (RAE) An evaluation of the *research and publication carried out in institutions of *higher education which is undertaken every four years in order to determine the level of funding which will be awarded. It is conducted jointly by the *Higher Education Funding Council for England, the *Scottish Funding Council, the *Higher Education Funding Council for Wales, and the Department for Employment and Learning, Northern Ireland. The assessment for each academic field is made by a specialist sub-panel. The research and publications of each department or faculty within the institution are scrutinized and evaluated against criteria set by the funding body. Each department, therefore, must decide which of its staff to enter for the exercise in order to gain as high a score as possible. Those departments or faculties whose score falls below a predetermined level will receive no government funding for research for the following four years. The quest for a high RAE rating will often influence decisions about academic appointments, as applicants with a lengthy and prestigious list of publications to their name will be much sought after. Some academics have suggested that the RAE is flawed in that it perpetuates inequalities of status between pre- and post-1992 universities. Since the emphasis in many of the latter has been on teaching rather than on research, some, it is claimed, are hampered in building up a sound research base as the most able researchers are drawn to posts where funding for research is assured. *See also* JOURNAL, ACADEMIC.

SEE WEB LINKS

- A list of subjects and fields for which there are sub-panels.

research fellow A post in a *university or other *higher education institution which is held on a short-term rather than permanent contract and is created specifically to enable the holder to carry out *research into a named field or topic. Such a post is often sponsored or funded by external bodies, and widely advertised.

research grant *See* RESEARCH.

research project *See* RESEARCH.

revenue support grant (RSG) The money devolved from central government to *local authorities each year to subsidize the services which the authority is responsible for providing. These include primary and secondary education. At the end of each calendar year the government issues a standard spending assessment (SSA) to all local authorities for the distribution of the RSG, which encapsulates the government's view of what the authority needs to expend to deliver a standard level of service. This includes an SSA specifically for expenditure on education within the authority. The revenue support grant was formerly known as the rate support grant.

review An inspection by the *Quality Assurance Agency of *higher education provision is euphemistically termed a 'review'.

reward *See* MOTIVATION.

rising fives The term 'rising fives' usually relates to children who are still 4 years old at the outset of a school term but will reach 5 before the term is over. A policy of admitting rising fives to a *reception class is thus one involving admissions each term to *primary school. This practice has been widespread in England for many years, but has been recently under review. *Local authorities are currently required to ensure that all children receive schooling from the start of the term *following* their fifth birthday. A.W.

Robbins Report (1963) The Report of the Committee on Higher Education, chaired by Lord Robbins (b. 1925) between 1961 and 1964. The Report recommended an expansion in *university provision to allow all suitably qualified candidates an opportunity for *higher education should they wish it. It proposed this be initiated by the founding of six new universities and by raising a number of existing colleges to university status. It also suggested raising the status of teacher training colleges by encouraging partnerships with universities and introducing a teaching qualification with degree status. Such colleges were to be renamed *colleges of education. Within 24 hours of the Report's publication, the government issued a *White Paper supporting many of its recommendations. Some recommendations, however, such as the suggestion that undergraduate degree courses be extended from three to four years and broadened in scope, did not find wide support. The success of the recommendations was reflected in the rapid expansion of university provision in the decade between 1965 and 1975. The Robbins Report has played a major role in shaping higher education provision as it exists today.

Rogers, Carl (1902–87) An American psychologist who wrote extensively about the psychology of learning. He discarded the term 'teacher' and used instead 'facilitator' in order both to stress the centrality of the learner in the learning process, and to argue against the formation of the traditional power relationship which assumes a higher status for the teacher in relation to the learner. Instead, he presented the learning process as one which is to the mutual benefit of both the learner and the facilitator of learning, arguing that 'the facilitation of significant learning rests upon certain attitudinal qualities which exist in the personal relationship between the facilitator and the learner' (Rogers 1983: 121). In claiming that a relationship of trust and respect is essential to successful learning, Rogers also argued that the facilitator–teacher should demonstrate an 'unconditional positive regard' for the learner. In other words, the teacher's attitude should be non-judgemental and accepting; and the learner should be made to feel valued and cared for. This is often cited as epitomizing the extreme application of *humanist learning theory. It was Rogers's belief that all organisms have a tendency towards 'actualization', the development of its full potential. In educational terms this suggests that the teacher's role is to facilitate the learner's progress towards this goal, rather than to deliver an externally imposed standard curriculum.

Further Reading: C. Rogers *Freedom to Learn for the 80s* (Merrill, 1983).

Rose Report (2006) The Rose Report on the teaching of reading skills in *primary schools identified five competencies which children should be able to demonstrate before they can progress to the successful acquisition of reading skills. These are:

- recognition of letters (and groups of letters such as digraphs) (*st*);
- the ability to sound out phonemes (*s*);
- the ability to hear and blend phonemes (*str*);
- the reading of phonically regular words (*sat*);
- the reading of some irregular words (*she*).

As well as stressing the importance of 'pre-reading skills' acquisition, the Report, whose full title was *An Independent Review of the Teaching of Early Reading*, was instrumental in encouraging the use of *synthetic phonics as the most effective approach to the teaching of reading to young pupils, suggesting that '"synthetic" phonics is the form of systematic phonic work that offers the vast majority of beginners the best route to becoming skilled readers' (para. 47).

Further Reading: Department for Education and Skills *Independent Review of the Teaching of Early Reading* (DfES, 2006).

SEE WEB LINKS

- Provides a summary of the Rose Report.

rote learning Learning which does not necessitate understanding, but is undertaken systematically and mechanistically, usually through repetition. Examples might be the chanting of multiplication tables, or the reciting of passages learned 'by heart' but with no accurate comprehension of content. Such activities were an integral part of education in the 19th and early 20th centuries, but find little acceptance today. To learn something by rote implies an *intention* to learn which is not present when, for example, the lyrics of a song or the sequence of numbers for a telephone call become committed to memory through repeated exposure or frequent use.

Rousseau, Jean-Jacques (1712–78) A Swiss philosopher who became known as an educational theorist, setting out his ideas in a semi-fictional work, *Émile;*

or, On Education (1762). Rousseau was interested in the idea of humans being able to live and learn more fully in a natural environment. The three *cognitive stages he identified were pre-12 years (survival), 12–16 years (reasoning and development of complex thought), and post-16 (adulthood); and he argued that each of these could be reached and more fully realized away from the artificial constraints of 'civilized' society. He claimed that virtue could be nourished through simple activity and gradual participation in society at the child's own pace; and argued that society and human nature were incompatible. His emphasis on protecting the 'innocence' of children reflects the Romantic notions of the philosopher John Locke (1632–1704) which were also to be found later in the work of the poet and mystic William Blake (1757–1827). He saw the *teacher as a facilitator, supporting an education appropriate to each stage of a child's development. In this sense he was an early exponent of individualized or *personalized learning. His approach was *child-centred, in the sense that he claimed a *curriculum should follow a child's own path of enquiry which might be very much like that of his eponymous character Émile, wandering through the countryside, becoming interested in the smells, sights, sounds, and textures of encountered objects and the simple responses a child makes. Rousseau recommended that a child's emotions should be educated before their reason, placing an emphasis on experience.

John Darling, in his book *Child-Centred Education and its Critics* (1994), argues that the history of modern educational theory can be traced back to Rousseau's theories. In practice, Rousseau's ideas to some extent resonate with current *early years *pedagogy. His notion that children could not calculate or demonstrate complex thinking before the age of 12 may reflect his own childhood education of solitude and self-learning, having been abandoned by his father when he was 10, after his mother died shortly after childbirth. Rousseau's ideas about education and child-rearing appear to conflict with his own practice as a parent, as he was not confident of his own fatherhood skills and gave up his five children to a foundling hospital, where he felt they would lead a more beneficial life. A.W.

Royal Society of Arts (RSA) *See* OCR.

rubric The written instructions provided for candidates as part of an *examination or test. It is now more colloquially referred to as **exam terminology**, and the ability to read it carefully and understand it accurately is an aspect of examination technique which teachers may formally cover with pupils prior to examinations.

Ruskin speech *See* GREAT DEBATE.

sabbatical A period of leave, with full pay, for the purpose of undertaking research or a course of study, or to write for publication. This arrangement is rarely available now outside *higher education; and even within that sector it is less common in some institutions than others. The original meaning conveyed by the word is of something which occurs every seven years, although current practice is much more variable. In the 1960s and 1970s it was not unusual for teachers in schools to be granted year-long sabbaticals, funded by their *local authority, to undertake professional development activity such as, for non-graduates, the gaining of a degree. More recently, in 2001, the *Department for Education and Skills introduced short, six-week centrally funded secondments for teachers to undertake development activities which will enhance their subject knowledge or the effectiveness of their performance. *See also* CONTINUING PROFESSIONAL DEVELOPMENT.

sanction Used in preference to the term 'punishment' to refer to measures taken by an institution or individual teacher in response to non-compliant or unacceptable *behaviour by learners. This includes the withholding of rewards or privileges, or more direct measures such as *detention. The imposition of sanctions and the giving of rewards are part of the behaviour management approach to classroom control.

sandwich course A course of study which involves a period of time, often a year, spent gaining practical experience in applying, and observing the practice of, the subject being learned. The practical experience constitutes the filling in the metaphorical sandwich, being preceded and followed by a period of study at the learner's college or university. Thus, an undergraduate degree which is taught as a sandwich course will normally take four years rather than the usual three, as the second or third year will be spent working outside the institution. An example of this might be a degree course in a modern language, where a year is spent abroad in the relevant country, improving the learner's language skills. Another would be a degree course in engineering which included a year spent working within the industry. Such an arrangement is distinct from a course involving *work experience, such as *initial teacher training, which normally runs concurrently with, or for limited periods between, studies in the institution.

schema As understood in current early childhood *pedagogy, a schema is 'a pattern of repeatable behaviour into which experiences are assimilated and that are generally co-ordinated' (Athey 1990). *Piaget first identified repeated behaviours as skills, which, once assimilated, are transferred to other activities and adapted, if necessary, to satisfy a child's drive to learn and succeed. An example of this might be the action of a push-button mechanism which activates sound or pictures. Once the child has learned this behaviour, this will be repeated when the child is offered the opportunity to interact with more sophisticated mechanisms.

Further Reading: C. Athey *Extending Thought in Young Children: A Parent–Teacher Partnership* (PCP, 1990) identifies commonly observed schema characteristics. A.W.

scheme of work A plan setting out how the *programme of study (PoS), *syllabus, or *curriculum will be translated into teaching and learning activities, including the sequencing of content, the amount of time spent on each topic, and how the specified learning *objectives will be assessed. Some schemes of work are drawn up centrally, such as those designed by the *Qualifications and Curriculum Authority which provide teachers with a template for translating *national curriculum PoSs into a series of *lesson plans. Others may be drawn up by teachers themselves, as is the case in many courses of *further and *higher education, where the creation of the scheme of work forms part of the planning process for the department, team, or the individual teacher.

scholarly activity In some *universities and *higher education institutions, teachers' conditions of service require that they be allowed a proportion of their working hours for scholarly activity, which may include research, reading, or writing.

scholarship 1. A high level of academic learning and skill in a recognized academic *discipline or field.

2. An award which may be offered to chosen students of exceptional ability who are seeking entry to a selective school or an institution of *higher education, and who have successfully passed an examination or interview conducted for the purpose of identifying worthy candidates.

3. A colloquial term at one time used for the *Eleven Plus examination.

school 1. Institution in which pupils are taught. These may be identified according to the age of the pupils: *pre-schools or *nursery schools, *infant schools, and *junior schools (collectively termed *primary schools), and secondary schools; or, in some local authorities, pre-schools or nursery schools, *first, *middle, and secondary schools. They may also be identified according to whether they are *maintained (state) schools or *public (private, fee-charging) schools; and whether they are selective (operate a process of *selection over pupil enrolment) or non-selective. Secondary schools may be designated *grammar schools or *comprehensive schools. Schools which are supported by recognized religious organizations are known as *faith or *denominational schools; and those with sponsorship from industry and commerce are called trust schools. Further categories are those of *special school for pupils with *special educational needs, and *specialist school, where there is an emphasis on a specific aspect of the *national curriculum, such as *information communication technology.

2. A subdivision of a college or university, roughly equivalent to a department, as in 'the School of Education'.

3. At Oxford University it can refer to a course leading to a *first degree, and to all those who work within that subject.

school adjudicator Under section 25 of the School Standards and Framework Act 1998, the admissions procedures of *maintained schools are subject to the scrutiny and ruling of adjudicators appointed by the *Secretary of State. Since 2007 the adjudicators may also direct schools to admit a pupil who has been excluded from, or refused admission by, every suitable school locally; and to direct the admission of *looked-after children. They do not, however, act on complaints from individual parents. *See also* CHOICE.

SEE WEB LINKS

- Provides details of adjudicators' main functions.

school admissions Despite the growing emphasis over the last quarter of the 20th century on the element of parental *choice in their child's schooling, admission to the first school of choice is not always possible if the school chosen is oversubscribed. Schools are required to have an admission policy which is both public and transparent, making clear the criteria which will be applied when selecting pupils for admission. Parental appeals against schools' admission decisions have risen sharply since the policy of parental choice replaced the previous system operated by *local authorities of allotting a catchment area to each school so that the choice of schools, in non-selective systems, was limited and determined by where pupils lived. *Admissions appeals can be made by parents against a school's decision not to admit their child. *See* SCHOOL ADJUDICATOR.

school boards Set up in Scotland through the School Boards (Scotland) Act 1998, these provided a forum for parental representation in Scottish schools. In August 2007 they were replaced by *parent councils. S.M.

School Certificate From 1917 the School Certificate was the national school-leaving qualification, taken at the age of 16 and requiring passes in five subjects. It was replaced by the *General Certificate of Education *Ordinary Level in 1951.

School Curriculum and Assessment Authority (SCAA) Formed as result of the *Education Act 1993 to take over the responsibilities of both the ***National Curriculum Council (NCC)** and the ***School Examinations and Assessment Council (SEAC)**, thus drawing together *curriculum and *assessment functions in one body. It was merged with the *National Council for Vocational Qualifications in 1997 to form the *Qualifications and Curriculum Authority, this time signalling a convergence between general or *academic education and *vocational education and training.

school development plan (SDP) Sets out the purpose and direction of future developments and projects, allowing schools an element of setting their own agenda rather than responding or reacting only to externally imposed policies and initiatives. The plan is drawn up in consultation with teachers, parents, governors, and sometimes pupils; and sets targets against which the school's progress may be measured, for example as part of the inspection process.

School Examinations and Assessment Council *See* SCHOOL CURRICULUM AND ASSESSMENT AUTHORITY.

school improvement partner (SIP) Acts for the *local authority and is the main channel of communication between the local authority and the school on matters of school improvement. The SIP supports the school by focusing on ways to improve pupils' progress and *attainment across all ability ranges, and by helping the school improve its overall performance through the development of strategies for raising standards of teaching and learning. The SIP also provides support in relation to school self-evaluation and the *school development plan.

SEE WEB LINKS

- Provides a full text edition of the SIP's brief.

school-leaving age *See* RAISING OF THE SCHOOL-LEAVING AGE.

school meals The *Education Act 1944 (*Butler Act) required all *local authorities to operate a school meals service to provide a midday meal in all schools, for which parents of pupils were charged a nominal weekly sum. This requirement was withdrawn by the Education Act 1980, as was the requirement that school meals meet a minimum nutritional standard, although meals for pupils whose families were on low incomes and in receipt of benefits continued to be provided free of charge. In line with the policy of introducing market competition into all aspects of public life, school meals services were put out by local authorities to tender. This led to what was widely recognized as a decline in nutritional standards. This was addressed in the School Standards and Framework Act 1998, which empowered the *Secretary of State to regulate minimum nutritional standards. These standards were put in place in 2002. Nevertheless, the continuing poor nutritional quality of some school meals was subsequently brought to public attention by a campaign conducted by the celebrity chef Jamie Oliver (b. 1975), who has been credited in some quarters with securing thereby an increase in government funding to ensure that minimum standards of nutrition can be met.

school profile One of the responsibilities of the governing body of a school is to publish online a school profile, which is designed to communicate with parents about the school's progress, priorities, and performance as measured against its *targets. This means of communicating progress against targets replaced the previous requirement on *governing bodies to produce an annual report to parents following the *Education Act 2005.

school record *Maintained schools are required to keep records of pupils' academic achievements and progress, including results of *national curriculum standard assessments at the end of *Key Stages 1, 2, and 3. The record for each pupil accompanies them through their compulsory schooling, passing from teacher to teacher in the *primary phase, and from school to school as they progress through the system or move to a different area. Under the provisions of the Data Protection Act 1998, pupils and parents are entitled to see what is recorded in the pupil's record. Most school records are now kept in electronic form.

school refuser *See* TRUANCY.

school report *See* REPORT.

SCOTLAND, EDUCATION IN

To an external observer, there would be nothing particularly distinctive about the structure of Scottish education, at least by comparison with that in other developed countries. Distinctiveness lies in interpretation.

The period of compulsory education lasts from 5 to 16. The primary stage occupies the first seven years of this, after which pupils transfer to secondary, which lasts four to six years. Most of this takes place in public institutions (nineteen out of twenty pupils), entry to which is not based on any formal measures of intelligence: the remainder attend private schools which charge fees and, at the secondary stage, are nearly all *selective. This structure of primary schooling was laid down in the last few decades of the 19th century; the pattern of secondaries emerged between the 1930s and the 1960s.

At each end of the period of schooling, Scotland has been participating recently in the international movement towards extending the period of attendance. The proportion of 4-year-olds in *nursery school rose from under 10 per cent in the early 1970s to over 95 per cent by the late 1990s. From ages 16 to 18, a growing proportion of pupils have chosen to remain in full-time education—an increase from around one-third in the early 1970s to three-quarters in 2008. Nearly all of that is at school: only about one in twenty of the age group spends this period in college.

Upon leaving school, around one in three enters full-time *higher education, and about one in four a full-time course of *vocational education. By age 21, the rate of participation in higher education has risen to around one-half, because many of those who take the vocational route use it to enter advanced courses. Fewer than one in ten of the higher education students leave Scotland for this study. The remainder attend institutions in two formally differentiated sectors. One is based in the same colleges as provide vocational non-advanced courses, and accounts for about 24 per cent of undergraduate students in higher education, attending one-year and two-year mainly vocational courses. The remainder mostly take four years to obtain a *degree, attending 21 higher education institutions. These institutions are formally equal, but in practice—through reputation based on historical legacies—divide into three sub-sectors: universities created in the early 1990s from former technological colleges (about 27 per cent of all undergraduate higher education students); four *universities founded in the 1960s, three of them also based on older technological colleges (18 per cent), and four universities which date from the 15th and 16th centuries (30 per cent). These types of higher education institution differ in prestige, in entry requirements, in the balance of their courses between *academic and vocational and between arts (or social science) and science (or technology), and in the amount of research which their staff carry out: broadly, the older the institution, the less dominated by applied science, the higher the entry requirements, and the more *research.

Since the 1960s there has been a massive rise in the proportion of the age group taking externally assessed *examinations in the last three years of secondary school, from one in four to almost all. Attainment in these examinations has been steadily rising, and this has encouraged school-leavers to stay on beyond the compulsory stage and to enter post-school courses. Part of the explanation of rising *attainment has been the rising aspirations of girls: by the late 1970s they had overtaken boys in attainment at the end of secondary schooling, and by the 1990s also in their rate of entry to higher education. Something the same has been true of people of various immigrant origins—Ireland and central Europe in the 19th and early 20th centuries, Asia and others parts of the former British empire in the second half of the 20th: their attainment and participation has risen and overtaken, as a proportion, that of the majority. There has also, since the 1990s, been some narrowing of *social class inequalities in attainment and participation. But all this equalization provides only part of the explanation of rising participation: all social groups have taken part to unprecedented extents in this educational revolution.

Nevertheless, if this structural account might seem familiar to an observer, the meanings attached indigenously are distinctive, as they are in any country, and they derive from history. The key feature of current interpretations of education in Scotland is uniformity. The secondary and primary sectors have standardized *curriculums, and the strength of the consensus around them is one reason why this is not imposed by law. The curriculum is broad, requiring pupils up to age 14 to study English, mathematics, science, social science, art, music, and religion, and to engage in physical exercise. Most of this breadth is maintained to age 16. There is uniformity also in the dominance of the public schools, non-selective and less socially segregated than most systems in developed societies (despite open enrolment since 1981); the association of about one in six of them with religious denominations (mainly the Roman Catholic Church) relates only to their general ethos, not, except in a few topics such as religious and moral education, to details of the curriculum or *assessment, and so represents a less strongly religious sector than in many other countries. And there is uniformity from the teachers themselves, over nine out of ten of whom have been educated in the quite small and homogeneous Scottish system of higher education.

The preference for uniformity is extending now to higher education. When the new Scottish Parliament took responsibility for Scottish education in 1999, one of its most prominent early acts was to abolish fees charged to undergraduates at the outset of a course. (They were replaced by, in effect, a graduate tax, the proceeds from which are used to subsidize *bursaries.) The state agency which funds higher and *further education has resisted pressure to concentrate research funding in only a few international centres, preferring research networks. Higher education remains predominantly public, in its governance (through legal regulation) and in its funding (more than 60 per cent from public funds).

These current predilections for a largely uniform, mainly public system were consolidated in the middle of the 20th century, when the consensus was established that the Scottish way of reconciling merit selection and equity was to favour individual selection within common institutions.

Thus, there would be mostly common schooling—to avoid the exacerbation of invidious social distinctions by institutional boundaries—but increasing amounts of formal *certification within them. In practice, then, social distinctions that remain are those created in society rather than those created by structures of educational provision: *gender or social class distinctions operate much more within schools than between them.

That mid-century settlement built upon the previous main wave of reform in the first few decades of the century. It responded to the international movement for universal secondary schooling by creating a single dominant concept of Scottish secondary education. That idea was firmly academic. It was the characteristic preparation required by the new professional classes, centred on literary studies and mathematics, including science and foreign languages, but only for a minority Latin. It became, in the 1920s, the curriculum not only of the older secondary schools inherited from the 19th century, but also of the much larger number of new secondaries created by public authorities before the First World War to cater mainly for the lower-middle class and the skilled working class. The curriculum was shaped by the *Scottish Leaving Certificate, which is the direct ancestor of today's school examinations; its credibility was strengthened by the even greater homogeneity of teacher culture then than today. Even in the 1930s, this senior secondary course catered for fewer than one-third of pupils, and only about one in twenty passed the full Certificate; but, over the next two decades, its dominant prestige came to subsume all attempts by policy-makers to create diverse tracks for the remainder. The merit-selective democracy of this process was aided by the absence in Scotland of anything like the dominant elite institutions found elsewhere.

These structures in turn drew upon a much older tradition of highly competitive but systematically public provision, dating ultimately to the Reformation, consolidated for universal elementary schooling in a key 1696 Act of the old Scottish Parliament, and renovated for it in 1872 and for the universities in Acts of 1858 and 1889. This tradition was not democratic in any 21st-century sense of the term; but it left three key legacies: it was public, it believed that open competition was the only way of reconciling excellence with equal human worth, and it venerated the academic.

Scottish debates about structures of education today cannot help being shaped by these predecessors. The Scottish Parliament has inaugurated unprecedented inquiry into the role of curricular breadth and standardization, academic learning, examinations, and public accountability. Reform of some sort is inevitable. But the attachment to uniformity, to public control, and to a singularly academic interpretation of worthwhile learning is not likely to wither readily. L.P.

History

During the medieval period, education in Scotland followed the pattern of European schooling, with the Roman Catholic Church organizing schooling. Church schools and grammar schools were founded in major towns, and in 1496 an Education Act introduced compulsory schooling for the eldest sons of nobles. The foundation of the universities of St Andrews in 1413, Glasgow in 1451, and Aberdeen in 1495 led an era of Enlightenment in education. The Protestant Reformation made literacy important as the means through which true believers could achieve spiritual enlightenment, and in 1616 the Privy Council commanded that every parish in Scotland should have a school (by the end of the 18th century this had been achieved in the majority of parishes). By the end of the 17th century a considerable proportion of the population was literate and the education system was more advanced than that in England and other European countries. The 18th century was a 'golden age' for Scottish education, contributing to advancement in intellectual enlightenment and the industrial revolution. Scottish universities attracted students from other parts of the country who were unable to study certain subject areas in Oxford and Cambridge universities owing to the more traditional nature of the courses available: this could be seen particularly in the field of medicine, where Scottish universities gained a better reputation. In 1872 education in Scotland became compulsory for all children between the ages of 5 and 13, and by 1888 the Leaving Certificate had been introduced and the leaving age raised to 14. The Leaving Certificate was replaced in 1962 by the Scottish Certificate of Education, and by the introduction of *Ordinary Grades (later replaced by *Standard Grades in the early 1990s) and *Highers. Corporal punishment was abolished in 1986. In 1999 the new Scottish Executive set up an Education Department and an Enterprise, Transport, and Lifelong Learning Department, which together took over the work of the Scottish Education Department. Currently, the Scottish curriculum is undergoing review and reform under the *Curriculum for Excellence initiative begun in 2004 which aims to create a single, coherent curriculum for children aged 3–18. In addition, the *McCrone Report of 2000 has had wide-ranging implications for and effect upon the conditions of teachers within the education system.

Structure

Scotland offers all 3- and 4-year-olds free nursery education. Primary education, for children aged 5–12, follows a national curriculum. The curriculum studied between the ages of 5 and 16 is broad, requiring study of English, mathematics, science, social science, art, music, and religion, as well as engagement in some form of physical activity. In addition, students may have access to qualifications in Scottish Gaelic. Indeed, more than 60 primary schools now teach Gaelic, the majority of these being located in the highlands or islands of Scotland. The curriculum is not set by law but has flexibility based upon the guidelines set by *Learning and Teaching Scotland under the aegis of the Scottish Parliament. There is no external testing for pupils in primary education; instead pupil attainment between the ages of 5 and 14 is assessed by teachers through the process of national assessment. Secondary education in Scotland begins for pupils at the age of 11 or 12 and runs for a compulsory four years, with two final years being optional. Pupils sit Standard Grade exams at the end of the fourth year of study. They will usually study between seven and nine subjects, and may choose to remain for another one or two years to study for **Access, Intermediate**, or Higher Grade exams in Year 5, after which they may go on to study for *Advanced Highers in Year 6, the qualifications necessary for access to a Scottish university.

The traditional four-year undergraduate courses allow for a broad first year curriculum with an in-depth focus from the second year, and lead to a *master's degree, although recently some Scottish universities have begun to offer alternative three-year courses leading to a *bachelor's degree. In 1999 the Scottish Executive abolished tuition fees for Scottish students. Instead students pay a one-off Graduate Endowment at the end of their course. Scottish students who wish to attend a university elsewhere in the UK will usually remain at school for a sixth year, completing the Advanced Higher—equivalent to the original sixth year study or an English *Advanced Level. Further education is provided at colleges or schools. Students may accumulate *National Units, which can be combined to build a *National Qualification. Many full-time National Qualification college courses are made up of groupings of National Units. Currently, under the direction of the Scottish Parliament, Scottish education is undergoing extensive reform, with the focus on the development of the Curriculum for Excellence initiative, with the goal of providing a more coherent and inclusive education for all which is linked with an emphasis on *lifelong learning. S.M.

Scottish Certificate of Education This replaced the *Scottish Leaving Certificate in 1962. S.M.

Scottish Council for Research in Education (SCRE) A body which supports *research and development in all aspects of education in Scotland. S.M.

Scottish Credit Accumulation and Transfer (SCOTCAT) A framework designed to make it easier for students to transfer educational *credit between Scottish institutions of higher education. SCOTCAT points are awarded as part of the *Scottish Credit and Qualifications Framework and are awarded based on time spent studying.

SEE WEB LINKS

- Sets out the format of SCOTCAT credits. S.M.

Scottish Credit and Qualifications Framework (SCQF) A framework which aims to help learners, employers, and providers of learning to see clearly how Scottish learning programmes and qualifications relate to each other in terms of level. In the SCQF there are twelve levels, ranging from level 1 (Access 1) to level 12, which is associated with postgraduate doctoral studies. *See also* NATIONAL QUALIFICATIONS FRAMEWORK.

SEE WEB LINKS

- Provides details of the Framework. S.M.

S

Scottish Enterprise, Highlands and Islands Enterprise Scottish Enterprise is Scotland's main economic development agency, funded by the Scottish government. This agency aims to develop Scotland's economic potential through supporting business development. The agency works with companies and individuals, as well as with *universities, *colleges, *local authorities, and other public sector bodies to achieve these goals. The Highlands and Islands Enterprise fulfils the same purpose in the highlands and islands of Scotland.

SEE WEB LINKS

- Provides details of the aims and activities of Scottish Enterprise.
- Provides details of the aims and activities of the Highlands and Islands Enterprise. S.M.

Scottish Examinations Board (SEB) Responsible for *assessment and *accreditation of Scottish examinations, the SEB was dissolved in 1997 and replaced by the *Scottish Qualifications Authority (SQA). S.M.

Scottish Executive Education Department (SEED) Set up at the time of devolution in 1999, SEED was the Civil Service department of the Scottish Executive with responsibility for education in Scotland. S.M.

Scottish Funding Council (SFC) The SFC allocates resources for teaching and learning, as well as for research and other activities in Scotland's colleges and universities, in support of the Scottish government's priorities for education. *See also* HIGHER EDUCATION FUNDING COUNCIL FOR ENGLAND. S.M.

Scottish Further Education Unit (SFEU) The SFEU contributes to the development of learning provision within Scottish *further education colleges by providing support for staff and the curriculum. S.M.

Scottish Group Award (SGA) The SGA consists of a number of courses and units which fit together to make a coherent *programme of study for older pupils and students. Group Awards are available at all five levels of study within *Higher Still (from Access level 2 to *Advanced Higher). A Group Award can be gained in one year of full-time study or built up over a longer period of time. Awards are made up of courses, *units, and external assessments combined to form a group which is recognized by employers, colleges, universities, and other providers of education and training. There are two types of SGA: **General Awards**, which do not specify mandatory subject content but do have set requirements in terms of the number of courses, units, and core skills which must be included; and **Named Awards**, which do specify certain subject requirements as well as a set number of courses, units, and core skills.

SEE WEB LINKS

- Provides details of SGAs. S.M.

Scottish Leaving Certificate Established in 1886, the Leaving Certificate was awarded to students leaving secondary school in Scotland who achieved a minimum standard of proficiency in education. This was replaced by the Scottish Certificate of Education in 1962. S.M.

Scottish Negotiating Committee for Teachers (SNCT) Introduced in 2001, SNCT is a tripartite body comprising members from teaching organizations, *local authorities, and the Scottish government, which oversees the implementation of the new conditions of service and pay laid down in the 2001 document *A Teaching Profession for the 21st Century*.

SEE WEB LINKS

- Provides details of the Committee's role. S.M.

Scottish Progression Award (SPA) A vocational qualification which recognizes and accredits the skills and knowledge used in the workplace. SPAs are designed to provide basic skills which will be attractive to employers and which candidates can build upon when working towards achieving a full *Scottish Vocational Qualification (SVQ). However, unlike SVQs, there is no requirement to produce evidence from the workplace. Students can receive accreditation through college, school, or training.

SEE WEB LINKS

- Provides an outline of this qualification and details of the subject areas in which it is currently available. S.M.

Scottish Qualification for Headship (SQH) First piloted in 1998, the SQH is the qualification required of those wishing to achieve headship of schools in Scotland. It is equivalent to the English *National Professional Qualification for Headship. *See also* HEADSHIP DEVELOPMENT. S.M.

Scottish Qualifications Authority (SQA) Established in 1997, the SQA is an executive non-departmental public body sponsored by the Scottish government Education Department. It is the national body in Scotland responsible for the development, *accreditation, *assessment, and *certification of qualifications other than degrees. It is also responsible for *vocational courses through its *Scottish Vocational Qualification department.

SEE WEB LINKS

- Lists the functions of the SQA. S.M.

Scottish Qualifications Certificate (SQC) Awarded to all students in Scotland on successful completion of courses, providing details of all *units gained and the marks awarded. S.M.

Scottish Vocational Education Council (Scotvec) The body responsible for assessment and accreditation of Scottish *vocational courses prior to 1997. It was replaced by the *Scottish Qualifications Authority. S.M.

Scottish Vocational Qualification (SVQ) Vocational qualifications awarded in Scotland. They are equivalent to *National Vocational Qualifications in England and Wales. *See also* SCOTVEC. S.M.

Secondary Heads Association (SHA) An association for *head teachers of both *maintained and *independent schools, formed in 1976 from an amalgamation of the Headmasters' Association and the Association of Headmistresses. *See also* TEACHERS' UNIONS.

secondary modern school *See* TRIPARTITE SYSTEM.

second marking The *assessment of a piece of student work by two teachers in order to ensure that the mark or grade awarded is accurate and reliable. It is a

process which is most valuable when the assessment method is vulnerable to some degree of subjectivity on the part of the marker; for example, in the assessment of essay-style answers or longer pieces of student work such as written *assignments and *dissertations. The second marking may be carried out as 'blind' marking, which means that neither teacher sees the comments or assessment decision of the other prior to arriving at their own decision. Alternatively, the second marker may have access to the first marker's comments and the grade or mark awarded. Second marking, or double marking, is an important feature of assessment in courses where the student outcome depends wholly or heavily on *continuous assessment.
See also MODERATION.

secondment The release of a teacher from their normal post for a limited period in order to allow them to take up a temporary post elsewhere, often to advise on good practice; or to undertake a relevant course of study or professional development. *See also* SABBATICAL.

Secretary of State for Education The member or members of the Cabinet responsible for the development and implementation of national education policy take their title from the government department which they are appointed to head. In 1964, when the Department of Education and Science (DES) was created, it was headed by the Secretary of State for Education and Science. The reorganization of the department in 1993 led to a change in title, with the DES becoming the Department for Education and the *minister responsible to the Secretary of State for Education. The merging of the DES and the Employment Department in 1995 necessitated a further change of title to Secretary of State for Education and Employment, heading the Department for Education and Employment. In 2001 the government department underwent a further change of name, becoming the *Department for Education and Skills (DfES) and headed by the Secretary of State for Education and Skills. In 2007 the DfES was replaced by two new government departments, each headed by their own secretary of state: the *Department for Children, Schools, and Families, and the *Department for Innovation, Universities, and Skills. The changes in title, both of department and of minister responsible, to some extent reflect governments' priorities and policies in education over the decades. In summary, then, the titles of secretaries of state responsible for education over the past half-century have been as follows:

1964–93	Secretary of State for Education and Science
1993–5	Secretary of State for Education
1995–2001	Secretary of State for Education and Employment
2001–7	Secretary of State for Education and Skills
2007–	Secretary of State for Children, Schools, and Families
2007–	Secretary of State for Innovation, Universities, and Skills

Cabinet responsibility, therefore, for education in schools has been separated from that for *post-compulsory education and training in the *higher education and the *lifelong learning sectors, and these policy responsibilities are now divided accordingly between the two secretaries of state. Working with each are junior ministers with delegated responsibility for specific areas of provision. As well as these elected colleagues, the secretaries of state have the support of a team of unelected civil servants to advise and support them on policy and other issues. *See also* WHITE PAPER.

Sector Skills Development Agency (SSDA) Set up by the *Department for Education and Skills in 2002, the SSDA is responsible for funding, supporting, and monitoring the network of sector skills councils. Its purpose is to involve employers in helping to shape the development of skills policy and the public supply of training across the UK. The Agency is a registered company which has an employer-led board that provides additional strategic support and advice. It is responsible for maintaining the standards across the sectors, for ensuring that skills provision is designed and developed to meet sector needs, and for promoting best practice and benchmarking between sectors.

SEE WEB LINKS

- Provides further details of the SSDA's role and function.

V.C., K.A.

selection The practice by *maintained secondary schools of selecting their intake of pupils, or (previously) of that selection being carried out by the *local authority through a process of testing pupils at *Eleven Plus. Following the *Education Act 1944 (*Butler Act), pupils were selected according to ability to go to the type of school considered best suited to them. In most local authorities this system of selection was replaced in the 1970s by a system of non-selective, *comprehensive secondary education, following the Education Act 1976. However, the policy of selection for secondary schooling was enabled to continue in some areas because the 1976 Act was superseded by the Education Act 1979, which made the abolition of selection optional rather than mandatory. It has been argued that the practice of selection at the age of 11 continues, not only in those areas where *grammar schools remain, but also as an inevitable result of *market competition within the schooling system, which has caused successful schools to become oversubscribed and therefore enabled them to operate some degree of selection over their intake. Moreover, the *specialist schools introduced in the 1990s are permitted to select up to 10 per cent of their pupil intake, based on testing of *aptitude for the specialist subjects, rather than on *ability, and thereby echoing the aims of the earlier *tripartite system.

self-assessment Under the **New Inspection Framework**, which came into operation in September 2005, schools are required to carry out a process of self-evaluation, which is documented in a self-evaluation form (SEF). *Ofsted teams use the school's SEF as a basis for planning their *inspection of the school, together with the school's previous Ofsted report and the school's documentation of its Performance Assessment (originally Performance Assessment and National (Contextual) Data), known as PANDA. The *lead inspector will evaluate the school's presentation of itself in the SEF, and examine how far this is compatible with the available evidence. Issues for inspection will arise from any apparent inconsistencies between the SEF's conclusions and the existing evidence, and from any significant weaknesses highlighted by the SEF, or from any obvious omissions. School self-assessment has meant that inspections can proceed with what has been termed 'a lighter touch', with visits from inspectors lasting a shorter time and involving a smaller team than previously. Inspections now focus on seeking clarification, if any is needed, of information contained in the SEF. Although this is only one document, as opposed to the four originally required, it is a lengthy one, containing 38 pages even before completion. It requires schools to evaluate their own progress against the appropriate inspection schedule, and to present the evidence, statistical or otherwise, on which they have made their evaluative judgements. It also requires schools to identify their own strengths and areas requiring development, and to explain how the former are being developed and the latter addressed. Schools are expected to update their self-evaluations at least annually, and to include feedback from pupils and parents about the school. If the SEF, in Ofsted's judgement, presents inadequate evidence, or does not make rigorous use of the evidence available, this may lead the inspectors to make judgements about the quality of management in the school. V.C., K.A.

self-assessment report Documents produced annually by all providers of *post-compulsory education as part of their quality assurance process. In larger institutions, those written at individual programme level contribute to programme area reports, which in turn feed into departmental reports, on which the organization's summary report is based. This summary will contain the following: an introduction, focusing on key improvements since the previous review of post-inspection development or action plans; information on progress on performance measures in the development of action plans; key strengths and areas for improvement for the institution, organized under the headings of the key questions of the *Common Inspection Framework (CIF), and for each curriculum area, where practicable; a table of grades awarded to CIF key questions and curriculum areas; and a summary of grades awarded for the observation of teaching, learning, and assessment. *See also* COLLEGE SELF-ASSESSMENT.

semester An alternative method of dividing up the academic year into periods of student activity, used by some institutions in preference to the three-*term model. It has been imported from the North American *higher education system, where the academic year consists of two semesters, each about fifteen weeks long, with lengthy breaks between them.

seminar A meeting between a *tutor and a small group of students for the purposes of teaching and learning. It can take a number of forms. For example, students may be asked to present their work or ideas to the rest of the group; or the tutor may encourage discussion of a relevant text or recent *lecture. *See also* TUTORIAL.

semiotics The study of signs and symbols, both individually and grouped together in sign systems. Sometimes referred to as **semiology**, it is an area of study which investigates the importance of language in the construction of meaning. Semiotics has become an important concept in the educational study of linguistics, sociology, media, film, and cultural studies, largely as the result of the work of C. S. Peirce (1839–1914) and Ferdinand de Saussure (1857–1913). Peirce, who preferred the term 'semiosis', proposed a triadic model which had within it the operation of three subjects in a chain of meaning. Thus, signs can be either **iconic** in that they resemble what they stand for, or **indexical** in that they have some causal connection with what they stand for, or **symbolic** in that they have no causal link with and do not resemble what they stand for, but work only through conventional association.

In his *Course in General Linguistics* (1916), Saussure proposed a dualistic model of meaning production, going against classical thought, which assumed a natural relationship between the object world and the linguistic sign, and proposing instead that this relationship was arbitrary. Two key terms used in semiotics are *parole*, the actual utterances of a language community, and *langue*, the underlying structure of language from which utterances are chosen.

This science of signs and meaning production as an academic study of language later informed the work of a range of theorists associated with **structuralism** such as Roland Barthes and Claude Lévi-Strauss. The study of semiotics suggests that the ideas (or *ideologies) we consider common sense and universal are in fact a matter of convention; the rules and conventions of language inform how we learn to perceive the world. Semiotics has been influential in shaping the approaches to teaching and educational research, particularly in *higher education. C.H.

senior curriculum team (SCT) The title sometimes given to the team of teachers in a secondary school who have combined responsibility for curriculum matters. This might consist, for example, of the *deputy head responsible for curriculum, the department or subject heads, the whole-school literacy coordinator, and any other teachers with a whole-school curriculum responsibility.

senior leadership team (SLT) The title usually given to the team of teachers and managers who have responsibility for the leadership of a school or college. This would include *principals, *head teachers, their *deputies and/or *assistants; department or *faculty heads; and others with institution-wide leadership responsibilities, such as *mentors and staff with professional development responsibilities. Sometimes the title 'senior leadership team' is used in preference to *'senior management team' (SMT), primarily in order to emphasize the idea of the institution as a team rather than as a group or organization which has to be 'managed' or controlled. This can mean that the role and purpose of an SLT may be indistinguishable from that implied by the term SMT. Although practical and academic distinctions have been clearly and often drawn between the functions of leadership and management, in the context of choosing the title for the senior team of a school or other educational institution, the distinction may be a semantic one whose choice is indicative of the approach or style determined by the governing body or the team concerned.

senior management team (SMT) *See* SENIOR LEADERSHIP TEAM.

senior teacher A role of increased responsibility for a subject area within a Scottish secondary school. The use of this term is now largely in decline.

S.M.

Service Children's Education (SCE) SCE provides schooling, in English, from the pre-school stage to sixth form for the dependent children living with Ministry of Defence personnel who are serving overseas. SCE schools follow the *national curriculum; and teachers, who are recruited mainly from the United Kingdom, have *qualified teacher status.

SEE WEB LINKS

- Provides full details of SCE.

sets Sub-groups of pupils from a larger mixed-ability class or cohort who have been grouped together according to their ability level in a particular subject. In *comprehensive secondary schools, where classes contain pupils from a wide ability range, sets may be used as a means of *differentiating by activity, task, or outcome, according to pupils' abilities and needs in specific subjects. It can be an alternative to the practice of segregating pupils into ability 'streams' or classes across the curriculum, and has the advantage of still allowing some subjects to be taught to the mixed-ability class.

Silver Book A colloquial term for *further education teachers' pay scale and conditions as they existed before the incorporation of further education *colleges in 1993. Until that time, conditions of service for teachers in the sector were enshrined in a printed document which had a silver cover and was commonly referred to as 'the Silver Book'. Following incorporation in 1993, when further education colleges were removed from local authority control, national pay and conditions were abolished, and individual colleges were required to negotiate salaries and conditions with their staff. Some teachers took the option to decline the revised conditions and retained instead their original terms of employment, which gave them shorter working days and longer holidays. However, this also meant that they had to forgo any incremental increases in salary. These teachers were referred to as 'Silver Book staff'. *See also* FURTHER AND HIGHER EDUCATION ACT 1992.

single-level tests As part of the *personalized learning initiative, *Standard Tasks (SATs) are being replaced by single-level, teacher-assessed tests for 7–14-year-olds, which will be applied, within limited parameters, according to pupil readiness rather than at a specified age. This development is presented as a response to concerns expressed by parents and teachers at the pressure imposed on children by the continued application of SATs. The revised approach, piloted under the title Making Good Progress, requires pupils in *Key Stages 2 and 3 to take tests of 50 minutes' duration in reading, writing, and mathematics. The tests operate twice a year so that teachers have a degree of flexibility to enter pupils when they believe they are able to attain a specified level. Unlike *national curriculum tests, in which the pupil has only to reach the grade's threshold in order to be awarded the grade, the revised tests require pupils to demonstrate that they have securely reached each level before the grade will be awarded. Under this single-level testing system, pupils making slow progress in English or mathematics receive one-to-one tutoring in those subjects. Schools will receive funding bonuses for successful results, and will work to targets aimed at increasing the number of pupils who progress through two levels in one key stage.

situated learning A model of learning first proposed by Jean Lave and Étienne Wenger, which suggests that learning is a social activity which arises from our engagement with our daily lives. They describe this process as one of participating in a **community of practice**, and argue that such communities are found everywhere, whether we are engaging with work, school, home, our civic or social involvements, or our leisure pursuits. In some communities of practice we are central players, while in others our role may be more peripheral. As we engage in these activities, we interact with others and with the wider world in terms of our socio-historical and economic context; and in so doing we necessarily adjust and tune the ways we relate. We can call this process 'learning'. It is a collective enterprise, and results in practices and behaviours which reflect our collective pursuits and are 'owned' by the 'community' which has been created by this shared endeavour. This is what Lave and Wenger term a 'community of practice'. Thus, situated learning is neither a form of education nor a set of *pedagogical practices, but is rather a way of framing the process of learning firmly within a context of lived experience, as something which takes place through participation in group involvement with daily life. It is a joint enterprise, engagement in which binds individuals into a social unit or 'community', one which develops, as do the individuals within it, over time. In practice, there is an argument for linking certain pedagogical practices or environments with situated learning. These might include, for example, learning undertaken in 'real' environments appropriate to the subject, such as horticulture taught in a garden or greenhouse, or *field trips organized to engage learning with practice in the 'real world'. However, as a model it calls into question several widely held assumptions about education and the learning process. For example, it challenges the idea that learning is an individual activity—something undertaken by individuals. It also challenges the idea that learning or education is a process which is separate from our everyday lives, and that it has a start and end point. Perhaps most of all, this approach calls into question the assumption that learning is always a result of teaching.

Further Reading: J. Lave and E. Wenger *Situated Learning: Legitimate Peripheral Participation* (Cambridge University Press, 1991).

sixth form college A *tertiary institution providing education for 16–19-year-olds, and covering broadly the same curriculum as that provided by a school sixth form. This includes a range of *General Certificate of Education *Advanced Levels (A levels), and *Vocational A levels or *diplomas. Sixth form colleges do not provide a skills-based vocational curriculum such as that found in *colleges of further education. Teachers in a sixth form college may have *qualified teacher status or *qualified teacher learning and skills status.

skills 1. An area of education and training concerned with *vocational qualifications and usually *assessed and *accredited through *National Vocational Qualifications. The term is reflected in current terminology for *further education (FE) and work-based training, which is often referred to collectively as the 'learning and skills sector'. The *Foster Report (2005) defined the role of FE colleges as that of skills training. This understanding of the term derives from the classification of learning into three domains, based on *Bloom's Taxonomy: the cognitive, the affective, and the psychomotor, of which the latter is concerned with the acquisition of physical or practical skills.

2. Skills need not be defined so narrowly, however. For example, one may apply skill to thinking (the cognitive domain) and to the sensitive handling of another's feelings (affective domain). *See also* KNOWLEDGE.

skills academies *See* NATIONAL SKILLS ACADEMIES.

skills agenda The focus on the improvement of the basic *vocational skills of the United Kingdom workforce in the first decade of the 21st century. The term was first coined in this context in 2003 in the *White Paper *21st Century Skills: Realising Our Potential*, which identified the need to raise skills levels to those of the more economically prosperous countries of the European Union. This theme was developed in two more White Papers: *14–19 Education and Skills* (2005) and *Getting on in Business, Getting on in Work* (2005). Sector skills councils and **Regional Skills Partnerships** have a central remit to work to this agenda through employer-led developments in unitized qualifications for the workplace; 14–19 vocational programmes; and the provision of funding to encourage employers to release staff for training. *See also* EMPLOYER ENGAGEMENT; 14–19 AGENDA; SKILLS; TRAIN TO GAIN; WORK-BASED LEARNING.

V.C., K.A.

Skills and Employment Action Plan An all-age skills programme operating in Wales and designed to address the skills deficit. This includes the National Basic Skills Strategy for Wales, Words Talk Numbers Count, which was launched in April 2005. The all-age approach recognizes the need for intervention at key points in the *lifelong learning cycle, and the strategy has supported the delivery of early years and family programmes, such as Language and Play programmes catering for parents and carers, including those whose first language is neither Welsh nor English. Age limits have been abolished for the *Modern Apprenticeship scheme, and a *work-based learning improvement plan has been introduced to boost quality and improve learning outcomes. A new Workforce Development Programme is tailored to the needs of individual businesses, and the ReACT programme provides targeted training support for those affected by major redundancies. H.G.

Skills for Life A national strategy for improving *adult literacy and numeracy in England. The Skills for Life Strategy Unit, originally called the Adult Basic Skills Strategy Unit, is part of the *Department for Innovation, Universities, and Skills, and is responsible for the strategy's implementation. The strategy includes the introduction of new national standards in literacy, numeracy, and language acquisition, new entry level qualifications, and national testing.

Skills in the UK *See* LEITCH REPORT.

Skinner, B. F. *See* BEHAVIOURIST.

social and emotional aspects of learning (SEAL) A resource for primary schools aimed to support them in the development of pupils' social and emotional skills. The framework and materials are designed to facilitate pupils' progression in these skills as they advance year by year through the school, and to involve parents and carers in their progress. This initiative encourages a whole-school approach as well as classroom activities, and incorporates a range of continuing professional development activities for teachers. Part of the *Primary National Strategy, SEAL is implemented with the support of Children's Service departments within all *local authorities.

social class A term which refers to societal hierarchies, expressed as the positioning of people within that society in relation to one another and determined largely by level of education and occupation and also to a great extent by the individual's economic value relative to other members of society. Social class is closely associated with culture and the cultural beliefs and practices of communities and, as such, forms an important part of personal identity. Because it is hierarchical, those individuals and communities who are at the bottom of the hierarchy are at increased risk of marginalization and social exclusion. Other characteristics which may lead to marginalization and social exclusion such as gender, race, sexuality, or disability, and which also form important aspects of personal identity, are heavily mediated by the social class of the individual. Social class is also closely related to power in society, since economic and political power is principally located with the middle classes—those who have been able to access high levels of education, exploit its advantages, and secure the economic rewards that this has offered.

Concerns around social class in an educational context are related to the significant class-based inequalities within the education system. These inequalities relate to a situation where young people have widely differing educational experiences—and achieve widely differing outcomes—based on the cultural values, beliefs, and practices associated with education within their community and their physical access (largely determined by catchment area) to higher or lower achieving schools which often offer different types of curriculum. The English education system has historically been complicit in the reproduction of class structures and ensures that young people reach the age of 16 with the credentials and education appropriate to class-specific occupations. These occupations and levels of credential reflect those that their parents achieved before them, an illustration of the notion of educational inheritance where those parents with limited educational and material resources are unable to generate academic profits for their children in the same way as those with more significant educational and material resources. Concerns related to access to education and educational outcomes within a class context exist in many education systems, particularly those of economically powerful countries with well-established universal access to education.

Although government defines social class according to a wide range of categories and sub-groups, it is unrealistic to discuss educational issues within the context of eight or more separate groupings, and in many texts a much broader differential is used and the terms 'working class' and 'middle class' (and occasionally 'underclass') are found. These relate to the social class of the parents of the young person, and are often used to illustrate inequalities in the education system. Hence, the term 'working class' has become synonymous with disadvantage and is used in the context of limited parental education and credentials, with occupations which might be defined as mundane, low-pay, and low-skill. However, this fails to differentiate the working class from the so-called underclass, which constitutes the children of parents who either have never worked or are, in the long term, economically inactive. The term 'underclass' is synonymous with poverty, social exclusion, and marginalization. In contrast, the term 'middle class' is often used to imply advantage and is related to higher levels of educational achievement and professional, technical, or managerial occupations which provide security of tenure, opportunities for advancement and career progression, and high economic returns. In addition to parental social class, a commonly used measure of disadvantage in educational research is the number of children within a school who are eligible for free school meals, or, after 16, the number who are in receipt of the means-tested *Educational Maintenance Allowance.

There are strong social class correlations in the outcomes of national examinations and assessments and in government school *league tables, in which schools in more affluent areas drawing from middle-class *catchments invariably dominate the top of the league, with the bottom dominated by schools in disadvantaged areas drawing from more socially excluded catchments. Some areas of education are more transparently class-specific than others. For example, *independent schools have a largely middle-class intake, while the English *further education colleges provide a predominantly skills-based curriculum to young people from lower social classes. It has been suggested that the present post-16 system in England offers tripartite 'pathways' which reflect the hierarchy of ancient Greek society described in Plato's *Republic* as well as contemporary social class structures. Within these pathways the academic 'gold standard' *General Certificate of Education *Advanced Levels, the full-time vocationally orientated level 3 programmes (e.g. BTEC National Diploma), and the occupationally based *National Vocational Qualification are the routes into higher education, training, and employment. However, the employment, salary, and thus the life opportunities which result from following the different routes are widely different, particularly for those who do not hold the necessary credentials to enter level 3 post-16, and who have to undertake lower-level vocational programmes. Historically, vocational programmes have tended to be regarded as of lower status than academic programmes. They are significant in the replication of classed (and gendered) inequalities and have been widely criticized for socializing young people into particular job roles.

Such class-based differentials also extend to *higher education, where, despite numerous policy initiatives intended to create more opportunities for less advantaged young people, proportionately more middle-class young people enter university. Of those working-class young people who do enter higher education, proportionately fewer attend high-status institutions and proportionately more undertake their higher education programme within a further education setting. They are statistically more likely to withdraw before completing their programme and statistically less likely to achieve higher grades.

Because social class is a characteristic deeply intertwined with personal identity and associated with embedded societal structures, values, and practices it often leads to discrimination. This is multifaceted and takes place at all levels from the use of playground insults such as 'snob' or 'chav' to the direction of (mainly working-class) low-achieving 16-year-olds to vocational programmes which are held in lower esteem and provide fewer opportunities in terms of future income and education than the academic programmes to which the higher-achieving (mainly middle-class) young people are directed. Because of the complex relationships between social class, inequality, and discrimination, it is a fundamental issue in debates around *social justice, equality, and inequality in education.

SEE WEB LINKS

- Provides government definition of categories and sub-groups of social class. L.A.

social interactionism As an approach to education this theory emphasizes the importance of the location of learning within a particular sociocultural environment, as well as the belief that learners are instrumental in constructing their own knowledge and understanding. Social interactionists adhere to the wider *constructivist theory of learning, and place an emphasis on the role which language plays as a medium of learner interaction, pointing out that it is through language that cultural and philosophical ideas are shared and developed. The contextualized and situational nature of learning is, according to the interactionists, a key element in driving cognitive development. This view takes account of the diversity of individuals within any learning group, particularly in the way they interpret or make sense of the world, and suggests that interaction between learners and between learner and teacher provide an important stimulus to learning, which would be missing in an *objectivist learning environment, where learners are passive and compliant recipients of learning. Pupils' self-concept—the view each of them has of herself or himself as an individual—is formed largely through interaction with others, and will change and develop according to the way they see themselves reflected in those interactions. This can affect pupil motivation and confidence, for example, if the view that is reflected back to them is a negative one in terms of their ability or attainment. This is one example of how the individual constructs their own meanings from their own interpretation of their social interactions. Learning based on an interactionist approach, therefore, presupposes a collaborative relationship between teacher and learner, rather than a relationship of learner dependency; and is likely to involve built-in opportunities for learners to discuss, collaborate, and become actively involved with the learning process. This model is above all predicated on the belief that meaning is created by the learner, rather than simply received unquestioningly from the teacher. *See also* VYGOTSKY.

SOCIAL JUSTICE

A term which refers to the good of the whole community, where that is taken to include both the good of each and the good of all, in an acknowledgement that one depends on the other. In Western thought the roots of the concept go back to both Plato and Aristotle. In *The Republic*, Plato drew attention to the connection between the virtuous individual and the socially harmonious state. Aristotle took these ideas further in his *Nicomachean Ethics* and *Politics*, where he introduced the idea of social justice as dependent on a fair distribution of goods in society.

Current ideas of social justice draw on these ideas and expand on them. Social justice is closely associated with fairness. It is also closely associated with individuals as members of the community in relation to respect:

self-respect and mutual respect. (It should be noted that in discussions of social justice, the terms 'self-esteem' and 'recognition' are more common than the terms 'self-respect' and 'mutual respect'.) Thus, social justice depends both on respect and also on a right distribution of benefits and responsibilities. It includes paying attention to individual perspectives at the same time as dealing with issues of discrimination, exclusion, and respect, especially on the grounds of (any or all of) race, *gender, sexuality, special needs, and *social class.

Since social justice could never be achieved once and for all, it is best understood as always in process. Working towards social justice means resolving possible tensions about the well-being of individuals, of whole societies, and of diverse social political groups. Inevitably, any resolution will be provisional. Human beings are creative and need room for individual expression and action. They have a diversity of cultures. So human societies are never static. As they change, so too do the tensions and balances between different interest groups and social sectors. Social justice is more a journey than a destination.

Equality is central to all ideas of social justice as fairness. At its simplest, equality means sameness: however, in relation to human beings and their societies, sameness is more a matter for judgement than measurement, simply because each person is a unique individual. Moreover, there is the question, Equality in or of what? For example, any judgement about what counts as equal resources has to take need into account. For instance, if disabled students are to enjoy equal education with the rest, they may sometimes require more resources than able-bodied ones, depending on the nature of the disability and the environment.

Key terms are **equal opportunity** and **equality of outcome**. A socially just society would ensure that no individual or social group had less opportunity to benefit from educational provision. It would also expect that no social group would, on average, achieve better or worse than other social groups. (Equality of outcome refers to social political groups. Of course, some individuals will—and should—achieve much more than others.) Thus, the different educational achievements of girls and boys is one example of a social justice issue. Another is the relatively high proportion of black boys who are excluded from school in the UK.

Self-identity is also a key concern for social justice. Respect for self and others affects but is also an effect of prejudice and discrimination experienced by a range of social groups. These include racism, sexism, homophobia, disability, class prejudice, and prejudice against outsiders to mainstream society such as travellers, refugees, and asylum seekers. Reasons for unfair discrimination also include religion, ethnic heritage, language, dialect, and coming from rural or inner-city areas. Most of these raise issues of a fair distribution of resources. However, they are also all issues of respect and therefore of self-identity.

Educators wishing to tackle social justice issues, whether as policy-makers, teachers, or researchers, need to pay attention to ways of working for social justice in context, focusing especially on self-esteem, empowerment, voice, partnership, consultation, and collaboration. They also need to focus on finding approaches to specific areas of disadvantage, including multicultural, intercultural, or anti-racist education, for instance, in the area of race. Similarly for gender, sexuality, special educational needs, and social class. These are all useful headings under which to make a social justice audit of teaching methods and strategies and also the processes of policy-making. Similarly, considerations of social justice are relevant in every curriculum area from mathematics to social studies. The curriculum areas where it may be easiest to address justice issues directly are citizenship and personal and social education. Another useful mechanism is through the equal opportunities policies in schools, colleges, and universities. *See also* INCLUSION.

Further Reading: S. Ball *The Education Debate* (Policy Press, 2008) explores the impact of education policy and ideas on social class divisions. M.G.

social skills Sometimes called 'social and life skills', these are concerned with the ability to interact and communicate appropriately with others in a variety of settings. Originally included as one of the 'core' skills (forerunners of *key skills) which formed part of the curriculum for young people on the *youth training programmes of the 1980s, it was considered to be one of the skills employers required to see in young job applicants. This range of skills is similar to that now embedded in the *national curriculum as part of *personal and social education.

Socratic questioning A form of questioning which aims not to test or assess, but to draw out the learner's *tacit knowledge. It takes its name from the Athenian philosopher Socrates (469–399 BC), who was said to use this approach in teaching his pupils.

SPECIAL EDUCATIONAL NEEDS (SEN)

The term 'special educational needs' became commonly used after the report published in 1978 by the Committee of Inquiry into the Education of Handicapped Children and Young People (the *Warnock Report). Prior to this, the terms 'handicapped' and 'retarded' were in common usage when describing young people with SEN. The main cause for seeking new terminology was to remove the negative focus of those words and the medical labelling of children used before the Report. It was also felt that the labels 'handicapped' and 'retarded' had a negative effect on the way people felt about themselves. The Code of Practice for SEN (revised 2001) sets out clear criteria and guidance for the assessment of SEN, but differing systems for interpretation of assessment data mean that one school's reasons for describing a student as having SEN may be quite different from another's. The term 'SEN' is generally applied where medical or cognitive disorders exist which create *barriers to learning and which require support for the learner on a long-term or ongoing basis. There are those who will require support on a temporary or indefinite basis owing to personal and family circumstances such as bereavement or a parent who is in prison: there is still much debate around whether or not it is appropriate to link students who require additional learning support owing to life circumstances with those who have cognitive disabilities under the banner of SEN. Not all children who are disabled as defined by the Disability Discrimination Act 2005 will have special educational needs. This debate widens with the introduction of *personalized learning which embraces methods of working with students with SEN and applies them to others. Some *local authorities are combining the term 'additional educational needs' with SEN when referring to provision for students who are experiencing barriers to their learning. Children with SEN will require in school interventions which are additional to or different from those provided as part of the school's usual approaches and strategy.

Further Reading: Department for Education and Skills *Code of Practice for Special Educational Needs (Revised)* DfES/581/2001 (DfES, 2001). T.B., L.E.

special educational needs coordinator (SENCO) is the person in a school responsible for implementing the Code of Practice for Special Educational Needs (SEN). The SENCO supports the head teacher in the strategic direction and development of *special educational needs provision and coordinates the development and implementation of policy. They must contribute to the in-service training of staff in matters relating to SEN. Other responsibilities held are to provide guidance and support for teachers in the school so that they are able to identify and assess students with *learning difficulties and set effective targets for individual students. The SENCO, in consultation with other key staff, usually writes *individual education plans containing relevant targets and strategies which act as guidance for those who implement the plans. It is the duty of the SENCO to ensure staff have all the information they need to plan for effective teaching to meet the needs of all pupils. They deploy staff and resources used to support pupils with SEN. A key role of the SENCO is to coordinate and chair *annual statutory review meetings for pupils who have *statements of special educational needs. This includes requesting advice from all involved adults, including parents and professionals from outside the education sector, preparing a detailed school advice document and writing the report following the review meeting. These tasks must be carried out in accordance with the guidance and timescales set out in the Code of Practice for SEN. The SENCO is the key link person with external agencies who support the school in the identification and assessment of any special needs in children. The SENCO is usually the school's contact for all multi-agency work with regard to SEN. The role of SENCO is complex and has in recent years been regarded as a senior management post. There are national standards for the role set by the Teacher Training Agency (now *Training and Development Agency for Schools) which were developed from the Code of Practice for SEN.

Further Reading: Department for Education and Skills *Code of Practice for Special Educational Needs (Revised)* DfES/581/2001 (DfES, 2001).

- Provides the full National Standards for SENCOs.

T.B., L.E.

Special Educational Needs and Disability Act 2001 (SENDA) An Act which repealed the exemption of education from the Disability Discrimination Act 1995 and made it unlawful for educational institutions in both the pre- and post-16 education sectors to discriminate against disabled pupils and students. Examples of discrimination would be refusing a place to a student with motor impairment simply because the school or college had no lift to the upper floor and providing learning materials in written format only for students with a learning difficulty affecting the ability to decode written language. The Act is all-embracing, covering admissions, education, and associated services (for example, school trips, student residential accommodation, and access to leisure facilities), but excludes requirements for the removal or alteration of physical features and the provision of auxiliary aids or services. The Act places a duty on the responsible body (normally governors) of all institutions to be anticipatory in making reasonable adjustments to existing provision.
See also ACCESSIBILITY PLANS.

T.B., L.E.

Special Educational Needs and Disability Tribunal (SENDIST) Established by the *Education Act 1993, the Special Educational Needs Tribunal had its remit extended by the *Special Educational Needs and Disability Act 2001 to allow it to consider claims of discrimination. The Tribunal is independent of influence from the government and has no connection with any local authority. It sits in private except in prescribed circumstances, to consider parents' appeals against the decision of local authorities about children's *special educational needs or to hear cases presented as discriminatory. The Tribunal can order local authorities to assess a child, issue a *statement of special educational needs, or make amendments to parts 2 (needs), 3 (provision), and 4 (placement) of an existing statement of special educational need. In claims of discrimination the Tribunal can order any action it thinks reasonable, although it cannot order the payment of financial compensation.

T.B., L.E.

specialist school A secondary school which specializes in the teaching of a particular area of the curriculum. From 1994 *maintained schools were able to apply for specialist status in design and technology, mathematics, and modern languages. This range was gradually expanded, so that schools may now apply for specialist status in arts, business and enterprise, engineering, humanities, languages, mathematics and computing, music, science, sports, and technology. Specialist schools are permitted to select up to 10 per cent of their pupil intake, based not on pupils' *ability, but on their *aptitude for the specialist subject.

SEE WEB LINKS

- Provides detailed information from the Department for Children, Schools, and Families on the role of specialist schools.

special measures Schools on special measures are those which have been identified by *Ofsted and the *Department for Children, Schools, and Families as giving cause for concern and being at risk of *failing. Schools on special measures may be given support in strengthening their leadership or in improving their teaching and learning, and thereby subsequently succeed in raising their performance. Some are given a *fresh start under a new name and a new *head teacher. Those which are judged unable to improve are closed down.

SEE WEB LINKS

- Provides details of government policy relating to schools in special measures.

special school A school that provides education for children and young people with complex or specific needs which generally cannot be fully met in the mainstream setting. Some special schools are generic in nature and cater for a wide spectrum of need while others offer education to discrete groups of learners such as those with a hearing impairment. Staff–student ratios are high and the setting will have enhanced resources. Funded by local authorities or private organizations, some schools offer residential placements or a 24-hour curriculum. Pupils on roll will usually have a *statement of special educational needs. Historically many pupils attended the same special school for the duration of their compulsory schooling, but more frequently now schools are organized into primary and secondary schools in line with mainstream education. T.B., L.E.

spelling The spelling of English is notoriously difficult, and the ability to spell accurately is usually only acquired by pupils over a number a years, rather than being a goal at some early stage of the education process. A major debate over the teaching of spelling has been whether a pupil's ability to write creatively will be stifled by an insistence on correct spelling. Some who lament inadequate *literacy levels among school-leavers believe that an emphasis on creativity over accuracy may be to blame. Others, such as George Bernard Shaw (1856–1950), have taken a more radical view, and suggested that all English spelling should be approached phonetically. Some pupils who have persistent and severe problems with spelling may be diagnosed as suffering from *dyslexia, while for others the difficulty may lie in their underexposure to the written word. *See also* READING.

spiral curriculum *See* CURRICULUM, SPIRAL.

sports day An annual event held by some schools in which pupils (and sometimes parents) compete in races and other competitive sporting events. In secondary schools where a house system exists, the competition may be between the houses. However, for many schools, and particularly those in the *primary sector, sports day has come to be less about competition and sporting excellence and more about inclusion and celebration.

staff development *See* CONTINUING PROFESSIONAL DEVELOPMENT; IN-SERVICE EDUCATION OF TEACHERS.

staff–student ratio (SSR) *See* CLASS SIZE; PUPIL–TEACHER RATIO.

stage not age A phrase used to summarize the approach implicit in the concept of a *personalized curriculum, and often used as a 'shorthand' for this approach by those professionals in schools and local authorities who are responsible for encouraging the implementation of personalization. It encapsulates the idea that a pupil should be provided with the learning experiences and curriculum content which are appropriate to the *stage of development which she or he has reached, rather than that all pupils be given an education which is standardized to 'fit' their chronological age.

stages A number of educationalists and psychologists have described human *cognitive development and the capacity for learning in terms of the individual's progress through a series of consecutive stages. *Piaget, for example, suggested that the human being goes through four main stages of cognitive development, each of which corresponds with a chronological stage in terms of the individual's age. His theory locates the first three of these stages in childhood and early adolescence, and has had a great influence on educational thinking and practice, particularly in the *primary phase of education. The stages which Piaget identified are as follows:

- Stage 1: Sensorimotor stage. This corresponds with infancy and has six sub-stages. Intelligence is manifested through motor activities, and knowledge of the world is based upon these physical experiences and interactions. Memory (or 'object permanence') is acquired at about 7 months; and as the infant's physical skills and mobility develop, so do their intellectual activity, including some language (or 'symbolic') ability.
- Stage 2: Pre-operational stage. This corresponds with the 'toddler' and early childhood period, and has two sub-stages. Intelligence is demonstrated through language use (or 'symbols'); and both memory and imagination develop. The child's thinking at this stage is egocentric and non-logical.
- Stage 3: Concrete operational stage. This corresponds with the years of primary schooling and early adolescence. Intelligence is demonstrated through the ability to manipulate symbols (language) in relation to objects. The tendency to think egocentrically diminishes as operational thinking develops.
- Stage 4: Formal operational stage. This corresponds with adolescence and adulthood, when intelligence is demonstrated through the ability to use symbols (language) logically in relation to abstract concepts. Early in this stage, during adolescence, there is often a temporary return to egocentric thinking. The formal operational stage is not reached by everyone; and some would argue that it is only attained by the minority of adults.

This idea of stages constitutes an important aspect of the *constructivist theory of learning. One of the implications this theory has for teaching is that children should not be expected to attempt learning which demands skills or abilities which are in advance of the stage at which they are currently functioning. Thus, in early childhood, for example, children should not be confronted with tasks which demand operational thinking. This is not to say, however, that teachers and parents should not challenge or stretch the child, but rather that such challenge should remain within the parameters appropriate to the child's developmental stage. More recent research has suggested that the link between developmental stage and chronological age may be less clearly defined than Piaget's original research suggested.

Where Piaget's theory focuses on cognitive development through infancy, childhood, and adolescence, *Erikson's description of personality growth as a series of stages is often used to inform the theoretical underpinning of the education of adults. Known as 'psychosocial stages', and complementing in some ways the psychosexual stages described by Freud, Erikson's stages are presented as a response to the demands of society, which, as the individual's development proceeds, trigger a series of personal conflicts or crises. Erikson identifies eight stages. The first three relate closely to Freud's psychosexual stages, as is evident from the terminology used, and are the oral, anal, and genital stages. The fourth stage, 'latency', covers the period when children are expected to acquire the skills which will equip them for adult life, and in Western society is coterminous with the period of primary schooling. The fifth stage, 'puberty and adolescence', confronts young people with the task of defining themselves and adapting to the roles imposed upon them by society. The three subsequent stages mark further adult rites of passage; and it is these which are sometimes used to inform *adult education theory. They are (6) young adulthood, when the individual must discover whether they are able to form intimate relationships; (7) adulthood, which presents the individual with the challenge of contributing to society ('generativity') or failing to contribute and instead 'stagnating'; and (8) maturity, the eighth and final stage, which presents the individual with the challenge of achieving 'integrity' and acceptance of self and one's place in the world, or failing to do so and falling into 'despair'. Erikson argues that it is not only the external demands of society which drive these crises or stages, but that there is also an inbuilt human developmental 'timetable' which determines the sequence and direction of individual personal development. His concept of a healthy or integrated personality is one which is in harmony with the society within which it is situated. On these grounds, his theory of stages has been criticized as conformist and as tending to reinforce, rather than interrogate in educational terms, the social status quo. *See also* STAGE NOT AGE.

Standard Assessment Tasks (SATs) *See* STANDARD TASKS.

Standard Grades Scotland's educational qualifications for students aged around 14–16 years. Standard Grade courses are taken over the third and fourth years of a student's secondary schooling. Students will typically study seven to nine subjects at Standard Grade. The Standard Grade replaced the Scottish *Ordinary Grade in the early 1990s. It is broadly equivalent to the *General Certificate of Secondary Education qualification taken in other parts of the UK.

S.M.

standardization The practice of ensuring that work is being assessed to the same *standard and against the same criteria by teachers, examiners, and *assessors in every institution. This is usually done through a process of *verification, by an external verifier or an external examiner.

standards A means of defining the quality—of work or of performance—which must be attained. In education there are two main levels at which standards are set and monitored: the national and the institutional. National standards are used to regulate both the quality of the educational and training process, and the levels of *attainment required in nationally recognized testing or qualifications. Thus, for example, the *national curriculum and its associated testing or assessment regime sets national, *key stage-specific standards for pupil achievement; and there are professional standards in place which define the training and performance requirements for teachers in schools, and which are applied nationally. On an institutional level there are standards set by individual schools and colleges in relation to, for example, student behaviour or attainment targets. The monitoring of national standards in English schools is part of the remit of the *Standards and Effectiveness Unit (SEU), which looks at pupil standards of attainment, and at overall school performance. The SEU is empowered to intervene where necessary in the interests of maintaining the required standards of performance. The monitoring of standards may also be carried out at an institutional level through a process of *verification, which is designed to ensure standardization across centres of delivery and assessment. 'Ensuring standards' and 'raising standards' have become key phrases in educational policy since the 1980s. *See also* Standards Unit.

Standards and Effectiveness Unit (SEU) Located within the *Department for Children, Schools, and Families, the unit has responsibility for implementing government policies relating to the raising of *standards in English schools. Its remit also includes the promotion of innovation and diversity, the improvement of pupil standards of attainment, and the monitoring of school performance. In relation to the latter, the Unit is empowered to intervene where necessary in the interests of maintaining the required standards of performance. Its responsibility also extends to the management of innovations such as the *National Literacy and *National Numeracy strategies and the *Excellence in Cities initiative.

SEE WEB LINKS

- Provides details of the organization of the SEU.

Standards and Verification UK (SVUK) Part of *Lifelong Learning UK, SVUK has responsibility for monitoring standards of teacher training leading to *qualified teacher learning and skills status for *further education and the rest of the *lifelong learning sector.

Standards Fund Administered by the Department for Children, Schools, and Families, to allow funding to be allocated to national priority areas and initiatives and to provide capital grants to schools, known as the **Schools Standards Grant**.

Standards Unit Following the UK government strategy for the development of the *learning and skills sector as outlined in **Success for All* (2002), a new Standards Unit was set up in 2003 at the *Department for Education and Skills. The role of the Standards Unit was to identify and disseminate best practice and to 'lead the transformation of teaching and learning and leadership across the learning and skills sector'. Teaching and learning frameworks were developed as resources in curriculum priority areas such as *Entry to Employment, science, construction, and business. The Standards Unit was then transferred to the *Learning and Skills Development Agency, which in 2006 was reorganized into the *Quality Improvement Agency. V.C., K.A.

Standard Tasks (SATs) Originally called **Standards Assessment Tasks**, but officially renamed **Standard Tasks** in 1990, SATs have informally retained their original abbreviated name, and have been an integral part of the *national curriculum assessment process. They require pupils in England to be tested in *Key Stage (KS) 1 at age 7 in English and mathematics, and the tests to be marked by the school and used as a basis for teachers to make an assessment of the *attainment *level at which the pupil is working. Pupils are tested again in KS2 at age 11, and in KS3 at age 14, in English, mathematics, and science. These tests are externally assessed and published nationally. SATs have been criticized by teachers and parents for imposing an unproductive level of pressure and stress on pupils. Partly as a result of this, the system which replaces them, *single-level testing, is intended to be more consistent with a *personalized learning, *'stage not age' approach to pupil assessment.

In Scotland there are no synchronous national assessments at *primary level. In the 5–14 curriculum each curricular area is divided into six levels, A–F. Assessment to attain these target levels can be taken when the teacher considers pupils ready. This is often completed as individuals or small groups; whole years do not sit tests. The levels are used as a confirmation of the student's current standard. In Wales there has been no testing at KS1 since 2002. A review of the testing and assessment arrangements for KS2 and 3 published in May 2004 recommended that tests should be phased out entirely by 2007/8. KS2 tests have been optional since 2005; KS3 tests became optional in 2006. External marking was offered for the first year of non-compulsory testing. In Northern Ireland national testing is an option in KS3.

statement of competence *See* COMPETENCE.

statemented *See* STATEMENT OF SPECIAL EDUCATIONAL NEEDS.

statementing officer An officer of the *local authority who writes *statements of *special educational needs. They will collate the multi-professional advice from the *statutory assessment process to establish the provision required to meet the student's needs and monitor their progress through the annual *statutory review. If the statementing officer agrees with recommendations for changes to the statement, following a statutory review, they will amend the statement to include the changes. T.B., L.E.

S

statement of special educational needs A legal document which is issued by the *local authority (LA) following a statutory assessment. Written advice will be sought from parents, educational professionals, medical agencies, the psychology service, and social services. Contributors must respond within six weeks. The views of the student should also be sought. A statement records personal details, including name and address, date of birth, and home language. A detailed description of the student's special needs follows. This is set out according to the areas of need identified during the assessment process. The LA will decide what special educational provision is required to meet the student's *special educational needs. Objectives are then written which relate to all areas of special needs described in the earlier part. Arrangements for monitoring progress towards the objectives are clearly set out. The main vehicle for review is the *statutory review, which must occur at least annually. The next section names the school where the special educational provision will be made. Parents may state a preference that their child is not educated in a mainstream school. If no preference is made, the LA must endeavour to place students in a mainstream school. An exception to this would be if this was not compatible with the education of other children. Other needs which could be identified by social services, health services, or other agencies are set out in the next part of the statement. Non-educational needs and provision are also recorded. Parents should be informed quickly of all decisions relating to the process as it affects their child. Regulations for the time limits are set out in detail in the Code of Practice for Special Educational Needs. The process for issuing a statement should usually be no more than 26 weeks.

Further Reading: Department for Education and Skills *Code of Practice for Special Educational Needs (Revised)* DfES/581/2001 (DfES, 2001). T.B., L.E.

state school *See* MAINTAINED SCHOOL.

statutory review A meeting held to monitor progress towards the objective set out in a *statement of special educational needs. It is appropriate to decide if any amendments to the description of needs or the provision described in the statement should be made. Statements must be reviewed at least annually, though it is possible to call interim meetings if necessary. All involved professionals and parents must be invited to the review. The views of the student must also be sought and recorded in the report from the meeting. Guidance for the timescales for the review can be found in the Code of Practice Special Educational Needs. Copies of the report are sent to all involved in the review and to the *local authority. T.B., L.E.

Steiner, Rudolf (1861–1925) An Austrian philosopher and head of the German Theosophical Society. Rudolf Steiner's most lasting and significant influence has been in the field of education. Having given a series of lectures on a range of theological and philosophical ideas to the workers of the Waldorf-Astoria cigarette factory in Stuttgart, he was asked to establish and lead a school for the children of the factory employees in 1919. There are now currently more than 600 independent Steiner Waldorf Schools in over 32 countries. In the UK they are most commonly referred to as 'Steiner schools'.

Steiner designed the school curriculum based on his notion of the three stages of a child's spirituality and the development of the body, spirit, and soul. He claimed that children learn through physical activity, imitation, and the development of temperament by watching adults who model required behaviours. For Steiner, there is no question of childhood being a preparation for life, but rather a spiritual and rhythmic journey when the natural fusion of the spirit (existing pre-birth) and body takes place. The Steiner Waldorf Schools, therefore, emphasize a carefully planned environment with activity, in the *early years, based on play with natural materials, oral storytelling of traditional fairy tales and role play, with a gentle introduction to reading and writing from the age of 7. Children sing, speak, model, paint, and perform household duties, absorbing the environment without transforming it, and developing an inner moral sense projected by family and school values.

One of the more unusual parts of the curriculum involves eurhythmy, which engages children in spiritual gestures to chanting and music. Steiner believed that eurhythmy enhanced coordination and strengthened the ability to listen. (Some of this may have informed current exercises included as part of *Brain Gym activity). He also claimed that such gestures developed the imagination and nourished the spirit. Steiner claimed that an education built on cooperation, love, and inner peace would be more beneficial to children's intellectual, moral, and creative well-being than one based on regimentation or coercion. Current practice in Steiner schools reflects this educational philosophy, with the same teacher educating children from 4 to 7, then 7 to 11. After the age of 11, in the UK, children in Steiner schools are able to follow the statutory *national curriculum.

Proponents of the Steiner approach to the education of young children have been vocal in their opposition to the *Early Years Foundation Stage curriculum, which sets learning targets for children aged 0–5, arguing that the imposition of this framework is incompatible with the Steiner approach to early years learning. A.W.

Strategic Area Review (StAR) StARs originated from the *White Paper **Success for All* (2002) strategy with the aim of providing accessible learning opportunities for those in the *post-compulsory education sector, to meet their ambitions and the needs of employment in their local communities. These Reviews use the Regional Boards which replaced local *Learning and Skills Councils (LSCs) to build networks between providers of post-compulsory education and training across the country. Local LSCs also work closely with *local authorities, employers, and schools in identifying local needs. It is also intended that the Reviews will promote building the skills base to its full capacity in the wider context of local and regional economy, and through national collaboration disseminate good practice in education and training.

SEE WEB LINKS

- Provides guidance on the implementation of reviews. V.C., K.A.

streaming Allocating pupils to different classes according to their ability, rather than teaching them in mixed-ability classes. This was a common practice in *grammar schools and secondary schools during the era of *selection between the 1940s and early 1970s, and was continued in some *comprehensive schools, despite the comprehensive principle of non-selection, since teaching pupils across the entire ability range in one class, it was claimed, was found in some cases to disadvantage both the more able pupils and those who needed additional support. Streaming is used more in secondary than in primary schools, although some primary schools do employ it. More usual in the primary sector is the organization of pupils by ability into *sets, particularly for English and mathematics.

student One who studies, usually in the *tertiary sector at college or university, although it is not unusual to refer to older pupils in schools as 'students', too.

Student Awards Agency for Scotland (SAAS) The Scottish government agency responsible for funding students who continue in education after 16.

S

The remit of SAAS is to provide financial support for eligible Scottish-domiciled students on courses of higher education throughout the United Kingdom.

SEE WEB LINKS

- Explains the SAAS remit and describes support available to Scottish students. S.M.

student loan *See* LOAN, STUDENT.

students' union 1. A society of students at a college or university which organizes social events and other activities and is represented on key institutional committees which deal with academic matters.

2. The building or bar on campus where students gather for social purposes. *See also* NATIONAL UNION OF STUDENTS.

study leave A period of paid leave granted to teachers in schools and in further and higher education for the purpose of undertaking a course of study related to their professional development. It is shorter than a *sabbatical, and may take the form of a release from duties for a few hours a week for a limited time in order for the teacher to attend a course. Study leave is not a right, and a strong case usually has to be made by the individual seeking it. *See also* SECONDMENT.

study skills The skills which learners need to possess in order to be able to study effectively. These include such disparate skills as time management, the ability to take relevant notes, listening skills, research skills, the ability to use information technology productively, and, of course, the ability to read and to write at the appropriate level. There has been a growing realization that students may need structured support in the development of study skills, and, to this end, guidance is now provided in most colleges and universities, as well as in schools, often in the form of workshops and tutorials.

study support Opportunities for supporting learning which are organized outside school hours and in which pupil participation is voluntary. Such activities and opportunities may be scheduled before or after the school day, during school holidays or at weekends, or during break times or lunchtime. They may typically include a breakfast club, which provides pupils with their breakfast as well as organized activities or time for study; a homework club where pupils have space and relative quiet in which to work; learning about learning, a service offering support and advice to pupils about the skills needed for thinking, studying, and revising; and subject-focused activities, such as clubs for those with an interest in science, literature, languages, or drama.

subject leader A teacher with school-wide responsibility for a particular curriculum area. It is a title most often used in *primary schools. An alternative form also in use is **subject coordinator**.

Success for All (2002) A strategy document published by the *Department for Education and Skills, which sets out proposals for reforms designed to enable *further education colleges and other training providers in the *lifelong learning sector to be more responsive to local and national training needs. This included the need for them to work more closely with employers, and to ensure that provision supported and encouraged principles of equality and diversity. It also stressed the need to develop systems of *e-learning in order to provide wider access to education and training. *See also* WHITE PAPER.

SEE WEB LINKS

- Provides the full text of this document.

sufficiency A term applied in the assessment of students' work or performance when the question arises of whether there is enough evidence of successful achievement to allow the *assessor to make an informed *assessment decision. It is commonly used in assessment for *vocational qualifications, where the question might be one of how many successful performances of a specific task constitute a sufficiency of evidence for the candidate to be judged competent to a national standard. Similar questions of sufficiency of evidence can arise over the assessment of written work, where it may be important to ascertain whether the learner can perform consistently at the required *standard.

summative assessment *Assessment which takes place at the end of a course of study and provides the final judgement on, or 'sums up', the candidate's performance. The most common form of summative assessment is the end examination.

Summerhill School A private school, founded by A. S. *Neill, an early proponent of pupil-centred democratic schooling in which children are acknowledged to have the right to make decisions about what and when they will learn. Founded in 1921 near Dresden, Germany, and now currently occupying a large Victorian house and grounds near the east coast in Suffolk, the school is run as a democratic community consisting of about 95 children aged between 5 and 18, with about one member of staff to every 20 children. All—staff and pupils alike—have equal status as members of that community. Although run mainly as a *co-educational *boarding school, drawing children from a diverse range of racial and cultural backgrounds, it also takes day pupils and provides a curriculum which includes *General Certificate of Secondary Education subjects. One of the ways in which it differs from a conventional school is that children are under no compulsion to attend lessons, and are provided with free access to communal areas where they can play, socialize, or engage in creative activities. The school timetable is created in response to the subject choices made by older pupils, and makes their preferred subjects available, although not mandatory. This democratic approach is based on A. S. Neill's philosophy that children learn self-confidence, tolerance, and consideration not from any externally imposed discipline, but from being given the freedom to think and choose for themselves. For the child, the most important right is considered to be the right to play. According to this approach, the decision to engage in formal learning should be a choice made freely, and therefore attendance at lessons should be optional.

The professional role and practice of the teachers within this community are also different in some respects from those required of teachers in conventional schooling environments. For example, they will offer one-to-one teaching for pupils who prefer this to a classroom approach; and they meet every day in order to discuss individual pupil progress and to plan the best response and provision for each child. As the philosophy on which the school is based rejects any imposition of hierarchy, teachers cannot use their authority as adults in order to impose values, nor their adult power to intervene in problem-solving. Instead of teacher-imposed sanctions, issues of discipline, bullying, and negative or disruptive behaviour are solved by community meetings or by 'ombudsmen' elected from within the community. The rejection of hierarchy also applies between pupils themselves, the older children having no more rights or authority than the very youngest.

The original Summerhill provision was part of an international school in Hellerau, outside Dresden, but was relocated by Neill in the first instance to Sonntagsberg in Austria, and then, in the early 1920s, to Lyme Regis in England, where it opened with five pupils. In 1927 it moved to its current site, still retaining the original name. During the Second World War the school was evacuated to Wales, while the premises in Suffolk were used by the army. Pupil figures fell in the 1950s; but interest in the school and in the philosophy of democratic, pupil-centred schooling was kindled by the UK publication in 1962 of Neill's book *Summerhill—a Radical Approach to Childhood*. The school continues to attract controversy, often depicted in the press as being excessively liberal in its attitude to learning and behaviour management. Its emphasis on individual fulfilment and goal-setting sets it at odds with two dominant current trends in state education: the *instrumentalist emphasis on education for employment or the good of the economy, and the growth of statutory testing and assessment. In 2006–7 the school was engaged in a much-publicized conflict of ideas with *Ofsted, which was finally resolved in the courts in Summerhill's favour.

The philosophy of Summerhill School is reflected in Neill's claim that 'The function of the child is to live his own life—not the life that his anxious parents think he should live, nor a life according to the purpose of the educator who thinks he knows best.'

Further Reading: A. S. Neill *Summerhill—a Radical Approach to Childhood* (Gollancz, 1962).

summer school 1. Informal, non-examined courses held in schools during the summer holidays, usually to help pupils improve their attainment in literacy or numeracy, or to undertake a range of creative or sporting activities. Attendance is not obligatory.

2. Residential summer schools are also held, usually on a suitable university *campus, by the *Open University in order to provide its students with an opportunity to interact and to engage in traditional modes of learning.

super-head A *head teacher who, because of their proven outstanding ability as leader and manager of their own school, is given responsibility for raising standards of achievement in other schools besides their own, or in a group or cluster of schools. The introduction of the 'super-head' (1997) or 'superhead' (2005) has been twice presented as an innovative measure by *secretaries of state responsible for education. In December 1997, during David Blunkett's term as Secretary of State for Education and Employment, it was announced that 'super-heads' would be introduced as part of the *Education Action Zone (EAZ) initiative, their role being to raise school standards at the group of schools within an EAZ area. These super-heads are chosen from among those head teachers who have a proven ability to raise standards in schools which were *failing or which were previously showing poor results, and they receive enhanced salaries, funded from the capital sums invested by the government in the EAZ.

The term 'super-head' was presented again as a policy initiative in 2002 under the Secretary of State, Estelle Morris, in the context of school partnerships and clusters. Heads with 'strategic vision', it was announced, would take control of a group of schools in an initiative to spread their expertise. Clusters of schools would operate under one governing body and one super-head, who would take responsibility for strategic planning, while each school would retain a head teacher with primary responsibility for teaching and learning.

The response from head teachers in general to the concept and creation of super-heads has been cautious, some welcoming the creation of an enhanced leadership role, equivalent to that of chief executive, while others have argued that effective leadership requires the head teacher to be a constant presence in their own school, and that in practical terms turning around the performance of a failing school or group of low-achieving schools is not a task which can readily be accomplished on a part-time basis.

supply teacher A teacher employed by the school on a temporary basis to cover the teaching of a member of staff who is absent. They may register with *local authorities, or with private supply agencies, and their services are called upon as needed.

support staff This can be used to describe a wide range of non-qualified teacher status staff, from *teaching assistants to technicians and administrators.

Sure Start A UK government programme announced as designed to deliver an optimal start in life for every child by bringing together early education, childcare, health, and family support. The responsibility for delivering this programme rests within the *Department for Children, Schools, and Families. Sure Start supports families, from the outset of pregnancy right through until children are 14, and up to age 16 for children with special needs. The guiding principles for service provision are: working *with* parents and children; services for everyone; flexibility at point of delivery; starting very early; operating in a way that is both respectful and transparent; providing community-driven and professionally coordinated services; and outcome-driven provision. These aims are now embedded within the *Every Child Matters agenda and the Children Act 2006.

The policies and programmes of Sure Start apply in England only, covering a wide range of programmes, both universal and those targeted on particular local areas or disadvantaged groups within England.

SEE WEB LINKS

- Provides further information.

A.W.

syllabus A specification of the content of a course of study. The term itself is closely associated with courses of general or academic study, such as the *General Certificate of Secondary Education. For the *vocationally focused *General National Vocational Qualification, on the other hand, the term used was not 'syllabus' but 'specification'. A single *curriculum may encompass several syllabuses, just as the *national curriculum encompasses the syllabus or *programme of study for each subject area. In drawing up a *scheme of work and individual *lesson plans, the teacher translates the contents of the syllabus into an appropriately sequenced series of lessons designed to enable learners to achieve the learning outcomes which the syllabus sets out.

synthetic phonics The approach to the teaching of *reading in *Key Stage 1 which is encouraged by policy-makers, advisers, and teachers. Synthetic *phonic work is defined by the following key features:

- letter/sound correspondences taught in clearly defined, incremental sequence (alphabetic principle);
- blending or synthesizing sounds in order, all through a word, in order to 'sound it out'—in other words, to read it;
- applying the skills of segmenting words into their constituent sounds in order to be able to spell words.

By listening to the sounds (or **phonemes**) which letters create, separately and when blended (or **synthesized**), the child is able to sound out not only immediately recognizable or familiar words, but also those which they may never have previously encountered. In this way, it is recognized that a listening child can be taught to become a reading child.

tabula rasa The mind in its original, uninformed state, before any learning begins. This concept is found in the philosophy of John Locke (1632–1704) and Jean-Jacques *Rousseau; but it is one which many educators do not accept, since it assumes that the mind is shaped solely by what is learned, and discounts the idea of individual predispositions or inherited characteristics. In this sense, it reflects the argument that nurture, not *nature, is of predominant importance in shaping an individual's cognitive skills. The literal meaning of this Latin phrase is a (writing) tablet scraped clean (of writing), suggesting that a young pupil's mind is open to be shaped as the teacher wishes.

tacit knowledge *Knowledge or understanding which the learner possesses, but which they are not aware they possess until the teacher helps them to articulate it by drawing it out, often with the technique of *Socratic questioning. This model of learning stands in direct contrast to approaches such as *rote learning, which begin with the assumption that all knowledge resides in the teacher and is transmitted to the learner, who must then memorize it. The recognition of tacit knowledge is also a recognition that the learner, not the teacher, plays the central role in the learning process. *See also* LEARNER-CENTRED.

targets Part of the vocabulary associated with improvement and raising standards. Successive governments have drawn up national targets for education and training, such as those embodied in the *National Targets for Education and Training, and in the 2006 *White Paper *Further Education: Raising Skills, Improving Life Chances*.

Individual schools in the maintained sector are also required at the beginning of each academic year to set targets for improving pupil performance at *Key Stage 2 and Key Stage 4 on an annual basis. This is one of the responsibilities of the governing body, which must also publish online a *school profile, which is designed for schools to communicate with parents about the school's progress, priorities, and performance as measured against its targets. This is in place of the annual report to parents, which was discontinued following the *Education Act 2005.

task An activity or piece of written work which is undertaken by the student in order that their achievement or progress may be assessed. An *assignment may be divided into a number of tasks, each carrying a stated number of marks and each of which the student is required to complete in order that their overall performance or *competence may be measured.

The word is also used in the term *Standard Task (originally Standard Assessment Task), which is used to describe *national curriculum *assessments of pupil attainment.

taught time In the context of schools, taught time represents the number of hours which pupils spend in lessons. A report produced by *Ofsted in 1994, with the eponymous title *Taught Time*, suggested that there was insufficient evidence of a correlation between levels of pupil achievement and length of teaching time to support arguments for an increase in the recommended minimum taught time in schools. It may be taken, however, to support the argument that the quality of learning is not solely dependent on the quantity of teaching. In *further and *higher education, taught time refers to the number of hours of active teacher contact, as opposed to hours of structured or supervised independent study, such as that undertaken in project work or for research. Thus, a *module at *master's level, for example, might be designated as involving the student in 120 hours of study, 30 of which are taught time.

Taunton Report (1868) Although distant in terms of time, the Taunton Report remains significant today in that it throws light on the origins of a peculiarly English educational characteristic, which some would claim persists in various guises: the ranking of educational needs according to *social class. The Report, produced as a result of the Taunton Commission into education, claimed that there were three grades of parents. In the 'first' grade were those who wished their children to receive schooling up to and beyond the age of 18, and who had 'no wish to displace the classics from their present position in the forefront of English education'. Significantly, such parents were considered unwilling for their children to receive an education aimed at preparing them for work. The 'second grade' of parents, who wished their children to be educated to the age of 16, were thought to approve of a curriculum which included not only Latin, but also 'a thorough knowledge of those subjects which can be turned to practical use in business'. This would include little that we would now term *vocational, but rather English, mathematics, natural science, and perhaps a modern language. The 'third grade' of parents, whose children might be educated to the age of 14, were considered to belong to 'a class distinctly lower in the scale', and to desire an education for their children which included no classics but only reading, writing, and arithmetic. This uncritical grading of educational provision according to social status seems shocking to us today; but two of its underlying assumptions—that curriculum subjects acquire increasing status the further removed they are from the world of work, and that prestige is attached to, and conclusions about social status drawn from, a school education to the age of 18—can still be seen as integral to common-sense assumptions about education and training a century and a half later. *See also* PARITY OF ESTEEM.

taxonomy The practice of classification, particularly in biology, where organisms are grouped according to similarities of structure or genes. In more general educational terms it most commonly refers to the classification of different orders of learning *objectives created in the 1950s by Benjamin Bloom (1913–99). *See also* BLOOM'S TAXONOMY.

Taylor Report (1977) Published as a result of the Taylor Inquiry set up in 1975, the Report recommended a greater involvement by *governors in curriculum issues within English and Welsh primary and secondary schools. It further suggested that members of governing bodies should be drawn in equal numbers from parents, representatives of both the *local authority and the local community, and *teachers. These recommendations can be seen as a step towards establishing the composition and active involvement of governing bodies as they exist today.

teacher Although most usually referring to one who teaches in a school, the title of 'teacher' also applies in a wider context to include professionals in other educational institutions, as well as those working outside such institutions who nevertheless have a *pedagogical role, such as giving instruction in the playing of a musical instrument. 'Teacher', therefore, may be used in both a specific (referring to a profession) and a more general (referring to an activity) sense. There is a growing tendency to refer to professionals teaching in *further education, too, as 'teachers'—for example, in *White Papers and in the professional standards for the sector—rather than as 'lecturers', by which title they were previously known; and the same trend is noticeable, although to a lesser extent, in the context of *higher education. This development may reflect a growing recognition both that effective teaching may involve more than the ability to deliver a lecture, and that educational professionals in universities and colleges are usually required to demonstrate a wider range of teaching skills than the term 'lecturer', when taken literally, would suggest. Thus, 'teacher' may be taken to cover a range of more specific terms which, as well as 'lecturer', include 'trainer', 'instructor', and 'tutor'.

Although, like most other professions, teaching requires a lengthy period of training and adherence to a professional code of conduct, many would argue that teachers are not normally accorded parity of status with other professions, such as the law and medicine. During the 1980s they were for a time subjected to what Stephen Ball (1990) refers to as a 'discourse of derision' when they appeared to be held culpable both by the popular press and in White Paper rhetoric for a number of national ills, including the high proportion of unskilled and unqualified school-leavers, an under-skilled workforce, and high levels of national unemployment. Nevertheless, well-qualified and highly motivated individuals continue to enter the profession in large numbers, most acknowledging that it provides them with an opportunity to bring about positive change in learners' lives. *See also* NEWLY QUALIFIED TEACHER; QUALIFIED TEACHER STATUS.

t

Further Reading: S. Ball *Politics and Policy Making in Education* (Routledge, 1990).

teacher assessment levels The formal *assessment of a pupil's performance made by the *teacher at the end of each *key stage in most *national curriculum subjects is expressed in terms of the level at which the pupil is currently working. Assessment is made against eight levels of attainment. Parents are informed of the level at which their child is working during Key Stages 1–3 through the child's school *report. At Key Stage 1 the pupil's level is based on the teacher's assessment. At Key Stages 2 and 3 the level will be based on the pupil's performance in national tests as well as on the teacher's assessment.

SEE WEB LINKS

- This page explains how teacher assessment operates, using the example of Key Stage 1.

teachers' conditions of service Conditions of service for schoolteachers are set out in an annual document by the *Secretary of State responsible for schools. This is known as the *School Teachers' Pay and Conditions Document*, and specifies the annual number of working hours (including teaching and other duties) for the individual teacher. In response to the rising number of administrative tasks which teachers were expected to undertake, a number of amendments to their conditions of service were introduced in 2004 in order to reallocate some non-teaching administrative duties to clerical or support staff within the school, and to allow guaranteed preparation and planning time to *primary school teachers.

teachers' pay *See* PAY, TEACHERS'.

teachers.tv A free digital television channel, launched in 2005, to provide teachers and other education professionals with relevant programmes which support their *continuing professional development. There is also an associated web site which provides details of current programming.

SEE WEB LINKS

- Programme details and related resources.

teachers' unions Organized national bodies formed to promote and protect teachers' interests and to negotiate the pay and working conditions of members. Most teachers' unions are sector-specific, the *National Union of Teachers and the *National Association of Schoolmasters Union of Women Teachers being two of the largest unions for schoolteachers in England and Wales, and the *University and College Union the largest for teachers in *colleges and *universities. Other major unions include the *Professional Association of Teachers, and, in Scotland, the *Educational Institute of Scotland. Separate unions exist for educational professionals who work in a management role. These include the *National Association of Head Teachers and the *Secondary Heads Association.

teacher training *See* QUALIFIED TEACHER STATUS.

Teacher Training Agency (TTA) *See* TRAINING AND DEVELOPMENT AGENCY FOR SCHOOLS.

teacher training skills tests Mandatory tests in *literacy, *numeracy, and *information communication technology undertaken by all trainee teachers intending to teach in the *primary or secondary sectors of education. They are designed to ensure that all teachers gaining *qualified teacher status (QTS) possess an appropriate level of skill in these three key areas. The introduction of the tests was proposed in the 2000 *Green Paper *Teachers: Meeting the Challenge of Change*, and the tests were first implemented during the academic year 2001/2. The tests are taken and assessed electronically, and all trainee teachers must successfully complete all three before they can be awarded QTS. The equivalent for teachers' training for the *further education sector are the *minimum core tests. There is currently no national key skills assessment required of teachers entering the *higher education sector.

teaching and learning responsibility (TLR) Responsibility which schools can allocate to individual teachers for specific issues relating to teaching and learning, which carry additional salary, calculated as **TLR points**. They were introduced in January 2006, and are available in two bandings. TLR1, the higher band, carries a higher maximum and minimum salary than TLR2. There can be different levels of TLR payment within one band, and the value of payments within the set minimum and maximum for each band is a matter for individual schools' discretion, so long as there is a £1 500 differential between each level of payment within the two. The governing body, in consultation with staff, make the decision about how many TLRs will be offered within the school, which bands they will be, and their value in terms of additional salary. TLR points are only awarded to teachers who have significant levels of responsibilities which are not part of every teacher's workload. For example, a teacher who has taken on the role of whole-school *literacy coordinator would fall into this category. One of the key criteria for awarding TLR points is that the teacher's additional duties must be focused on teaching and learning (rather than, for example, administration or management), and must involve the leadership or development of a curriculum area, or of pupil development across the curriculum. To be awarded TLR points in the higher band, a teacher must also have line management responsibility for a significant number of other staff. The TLR replaced the previous system of Management Allowances used in schools. *See also* PAY, TEACHERS'.

teaching assistant (TA) Sometimes, but decreasingly, referred to as 'classroom assistant', a TA is an adult employed to assist a qualified teacher in the classroom. They may have a general role in the classroom or may be assigned to assist a particular student who has a *statement of special needs. The responsibilities of a teaching assistant can vary greatly. Typical activities might include preparing resources for lessons, putting up displays, administrative tasks such as photocopying or marking, and working with individual children.

teaching practice (TP) Trainee teachers receiving their initial teacher education for the *primary, secondary, or *further education sectors are required to undertake a period of practical experience in a *school (which is known as **school based training**) or *college appropriate to the sector in which they plan to teach. During this they are expected to observe the teaching and other professional practices of qualified and experienced teachers, and to carry out teaching themselves, under supervision, for gradually increased periods of time. This allows them to apply and reflect upon the theoretical knowledge and understanding which they have gained during their training in college or *university. Their performance in their teaching practice *placement is assessed by their college or university tutor and by a designated member of staff in the placement school or college, who may also be the trainee teacher's *mentor. In order to be considered for *qualified teacher status, the trainee teacher must reach the required standard of attainment in their teaching practice as well as in their theoretical work.

teaching style Just as pupils and students can be said to have differing *learning styles, so teachers will vary in the style of teaching with which they are most comfortable. For example, where one teacher possesses the skills best suited to deliver a lecture to a large group of learners, another may feel that their strength lies in working at an individual level with small groups of learners, using such techniques as question and answer. Whatever the individual teacher's preferred teaching style, however, they are expected, as professionals, to develop and use a wide range of approaches and styles which are appropriate both to the needs of their learners and to the nature and level of their subject. Nevertheless, most teachers will admit to having a preferred style of teaching with which they feel at their most confident. *See also* METHOD.

teaching to the test Both teachers and parents have expressed concerns that the growing pressures exerted by national regimes of testing and examinations are leading teachers to focus too narrowly on the knowledge necessary to enable learners to pass the test, rather than developing in them an understanding of the subject and its context within the wider field of knowledge. Teaching in this way has become known as 'teaching to the test'. Many educationalists and teachers claim that such an instrumental approach stifles enquiry and is detrimental to the education process.

SEE WEB LINKS

- A report on research into the effects of teaching to the test.

team teaching A strategy which involves two or more teachers working simultaneously with the same group of learners. This might be employed for practical reasons in particularly large classes when the *pupil–teacher ratio justifies the deployment of more than one teacher; or on educational grounds where the subject expertise of more than one teacher is necessary for the students' learning of a specific topic. Team teaching is also useful for conducting peer evaluations, since it allows teachers an opportunity to provide reciprocal feedback on one another's performance.

Technical and Vocational Education Initiative (TVEI) An initiative set up in 1983 and aimed at supporting school and college provision of technical and *pre-vocational courses for 14–18-year-old pupils. Funded by the Department of Employment (DoE), and operating through locally organized advisory teams, TVEI also promoted **core skills**, including those in communication, numeracy, and information technology, which were the forerunners to today's *key skills. Although the TVEI was formally linked to the *Manpower Services Commission and later the *Training and Enterprise Council through their common connection with the DoE, local TVEI teams often worked very closely with their *local authority advisory service for schools. In many areas they extended their remit to provide training and policy advice on equal opportunities issues. Their funding began to be withdrawn from 1991, which brought the initiative to a gradual end.

Technological Baccalaureate *See baccalauréat.*

technology 1. Educational technology encompasses the strategies and techniques relating to the learning process, as well as the equipment and resources used to support it.

2. A *national curriculum subject introduced in 1989 and combining the subject areas of craft, design, and technology, art, business studies, home economics, and information communication technology. It has now become known as **Design and Technology**.

term Traditionally there are three terms in the academic year, during which pupils or students are expected to attend for classes. These are usually referred to as Autumn, Winter, and Summer terms, although some universities use alternative, traditional names, such as *Michaelmas Term for the Autumn Term. The academic year begins at the commencement of the Autumn Term and ends at the close of the Summer Term, with breaks at Christmas, Easter, and July–August. School terms are usually longer than college or university terms, and are punctuated by *half-term breaks, usually of a week's duration round about the term's mid-point. In 2001 the Independent Commission on the Organization of the School Year recommended that schools should adopt a six-term year, incorporating a shorter summer break. This was to be in place by 2005, but is proving contentious and difficult to implement in many *local authority areas. Those who support the idea of reorganizing school terms in this way suggest that it would have advantages for the timing and assessment of public examinations such as the *General Certificate of Secondary Education and *General Certificate of Education *Advanced Level.

terminal examination Also known colloquially as an **end exam**, the terminal examination is one which takes place on completion of the course of study. Examples include *examinations for the award of a *degree at the end of the period of *undergraduate studies; and the external testing in *General Certificate of Secondary Education subjects which takes place at the end of *Key Stage 4. A terminal examination is a means of carrying out a *summative assessment, rather than an ongoing *formative evaluation of the candidate's performance.

terminate To end formally a student's enrolment on a course at college or university, either because they have not completed the required work, or because they have failed to reach the required standard. At many colleges of further or higher education, student work which fails to meet the necessary criteria will be 'referred' back to the student for a second attempt, although in such cases it is normal to award no more than the minimum pass mark if the student's resubmission is successful. The student may be 'failed and terminated' if their work still fails to meet the grade. Despite its associations, termination in this context is not so quite so sinister a matter as the word might suggest.

tertiary college An institution which provides both a general sixth form *curriculum and *vocational *further education for students aged 16–19. The name derives from the fact that such colleges provide the third stage of education, after *primary and secondary. They are distinct from general further education *colleges in that they cater for a specific age group and offer a less extensive and varied curriculum.

testing The process of assessing and measuring a learner's attainment in a task, a lesson, a subject, or a *programme of study. In schools it is a term most commonly associated with the national testing which takes place at the end of each *key stage. The trend towards extensive national testing, while applauded by some educators as contributing to a raising of achievement, is viewed less favourably by others who consider it imposes a pressure on pupils and teachers alike, which is detrimental to the learning process and the purposes of education. *See also* STANDARD TASKS.

Te Whaariki The New Zealand Ministry of Education early childhood curriculum policy statement, published in 1996. It is a framework for providing children's early learning and development within a sociocultural context. It emphasizes the learning partnership between teachers, parents, families, and children, and is the bicultural, incorporating Maori as well as Western cultural values. It represents a national curriculum for the early childhood sector in New Zealand, and is intended to encourage the aspirations of children as competent, confident learners and communicators who know that they can make a valued contribution to society. Its philosophy closely reflects that which underpins the development of *Reggio Emilia schooling, and it has been influential in the design of the UK *Birth to Three Matters framework.

Its four broad principles of empowerment, holistic development, family and community, and relationships are interwoven; hence Te Whaariki: a Maori word meaning a woven mat for all to stand on. Within those principles there are five strands: well-being, belonging, contribution, communication, and exploration. The principles and strands are assessed through narrative observations, or learning stories, of children's activities and dispositions, with additional evidence of photographic records to highlight learning processes.

This curriculum framework is closely aligned to the experiential and philosophical ideas of *Rousseau, *Dewey, *Isaacs, *Vygotsky, and *Malaguzzi, and has therefore attracted international interest among *early years practitioners.

Further Reading: Ministry of Education *Te Whaariki: He Whaariki Matauranga mo nga Moi Aoteroa. Early Childhood Education* (Learning Media, 1996).

SEE WEB LINKS

- This presents the theoretical origins of the Te Whaariki curriculum in New Zealand. A.W.

thesis 1. A lengthy piece of academic writing presenting an argument based on research, and presented for *assessment towards an academic award at *postgraduate level, such as a *master's degree or a *doctorate. A thesis at this level is usually expected to contribute something new to existing knowledge within its field.

2. An original idea or contribution to knowledge, for which a carefully argued case is presented, usually, but not always, in the form of sense 1 above.

Thus, the term may refer to the written document or to the argument contained within the text. *See also* DISSERTATION.

thinking skills Incorporated into the teaching of *national curriculum subjects, particularly in *primary schools (*Key Stages 1 and 2), the development of thinking skills in young pupils is thought to improve the quality of their learning and raise their standard of attainment in school-based tests. The term itself covers a range of different approaches, exercises, and activities, the common elements of which usually include problem-solving and classroom discussion. Most approaches stress the importance of language and articulation, and some use specific teaching strategies to develop pupils' *cognitive skills. In the UK in the 1980s and 1990s the **Cognitive Acceleration** through Science Education project provided evidence to suggest that the development of thinking skills improved Key Stage 3 pupils' attainment in science; and this project has now been extended into other national curriculum subject areas.

Of all the names associated with the development of thinking skills, it is perhaps that of Edward de Bono (b. 1933)—and his concept of *lateral thinking as a tool for problem-solving—which is most familiar in the UK. Other approaches include that of the American philosopher Matthew Lipman (b. 1922), who founded the Institute for the Advancement of Philosophy for Children in New Jersey. His belief that young pupils were generally encouraged to accept facts and opinions from teachers without questioning these for themselves led him to develop an approach to the teaching of thinking skills which involves classes of pupils and their teachers reading specially constructed stories, or 'novels', together and exploring the questions or anomalies which these give rise to through guided discussions. The questions addressed arise from the children's curiosity rather than from any pre-planned agenda from the teacher. This approach to thinking skills involves children in exploratory thinking as well as discussion with their teacher and their peers. It is known as **philosophy for children**.

Another key name in the development of thinking skills is that of Reuven Feuerstein (b. 1921), who worked on the cognitive assessment of young immigrants entering Israel at the end of the Second World War. His project was to improve young learners' performance in cognitive tests. This led to the development of a programme of activities which could be used to improve children's learning process, providing appropriate activities to address each different area of difficulty and to enrich learning. These activities were known as 'instruments'; and thus Feuerstein's approach became known as the **instrumental enrichment** programme.

Lateral thinking, cognitive acceleration, philosophy for children, and instrumental enrichment are only some of the approaches which may inform the teaching of thinking skills in schools.

Further Reading: C. McGuinness *From Thinking Skills to Thinking Classrooms: A Review and Evaluation of Approaches for Developing Pupils' Thinking* (DfEE, 1999); M. Lipman *Thinking in Education* (Cambridge University Press, 1991).

threshold *See* PERFORMANCE-RELATED PAY.

tiering The divisions which apply to the formal assessment of *General Certificate of Secondary Education subjects, and which allow for the provision of *differentiated tasks. Its purpose is to enable candidates to achieve at a level appropriate to their ability. The lower tier covers grades C–G, and the higher-tier grades A*–D, allowing an overlap in grades C–D. Candidates are entered for one or other tier, according to their expected *attainment *level.

timetable The formal organization of teachers' and learners' time, and the allocation and coordination of timings, accommodation, and other resources within an educational institution. The timetable provides information about who should be where, and at what time. Individual learners and teachers each have their own timetable showing how their formal teaching or learning time will be spent. These may cover a day, a week, a *term, a year, or a programme covering several years. The institutional timetable is a collation and summary of all this information. In some organizations or departments a specific member of staff has responsibility for drawing up and coordinating timetables, although the process is more usually carried out now electronically through the use of specialized software. This task is known as 'timetabling'.

Tomlinson Report (1996) The Tomlinson Report *Inclusive Learning* played a key role in the *post-compulsory sector's *widening participation agenda. Where the *Kennedy Report of 1997 examined ways of improving learning opportunities for all, the Tomlinson Report explored widening participation specifically for learners with *learning difficulties or disabilities. Tomlinson found that students with *special educational needs were underachieving in the post-compulsory sector; were unable to access the wider curriculum; and were, for the most part, lacking in confidence, possibly because of their previous school experience of education and learning. The Report found that historically learners with learning difficulties or disabilities were excluded from mainstream opportunities in the post-compulsory sector. It also found that this form of exclusion affected the culture of learning providers such as *further education colleges.

Tomlinson recommended that the responsibility should be on the educational institution to empathize and respond to the individual, and to address the needs of that individual learner. Among the Report's recommendations was a requirement that institutions should publish their own disability statements, with information regarding entry and openness of access, which should operate regardless of age, gender, ethnicity, or disability. The Report envisaged that such a focus on inclusive learning would improve the quality of learner experience for students with difficulties or disabilities, and, indeed, change the culture of educational establishments by focusing on planning with and supporting the needs of individuals. V.C., K.A.

Tomlinson Report (2004) Entitled *14–19 Curriculum and Qualification Reform: Final Report of the Working Group on 14–19 Reform* (Department for Education and Skills, 2004), the Report of the group led by Sir Mike Tomlinson was instrumental in the introduction of the *14–19 Diploma. It suggested that such a diploma should be introduced over a ten-year period from 2005 and should eventually replace all existing public examinations at *National Qualifications Framework levels 2 and 3, including the *General Certificate of Secondary Education, *General Certificate of Education *Advanced Levels, and equivalent vocational qualifications. Other radical reforms recommended in the Report included the replacement of all coursework by one extended **project** undertaken by each pupil in *Key Stage 4, and a substantial reduction in the number of examinations which pupils are required to take. It was also influential in the introduction of the *personalized curriculum, suggesting that pupils should be encouraged to progress at their own rate rather than be constrained to progress in cohorts organized according to age group.

topic An integrated, thematic approach to learning, implemented mainly in *primary schools, which uses a particular focus such as 'water' or 'Romans' through which to develop pupils' knowledge and understanding of required *national curriculum subjects such as mathematics and English, as well as to encourage their creative and imaginative skills.

trainee Someone undergoing *training. It has come to be used in preference to 'student' for learners on *vocational programmes, and is part of the vocabulary of *National Vocational Qualifications. It is also applied by government agencies such as the *Training and Development Agency to student teachers. Its use raises the questions of how we define the difference between a student and a trainee and of whether there is a value judgement—for example, about status—implicit within the distinction between provision which is described as 'education' and that which is described as 'training'.

training Usually applied to *vocational learning or learning of a practical rather than a theoretical nature. There are, however, anomalies in this regard, since it is usual to refer to 'trainee teachers' and 'trainee doctors', contexts in which a substantial body of theoretical learning is involved as well as practical skills. Perhaps the broadest distinction to be made between education and training is that the latter is instrumental in preparing the learner for a specific task, job, or profession, while education has a more general, developmental purpose as envisaged in the concept of *liberal education. *See also* TRAINEE.

Training and Development Agency for Schools (TDA) An executive, non-departmental public body of the *Department for Children, Schools, and Families responsible for building and supporting a well-trained and qualified workforce of teachers and school support staff. It was developed from the Teacher Training Agency, and took over the work of that body in September 2005 as a result of the *Education Act 2005, but with an extended remit, which included the whole of the school workforce, from catering staff and caretakers to curriculum heads. Its board is appointed by the *Secretary of State for Children, Schools, and Families. Its role includes encouraging recruitment of able and committed teachers; improving and monitoring the standard of all routes into the teaching profession, including *initial teacher training programmes and postgraduate qualifications in teaching; and ensuring schools are kept informed and well supported on issues of *continuing professional development for teachers.

SEE WEB LINKS

- Provides links to a full range of TDA plans, policies, and reports.

Training and Enterprise Council (TEC) In 1991 local TECs took over the work of the *Manpower Services Commission in administering the government budget for *vocational training at a local level, with the aim of giving all school-leavers at 16 the opportunity for vocational education and training. Representatives of local businesses and the *local authority made up the majority on the TEC's executive board, with minimal representation of those involved in local educational provision. In Scotland the equivalent organization was known as the **Local Enterprise Company (LEC)**. TECs were replaced in 2001 by local *Learning and Skills Councils, although many of the same personnel were retained.

training college *See* COLLEGE OF EDUCATION.

Training for Work (TfW) Run by Scottish Enterprise, TfW provides training support for people in Scotland who are unemployed or are actively looking for work. The programme is targeted at adults aged 25 and over. S.M.

training school A secondary school which, in partnership with a local *university or other *higher education institution involved in teacher training, develops strategies for *initial teacher training and trains their staff to develop *mentoring skills with which to support trainee teachers who undertake training within the school. In return for taking on this role, schools are offered additional funding. The scheme was recommended in the 1998 *Green Paper *Teachers: Meeting the Challenge of Change*, and was introduced in 2000. *See also* TEACHING PRACTICE.

Train to Gain A *Learning and Skills Council funded scheme in the UK, which includes learners who were part of the *employer training pilots. The scheme was introduced in 2006 to help develop a skilled workforce. Impartial skills brokers advise employers on how to access relevant training for their employees, including *literacy and *numeracy development, which will improve the success of their enterprises. Such training is planned to be flexible and responsive to the needs of individual businesses. Some training within the scheme attracts subsidized funding, for example *Skills for Life qualifications; first full qualifications at level 2 on the *National Qualifications Framework, such as *National Vocational Qualifications, BTEC First Diplomas, or five *General Certificate of Secondary Education subjects; *Young Apprenticeships; and some level 3 qualifications. *See also* BUSINESS AND TECHNOLOGY EDUCATION COUNCIL.

SEE WEB LINKS

- Provides further details of how the scheme operates.

Transfer Test A term referring to the *Eleven Plus tests in Northern Ireland which have survived as part of the system of academic selection. These tests continued in practice until autumn 2008. The **Burns Report** of 2001 stated, 'we have been left in no doubt that the eleven-plus transfer tests are socially divisive, damage self-esteem, place unreasonable pressures on pupils, primary teachers, and parents, disrupt teaching and learning at an important stage in the primary curriculum and reinforce inequality of opportunity'. It is interesting to note, however, that results at *General Certificate of Secondary Education and *Advanced Level are significantly better in Northern Ireland than England and Wales, although it has not been proven that these statistics have any causal relationship with the continued practice of *selection.

SEE WEB LINKS

- Gives full text of the Burns Report. J.H.

transition The progression of pupils from one stage or school to another; most notably, from *primary to secondary school. It is recognized that the challenges this presents can prove stressful for many pupils, as it usually involves exchanging their position as an older child in a smaller school for that of a younger child in a much larger one. Moreover, pupils at this stage must often exchange the security of one teacher and one classroom for a system in which they will be taught by several different teachers every day, and expected to move from classroom to classroom in the process. To acknowledge and ease this difficult transition, schools may adopt a number of strategies, such as the provision by secondary schools of 'taster' visits for primary pupils so that they may familiarize themselves with the school they will soon be attending; and visits by secondary teachers to primary schools to introduce themselves to pupils who will shortly be making the transition. One of the arguments used in the *Plowden Report in support of introducing *middle schools was that they would ease the transition by introducing gradual change in the 'middle years' rather than the abrupt transplanting of pupils at 11. Transition applies to any stage of progression, including that from secondary school to *further or *higher education.

tripartite system The division of the secondary sector into three types of school: *grammar schools, technical schools, and modern schools, as suggested in the **Spens Report** (1938). Following the *Education Act 1944 (*Butler Act), *local authorities were permitted to provide a range of secondary schooling. Some opted for the tripartite system, while others established a dual system of grammar and secondary modern schools. Both involved the selection of pupils by ability at 11, which aimed to provide each child with the secondary education best suited to their *abilities and *aptitudes. Within authorities operating a tripartite system these abilities were classified as academic (grammar schools), technical (technical schools), and practical (secondary modern schools). The system was replaced by non-selective, *comprehensive secondary education in most local authority areas during the 1970s following the Education Act 1976. *See also* BIPARTITE SYSTEM.

tripos A course of study leading to an *honours degree at Cambridge University, where the student is required to pass two tripos examinations in order to be awarded their *Bachelor of Arts. The name refers to the three-legged stool on which, in medieval times, graduates sat to deliver a satirical speech at their degree ceremony.

truancy The persistent failure to attend compulsory schooling. Many secondary schools report this as a growing problem, with pupils who truant now being referred to as **school refusers**. Schools are required by law to report on truancy numbers, and to work with local education welfare officers to address problems of attendance with individual pupils and their parents or carers. In *White Paper rhetoric, truancy has been associated with subsequent unemployment and even criminality. On the whole, school refusers are often among the lowest of achievers, particularly in the *key skills of *numeracy and communication; although the causal relationship between truancy and low achievement is not clear-cut, in the sense of whether pupils play truant because they are low achievers or are low achievers because they truant. Parents of persistent truants can be prosecuted and fined or sentenced to a term of imprisonment.

tuition fees *See* FEES.

tutor In schools, *teachers responsible for supporting the work or welfare of a group of pupils may be designated a tutor, as in 'form tutor' and 'year tutor'. In *further and *higher education a tutor is responsible for overseeing the workload of a student or group of students, and for providing support in matters relating to their studies. Trainee teachers on *teaching practice, for example, have a tutor to advise them and to monitor their progress in their *placement. A tutor may also be a subject specialist who guides or advises the student in a specific aspect of their academic discipline, such as supporting students through their *master's degree or *doctoral studies. Like the term 'teacher', 'tutor' cannot be defined by one specific role. Broadly, it could be said that tutoring involves providing support for learning, often for individuals or relatively small groups of learners, while teaching suggests a more actively didactic role. *See also* TUTORIAL.

tutorial A meeting between *tutor and one or more students (sometimes referred to as tutees) which focuses on some aspect of the students' learning or *assessment. They are an integral part of *higher education provision, but are also used in *further education and in some schools. In terms of time and resources, tutorials are considered costly because they normally involve tutors working with relatively small numbers of students. Perhaps for this reason, the inclusion of extensive tutorial support in students' *timetables is becoming increasingly problematic in some higher education departments.

UHI Millennium Institute *See* DISTANCE LEARNING.

underachiever Someone whose *academic performance falls measurably below what might be expected from what is known of their *ability, learning potential, or *intelligence. Reasons for underachievement can include language or cultural difficulties, where the learner's ability to express themselves is hampered by their lack of language skills or lack of familiarity with culturally specific concepts and ideas. Emotional problems or difficulties in the home environment can also be the cause of underachievement, as can lack of motivation or a curriculum which does not challenge or engage.

undergraduate A student on a *higher education course which leads to the award of a first *degree or *bachelor's degree. On achieving their degree—in other words, going through the process of **graduating**—they are referred to as *graduates. Undergraduate can also be used as an adjective to describe the level of study for a first degree, as in the phrase, 'an undergraduate programme'.

Undergraduate Credit and Teacher Associate schemes Joint schemes launched by the Teacher Training Agency in 1992 and taken over by its successor, the *Training and Development Agency, to provide up to 3 000 undergraduate students with the opportunity to gain supervised teaching experience in schools at the same time as studying for their degree. Training on the job was provided variously by or through local authorities, schools, and the undergraduate's own university or college. The experience and training could then be used as credit towards the completion of a teacher training programme if the student subsequently decided to enter the teaching profession.

unit A component or subdivision of a course or *programme of study, which may be taught or assessed as a discrete section of the whole. The term was also used in a very specific sense from 1993 to describe the component parts of a *General National Vocational Qualification (GNVQ), which were separately assessed and could be accumulated over time in order to gain the full GNVQ award. In the process of tailoring the design of the GNVQ and the *modular *Advanced Level (A level) to become more compatible for the implementation of *Curriculum 2000, the term 'unit' was gradually dropped in favour of 'module', so that the *Vocational A level, which succeeded the GNVQ, was subdivided into modules rather than units. The term is still in use in the wider context of educational and training programmes, however, as in the phrases 'unit of study' and 'unit of assessment'.

Universities and Colleges Admissions Service (UCAS) The organization which processes candidates' applications for a place at a *university or other *higher education institution to study for a first *degree, a university *diploma, or a *Higher National Diploma. It was formed in 1992 as a consequence of the merger between the Universities Central Council on Admissions (UCCA) and the Polytechnics Central Admissions Systems (PCAS), which followed as a result of the *Further and Higher Education Act 1992, which granted polytechnics university status. UCAS is also responsible for the work of the *Graduate Teacher Training Registry. Applicants to higher education who have yet to sit their *Advanced Levels (A levels) will normally be offered a place which is conditional on their achieving the required number of A level points. Those whose results fail to gain them their conditional place, or those who have waited until after their results to make their application, may go through the UCAS **clearing** process, which aims to match suitable applicants to places which remain unfilled.

SEE WEB LINKS

- An explanation of how the clearing system works.

university An institution of *higher education with the authority to confer degrees and which has been granted university status. Since the *Further and Higher Education Act 1992, which gave university status to polytechnics, most major towns and cities can boast a university, and sometimes more than one. The proliferation of universities has catered for the steep rise in the percentage of young people going on to higher education, for which the current government target is 50 per cent. Until relatively recently, however, a university education was accessible to the very few. The first universities to be established in England were Oxford and Cambridge, which were both founded in the 13th century. In Scotland, St Andrews, Aberdeen, and Glasgow were the earliest, dating back to the 15th century; Edinburgh was established in 1582. It was not until the 19th century that university provision began to be extended, largely funded by private benefactors, in some of the major cities. Following the Second World War, there was a very rapid expansion, including the founding of the universities of York, Warwick, and Lancaster in the 1960s. These universities were known as 'new universities' to distinguish them from the older institutions such as Oxford, Cambridge, Glasgow, and Durham, and the *red-brick universities founded at the turn of the century. With the abolition of the *binary system in 1992, the total number of universities again rose considerably. In England the nominal head of a university is known as the chancellor, and is normally a public figure. The executive head is usually known as the vice-chancellor, who, together with the board of governors, is ultimately responsible for the operation of the university as a corporate business.

University and College Union (UCU) The union for professionals in the *post-compulsory education sectors of *further and *higher education, including managers, administrators, researchers, and librarians as well as teaching staff. Established in 2006 by the amalgamation of the *National Association of Teachers in Further and Higher Education (NATFHE) and the *Association of University Teachers (AUT), it is currently the largest union of its kind worldwide.

SEE WEB LINKS

- A detailed history of NATFHE and the AUT and their eventual amalgamation as UCU.

university college A college which provides *higher education but which does not have a charter to confer *degrees. Such colleges operate in partnership with a university or other college of higher education, and it is from the partner institution that the university college's *graduates gain their degree.

university entrance Still the most usual route for progression to *undergraduate studies at *university are *General Certificate of Education *Advanced Levels (A levels). The minimum requirement is normally two A level passes, but most universities, through their faculties or departments, stipulate a specific minimum number of points which must be gained to secure a place, which are calculated on the basis of the A level grades achieved. The number of points required will differ from subject to subject, depending upon the demand for places. Places for which there is a high level of competition, such as medicine, will normally require a higher point score than those which consistently under-recruit. As well as the A level route, most universities accept alternative entry qualifications for adult students, such as the *Access to Higher Education qualification. The Open University, as its name suggests, accepts students with no formal entry qualifications. *See also* ACCESS COURSE.

SEE WEB LINKS

- Gives point scores for a range of national qualifications, including A levels.

University for Industry (UfI) Established in 1998 and in operation since 1999, the UfI offers *e-learning in *basic skills, *information technology, *vocationally specific skills training for the workforce, and skills in the management of business. By 2007 almost a quarter of a million businesses had accessed the UfI for skills training, which is delivered through *Learndirect. It is a virtual university, in the sense that it has no *campus but communicates with clients and learners through the telephone and online, as well as having local learning centres operating in publicly accessible places such as libraries and shopping malls. It works in partnership with other universities, with private training providers, and with colleges for the delivery and *validation of programmes.

SEE WEB LINKS

- Access to detailed lists of the UfI's objectives.

University of the Third Age (U3A) In the UK, U3A is a self-help *adult education organization consisting of local groups nationwide, each called a U3A, which operate as learning cooperatives. Aimed at and organized by those who have reached 'the third age'—in other words, who have retired from paid employment—U3As draw upon their own membership as a learning resource in order to learn in fields of their choice. The role of learner is more important than the role of 'teacher', which often revolves or is shared among the group to take account of individuals' experience, expertise, and gathered wisdom. There is no externally set syllabus. Currently, over 300 areas of interest are available and members attend interest groups in fields as disparate as computing, philosophy, and walking. Fine distinctions are not made between educational and recreation activities; it is social learning and companionship which are emphasized. There are no admission requirements and no assessments are involved nor awards conferred. U3A has been in existence in the UK since 1982.

Each local group is an operationally independent charity run on a voluntary basis with a committee functioning as trustees. U3As have representation on the National Executive Committee via their regional representative. The national umbrella organization, the **Third Age Trust (TAT)**, provides not only services such as a learning resource centre, other learning support including a handbook for interest group leaders, and indemnity insurance, but also enriching activities such as summer schools and online courses. U3A is an international movement founded in Toulouse, where, in 1972, the city's university provided a successful summer school for retired people which prefaced the first Université du Troisième Âge. The French model of the U3A is quite different from that operated in the UK. There, courses are provided by learned institutions for students. Internationally five models of U3A have been identified, all of which are dedicated to the ideal of providing non-award-bearing learning opportunities for those in the third age of life. The international body linking U3As, the International Association of Universities of the Third Age, is based in Paris and promotes understanding and the maintenance and development of third age learning. *See also* LATER LIFE LEARNING.

upper school This term usually refers to Years 12 and 13 in a secondary school, to distinguish older pupils from those in compulsory education in *Key Stages 3 and 4, which may be referred to as 'lower school'. This meaning probably originates from a similar usage in traditional public, fee-paying schools.

vacation Also referred to as school holidays, these are the periods of time between *terms when a school, college, or university does not hold full-time classes. Traditionally the three main vacations are at Christmas, Easter, and Summer. Colleges and universities do not 'close' during periods of vacation (except for statutory bank holidays), and teaching staff are not automatically entitled to take leave during these breaks in teaching although they constitute a vacation for full-time students. In schools, teachers may be required to attend during vacations for meetings and *continuing professional development events. *See also* TERM.

validation The process by which degrees and other awards are approved by *universities or other *awarding bodies, both for programmes of study within the awarding institution itself, where this is appropriate, and for those taught in partner institutions, such as *colleges of further education, where the qualification awarded is in the university's or the awarding body's name. In order to be validated, such programmes and awards must go through a formal validation procedure, the purpose of which is to ensure that all aspects of quality assurance are in place with regard to the content, teaching, administration, resourcing, and assessment of the programme. To this end, a **validation document** is usually prepared, explaining how all these aspects will be covered. In the case of university-validated awards, this is submitted to a **validation panel** made up of relevant university staff and including one or more external members from other universities or academic bodies. The decision-making process which ensues is known as the **validation event**. If the programme being considered for validation is to be delivered by an institution other than the awarding body, for example in a local college, an inspection of the site and its facilities may form part of the validation process.

validity *See* ASSESSMENT.

value added The difference a *school, *college, or *university has made in the education of its learners compared to the provision of an equivalent institution. Recognition of value added is an alternative—and some would argue fairer—method of making comparisons between the performance of institutions in the same sector than comparing data such as *examination results or the scores for *national curriculum tests, since it takes into account the starting point of learners and the actual progress made, or, as it is sometimes expressed, 'the distance travelled', rather than simply the level of achievement attained. Thus, for example, schools which recruit less able or less advantaged pupils can be recognized for their achievement, if value added is taken into consideration, in a way which they would not be in a simple quantitative comparison of scores with a *selective school recruiting only pupils of high ability.

verification The process carried out by an *awarding body in order to ensure that the processes of *assessment are being carried out in accordance with the body's regulations and requirements. This normally includes scrutinizing the procedures for assessment, *moderation, *second marking, and the recording of assessment decisions. It is involved not with checking the assessment decisions, but rather the procedures by which they are arrived at. Those appointed to carry out this role on behalf of the awarding body are known as **external verifiers**. In some cases there may be a process of internal verification prior to the external verifier's visit. This will be carried out by a member of the teaching team, who, for the purpose of this role, is known as the **internal verifier**. The role of the verifier is distinct from that of examiner or moderator, since it focuses on processes rather than outcomes.

verifier *See* VERIFICATION.

vertical grouping The grouping of children of various ages, usually in primary education, for the purposes of, for example, project work. This is also known as 'family grouping'. Where vertical grouping is a standard arrangement, the pupil will remain with the same teacher throughout their time at the school, rather than moving 'up' a class at the beginning of each year.

vice-chancellor *See* UNIVERSITY.

virement The practice of transferring funds from one internal budget to another. The internal financial structure and organization of an educational institution is often divided into departments or functions, each with their own budget and accounts. Under some circumstances, money may be **vired** from one to another.

virtual learning environment (VLE) A computer software tool which enables teachers to permit controlled access to the materials, processes, and administrative systems that support their programmes, to track students' progress on them, and to develop communications networks with (and among) students, fellow teachers, and support specialists for feedback and guidance. It is a means by which *e-learning may be delivered and supported. Institutions may build their own platforms for virtual courses, or engage commercial companies to develop appropriate systems. All learners' details would then be entered onto a central database, from which tutors would enrol chosen students onto specific courses. One of the chief benefits of a VLE is that students can study using any computer with Internet access, allowing online or *blended learning. A virtual learning environment can also be a subsystem of a *managed learning environment. *See also* INFORMATION AND LEARNING TECHNOLOGY.

V.C., K.A.

vision Closely linked to, or embodied in, the *mission statement, particularly of *colleges and universities, and embodying a summary of the institution's purpose and direction, 'vision' is one of many examples of business language usage which have become part of the vocabulary of education. Senge (1990) describes vision as an articulation of the envisioned future which the institution wishes to create, while Barrett (1998) suggests it is a statement of how the institution will achieve fulfilment of purpose. Both of these theorists are writing in the context of the management of large business organizations. In colleges and universities the organizational vision is decided by those with executive power.

Further Reading: R. Barrett *Liberating the Corporate Soul* (Butterworth Heinemann, 1998) and P. Senge *The Fifth Discipline* (Random House, 1990) both provide further discussion of corporate vision relevant in the context of educational institutions.

viva The abbreviated and more popularly used form of **viva voce**, an *oral examination used as a matter of course in the assessment process for higher degrees, notably the Doctor of Philosophy (Ph.D. or D.Phil.) and Master of Philosophy (M.Phil.), but also for other examinations, particularly where the candidate's result is *borderline. A panel for the Ph.D. viva will consist of a minimum of two examiners who are recognized experts in the candidate's field. At least one of them will be appointed from outside the university or higher education institution where the candidate is registered. He or she is known as the **external examiner**. In addition, at least one will be appointed from inside the institution, and is known as the **internal examiner**. The candidate is required to defend his or her thesis in the face of questions from the examiners. Some institutions now also appoint an internal member of staff as chair in order to ensure that the viva is conducted in accordance with institutional regulations. *See also* DOCTORATE.

vocational Directly related to employment, usually in a specified sector or trade. Education is referred to as vocational if it involves skills training or if it prepares the learner to enter directly into skilled or semi-skilled employment. This is to distinguish it from *academic or general education, such as *Advanced Level and *General Certificate of Secondary Education; and from **general vocational education**, of the type offered by the *General National Vocational Qualification in the 1990s, which is designed to equip learners with a transferable set of skills necessary for entering the world of work across a broad sector of employment. Therefore, we can broadly map two kinds of education: education for the development of the individual, which is known as general, *liberal, or academic, and education for work, now termed vocational or skills training. Research suggests that vocational qualifications are, on the whole, still accorded rather less esteem than general, academic ones, despite the introduction of equivalence levels, as set out in the *National Qualifications Framework. The distinction between vocational and academic education is sometimes referred to as the **vocational–academic divide**, to denote the difference in status between the two. The reasons for this lack of parity are largely historical.

In the 18th and early 19th centuries, education beyond a very basic level was accessed by an elite which was mostly male, and its purpose was to produce the cultured gentleman. With the growth of industries there came the recognition that a range of knowledge beyond the gentleman's education in Latin and Greek would be essential to the country's industrial progress, but it was considered that an education of this sort was only suitable for those who must take paid employment. As a consequence, what was referred to as 'useful' knowledge became associated with trade and the artisan class. Thus, a classical education, also referred to as a liberal education in the sense of broad and life-enhancing, remained associated with an elite; while, in contrast, a scientific or vocational education was considered to be narrower in purpose, equipping the learner only with the skills to earn their living. Despite successive governments' policy statements from the 1980s to the present day stressing the need for *parity of esteem between the two, the vocational–academic divide is still apparent, for example in the disparity of pay and status between teachers in the further education sector and those in schools. A further distinction related to the divide is that between 'training' and 'education', with 'training' more usually associated with the vocational curriculum. Definitions of the two, as well as the contexts in which they are used, tend to reinforce the view that training is concerned with a lower order of skills and knowledge. An extreme example would be that we speak of 'animal training' rather than 'animal education'. However, an education and training which leads to professional qualifications in medicine, law, and the Church, while still spoken of as 'vocational' (in the sense that those entering these professions are said to have a vocation for them), is accorded high, rather than low, status. No doubt the operational word here is 'professional', but it is also significant that all three of these 'vocational' training routes have traditionally involved a substantial degree of classical learning—a knowledge of Latin, for example—originally associated with a high-status education.

It is interesting to note that although historically an academic education was considered to be liberal and 'broad', while education for the purposes of work was thought of as focused and 'narrow', the application of these two terms is today quite the reverse, the academic route being described as narrow and the introduction of vocational elements into the curriculum for 14–19-year-olds, for example through the 14–19 Diplomas, being presented as a broadening of that curriculum. *See also* MECHANICS' INSTITUTES; NATIONAL VOCATIONAL QUALIFICATION.

Vocational Advanced Level (Vocational A level) Originally known as the Advanced *General National Vocational Qualification (GNVQ) and given its current title in 2002, this was a development which closely echoed the recommendation in the 1996 **Dearing Review of Qualifications for 16–19-Year-Olds* that GNVQs be renamed 'Applied A Levels'. In both cases the rationale for the change of name was the need to establish greater *parity of esteem with traditional A levels. The Vocational A level has a similar structure and assessment process to that of the modular *General Certificate of Education (GCE) *Advanced Level, and has a credit value of half the original Advanced GNVQ. Students, if they wish, may take a combination of Vocational and GCE A levels. The Vocational A levels are taught in both sixth forms and *further education colleges and focus on general vocational areas such as business and art and design. Like GCE A levels, they may be used as a progression route into *higher education.

vocational awarding bodies *See* AWARDING BODY.

vocational education and training (VET) An alternative title for the *further education sector. Others are *learning and skills sector (except in Scotland), continuing education, and the *lifelong learning sector. *See also* VOCATIONAL.

voice output communication aid (VOCA) A device holding electronically stored speech specifically designed to enable individuals without natural speech to communicate. Speech is stored either digitally or via a speech synthesizer. These can be used by learners who would not otherwise be able to communicate. There is a range of VOCAs available; some are dedicated communication devices while others are laptop computers with specialist software installed. Frequently computer-based devices are programmed to include additional features such as an environmental control system. How the device is accessed is dependent on the needs of the user and can be via direct touch, specialist switches, light pointers, or infrared sensors. *See also* AUGMENTATIVE AND ALTERNATIVE COMMUNICATION. T.B., L.E.

voluntary organizations Groups of like-minded people who work towards a common cause. Organizations may have charitable status, operate without profit, be staffed by unpaid volunteers, or have a governing body which does not receive payment. The number of such organizations in the United Kingdom totals over 250 000 with many whose work is allied to the education sector. These allied voluntary organizations are used extensively by schools as sources of ideas, providers of teaching and learning resources, and givers of advice and guidance. Some organizations offer direct support to pupils and parents on issues relating to the safety of children. T.B., L.E.

Voluntary Service Overseas (VSO) An organization whose purpose is to bring aid and support to developing countries, often in the form of education and training projects. It recruits volunteer teachers and trainers in the United Kingdom on fixed-term contracts and pays them a minimum salary, usually at the going rate for teachers in the country where they are working.

SEE WEB LINKS

- Provides a list of subjects and skills in which teachers or trainers are needed.

Vygotsky, Lev (1896–1934) A Russian psychologist who defined one of the most important concepts of educational theory currently embedded in contemporary approaches to teaching and learning: the **zone of proximal development (ZPD)**. The majority of *teachers now recognize that if students, young and old, are given tasks to accomplish that are just beyond their actual *competence, but are able to secure the support of others, it is likely that they will be able to manage the task better than if they are left alone to struggle with it. The teacher's skill is to observe carefully and monitor a student's progress in order to provide a task within the proximal reach of that learner and to suggest who their learning partner might be to provide a **scaffold**, or support, to enable this achievement. This social strategy development theory of learning focuses on the connections between people and the cultural context in which they act, and requires learning to become a reciprocal experience for the students and teacher, thus creating a community of learners. This approach represents a contrast to previously established principles of the individual construction of knowledge, as proposed by *Piaget. Vygotsky's ideas took some time to be translated into English, and therefore his controversial influence continues to challenge established psychological and educational theory of age–stage development.

V

In recent years, Vygotsky's educational theories have been applied in the *pre-schools of *Reggio Emilia, where *dialogic teaching and thinking between children and peers, children and adults, and teachers and parents is fundamental to the project-based *curriculum. Deep *reflection on this continuous narrative of learning requires teachers to be researchers into children's understanding, and is similar to *Dewey's belief that teachers must use their greater knowledge of the world to help make sense of it for the children, and thus stretch their active and emerging competencies.

Further Reading: L. Vygotsky *Mind in Society* (Harvard University Press, 1978). A.W.

WALES, EDUCATION IN

The third term of the National Assembly for Wales began in May 2007, following the elections. Education is a significant area of responsibility devolved to the Assembly, covering *early years and *schools, family policy, *further education (FE) and *higher education (HE), *adult and *community education, qualifications, and the careers service. Notably, teachers' *pay and conditions of service and pensions remain the responsibility of the *Department for Children, Schools, and Families at Westminster, as does the maintenance of the database of teachers' records, though teacher training and support are devolved to the Assembly. Education in particular is an area where the Assembly has been very proactive in developing distinctive policies, and there have been several changes in the administrative process to support that development. During 2006 the Welsh Assembly department responsible for education and training was expanded to assume responsibility for all education and training with the exception of HE in higher education institutions (HEIs) and in certain instances in *colleges of further education. Funding for these is the responsibility of the *Higher Education Funding Council for Wales.

The *Education Act 2002 provided Wales with the opportunity to develop its educational policy along lines which differ in a number of ways from that elsewhere in the UK. That development has been seen clearly as part of the aim to break down barriers between departments, as exemplified in the Assembly document *A Winning Wales* (2002), which covers education and economic development, giving a sense of the potential for cohesive policies across boundaries in a small country. *A Winning Wales* is one of a number of ambitious documents setting the strategy for the devolved Assembly; those relating to education in particular are *The Learning Country* (2001) and *The Learning Country: Vision into Action* (2006). The first sets out a ten-year strategy for education in Wales, covering all ages, with the emphasis on a continuum of learning from *pre-school through to *lifelong learning and *skills updates. The second reinforces the original document, giving an overview of progress so far and updating the strategy.

Certain key issues, such as *widening participation in *post-compulsory education, are central drivers across all the jurisdictions, though the strategies for implementation are often distinctive. In the *widening access agenda, for example, geographical and demographic features in Wales are reflected in the Reaching Wider initiative (2002), whereby the Funding Council supports broad groupings of HEIs in delivering initiatives which respond appropriately to local and regional factors. Other policies which are common throughout the UK include enhanced early years provision, improvements in buildings and environment, and the aspiration to reconnect with disaffected children and young people. In a number of instances, however, Wales has either adopted different methods of achieving those goals or has developed distinctive initiatives such as the *Welsh Baccalaureate.

Over recent years the Minister for Education has commissioned a series of in-depth reports in a number of areas. The emphasis in the guidance for all of these has been on evidence-based recommendations, and resource has been invested to enable a significant level of research and analysis to support the process. Studies and pilots have been carried out in relation to the initiatives at pre-school and school stages, with the implementation of programmes such as *Flying Start (2007) for early years education.

A report on full-time HE provision made recommendations for student support, funding, and fees, proposing a variable fees structure and a clear, enabling support system. This resulted in an Assembly vote which introduced the Wales-specific fee remission grant of up to £1 800 for all Welsh-domiciled students choosing to study at a Welsh HEI, thus effectively reducing their fee commitment to £1 200, with the differential between that and a maximum of £3 000 as decided by the institution. The fee remission grant is non-means-tested and those students have access to the £1 200 student loan through the usual channels.

Part-time students constitute 41 per cent of all student enrolments in Welsh HEIs. The balance between full- and part-time varies enormously between institutions, but the overall percentage is significant. In 2006 a report on part-time HE study was published, and subsequently ratified by the Assembly, recommending increased student support for part-time students and advising that additional funding should be given to institutions, allocated in proportion to their numbers of part-time students, to enable them to respond to local and regional factors in the provision of courses. The new regimes for both part- and full-time HE were implemented in the same academic year, beginning September–October 2007.

Some important issues to be addressed by the education sector in Wales include falling rolls in schools, which is a particular challenge in some of the more rural areas; challenges around the Welsh-medium policy; the *transition phase between primary and secondary; and funding levels, especially for post-16 education.

Support for the teaching profession is a priority in Wales, with the *Newly Qualified Teachers programme and certificate, and the ongoing support offered to teachers in Years 2 and 3 of their professional life. There is also provision for additional training for teaching through the medium of Welsh, particularly at the school stage. Indeed, the Welsh language is important to the education strategy of the Welsh Assembly, with the number of Welsh-medium schools increasing. There are, however, problems around some ambitious targets in relation to the Welsh language, particularly at HE level.

Considerable effort has been invested in the early years and foundation stage, with the Flying Start programme providing part-time places for 3-year-olds whose parents want them to enrol and pilot schemes in structured activity learning for the 3–7-year age groups. All *infant class sizes now conform to the statutory limit. The strategy on assessment means there are no tests at *Key Stage 1, and a recent report recommended that assessment at Key Stages 2 and 3 should also be phased out. The appointment of a Children's Commissioner has been an important step forward and again indicates the aspiration for joined-up, pan-Wales thinking. The dispersed population in some parts of Wales creates particular challenges such as in the support for children with *special educational needs, where maintaining a full range of services can be difficult for some of the smaller rural local authorities. To meet that challenge, the National Steering Group for SEN in Wales was established with an all-Wales remit, allowing for collaboration between authorities, but also for *peripatetic services.

At secondary stage there have been some interesting initiatives, notably the Learning Pathways for 14–19-year-olds. The approach here is to develop a variety of learning routes geared to the individual with support from learning coaches for advice and guidance. The development of the Welsh Baccalaureate has been an important and successful Welsh initiative, and has established a qualification which is now accepted by the *Universities and Colleges Admissions Service as part of the qualification calculations for entry to university.

The development of the *Credit and Qualifications Framework for Wales (CQFW) is a further example of the aspirations towards cohesion of provision and support of the learner. From 2005 all accredited learning, including mainstream qualifications offered in Wales, has gradually been brought into the single unifying structure of the CQFW. The Framework is designed to create flexibility for the learner and to offer a guide to comparable and equivalent levels of achievement and qualifications whether these are gained through learning in the workplace, the community, at school, at college, or at university.

For both the FE and the HE sectors, a major factor has been the clear policy of significant movement towards collaboration and reconfiguration. There have been some notable developments in sustainable collaboration, such as the merger between the University College of Medicine and Cardiff University, and the move by the Royal College of Music and Drama to become an Associate of the University of Glamorgan. H.G.

Warnock Report (1978) The report of the Committee of Inquiry into the Education of Handicapped Children and Young People, chaired by Mary Warnock, and viewed as revolutionary at the time of its publication. The Report was to change radically the educational picture for children with disabilities as most of the recommendations became enshrined in law in the *Education Act 1981. The Report introduced the term *special educational need to identify any child needing extra or different support, and argued that 20 per cent of children have special needs at least for some part of their educational career. It further introduced new terms to identify groups of children with the intention of moving away from the previous medical labelling of children: these were 'speech and language disorders', 'visual disability and hearing disability', 'emotional and behavioural disorders', and 'learning difficulties: specific, mild, moderate and severe'. The Report recommended that segregated 'special' schools should be for those with the most complex and multiple disabilities which were long-term, and that mainstream schools should develop to meet the needs of all other children. It put forward three models for the *integration of children with disabilities—**locational**, **social**, and **functional integration**. This recommendation for mainstreaming children had criteria attached: parents should be in agreement with the placement; the child's educational needs were capable of being met in a mainstream school; the local education authority was using its resources efficiently; and the education of other children was not affected. To help facilitate the integration of children the Report recommended an expansion in special needs advisory and support services. With the aim of protecting the educational needs of the most severely disabled and ensuring they received appropriate resources to make progress, the Report recommended *statements of special needs. These statements were to be issued by local authorities to individual children only after a five-stage assessment process had been followed. Once issued the local authority had a statutory duty to make the provision listed on the statement. T.B., L.E.

weighting When the overall *assessment of a candidate's *coursework or *examination performance is based on a series of tasks which have each been awarded a mark or grade, it must be clear whether each of those contributory marks or grades counts equally towards the final one awarded, or whether some tasks carry more 'weight' than others. So, for example, in an examination which consists of four tasks, each of equal difficulty and therefore weighted equally, they will each count as 25 per cent of the overall mark or grade. However, if, of the four tasks, one is more challenging or requires a longer answer than the others, the percentage marks it carries should be weighted accordingly.

Welsh Baccalaureate A new, broader post-16 qualification piloted since 2003 and offered at Advanced and Intermediate levels from September 2007 in 76 approved centres. The *Universities and Colleges Admissions Service allocates 120 tariff points to the core qualification. Students who successfully complete the Welsh Baccalaureate at Advanced Level will therefore have the equivalent of an A grade *General Certificate of Education *Advanced Level in addition to the points they earn from their optional studies. H.G.

Welsh-medium education A policy priority for the Welsh Assembly working through a number of public bodies, including *Estyn, the education services provider **WJEC**, and in particular the **Welsh Language Board**, which has responsibility for the promotion and development of Welsh-medium education. The Board's Education and Training Department reviews *local authority policies, approves and monitors the implementation of their Welsh Language Schemes, and maintains a strategic overview of Welsh-medium education and training. The

Board allocates grants to local authorities on an annual basis to support the teaching of Welsh. In the post-16 sector the Assembly Bilingual Learning Unit aims to promote bilingualism and Welsh-medium education and training in *colleges of further education and workplace training providers, and there is an ambitious target for Welsh-medium delivery in higher education institutions. H.G.

White Paper A government discussion document which sets out government policy on a specific issue. It is usually the precursor of legislation, and as a type of command paper it is often the subject of statements or debates in the House of Commons. It is issued by a government department and contains detailed proposals for legislation. It represents the final stage in the process of creating legislation before the government introduces its proposals to Parliament in the form of a bill. For example, the 1991 White Paper *Education and Training for the 21st Century* set out the government's argument that *colleges of further education would operate more effectively if they were given freedom from *local authority control, and was followed in 1992 by the *Further and Higher Education Act, which legislated to bring this about. White Papers are often prefaced by a statement in the House from the *secretary of state of the government department sponsoring the proposals. In the case of education White Papers, this will be either the Secretary of State for Schools, Children, and Families, or the Secretary of State for Innovation, Universities, and Skills. A White Paper is sometimes produced following the consultation process which is undertaken when the government issues a *Green Paper.

Over the past three decades there has been frequent publication of White Papers on all aspects of education, reflecting the frequent policy developments and the rapid rate of change in every sector of the education system. Examples of landmark White Papers are:

1981 *A New Training Initiative: A Programme for Action*, which set out the argument for a year's work-related training scheme for all school-leavers, a policy which eventually led to the *Youth Training Scheme
1992 *Choice and Diversity: A Framework for Schools* argues for new arrangements for the inspection of schools, which resulted in the setting up of *Ofsted
2001 *Schools: Achieving Success*
2003 *The Future of Higher Education*
21st Century Skills: Realising Our Potential
2005 *Skills: Getting On in Business, Getting On at Work*
14–19 Education and Skills sets out the argument for allowing some 14–16-year-olds to undertake part of their learning in colleges of further education, which resulted in this becoming a widespread practice
Higher Standards, Better Schools for All
2006 *FE Reform: Raising Skills, Improving Life Chances*
2007 *Care Matters: Time for Change*
The Children's Plan: Building Brighter Futures

See also EDUCATION ACT.

SEE WEB LINKS

- Provides a full list of recent White Papers on education, and access to both full text and summary versions.

W

widening access Part of the *widening participation agenda, the drive to widen access to education focuses particularly on those potential learners who find themselves excluded from educational or training opportunities by difficulties to do with their access to it, rather than out of choice. Such difficulties might include access in the literal sense, for those who live some distance away from provision or who have a disability which affects their mobility or ability to gain entry to the *campus or buildings where learning is offered. They might also include cultural or language issues which make it difficult for the potential learner to access information about provision or to attend classes at the institution concerned. Adults in full-time work may also have difficulty in attending courses which are taught during their working hours. Awareness of issues over access has led to an expansion in outreach classes and community education, and in the development of *distance learning, *blended learning, and *e-learning models. *See also* INCLUSION; INCLUSIVITY; KENNEDY REPORT; WARNOCK REPORT.

widening participation Encouraging people to enter *further and *higher education who have previously been under-represented in these sectors. This includes people from a wider range of educational, social, ethnic, and cultural backgrounds, and from a wider range of abilities and skills. A drive to widen participation in *post-compulsory education and training is presented as part of the government's policy to create a more highly skilled workforce. To this end, specific targets were set in the 2006 *White Paper *Further Education: Raising Skills, Improving Life Chances*, which include:

- participation rates by 16–19-year-olds to increase by 15 per cent by 2015;
- the number of adults gaining a *National Qualifications Framework level 2 qualification to reach at least 3.6 million by 2010;
- 50 per cent of all 18–30-year-olds to be participating in *higher education by 2010.

Concerns have been raised by some educationalists over the apparent contradiction at the heart of a policy which aims both to widen participation and at the same time to raise standards of achievement.

Widening participation and access is a focus for Scottish universities. In 2001 every higher education institution signed a seven-point commitment to improving social inclusion in higher education (*Commitment to Inclusion*, March 2001). This issue has been addressed in the 2005 *Learning for All* document by the Scottish Funding Council. *See also* INCLUSIVITY; KENNEDY REPORT.

SEE WEB LINKS

- Provides a downloadable version of *Learning for All.*

work-based learning (WBL) The development and assessment of skills within and directly related to the workplace. Many learners have been able to gain work-related qualifications in the form of *National Vocational Qualifications, which recognize the competencies gained in the workplace. Traditionally, *further education colleges have provided employers with the support and underpinning knowledge and assessment for WBL, but it can be facilitated through part-time study at non-workplace locations, such as schools, further education colleges, and training providers, or through full-time learning within the work setting.

Modes of WBL are numerous: Increased Flexibility, which funds partnerships between further education colleges, schools, and providers of work-based learning, and *Young Apprenticeship programmes both offer a taste of WBL within the school curriculum at *Key Stage 4; *Entry to Employment supports and prepares young learners who are not yet ready to undertake a Young Apprenticeship scheme. *Foundation degrees were launched by the UK government in 2000 to meet the needs of employers, especially in developing the higher levels of technical skill required to enable the workforce to satisfy regional, national, and global demands. The foundation degree programme also allows for progression to an honours degree, linking work-based with more traditional higher education. These degrees are designed to be delivered in a flexible manner using learning in the workplace supported by a further education college or university, and with the use of *e-learning. V.C., K.A.

work cards Usually designed by the teacher and used in *primary schools, these are cards which provide information and the briefing for a related activity or activities. They are a means of facilitating *individual learning undertaken at the learner's own pace, and also allow for *differentiation of activity. They enable the teacher to allocate learning tasks of different types and levels to individual pupils within a class, rather than requiring all pupils to be always working at the same pace and level. *See also* PERSONALIZED LEARNING.

Workers' Educational Association (WEA) Part of the *adult education sector with its roots in the self-improvement movement of the 19th century, a movement whose aim was to raise the level of intellectual achievement of the working classes. In the 1960s, 1970s, and 1980s, however, it became for a time more closely associated with the middle classes and the concept of education for leisure. It is a registered charity operating through 650 local branches which run classes in a variety of subjects, from English literature to reflexology, mainly taught by teachers, lecturers, and other experts who are contracted on an hourly basis. Founded in 1903 and organized through *universities, the Cooperative Society, and trade unions, it became widely regarded as part of the labour movement between the First and Second World Wars. As it gained its 'middle-class' image, however, it also gained financial support from central government, some direct and some through *local authorities. This enabled local branches to subsidize their courses and thereby keep the cost of fees down. In 1993 the WEA came under the aegis of the *Further Education Funding Council in terms of its funding, and from this point it was required to bid for financial support against providers such as further education *colleges and private vocational training agencies. As the criteria for funding became increasingly concentrated on provision which led to *National Qualifications Framework qualifications, and as local authorities' role in funding was eroded, the WEA was no longer able to subsidize fees at the same level. This had repercussions on levels of recruitment and the range of courses it was able to offer. In 2007 it ran over 10 000 courses, providing for over 110 000 adults.

SEE WEB LINKS

- The WEA's mission, aims, and values.

work experience The placement of a pupil, student, or trainee in a work environment where they will gain supervised experience of working within that business, company, or organization. It was an integral part of early youth training programmes such as the *Youth Opportunities Programme and the *Youth Training Scheme, where the trainee was placed with an employer to receive on-the-job training—that is, training of a practical, experiential kind—and attended a further education *college or other training provider for part of the week in order to receive off-the-job training, which often included the underpinning theoretical component of the work skills they were acquiring. This pattern of attendance was similar to the *day release arrangements which operated for trainees in employment. Work experience was extended into some full-time *programmes of study in *further education in the 1980s, notably *Business and Technology Education Council courses in vocational areas such as business education. In schools it is now common practice to encourage pupils to undertake one or two weeks of closely supervised work experience at the end of Year 10. In *higher education, some four-year degree courses include a year of work experience, and are often referred to as *sandwich courses, the year in work representing the filling in the middle. For some qualifications the experience of work is an integral and essential component, as, for example, for a degree in medicine. Students studying for language degrees are normally encouraged or required to spend a year overseas as part of their programme, practising the language they are studying while at the same time gaining work experience, often as an English language assistant in a school.

Year 11 Information System (Yellis) This system provides tests which are used nationally by secondary schools to gauge the potential of their *Key Stage 4 pupils. Schools choose whether or not to participate in this type of standardized assessment. Test results can be used by secondary schools as a baseline for *value added measures. They are also used to predict *General Certificate of Secondary Education grades for core GCSE subjects. Yellis tests provide an alternative baseline to Key Stage 3 *Standard Task results, which are the outcome of specific learning and instruction, rather than innate potential. Yellis produces baseline tests for Years 10 and 11. These tests are assessed externally by Yellis and results are returned to the school shortly afterwards. *See also* Cognitive Abilities Test; Middle Years Information System. I.F.W.

Yellis *See* Year 11 Information System.

Yellow Book The informal title given to a report compiled by advisers in the Department of Education and Science in 1975 on national standards in education. It was broadly critical of standards in both primary and secondary schools. Elements of this report informed the **Ruskin College speech** given by James Callaghan (Prime Minister 1976–9) in 1976 which is credited with opening the continuing *Great Debate on education and training.

Young Apprenticeship The Young *Apprenticeship programme comes within the framework of the UK government's 14–19 and Skills agendas. The programme offers an opportunity for able 14–16-year-olds to combine the practical application of skills and knowledge in a *vocational context, with the chance to gain qualifications that relate to specific occupational areas. It is seen as an addition to the range of vocational options at *Key Stage 4, where pupils can follow specific vocational programmes outside school, in partnerships with employers and involving long-term work placements.

The first cohort of 1 000 learners started their two-year programme in September 2004 in art and design, business administration, engineering, health and social care, and the motor industry. For the second cohort, the programmes expanded to include sports management, leadership, and coaching; performing arts; hospitality; and textiles. *See also* Modern Apprenticeship. V.C., K.A.

Youth Council for Northern Ireland The Youth Council for Northern Ireland was established under the Youth Service (NI) Order 1989, and the legislation defines its functions as follows: to advise the Department of Education, education and library boards, and other bodies on the development of the Youth Service; to encourage cross-community activity by the Youth Service; to encourage the provision of facilities for the Youth Service and facilities which are especially beneficial to young persons; to encourage and assist the coordination and efficient use of the resources of the Youth Service; and to grant aid to regional voluntary youth organizations towards their administration. J.H.

youth offending team (YOT) Youth offending teams are multi-agency teams set up in each *local authority area. They comprise representatives from education, health, the police, the probation service, social services, housing officers, and the drugs and alcohol misuse team; each team is led by a youth offending team manager. This multi-agency approach ensures thorough assessment, planning, and delivery of appropriate support to young offenders. The main role of a youth offending team is to work with young people aged 10–18 who are subject to court orders either in the community or in custodial situations. There is currently a new initiative for teams to work with children aged 8–13 who are identified as at 'risk of offending'; this is called the Youth Inclusion Support Programme. T.B., L.E.

Youth Opportunities Programme (YOP) A forerunner of the *Youth Training Scheme (YTS) and the first national training programme for 16–18-year-olds not in education or work. Established in 1981 as part of the training agenda for school-leavers and adults set out in the 1981 *White Paper *A New Training Initiative*, YOP provided a programme of individual *work experience combined with attendance at further education classes with a generalized *vocational focus. The programme was short-lived and was succeeded within two years by YTS.

Youth Training Scheme (YTS) YTS replaced the *Youth Opportunities Scheme (YOP) in 1983 and became the mainstay of the national training agenda set in 1981 by the *White Paper *A New Training Initiative*. Like YOP, it involved substantial (in terms of time) *work experience which was intended to provide **on-the-job training**, as well as requiring the trainee to complete a programme of *vocationally related skills delivered in *colleges of further education, private training agencies, or—in organizations with the facility to accommodate this—in the workplace. The **off-the-job** *curriculum also included such transferable core skills as communication, numeracy, and a set of skills known as 'social and life skills'. Trainees were paid a nominal 'wage' for which employers were subsidized by government funds paid through the local *Manpower Services Commission, and later through the local *Training and Enterprise Council. By 1988 there were over 500 000 contracted placements on the scheme. Criticisms of the programme included the allegation that many trainees were gaining little valuable experience in the workplace, were being given menial or meaningless tasks, and were failing to gain real employment on completing the scheme, and the suggestion that the scheme was intended as a means of omitting the numbers of unemployed school-leavers from the national unemployment figures. On the other hand, many of those involved, both organizations and trainees, claimed that it provided valuable experience and a genuine route into employment for young people. It was replaced by Youth Training in 1989. *See also* KEY SKILLS.

zero tolerance A refusal to permit or tolerate *behaviour which is inappropriate, illegal, or unethical. In schools and other educational institutions this will include behaviours such as *bullying, and racial or sexual harassment, and may also include, for example, the use of offensive language, the use of mobile phones in class, and the wearing of certain types of dress or jewellery. The term itself is part of the rhetoric of recent policy debates about law and order. It is also closely linked to the **Respect** agenda. Thus, governments, too, will express their zero tolerance of certain behaviours, such as street violence. Some schools and colleges operate what is referred to as a 'zero tolerance policy' in order to enforce acceptable behaviour and adherence to the law and rules of the institution. Such a policy sets out clearly the behaviours which are specifically prohibited and their consequences—usually *exclusion or suspension. *See also* SANCTION.

zone of proximal development (ZPD) *See* VYGOTSKY.

Appendix 1

Time Line

1833	The Factory Act introduces a mandatory two hours of schooling each day for children
1840	The Grammar Schools Act permits grammar schools to introduce subjects other than the classical languages into their curriculum
1856	A government Education Department is created
1868	The Taunton Report recommends three grades of provision in grammar schools according to pupils' social class
1870	The Elementary Education Act establishes school boards empowered to create new schools and fund schooling for children of the poor
1880	The Education Act makes school compulsory for children up to the age of 10
1902	The Education Act abolishes school boards and replaces them with local educational authorities whose role is to manage school funding, employ teachers, and allocate school places
1917	School Certificate is introduced
1918	The Education Act makes school compulsory for children up to the age of 14
1944	The Education Act introduces the tripartite system; secondary education becomes free in maintained schools and the school-leaving age rises to 15
1951	The General Certificate of Education at Ordinary and Advanced Level replaces School Certificate and Higher School Certificate
1964	The Department of Education and Science is established
1965	Comprehensive schooling is recommended in government Circular 10/65. The Certificate of Secondary Education is introduced
1967	The Plowden Report on children and primary schools
1973	The school-leaving age is raised to 16
1976	The Education Act requires local authorities to submit plans for comprehensive education
1979	The Education Act repeals the 1976 Act
1981	The White Paper *A New Training Initiative: A Programme for Action* sets out the argument for a year's work-related training scheme for all

school-leavers, a policy which eventually leads to the Youth Training Scheme

1986 The Education Act requires maintained schools to increase parental representation on their governing body

1988 The Education Reform Act introduces the national curriculum; the General Certificate of Secondary Education replaces GCE Ordinary Levels and the Certificate of Secondary Education

1992 The White Paper *Choice and Diversity: A Framework for Schools* argues for new arrangements for the inspection of schools, which results in the setting up of Ofsted

1993 The Department for Education replaces the Department of Education and Science

1994 The Education Act introduces the Teacher Training Agency

1995 The Department for Education and the Employment Department merge to become the Department for Education and Employment

1996 *Dearing Review of Qualifications for 16–19 Year Olds*

1997 The National Literacy Strategy is introduced
Kennedy Report, *Learning Works*

1998 The General Teaching Council is established

1999 Moser Report, *A Fresh Start: Improving Literacy and Numeracy*

2000 The Learning and Skills Council replaces the Further Education Funding Council and the Training and Enterprise Councils
Curriculum 2000 is introduced

2001 The Department for Education and Skills replaces the Department for Education and Employment

2002 City academies are introduced

2003 The Green Paper *Every Child Matters* stresses the need for accountability and integration between services and organizations in support of young people

2005 The White Paper *14–19 Education and Skills* sets out the argument for allowing some 14–16-year-olds to undertake part of their learning in colleges of further education, which becomes widespread practice

The White Paper *Higher Standards, Better Schools for All: More Choice for Parents and Pupils* argues for the need to create a system of independent non-fee-paying state schools in which schools can decide whether they wish to acquire a self-governing trust or become a self-governing foundation school; for parents to receive regular meaningful reports during the school year; for more grouping and setting by subject ability; for clarification of the legal right of teachers to discipline pupils

2006 The Education and Inspections Act enables all schools to become trust schools by forming links with external partners; enables local authorities to take on a new strategic role including appointing school improvement partners for maintained schools; introduces a tighter admissions framework; requires local authorities to provide free transport for the most disadvantaged families; introduces new specialized diplomas for young people; provides new nutritional standards for food and drink served in maintained schools; merges several existing inspectorates into a single inspectorate to cover the full range of services for children and young people, as well as lifelong learning

The White Paper *Further Education: Raising Skills, Improving Life Chances* confirms further education's role as one of skills training; sets national qualification targets; introduces regulatory continuing professional development for teachers in further education; reforms funding for 14–19 learning

2007 The Department for Education and Skills is replaced by two new departments: the Department for Children, Schools, and Families and the Department for Innovation, Universities, and Skills

The Further Education and Training Act implements the proposals set out in the Foster Report (2005) and the White Paper *Further Education: Raising Skills, Improving Life Chances* (2006); sets in motion the restructuring of the Learning and Skills Council; grants English colleges of further education the right to award foundation degrees

2008 The White Paper *Innovation Nation* emphasizes higher education's role in supporting the national economy

Appendix 2

Educational Provision in Some Other English-Speaking Countries

Regulation and administration

Australia	The Department of Education, Employment, and Workplace Relations (DEEWR) provides national leadership in developing and implementing policies. Each state and territory has its own Department of Education which collaborates with the DEEWR and is responsible for the regulation of educational provision SEE WEB LINKS
Canada	There is no national or federal ministry of education, although there is federal involvement in some aspects of provision such as vocational training which can be subsidized by the federal Department of Labour. Each province and territory has its own ministry or department responsible for elementary, secondary, and post-secondary provision and policy SEE WEB LINKS
New Zealand	The Ministry of Education is responsible for education policy, administration, and regulation across all sectors SEE WEB LINKS
North America	There is no national or federal ministry of education. Control and funding comes from three levels: federal, state, and local. The state and national governments have a power-sharing arrangement, with the states exercising most of the control. At the primary and secondary school levels, curriculums, allocation of funding, teaching, and other policies are set through locally elected school boards with jurisdiction over school districts SEE WEB LINKS
South Africa	A national framework for school policy is provided by the national Department of Education, which is responsible for national education and training as a whole, including higher education. Each of the nine provinces has its own Department of Education, which has direct administrative responsibility for schools SEE WEB LINKS

Compulsory provision and early years

Australia	Pre-school provision varies according to the state or territory, and is often in kindergartens attached to primary schools. Education is compulsory for ages 6–16 (15 in Tasmania), and is delivered through:

	• primary school: Years 1–6/7 (ages 6–12/13) (depending on state) • secondary school, high school: Years 7/8–12 (ages 12/13–18) (open and selective) Sixty-six per cent of provision is in government-funded schools; the rest is in fee-paying independent schools. Both government and independent schools adhere to the same curriculum framework
Canada (outside Quebec)	Pre-school provision (Grade K) is in kindergarten (or equivalent) and varies according to province. Education is compulsory for ages 6–16 (18 in Ontario, 15 in Alberta): • elementary school: Grades 1–6/7/8 (ages 6–11/12/13) (depending on province) • junior high school/middle school/intermediate school: Grades 7–9 (ages 12–15) • high school: Grades 10–12+ (ages 15/16–21 and under) Eight per cent of pupils attend private schools
New Zealand	Pre-school provision consists of kindergartens (ages 3–5), kohanga reo, and early childhood centres (ages 0–5). Education is compulsory for ages 6–16 (15 with parental permission), and is delivered through: • primary school: Years 1–6 (ages 5–13) • intermediate school: Years 7–8 (ages 11–13) • secondary school: Years 9–13 (ages 13–18) Some schools cater for pupils across two or all of these groups. Most pupils start school at 5 and remain until 18. Students with special educational needs can stay in school until 21. Eighty-six per cent of provision is in state schools; the rest is in integrated or private schools
North America	There are no mandatory public pre-school or crèche programmes. Education is compulsory for ages 6–16 or 18, depending on the state. Compulsory provision is divided into three levels: elementary school, middle school, and high school. Grade levels in each vary from state to state: • elementary school: Kindergarten Grade–5th/6th Grade (ages 5/6–11) • middle school: 6th–8th Grade (ages 11–14) • high school: 9th–12th Grade (ages 15–18) Students may attend public, private, or home schools. Approximately 85 per cent of students attend the public schools
South Africa	Grade 0 (or Grade R) is reception year for 6-year-olds, provided in nurseries or primary schools. Education is compulsory for ages 7–15 (or completion of Grade 9) and is delivered through:

- primary school: Grades 0–6 (ages 6–12)
- high school: Grades 7–12 (ages 12–18)

Ninety-five per cent of provision is in government-funded schools; the rest is in fee-paying independent schools. Government and independent schools adhere to the same curriculum framework

Post-compulsory education

Australia — Higher education takes place in universities. Bachelor's degrees take three to four years. Associate degrees (roughly equivalent to the UK's foundation degree) take two years. Both are assessed through coursework. Technical and further education (TAFE) is provided in institutes of technical and further education (which may also offer higher education courses) and registered training organizations (RTOs). TAFE institutions and RTOs must comply with the Australian Quality Training Framework (AQTF)

Canada — Higher education takes place mainly in universities. Bachelor's degrees normally take three years, or four years with honours. Vocational education is provided in community colleges and technical colleges, some of which may also offer higher education courses leading to a degree

New Zealand — Higher education takes place in universities, colleges of education, polytechnics, and wananga. A bachelor's degree normally takes three years, with an additional year for honours. Vocational education takes place in polytechnics and technical colleges

North America — Post-secondary education in the United States is known as college or university and commonly consists of four years of study leading to a bachelor's degree. Vocational education is provided by community colleges, which may also offer higher awards such as the associate's degree

South Africa — Higher education takes place in universities and at private institutions, registered with the Department of Education, offering specific degrees and diplomas. Further education and training (FET) is provided both in Grades 10–12 of secondary school and in further education and training institutions and colleges

Qualifications framework and key awards

Australia — Qualifications are classified in a national Australian Qualifications Framework (AQF). The major school-leaving qualification is the Senior Secondary Certificate of Education (SSCE), which requires two years' additional study following Year 10, and prepares students to enter higher education or technical and further education. There is testing of literacy and

	numeracy in primary and secondary schools, which varies from state to state. Although universities regulate much of their own provision, vocational education and training (VET) is regulated by AQF
Canada	There is no federal framework for qualifications or testing because of the distributed nature of jurisdiction for education. The main school-leaving qualification is the High School Diploma, which is the minimum qualification required for entry to governmental jobs and to higher education
New Zealand	The New Zealand Qualifications Authority co-ordinates qualifications in the secondary and tertiary sectors through the National Qualifications Framework (NQF) The National Certificate of Educational Achievement (NCEA) is New Zealand's main national qualification for secondary school students and is part of the NQF. Entry to universities is open, requiring only the minimum NCEA. However, many universities operate a selective admissions procedure
North America	There is no federal framework for qualifications. At the primary and secondary school levels, curriculums are set through the locally elected school boards. There is standardized testing under the No Child Left Behind Act, which requires that all American states must test students in public (i.e. state) schools to ensure that they are achieving the desired level of minimum education. The main school-leaving qualifications are the High School Diploma or the General Educational Development (GED) test certificate
South Africa	There is a National Qualifications Framework (NQF) which encompasses three bands of education and training: general education and training (including adult basic education), further education and training (FET), and higher education and training (HET).The main school-leaving qualifications are the Matriculation endorsement (matric), in which three subjects must be passed at the higher level for entry to higher education; and Standard Senior Certificate, necessary for progression to technical qualifications